D1538782

WINCHESTER REPEATING ARMS COMPANY

Its History & Development from 1865 to 1981

by HERBERT G. HOUZE

The tradename and trademark "WINCHESTER" is owned
by Olin Corporation and is used with Olin Corporation's
express permission. Neither the author, nor the publisher,
are sponsored by or associated with Olin Corporation.

© 1994 by Herbert G. Houze

Published by

**krause
publications**

700 E. State Street • Iola, WI 54990-0001
Telephone: 715/445-2214

Library of Congress Catalog Number: 93-80097
ISBN: 0-87341-285-0
Printed in the United States of America

DEDICATION

To my family, Alec, Andrew, Jennifer and Lynn, for their unending patience and support during the time this book was being written.

CONTENTS

Acknowledgements

During the course of writing this study, assistance and information was received from a great number of individuals. While I have tried to record the names of all those contributors, I fear that many have been accidentally overlooked and, consequently, omitted from the list below. To them I offer my sincere apologies, and to those mentioned, my profound thanks.

The principal debt of gratitude must be extended to Olin Corporation and the Buffalo Bill Historical Center, the two largest repositories of the former Winchester Repeating Arms Company's records. Without their cooperation this book could not have been written. At Olin Corporation, I would like to thank Melvin Neisloss, former secretary to the company; Bruce E. Burdick, senior counsel; Thomas E. Hall, former curator of the Winchester Gun Museum; Thomas E. Henshaw; and John Walsh.

At the Buffalo Bill Historical Center, the following were of particular help: Dr. Paul Fees, senior curator; Howard M. Madaus, the Robert W. Woodruff Firearms Chair of the Cody Firearms Museum; Christina Stopka, librarian; Frances Clymer, associate librarian; Joan Murra, library assistant; Devendra Shrikande, photographer; and Lucille Warters, assistant photographer. In addition, I would like to express my appreciation to the Historical Center for their granting me permission to publish photographs and extracts of material in their collections.

Mention must also be made of the cooperation offered by the following institutions: the Baker Library, Harvard University for providing extracts from the records of the R.G. Dun Company, and to Dun & Bradstreet Company for permission to publish those extracts; the British Patent Office; and the National Archives of the United States.

Among the many private parties who provided invaluable information were Howard L. Blackmore, John C. Davies, Charles Dupont, R.C. Romanella and the heirs of General Schurz.

Special thanks are also due to Dena Hollowell for transcribing my manuscript into readable form; Lynn Houze and Ned Schwing for reading the completed text and offering valuable suggestions for its improvement; and to Patricia Klug, Mary Sieber, as well as Ron Kowalke of Krause Publications for transforming it into the present book.

Finally, I wish to thank the administrators of the Kinnucan Arms Chair of the Cody Firearms Museum for their generous financial assistance in partially underwriting the costs associated with the photographs reproduced in this book.

Photograph Credits

With the exception of those illustrations noted as having been supplied by Olin Corporation, or otherwise credited, all the photographs reproduced in this book were taken by Devendra Shrikande and Lucille Warters.

Preface

By the end of the U.S. Civil War, an entirely new lexicon of words and phrases associated with that conflict had entered the American language. Terms such as ironclad, monitor, Napoleon, Parrott Rifle, torpedo and so forth, became, by virtue of their constant presence in the reports and stories about the war published in the popular press, as familiar to those at home as to the combatants themselves.

To no less an extent, the names of the various small arms used by the troops in the field also achieved a measure of notoriety. While the public at large might not have been able to intelligently discuss the relative merits of the Sharps breech-loading rifle over the muzzle-loading Springfield rifle musket, or to accurately describe the physical differences between Colt and Remington revolvers, they nonetheless were intimately aware of the arms' names. Other weapons, especially those of more modern or novel design, such as the Gatling Gun, also captured the public's imagination.

One of the major beneficiaries of the press' attention to arms of modern design was the Henry rifle. Praised by those who used it and feared by those who had it used against them, the Henry rifle quickly gained fame after its introduction into service in 1862. The public's fascination with both the rifle and the exploits of those who used it eventually led to the name "Henry" becoming a generic term for any repeating cartridge rifle with a magazine located beneath the barrel. Even after the close of the war, the term continued to be used in the same fashion as before. By 1870, however, it had been eclipsed by another phrase.

Through advertising, reports in the press about the westward expansion, and stories relating to the Indian Wars, a new byword for repeating rifles gradually emerged, the name "Winchester." In the almost century and a quarter since then, the word Winchester is still not only synonymous with repeating rifles, but also has had its meaning expanded to include all the various types of arms manufactured by the Winchester Repeating Arms Company over the intervening years. Moreover, the term still carries with it the same assurance of quality and reliability that characterized the original products of Oliver F. Winchester and his immediate successors.

Recognizing that it was important to preserve the history of the Winchester company, its owner, Olin Industries, commissioned Professor Harold F. Williamson of Yale University, in 1946, to write a corporate study of the company's origins and development. Completed in 1948, Williamson's work was published in 1952 as Winchester The Gun That Won The West.

During the four-and-a-half decades since that book was published, however, a considerable amount of new information has come to light concerning the Winchester company's operations between 1865 and 1945. While much of what has been found is inconsequential in nature, the content of some of the documents radically challenges many commonly held beliefs about the company's development.

Indeed, it is now evident that some of the basic tenets of Winchester history must be revised. This is especially true concerning the circumstances surrounding the founding of the firm and its early operations. Interestingly, though, some of the new documentary material deals with developmental programs that took place this century which have either escaped examination before or whose true significance has not been appreciated. Likewise, a number of financial and production reports alter currently held perceptions about the company's activities during the same period. The net effect of integrating the new material with what was previously known is the creation of a new corporate history which completely presents the various efforts undertaken by the Winchester Repeating Arms

Company between 1865 and 1945, to maintain or increase its position within the American and overseas arms markets. Similarly, by continuing the study of the firm's operations up to the sale of the company in 1981, the full history of the company can be reconstructed.

The purpose of this book, therefore, is to present a revised history of the Winchester Repeating Arms Company's development, incorporating not only the material included in Williamson's pioneering work, but also the information that has been uncovered since then, together with the company's activities after 1948, so that those interested in the firm may better appreciate its operations and growth.

THE ORIGINS OF THE WINCHESTER ARMS COMPANY

Although it is a matter of the purest speculation, one must wonder whether or not the name Winchester would be so closely associated with firearms today had the Volcanic Repeating Arms Company proved to be successful. For it was the circumstances of that company's failure which propelled Oliver F. Winchester from being merely a company stockholder and corporate officer into an active participant in the arms industry. Ultimately, this turn of events was to lead to the formation of one of the world's largest and most respected firearms manufacturing companies: the Winchester Repeating Arms Company.

While the collapse of the Volcanic Repeating Arms Company has been generally attributed to poor financial management, aggravated by poor sales, the root cause was its over capitalization in machinery during the concern's set-up in 1855[1]. By spending the greater portion of the monies it raised through stock subscription on capital equipment, the firm did not have sufficient reserves to cover its operating expenses when sales did not meet expectations. Consequently, it was forced to borrow money from its officers to meet these shortfalls beginning in mid-1856[2]. Unlike those funds generated by stock sales, which were for all practical purposes unsecured, the

> ### ■ Oliver F. Winchester
> ### (Nov. 30, 1810 - Dec. 10, 1880)
>
> Like his contemporary Samuel Colt, Oliver F. Winchester's earliest business ventures were not successful. Indeed, by the time he moved from Baltimore, Maryland, to New Haven, Connecticut, in 1845, he was virtually penniless. His self-confidence and energy had, however, not been adversely affected by the reversal of his fortune, and over the next ten years he slowly recovered to become one of New Haven's wealthiest citizens.

loans were guaranteed by mortgages issued against the company's assets. Based upon surviving corporate records, the primary lenders during this period were the firm's president, Nelson H. Gaston, and its vice president, Oliver F. Winchester, although other officers evidently contributed small amounts at one time or another[3].

By late 1856, the situation had deteriorated to such an extent that the company was borrowing money, not only to meet payroll costs, but also merely to retire previous debt[4]. While it is evident that Gaston and Winchester were prepared to subsidize the company until such a time as sales did increase, Gaston's sudden death in December 1856[5] brought the matter to a head. Faced with the prospect of having to lend the

company approximately $24,000 to redeem Gaston's advances, Winchester entered into an agreement with the executors of Gaston's estate to force the bankruptcy of the Volcanic Repeating Arms Company themselves[6]. In this manner, their interests would be protected even if an outside creditor filed a claim. Consequently, when two thirty-day payment drafts issued to himself and Gaston fell due on Jan. 10 and 13, respectively, Winchester declined to lend the Volcanic company the money needed to cover them[7]. When they were not honored, Winchester and Gaston's executors initiated legal proceedings to foreclose on their mortgages. The receipt of their writs of attachment on Feb. 2 and 3, 1857[8], was the catalyst which forced the directors of the Volcanic company to declare their firm insolvent[9].

On Feb. 4, in compliance with bankruptcy proceedings, the Volcanic Repeating Arms Company transferred all their assets to two trustees, Samuel L. Talcott and Gardner Morse, and petitioned the Probate Court of New Haven, Connecticut for permission to liquidate the company's assets[10]. Immediately, Winchester began protecting his claim and that of Gaston's estate (which he had by then assumed) by lending the company's trustees such funds as were necessary to redeem other loans which were secured by mortgages or that could be recovered by legal action involving the attachment of the company's assets[11]. He also advanced the trustees the money needed to pay off the company's obligations to Courtland Palmer, Horace Smith and Daniel B. Wesson, so that their patents were fully paid for and totally under the control of the trustees[12]. As a result of this maneuver, Winchester became the sole mortgage holder of the former Volcanic Repeating Arms Company, at a cost which ultimately amounted to $35,438.74[13].

> The products of the Volcanic Repeating Arms Company never achieved the success the firm had hoped for, despite the receipt of glowing testimonials such as the following: "I consider the Volcanic Repeating Pistol the plus ultra of Repeating or Revolving Arms, and far superior in many respects to Colt's much extolled revolver." (C.F.W. Behm, March 10, 1855)

On Feb. 18, the Probate Court approved the appointment of Talcott and Morse as the Volcanic company's executors and ordered them to prepare a list of all creditors, mortgage claims and assets[14]. Eli Whitney, Henry Munson and Charles Ball were also appointed by the court at that time to appraise the company's property[15].

On March 13, Talcott and Morse presented their report, which indicated that the former Volcanic Repeating Arms Company's total assets amounted to $57,714.53 against which the following mortgages totalling $65,632.06 were held[16]:

Oliver F. Winchester	$30,673.80
Nelson H. Gaston	$24,317.04
Tradesmens Bank of New Haven	$10,641.22

Judge Cyprian Willcox then instructed Talcott and Morse to sell the assets of the company either by public or private sale so that the mortgage claims could be paid[17]. On March 31, 1856, Talcott and Morse carried out the court's instructions, and Oliver F. Winchester purchased the right to redeem both his mortgage and that of Gaston's for $805[18]. He also purchased 2,000 arms in the process of being finished for $2,000, three lathes not included in the mortgage claims for $475 and miscellaneous other items for $500[19]. His agents, E. Benjamin and B.F. Parder, purchased an additional $628.25 worth of material including 102 pistols at $5 each[20]. As a result of these purchases and two subsequent payments to Courtland Palmer, Winchester became the sole owner of the Volcanic company's assets at a total cost to him of $40,242.51[21].

Having gained complete control of the former Volcanic company's manufacturing capabilities, Winchester then set about organizing a new company. Prior to doing so, however, he secured clear claim to his new property by paying off Gaston's estate and by renegotiating the mortgage the Tradesmens Bank held against the old Volcanic company, which they stood to lose under the settlement agreement[22]. Winchester then met with William Story and J.W. King to form a successor to the old firm. The articles of association for this new company, to be called the New Haven Arms Company, were signed on April 3, 1857[23]. While production began almost immediately thereafter, the company was not formally organized until May 1, when sufficient monies had been paid into its treasury so that it could purchase from Winchester for $15,000 the rights to use the patents he had acquired from the Volcanic company and their machinery, as well as work in progress, for an additional $25,000[24]. Ironically, the greater part of the money given to Winchester was his own as he purchased 800 shares in the new company at a cost of $20,000[25]. The balance of the machinery and patent rights purchase was funded by stock purchases by Story, King and Samuel Talcott[26].

Though small in comparison with such operations as the Colt's Patent Fire Arms Manufacturing Company in Hartford, Connecticut and E. Remington & Sons in Ilion, New York, the New Haven Arms Company's factory was formidably equipped when it began formal production under the superintendency of Hollis Smith[27], in May 1857, as the following list of machinery in place there demonstrates[28]:

- 10 Robertson's Milling Machines
- 1 Chickopee Index Milling Machine
- 2 Jigging or Edging Machines
- 1 Robertson's Drill Press
- 2 Robbins & Lawrence Drill Presses
- 1 Robbins & Lawrence Small Drill Press
- 2 Shepard, Lathe & Company Planing Machines
- 1 White & West Rifling Machine
- 1 Hicks' Vibrating Breeching Press
- 1 Screw Press
- 2 Reaming Machines
- 1 Polishing Machine
- 1 Screw Cutting Machine
- 2 Seven Foot Screw Lathes
- 3 Six Foot Screw Lathes
- 7 Five Foot Common Lathes
- 5 Hand Lathes
- 6 Fitters Lathes
- 2 Boring Machines
- 1 Checking Machine
- 1 Chucking Lathe
- 3 Polishing Stands
- 1 Crittenden and Tibballs Rule Machine
- 1 Hicks' Vibrating Machine
- 1 Drop Press
- 4 Spindle Drill Presses (White and West)
- 3 Lathes
- 1 Four Hammer Drop Press
- 2 Grindstones
- 2 Ball Wedging Machines
- 1 Loading Machine

In addition, the company held the rights to manufacture arms under the following patents[29]:

Patent issued to William R. Palmer, assignee of Walter Hunt, dated February 16th 1850 and marked Re-issue No. 163, for "method of attaching a ball to a cartridge"

Patent issued to George A. Arrowsmith, assignee of Walter Hunt, dated February 16, 1850, marked Re-issue No. 164, for "Loaded Ball"

Patent issued to George A. Arrowsmith, assignee of Lewis Jennings, dated December 25th 1849, for "Improvements in breech- loading firearms" and marked No. 6973

Patent issued to George A. Arrowsmith, assignee of Walter Hunt, dated August 21st, 1849, for "combined piston breech and firing cock repeating gun" marked No. 6663

Patent issued to Courtland Palmer, assignee of Horace Smith, dated August 26th, 1851, for

"improvements in breech-loading fire-arms", marked No. 8317

Patent issued to Horace Smith and Daniel B.Wesson, dated August 8th, 1854, for "Improvement in cartridges", marked No. 11496

Patent issued to Horace Smith and Daniel B. Wesson, dated October 10th 1854, for "Improvement in fire-arms", marked Re-issue No. 279 (Plate 1)

Patent issued to the Volcanic Repeating Arms Company aforesaid, assignee of Horace Smith and Daniel B. Wesson, for "Improved Primers for Cartridges of Fire Arms", marked No. 14147

Initially, the company worked on the completion of the 2,000 arms left in pro-

cess by the old Volcanic company. That the firm was reasonably successful in marketing these arms, as well as the 500 pistols Winchester had secured, is demonstrated by a record of the company's sales for the period of May through September 1857[30]:

The importance of these figures is that they indicate that a substantial number of the arms acquired from the inventory of the Volcanic firm were disposed of relatively quickly, and by virtue of the cost figures first appearing in the August entry that production of at least one new model had begun. The final expansion of the company's product line to include seven distinct models of pistols (Plate 2) and carbines (Plate 3) was

Plate 1

*O*riginal specification drawing for Horace Smith and Daniel B. Wesson's U.S. Patent Number 10535 issued Feb. 14, 1854, and reissued Oct. 10, 1854 (Number 279). Record Group Number 241, National Archives of the United States, Washington, D.C. Photograph Courtesy of the National Archives.

	Gross	Net	Cost	Sold	Profit
May	$11328.75	10270.42			
June	753.77	563.94			
July	698.20	580.40			
Aug	1188.53	1022.63	232.12	297.60	65.48
Sept	1456.20	208.30	260.90	52.60	

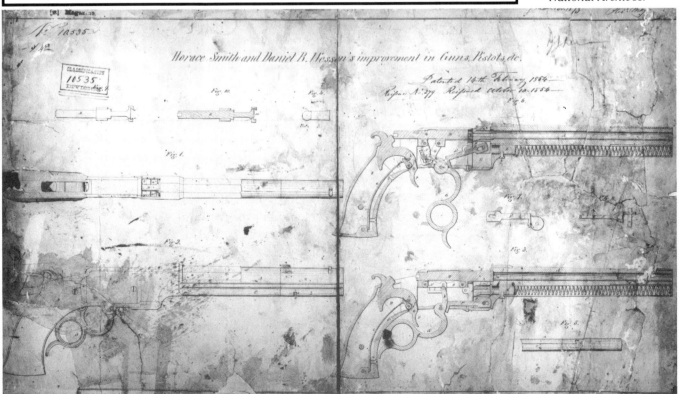

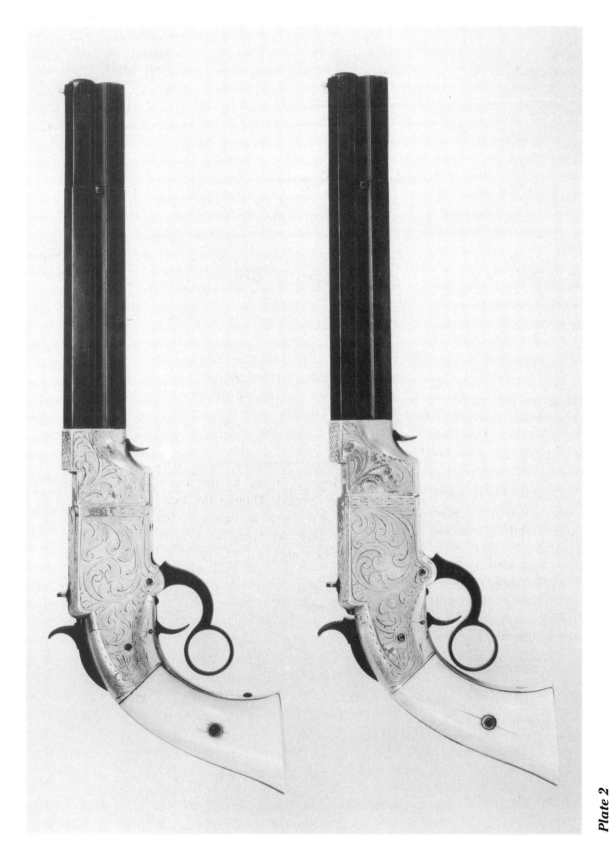

Plate 2

Pair of engraved and silver-plated New Haven Arms Company .38 caliber pistols fitted with ivory grips, originally owned by Oliver F. Winchester. Winchester Family Collection. Olin Corporation photograph.

not to be completed until some eighteen months later[31].

A further indication of the New Haven Arms Company's prosperity during this period is that Winchester paid off all the debt he had assumed with the Tradesmens Bank on account of the Volcanic Repeating Arms Company prior to Nov. 1, 1857[32].

In April or May 1858, Hollis Smith retired as the New Haven Arms Company's factory superintendent, and Benjamin Tyler Henry (Plate 5) was hired as his replacement[33]. Faced with declining sales due to what Winchester termed a "strong prejudice[34]" against the Volcanic style arms, Henry was instructed to begin experiments which might lead to

> No more popular than those arms made by the Volcanic Repeating Arms Company, the early products of the New Haven Arms Company were, nevertheless, advertised in October 1859 as being both a "triumph of genius" and "the most powerful and effective weapon of defense ever invented."

the alteration of the Smith & Wesson system so that metallic cartridges could be used in it. By mid-1859, Henry had developed a satisfactory solution to the problem (Plate 6) and had produced at least one working sample of a .38" caliber carbine (Color Plate 2)[35]. Realizing that arms of this caliber would probably not be of much economic value, Winchester directed Henry to develop a larger bore version. Though the exact date is unknown, it is believed that Henry completed work on the .44" caliber rimfire cartridge and the rifle chambered for it in early 1860, at which time drawings of the completed sample, as well as the tooling necessary to manufacture it, were begun[36]. It was not until mid-1860, though, that the completed sample together with drawings of it were forwarded to Washington to support Henry's patent application (granted Oct. 16, 1860, Plate 7)[37].

Due to the financial obligations Winchester had incurred together with John M. Davies in the expansion of their shirt manufacturing company (Color Plate 3) beginning in 1860[38], he was not in the position to immediately fund the cost of retooling the New Haven Arms Company's plant so that

Plate 3

A New Haven Arms Company .38 caliber carbine in its original paper carton. Olin Corporation photograph.

production of the new rifle could begin. Rather, production was delayed until sufficient funds were received in the company's accounts. One effort made to generate money in 1860 involved the firm's agreement to manufacture 3,000 percussion revolvers based upon John Walch's United States Patent Number 22905, issued on Feb. 8, 1859, for the Walch Fire-Arms Company of New York[39]. While it was anticipated that this contract would generate $8,000 in profit from the total contract price of $26,000, the Walch company failed prior to the completion of the contract and the New Haven Arms Company upon suit only received the revolvers as compensation[40].

By April 1861, however, Winchester's personal finances had improved sufficiently enough to allow him to advance the company the money needed to begin construction of the tools and fixtures needed to manufacture the Henry rifle.

Plate 4

Photograph of the New Haven Arms Company's factory at 9 Artisan Street, New Haven, circa 1858 or 1859. The gentleman at the window is believed to be O.F. Winchester, and the man at the door B.T. Henry. Three of the employees pictured are holding pistols (the man at far left with two; sixth from left one; and seventh from left one). The man fourth from the left is holding a carbine to his left shoulder. Olin Corporation photograph.

■ Benjamin Tyler Henry

Born on March 22, 1821, in Claremont, New Hampshire, Benjamin Tyler Henry entered the employ of Oliver F. Winchester as a master mechanic at the New Haven Shirt Manufacturing Company in the mid-1850s. He then was employed as superintendent of the New Haven Arms Company, where he developed the repeating cartridge rifle which was to make his name famous. After parting company with Winchester in 1864, Henry worked as a general gunsmith in New Haven. He died in relative obscurity on June 8, 1898, his fame having been eclipsed some five decades earlier.

Plate 5
Photograph of Benjamin Tyler Henry believed to have been taken circa 1863. Olin Corporation photograph.

Although absolute evidence is lacking, it would appear that this work was not done in New Haven, but rather, Hartford, Connecticut, at the Colt's Patent Fire Arms Manufacturing Company. The basis for this conclusion is the following receipt signed by Elisha K. Root[41] (upper right):

Given the date and amount, some consideration should also be given to the possibility that the Colt company may have manufactured the first production run of Henry rifles that had iron frames. Certainly, the amount being paid out suggests strongly that more than tools and fixtures was involved. However, until further documentation comes to light, this must remain a matter of speculation.

The date production of the brass frame Henry rifle (Plate 8) began in New Haven can, however, be fixed with certainty to the early spring 1862. On April 24 of that year, Winchester wrote E.K. Root at the Colt company, as follows[42]:

"I send you to-day by Adams' Express Co. three of our rifles and one hundred cartridges fro each. One of these you will please accept for yourself; and present one of each of the others, with my best respects, to Mr. Jarvis and Mr. Lord".

The rifle given to Root later passed into the Colt Factory Museum, and its inventory record notes that it bore the serial number 205. Further corroboration of the early 1862 commencement of production is provided by rifle serial number 228, which was presented by Winchester on May 2, 1862, to and is still accompanied by the letter at right[43]:

By July 1862, a sufficient quantity of the new rifles had been completed so that back orders had been filled and general marketing of the rifle could begin. A copy of the letter circulated to dealers and other interested parties at that time described the new rifle as

---

Colt's Patent Fire Arms Manufacturing Company
Hartford, Conn.

May 11, 1861

Mr. O.F. Winchester, Esq.
New Haven

Patent Arms Acct	$4,200.00
Recd	2,300.00
	$1,900.00

New Haven Conn.
May 2, 1862

General Schurz
Washington

Dear General

Please accept with my compliments, one of our new rifles which has been sent to you this day by Adams' Express in care of the Willard Hotel.

As you will see it is much improved over our previous models and is well suited for military use.

Yours, very truly

O.F. Winchester, Prest

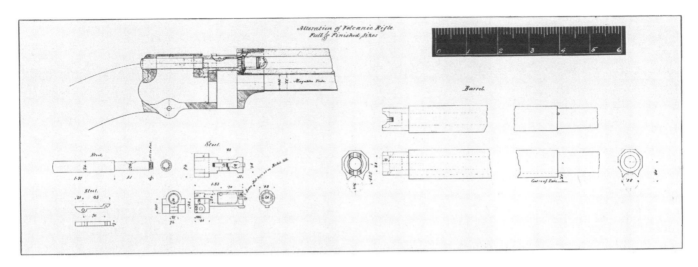

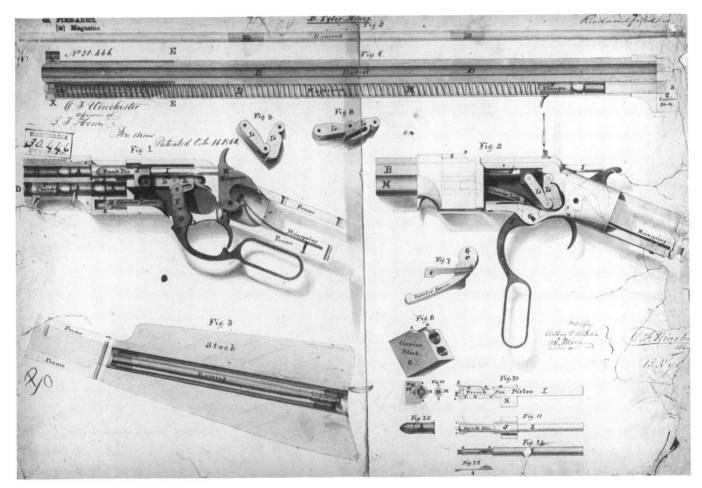

Top: Plate 6

*D*esign drawing prepared in mid-1859, to demonstrate the modification of a New Haven Arms Company carbine receiver for use with metallic rimfire cartridges of .38 or .40 caliber. Winchester Arms Collection Archives, Cody Firearms Museum, Buffalo Bill Historical Center. Olin Corporation photograph.

Bottom: Plate 7

*O*riginal specification drawing for Benjamin Tyler Henry's U.S. Patent Number 30446 issued Oct. 16, 1860. Record Group number 241, National Archives of the United States, Washington, D.C. Photograph courtesy of the National Archives.

"the most powerful weapon of its size produced, and of greater accuracy and rapidity[44]", and fixed its price at $42.

Despite the promise held by the Henry rifle, the New Haven Arms Company continued to be plagued by debt and lack of investor interest. By October 1862, Winchester's personal loans to the company amounted to approximately $22,000 and other parties held just over $50,000 worth of the company's notes[45]. The financial picture did begin to brighten, however, in early 1863, when sales and orders increased.

The realization of the Henry rifles's true profit potential was to elude the New Haven Arms Company for the first two-and-a-half years of the rifle's production. Under an agreement negotiated in May 1859, Benjamin Tyler Henry had a five-year exclusive contract to manufacture arms for the company[46]. Based upon the surviving payroll records of the firm, it appears that he never substantially increased the work force under his control even when the company had purchased additional machin-ery and orders warranted increased production[47]. The reasons for his inaction are at present unknown, but they may have involved his wish to draw both a straight salary as well as the profits from providing contract employees as long as possible. Whatever the case, the delays incurred between the receipt of orders and actual delivery of rifles caused an ever-increasing amount of friction between Winchester and Henry. Tension between the two was heightened in December 1863, when Winchester personally leased the old Dwight, Chapin & Company armory in Bridgeport, Connecticut (Plate 9) from its owners, Wheeler and Wilson of New Haven,

Plate 8

Illustration of a First Pattern Henry Rifle used on the cover of the New Haven Arms Company's 1863 catalog. Olin Corporation photograph.

While General Carl Schurz's military career during the Civil War has now been largely forgotten, the remarks he made on Oct. 17, 1899 in Chicago will always ensure that the man himself is never forgotten. "Our country, right or wrong. When right, to be kept right; when wrong, to be put right."

with the sole purpose of expanding Henry rifle production[48]. Utilizing his own funds, Winchester purchased sufficient machinery to double production and contracted with Luke Wheelock to supervise its installation during December 1863 and January 1864[49]. However, production at the Bridgeport facility was to be put off until Henry's contract with the New Haven Arms Company expired.

Although Henry left the company in mid-May 1864, his contract to produce arms was honored until its expiration one month later[50]. Immediately thereafter, though, the work force was reorganized and substantially enlarged. C.M. Manning was appointed superintendent of the New Haven factory, and Allen Bowe was given the same position in Bridgeport[51]. In comparison with the period of April 17 to May 14, when Henry employed 33 people to manufacture arms and the company itself had 18 employees, the company's payroll book indicates that in July 1864, a total of 65 persons were employed at the factory, and in August that number had increased to 67. By September, the Bridgeport plant was in full production and the company's total work force had been enlarged to 100 people[52].

The importance of the ammunition division to the company's welfare at this time is perhaps best demonstrated by the fact that of the 100 people employed in September, 37 were women engaged in making cartridges under George A. Stetson's control[53]. As

Plate 9

The Dwight, Chapin & Company Armory in Bridgeport, Connecticut, leased by O.F. Winchester in December 1863. Olin Corporation photograph.

19

orders for ammunition increased, the percentage of the company's employees working solely on ammunition increased to fifty-five percent[54].

In contrast to operations under Henry, when arms were manufactured under a contract system, the New Haven Arms Company after June 11, 1864, was solely responsible for manufacturing and paying all employees. Evidently, the experience with Henry had disillusioned the company's directors from reinstituting the contract form of production.

While Winchester had evidently given some thought to the expansion of the company's product line to include carbines and .50" caliber muskets as early as July 1863[55], it was not until mid-1864 that the subject was given any

Described in newspapers such as the **Louisville Democrat** as "the best weapon yet devised by the wit of man," a truer appreciation of the Henry Rifle's worth is to be found in the following statement made by a Confederate soldier captured at the Battle of the Rome Cross Roads on May 16, 1864: "Sir, there is no use in the South fighting men armed as yours are armed."

Plate 10

B*avarian Contract Henry Rifle with George W. Briggs' altered magazine loading port, serial number 181. Winchester Arms Collection (Inv. No. W121), Cody Firearms Museum, Buffalo Bill Historical Center. Olin Corporation photograph.*

Plate 11

P*hotograph of Oliver F. Winchester believed to have been taken in 1864. Olin Corporation photograph.*

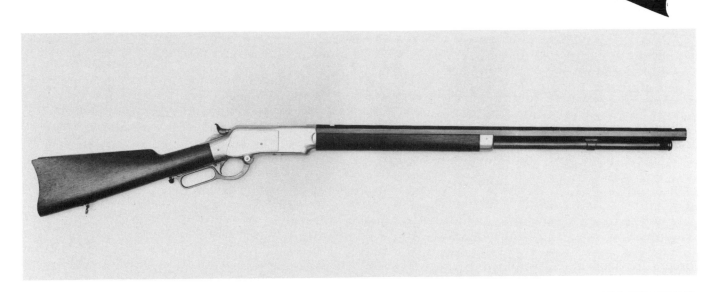

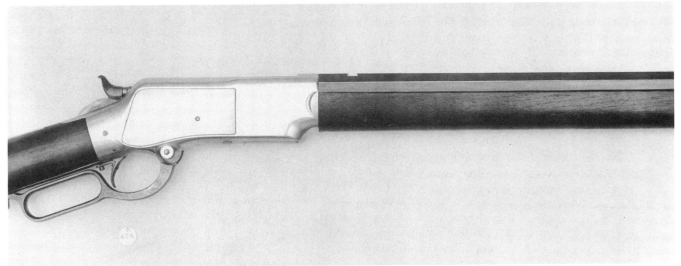

serious attention. As the Henry rifle saw ever-increasing field use in the Civil War it became evident that its design contained two major flaws. If the rifle were exposed to mud or rain, the rotating collar which allowed the magazine to be charged had a tendency to rust in place, if not properly lubricated; and the magazine tube itself could be fouled by mud or dust entering through the open slot so that cartridges would not feed properly[56]. While these problems would not have been of great consequence in an arm designed for the civilian market, in a military rifle the results could be disastrous. Consequently, the New Haven factory's chief designer, George W. Briggs, was given the task of redesigning the loading sys-

tem so that the problems were either eliminated or at least partially alleviated[57].

The first design to be developed to correct these problems was incorporated in the 500 Henry rifles (Plate 10) produced under contract for the Kingdom of Bavaria at the Bridgeport plant in late 1864[58]. In place of the rotating muzzle collar used in the standard Henry rifle, Briggs fitted the magazine with a sliding cover which fit over an aperture cut in the magazine tube approximately 6-3/4 inches from the muzzle. To charge the magazine, the cartridge follower was moved forward, as in the Henry, until it was past the sliding loading port cover. The cover itself was then moved forward out of alignment

Top: Plate 12

An 11.3mm caliber lever action rifle incorporating O.F. Winchester's sliding magazine tube loading system built by Weber-Ruesch of Zurich, Switzerland, in March or April 1865. Winchester Arms Collection (Inv. No. W266), Cody Firearms Museum. Olin Corporation photograph.

Bottom: Plate 13

Detail of the Weber-Ruesch rifle illustrated in Plate 12. Olin Corporation photograph.

with the loading aperture and rotated slightly to lock it in an open position, thereby also preventing the cartridge follower from moving rearward under pressure from the magazine spring. Cartridges could then be directly fed into the magazine. When charging was complete, the sliding cover was unlocked and moved rearward to its closed position[59]. While the majority of the Bavarian contract Henry rifles have manually operated loading port covers, several examples are fitted with covers having a small internal lug, which is briefly engaged by the cartridge follower during its rearward travel after the cover has been unlocked and causes the cover to be automatically closed[60].

Though a marked improvement over the basic Henry magazine design, the Bavarian rifles still embodied one of the earlier rifle's failings: the open slot cut in the magazine tube. Consequently, the design was not adopted for general production.

While it has been commonly assumed that Winchester (Plate 11) was involved in the day-to-day operations of the New Haven Arms Company during 1863 and 1864, his almost total involvement with his partnership with John M. Davies at this time precluded anything greater than a supervisory role[61]. By December 1864, however, the fortunes of the Winchester-Davies Company had increased to such an extent that both partners

Top: Plate 14

A 16 gauge lever action shotgun incorporating O.F. Winchester's sliding magazine tube loading system built by Weber-Ruesch of Zurich, Switzerland, in March or April 1865. Winchester Arms Collection (Inv. No. W532), Cody Firearms Museum. Olin Corporation photograph.

Bottom: Plate 15

Detail of the Weber-Ruesch shotgun illustrated in Plate 14. Olin Corporation photograph.

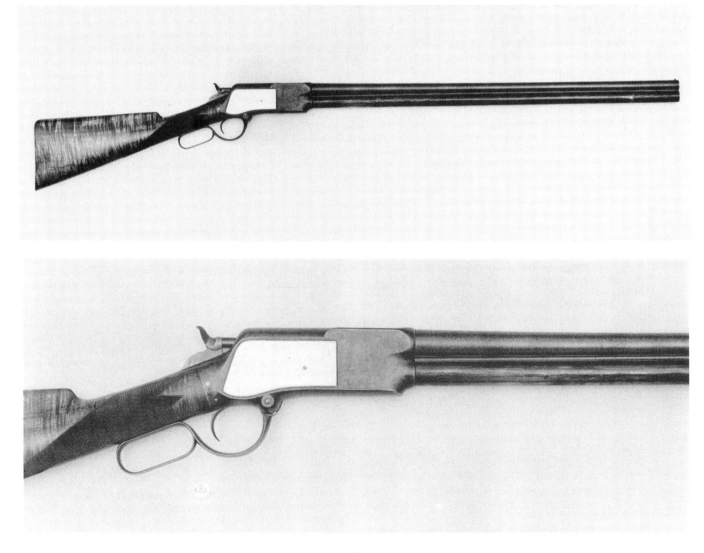

decided they could safely transfer management of the firm to their respective sons[62]. On Jan. 1, 1865, Winchester and John M. Davies announced their retirement, and shortly thereafter, Winchester left for Europe, arriving in Naples, Italy on or about the 15th of that month[63].

Whether or not Winchester took samples of the Henry rifle with him on his trip is unknown, but the likelihood is that he did. It is certain, though, that he gave considerable thought to the problem of that rifle's magazine design while he was abroad. The basis of this statement is that Winchester contracted with the Zurich armsmaker Weber Ruesch to build a rifle (Plates 12 and 13) and shotgun (Plates 14 and 15) in March or April 1865, with Henry-style actions but an entirely different magazine design[64]. The magazine developed by Winchester (Plate 16) was constructed in two parts consisting of a fixed outer sleeve and a sliding tube having captive spring and cartridge follower which fitted into the sleeve. To load, it was necessary to withdraw the tube, fill the magazine sleeve with cartridges and then insert the tube back into the sleeve. While both the 11.3mm caliber rifle and the 16 gauge shotgun made by Weber-Ruesch have magazines of this design, the method of locking the inner tube in place differs. The rifle's inner magazine tube has a knurled tip having a raised partial rib around its forward circumference. When the tube is inserted into the magazine sleeve, the tip can be rotated so that the raised rib engages a slot cut in the bottom of the barrel, thus locking the tube in place. In contrast, the shotgun's inner tube is held in place solely by friction. Apart from their magazines, both Bernard arms are noteworthy in that their receivers are not fitted with dovetailed side panels, but rather, sideplates secured by transverse screws[65]. From the viewpoint of manufacture, this arrangement involved far less

machining than the old design, and was subsequently adopted for use on all sample and limited production arms made up to 1873. The sideplates of the shotgun are of particular interest, as they are made of an aluminum alloy, one of the first applications of this metal in arms making[66].

While in Paris, during the second half of April, Winchester met with M. Francois de Suzanne, who informed him that the French government would be willing to purchase, for export abroad, 1,000 Henry rifles incorporating "such improvements as may be made[67]" subject to normal review procedures.

By the beginning of May 1865, Winchester was again in Zurich, Switzerland. While it was his intention to travel from there to the Rhine Falls at Schaffhausen, the spas at Baden-Baden, Cologne, Liege and finally London, before returning to the United States[68], those plans were forestalled by a dispatch he received in Zurich, which informed him that the secretary of the New Haven Arms Company, Charles W. Nott, in collaboration with Benjamin Tyler Henry (still a stockholder in the firm) had used a power of attorney, signed by Winchester prior to his departure to Europe, to petition the Connecticut State Legislature to change the name

■ John M. Davies

Characterized as "a man of capital and character," John M. Davies was a prominent New York businessman before moving to New Haven, Connecticut in 1860. A long-standing personal friend of Oliver F. Winchester, Davies first went into partnership with Winchester in the early 1850s, when they established the New Haven Shirt Manufacturing Company. By the time of the Civil War, that concern had grown from a very small shop into a business with a net worth in excess of $1 million. Davies' subsequent partnerships with Winchester in the arms business proved to be equally successful, and by the time of his death in 1874, he was a multimillionaire.

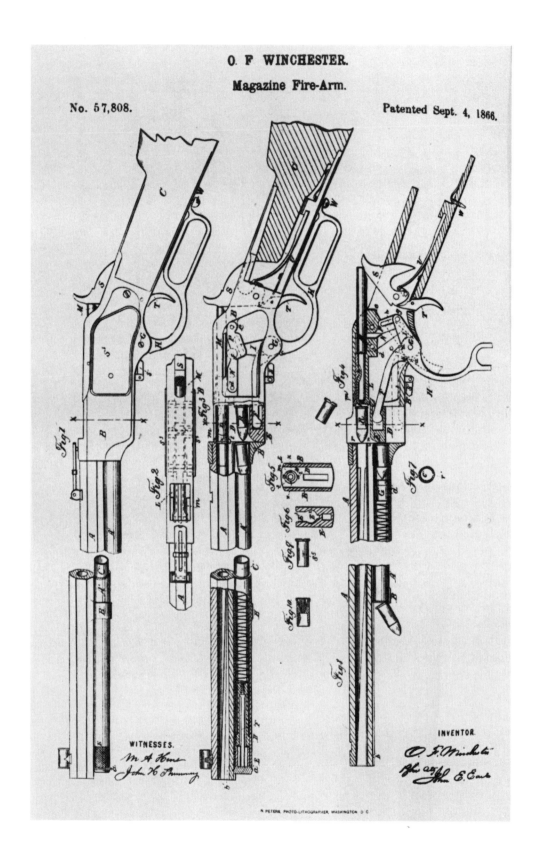

Plate 16

Specification drawings enrolled with O.F. Winchester's U.S. Patent Number 57808 issued on Sept. 4, 1866. Winchester Arms Collection Archives, Cody Firearms Museum.

of the New Haven Arms Company to the Henry Repeating Rifle Company[69].

Infuriated, Winchester cabled his London bankers, Baring Brothers, to immediately notify his partner in New Haven, John M. Davies, to[70]:

"...present all those mortgages and liens now in my possession or held by my son, William Winchester, against the company formerly called the New Haven Arms Company, to its successor in business, the Henry Rifle Company [sic] for immediate collection."

Although Winchester could not, without some public embarrassment, prevent the name change from becoming a fait accompli, since the power of attorney used was legitimate, he could prevent the new company from operating under the Henry banner. By presenting the notes he held against the property of the New Haven Arms Company, Winchester effectively diverted the attention of the dissident stockholders from any thought of normal business operations to the very real prospect that their new company would soon be forced into bankruptcy.

Based upon the alacrity with which subsequent events occurred, Oliver F. Winchester had, by the time he returned to the United States in early June 1865[71], abandoned his plan to openly challenge the New Haven Arms Company's name change, and instead, settled upon the simple expediency of establishing his own privately owned company to manufacture an improvement of the Henry design.

While this solution would appear at first glance to have been a rather expensive undertaking for Winchester, it was, in reality, not. As he personally held the lease on the Bridgeport factory and had equipped it at his own expense[72], Winchester merely needed to refuse the New Haven Arms Company further use of the property and then recover the mortgage note for its machinery to accomplish his aims. At a meeting of the New Haven Arms Company's officers and stockholders held prior to July 1, 1865[73], Winchester made his intentions known. The privatization of the Bridgeport plant served another of Winchester's purposes, apart from just providing him with a manufacturing site. Its separation from the New Haven Arms Company reduced that firm's production capabilities by better than fifty percent, thereby clouding, if not crippling, any hopes the dissident stockholders had of securing outside financing to buy out Winchester's interest in the company[74]. Consequently, Winchester did not feel that there was any compelling need to force the issue of the name change, especially since the Henry Repeating Rifle Company needed $300,000 in new capital before it could begin operations[75]. Winchester did, however, believe that it was necessary to maintain his position as president of the New Haven Company. He, therefore, forced a vote on the matter as well as a vote on Nott's continued presence as secretary[76]. By virtue of his own stock holdings, combined with his son's and John M. Davies', Winchester was easily reelected. Nott, as might be expected, did not fare as well. To replace him as company secretary, Davies nominated Henry A. Chapin[77], who was a staunch ally of Winchester's. Having secured operational control of the New Haven company, Winchester was then in the position to direct its fortunes in addition to those of his own company.

Endnotes

1. The company's extensive investment in machinery and tooling is demonstrated by the list of property attached by Gaston's heirs and Winchester on Feb. 3, 1857. Writ of Attachment, File 1, Item 6, Documents Relating to the Volcanic Repeating Arms Company, etc. Winchester Arms Collection Archives, Cody Firearms Museum, Buffalo Bill Historical Center, Cody, Wyoming.

2. Statement of claims filed by N.H. Gaston's heir and O.F. Winchester against the Volcanic Repeating Arms Company. Ibid, File 2, Items 6-9 and File 3, Item 11.

3. Probate Court Report dated Aug. 24, 1857. Ibid, File 2, Item 9.

4. Ibid.

5. Upon Gaston's death, all notes he held against the company became immediately payable.

6. This statement is based upon the fact that both the Gaston estate and Winchester writs of attachment were filed on the same day. Volcanic Documents, op. cit., File 1, Items 6 and 7.

7. Ibid.

8. Ibid.

9. Appointment of Receivers dated Feb. 3, 1857. Ibid, File 1, Item 10.

10. Petition for the Volcanic Repeating Arms Company to be declared insolvent filed by the Tradesmans Bank of New Haven. Ibid, File 2, Item 18.

11. Statement of payments made to the receivers of the Volcanic Repeating Arms Company to cover outstanding obligations to March 31, 1857. Ibid, File 1, Item 15.

12. Ibid.

13. Ibid.

14. Probate Court Order dated March 13, 1857. Ibid, File 1, Item 19.

15. Probate Court Appointment of Appraisers dated Feb. 18, 1857. Ibid, File 1, Item 12.

16. Statement of Appraisers dated March 13, 1857. Ibid, File 1, Item 12.

17. Probate Court Order of Sale dated March 13, 1857. Ibid, File 1, Item 12.

18. Contract to Purchase Machinery dated March 31, 1857. Ibid, File 1, Item 13.

19. Statement of Purchases made by O.F. Winchester from the Volcanic Repeating Arms Company Estate (undated). Ibid, File 2, Item 7.

20. Ibid.

21. Ibid.

22. Statement of Accounts Paid by O.F. Winchester. prepared in late March 1857. Ibid, File 2, Item 1.

23. Harold F. Williamson, **Winchester: The Gun That Won The West** (Combat Forces Press; Washington, D.C.: 1952), page 21.

24. Bill and Assignment of Sale Executed by O.F. Winchester dated May 1, 1857. Volcanic Documents, op. cit., File 2, Item 10.

25. Statement of Account of O.F. Winchester with the New Haven Arms Company for April and May 1857. Ibid, File 2, Item 11.

26. Ibid.

27. Miscellaneous Notes Regarding the New Haven Arms Company (circa 1900), page 1. New Haven Arms Company File, Winchester Arms Collection Archives, Cody Firearms Museum.

28. This is the same machinery purchased by Winchester on March 31, 1857, from the Volcanic Repeating Arms Company Estate. Volcanic Documents, op. cit., File 2, Items 6-9.

29. Transfer of Patents dated March 31, 1857. Ibid, File 1, Item 14; and Bill of Assignment dated May 1, 1857. Ibid, File 2, Item 10.

30. Verso of Accounts Paid by O.F. Winchester and Estate of N.H. Gaston as of March 31, 1857. Ibid, File 1, Item 15.

31. New Haven Arms Company advertising pamphlet dated May 1, 1859 (reproduced in R. Bruce McDowell, **Evolution of the Winchester** [Armory Publications; Tacoma, WA: 1985], page 113).

32. See Notes 11 and 30.

33. Synopsis of Benjamin Tyler Henry's employment with the New Haven Arms Company. New Haven Arms Company File, op. cit.

34. Letter from O.F. Winchester to E.B. Martin dated Oct. 19, 1862. New Haven Arms Company Letter Press Book (May 1, 1857 to Dec. 12, 1863), pages 118-120. Winchester Arms Collection Archives, Cody Firearms Museum.

35. A detailed elevations drawing and detached receiver of this rifle are preserved in the Winchester Arms Collection, Cody Firearms Museum. For further corroboration of the date cartridge experimentation took place, see **"In the matter of the application of B. TYLER HENRY, for an extension of Letters Patent, granted to him Oct. 16, 1860, reissued Dec. 8, 1868, for magazine Firearms," Brief on the Part of Applicant, Before the Hon. Commissioner of Patents, Sept. 21, 1874** (U.S. Government Printing Office; Washington, D.C.: 1874).

36. Two engineering drawings dated Jan. 12 and 23, 1860, are known to exist in private collections. Cf., Winchester-Martin letter cited in Note 35.

37. United States Patent Number 30446, issued Oct. 16, 1860 (the application for which is believed to have been filed on either May 15 or 16, 1860).

38. The Winchester-Davies factory was substantially enlarged in 1860, resulting in a heavy expenditure of capital for new machinery. Records of the R.G. Dun Company, Connecticut, Volume 39, page 208, Baker Library, Harvard University, Boston, Massachusetts.

39. Winchester-Martin letter, op. cit., page 118.

40. Ibid, pages 118-119.

41. Formerly in the collection of James L. Mitchell, sold by the Richard A. Bourne, Co., Inc., March 17-18, 1982, Lot 862 (part). Present location unknown.

42. Ibid, Lot 700. Present location unknown.

43. In the possession of General Schurz's descendants. For an account of Schurz's civilian and military life, see Kathryn E. O'Brien, **The Great and the Gracious on Millionaire's Row** (North Country Books, Inc.; Utica, NY: 1978), pages 136-144. Schurz served as U.S. Ambassador to the Court of Spain and returned to the United States after the First Battle of Bull Run. He was a friend of President Lincoln's and apparently personally reported to Lincoln throughout his Civil War career.

44. New Haven Arms Company File, op. cit.

45. Winchester-Martin letter, op. cit., page 119.

46. See note 33.

47. This statement is based upon subsequent events and a survey of the New Haven Arms Company Payroll Book (Jan. 24, 1863 to July 7, 1866). Winchester Arms Collection Archives, Cody Firearms Museum.

48. Letter from O.F. Winchester to T.C. Watson dated Nov. 17, 1862, reading in part, "If the third proposition only should be accepted we propose to manufacture them at our Armory in Bridgeport." New Haven Arms Company Letter Press Book, op. cit., page 481.

49. New Haven Arms Company Payroll Book, op. cit., Jan. 23, 1864. Regarding machinery, a notation recording a loan made by John M. Davies to O.F. Winchester on December 8, 1863, for "rifle machinery" is recorded in "Summary of Monies Invested by John M. Davies 1858-1870", page 5. Davies Estate Records, Davies Family Papers, New York, New York.

50. New Haven Arms Company Payroll Book, op. cit., June 11, 1864.

51. Ibid, May 14, July 9 and Aug. 6, 1864.

52. Ibid, Sept. 5, 1864.

53. Ibid.

54. Ibid, Sept. 5 to Dec. 24, 1864.

55. Letter from O.F. Winchester to the Honorable Joel Hayden dated June 12, 1863. New Haven Arms Company Letter Press Book, op. cit., pages 290-291.

56. Williamson, op. cit., pages 34 and 49. Also, Winchester's Repeating Fire Arms (Winchester Repeating Arms Company; New Haven, CT: 1867), pages 8-12.

57. The attribution of this design to Briggs is based not only on its construction, but also, a pencil sketch of what appears to be the same system which is initialled "GWB" preserved in the Winchester Arms Collection Archives.

58. **Die Entwicklungsgeschichte der WINCHESTER Gewehre** (Weber- Ruesch; Zurich: n.d.), page 3. For further information regarding this source see Note 64 following.

59. See the Bavarian Contract Henry rifle, serial number 181 in the Winchester Arms Collection (Inv. No. W121).

60. For example, serial number 170, preserved in a private Swiss collection (personal communication from its owner).

61. The complexity of the Winchester-Davies partnership's operations is demonstrated by various entries in the records of the R.G. Dun Company, op. cit., Connecticut, Volume 40, pages 208 and 426.

62. Ibid, page 426.

63. John M. Davies, Manuscript Diary for the period Jan. 2, 1865 to Dec. 28, 1866. Entry dated Jan. 15, 1865. Davies Family Papers, loc. cit.

64. Entwicklungsgeschichte der Winchester, op. cit, pages 4 and 5. This 22 page pamphlet (hereafter referred to as Weber-Ruesch) discusses the relationship of Weber-Ruesch with O.F. Winchester and the Winchester Repeating Arms Company from 1858 to approximately 1883. Though undated, it is believed that the pamphlet was printed in 1883 as mention is made of the "neues modell" Hotchkiss rifle with William Mason's improvement as about to enter production.

65. Inventory Numbers W266 and W532, Winchester Arms Collection, Cody Firearms Museum. Cf., T.C. Johnson, F.F. Burton, E. Pugsley, T.E. Hall, et al., **Inventory of the Winchester Repeating Arms Company Firearms Reference Collection** (Lynham Sayce Co.; Salt Lake City, UT: 1991), pages 52 and 88.

66. Inventory Number W532, Ibid, page 88.

67. Davies Diary, op. cit., entry dated June 4, 1865. This entry reads in part "...visit to Paris profitable the French ordered 1000 rifles for Mexico having such improvements as may be made shortly...." The letter press book maintained by de Suzanne contains a letter of thanks to Winchester mentioning his recent "courtesies" that is dated April 26, 1865 (Francois de Suzanne, Letters-3, page 43. Manuscript Book Number 26, de Suzanne Family Papers).

68. Letter from Jane Winchester addressed "Dear Sarah" and dated April 20, 1865. Davies Family Papers.

69. The petition was submitted to the Connecticut State Legislature in May 1865, and published on July 7, 1865.

70. The full text of the letter was copied by Davies in his diary under the date May 21, 1865, presumably the day it was received. Davies Diary, op. cit., entry dated May 21, 1865.

71. The exact date of Winchester's return to the United States is unknown. However, Davies began mentioning dinners and meetings with Winchester as early as June 4, 1865 in his diary (op. cit.) and letters written by Winchester bearing the New Haven headline are known to exist with dates beginning June 10, 1865.

72. Cf., Notes 48, 49, 73 and 74.

73. It is believed that this meeting took place in June 29, 1865, at the offices of the Winchester-Davies Company (Davies Diary, op. cit., undated entry between those of June 27 and 30, 1865). Also the articles of agreement for the Winchester Arms Company were signed July 1, 1865 (Ibid, entry dated July 1, 1865).

74. Ibid.

75. Per the conditions of the Henry Repeating Rifle Company's charter granted by the Connecticut State Legislature.

76. See Note 73.

77. Ibid.

CHAPTER 1

OPERATIONS FROM 1865-1866 AND 1866-1871

On July 1, 1865, Oliver F. Winchester, William Wirt Winchester and John M. Davies signed the articles of association which established the Winchester Arms Company in Bridgeport, Connecticut[1], and hired Nelson King (Plate 17) to be its superintendent[2].

To prevent any meddlesome interference by Benjamin Tyler Henry, it was decided that the immediate goal of the company was to develop an improved version of the Henry rifle, which was sufficiently different in design as to preclude any claims being lodged against it by Henry. This decision also prevented any appearance of impropriety on Winchester's part with respect to his continued association with the New Haven Arms Company, or accusations of unfair competition. The Henry rifle and the company that produced it were to succeed or fail on their own merits.

Based upon surviving engineering drawings and sample arms, the first replacement design to be developed in Bridgeport was that created by James D. Smith, the factory's assistant superintendent[3]. In place of the magazine design used in the Henry rifle and its antecedent Volcanic arms, Smith proposed a closed magazine, housed within a wood forestock, which could be charged through a hinged loading port located in the bottom of the

Plate 17
Photograph of Nelson King believed to have been taken circa 1870. Olin Corporation photograph.

receiver immediately below the cartridge carrier. When the action was fully open, the arm was to be inverted and the loading port unlatched so that cartridges could be fed directly into the magazine. To prevent the rearward movement of cartridges during the loading process, a small section of the cartridge carrier remained in alignment with the magazine tube to provide a shoulder against which the upper rim of the rearmost cartridge in the magazine could rest[4]. Smith also designed a new finger lever catch, which utilized a pivoted and spring-loaded hook mounted in the rear bow of the lever. When the lever was closed, the upper arm of this hook engaged a slot cut in the lower tang. To release the catch, it

was necessary to apply direct pressure to the hook's lower arm that protruded from the lever bow.

In addition to the positive finger lever catch, Smith's design incorporated a safety to prevent the accidental discharge of the arm during the final upward movement of the finger lever when the hammer was no longer held

Top: Plate 18

*D*etail of a full-length design drawing illustrating James D. Smith's loading system, dated July 30, 1865. R.C. Romanella Collection, Geneva, Switzerland.

Bottom: Plate 19

*J*ames D. Smith sample .50 caliber musket made in August or September 1865. Winchester Arms Collection (Inv. No. W253), Cody Firearms Museum. Olin Corporation photograph.

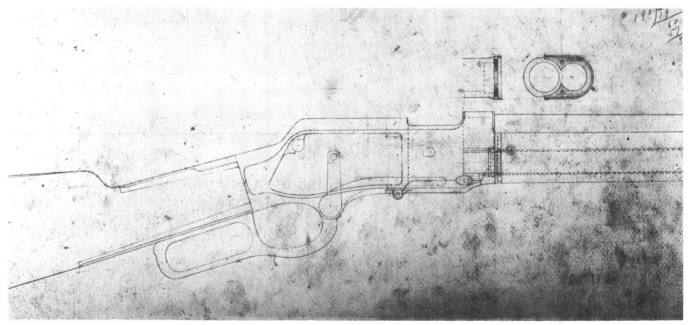

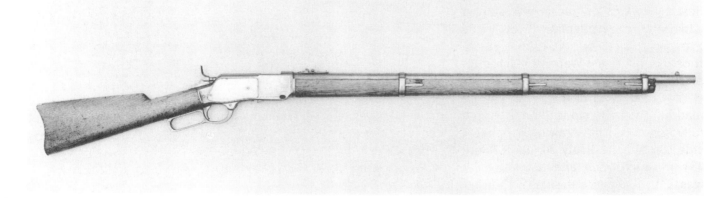

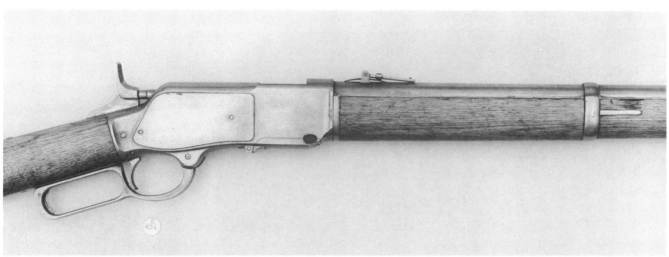

in cocked position by the bolt. At the point when the hammer was released by the bolt, the position of the finger lever was such that an extension milled on the rear surface of the trigger could prevent the latter's rearward movement until the lever was fully closed. To further ensure this safety's operation, the clearance between the trigger and the finger lever was reduced so that the trigger could only release the sear when the extension entered a slot cut in the lever itself. To reduce potential production costs, Smith made use of a separate lower tang, which was secured to the receiver by two screws as well as the hammer bolt and trigger pin[5]. As a precaution against any claim being filed by Henry, Smith also redesigned the bolt, firing pin, cartridge extractor and cartridge carrier, so that they not only varied from Henry's, but also, had a more positive action[6]. One other important feature of the Smith design was that the receiver was fitted with detachable sideplates secured by a transverse screw similar in form to those found on the Weber Ruesch samples made for Winchester.

The initial form of the musket to be made on Smith's plan is illustrated in a full-length elevation drawing of its right side that is dated July 30, 1865 (Plate 18). At some point after this drawing was completed, the design of the fore end was slightly altered by the deletion of the cross bolt securing the stock to the barrel and magazine tube just forward of the receiver. Evidently, it was found that the forestock could be safely held in position by the metal base plate, which fit into a recess on the forward face of the receiver and by the barrel bands. This modification is demonstrated in the .50 rimfire caliber sample musket (Plates 19-21 and Color Plate 4) preserved in the Winchester Arms Collection of the Cody Firearms Museum (Inv. No. W253)[7].

In contrast to the musket, the carbine based upon Smith's design had a loading port set into a recess cut in the lower surface of the receiver so that it was flush with the receiver's edges. In addition, the pivoted finger lever catch was abandoned due to the reduced length of the lever, in favor of the rotating stud catch employed in the Henry rifle. Although the model submitted to the United States Patent Office was built on a modified Henry receiver[8], the patent specification drawings (Plate 22) indicate that some sample carbines were built with detachable sideplate

Right: Plate 21

*D*etail of the Smith musket illustrated in Plate 19 with the loading port cover open. Olin Corporation photograph.

Top: Plate 20

*D*etail of the Smith musket illustrated in Plate 19. Olin Corporation photograph.

31

receivers and Smith's improved lockwork[9].

While the exact number of samples made of Smith's design is unknown, it probably did not exceed six or eight, given the number needed for development work and subsequent patent applications.

Despite the fact that the sample arms based upon Smith's design were substantial improvements over the Henry rifle and corrected all its deficiencies, the pattern was never adopted for production. Although a number of factors probably influenced this decision[10], the major reason may have been the extensive retooling its manufacture would have required.

The second and simplest modification of the Henry rifle to be developed was that designed by George W. Briggs in September 1865, while on leave from the New Haven Arms Company[11]. In many respects, his design represented a synthesis of the loading port he had previously incorporated in the Bavarian-contract Henry rifles and Oliver F. Winchester's removable magazine tube. However, unlike both of the latter, which had either a fixed magazine or fixed outer housing for one, Briggs simply recommended that a sliding magazine tube that could be moved forward for loading be used. To prevent the cartridges pressed into the magazine from escaping during loading, Briggs designed the magazine's rear locking catch so that a stud on its inner surface

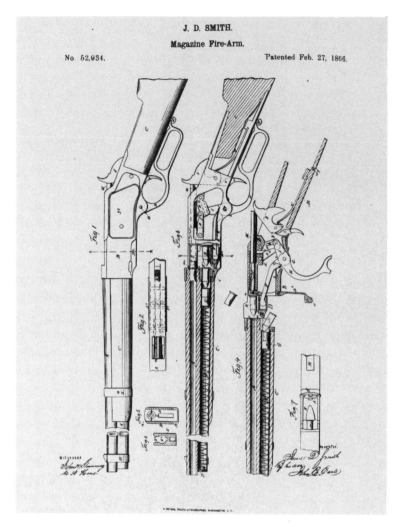

Top: Plate 22

Specification drawings enrolled with James D. Smith's U.S. Patent Number 52934 issued Feb. 27, 1866. Winchester Arms Collection Archives, Cody Firearms Museum.

Bottom: Plate 23

George W. Briggs' sample .44 caliber rifle made in September 1865. Winchester Arms Collection (Inv. No. W243), Cody Firearms Museum. Olin Corporation photograph.

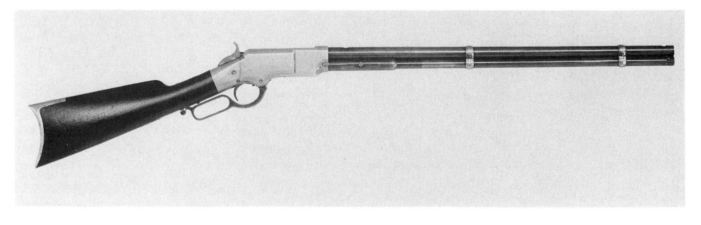

would partly enter the tube itself when the latter was moved forward. When unlocked, the locking catch's spring forced the catch's rear arm against the rear section of the magazine tube so that the stud on its interior side passed through a slot and came into alignment with the axis of the tube.

As cartridges were fed in, their cases slid over the angled leading edge of the stud, pivoting it outward. However, at the point when their rims passed by it, the stud snapped back into position and prevented any rearward movement of those cartridges in the magazine. When the magazine was closed, the stud detent pivoted out of alignment with the cartridges as the locking catch moved into contact with the receiver,

thus allowing them to move freely rearward. In case the rear magazine locking catch accidentally disengaged, Briggs fitted the forward end of the magazine tube with a rotating tip that had a raised lug which fit into a slot cut in the barrel beneath the muzzle. By simply turning the tip so that the lug entered the barrel slot when the magazine was closed, the tube could be securely locked in position.

Top: Plate 24

Detail of the Briggs rifle illustrated in Plate 23. Olin Corporation photograph.

Bottom: Plate 25

Detail of the Briggs rifle illustrated in Plate 23 with the magazine tube in its forward loading position. Olin Corporation photograph.

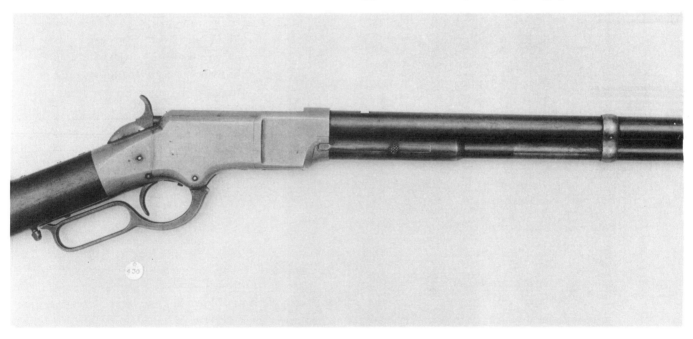

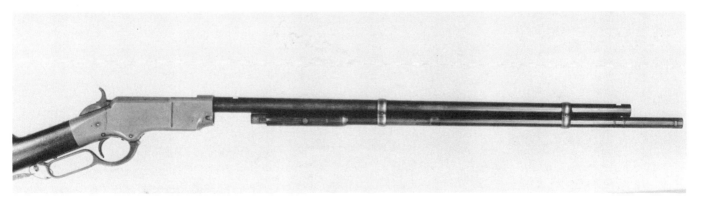

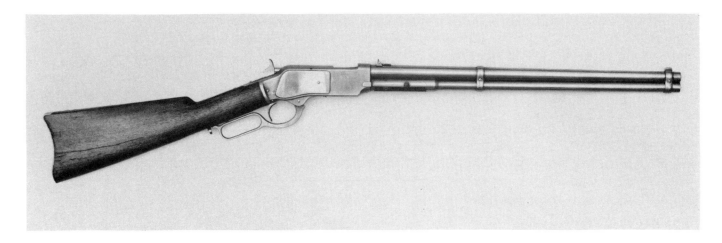

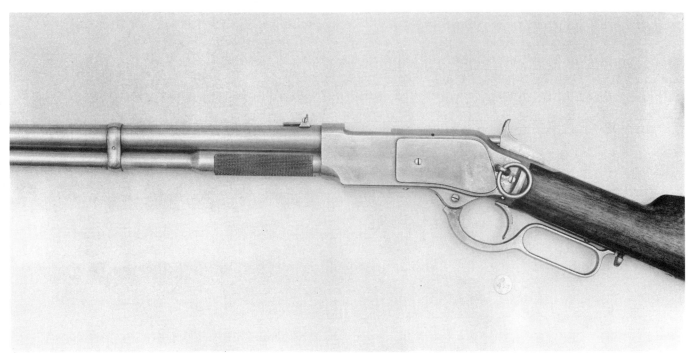

The first samples made of this design were built upon standard Henry rifle actions, which were fitted with round barrels and modified to accept the Briggs pattern magazine (Plates 23-25)[12]. Subsequent samples, however, utilized Smith pattern receivers with detachable sideplates and incorporated all his lockwork improvements. Based upon the sample carbine, serial number 1, in the Winchester Arms Collection (Inv. No. W257)[13] and later patent specification drawings (Plate 28), these arms were not fitted with Smith's finger lever catch, but rather, had Henry-style catches.

The third improvement to be developed in the early autumn of 1865 closely paralleled Briggs' work. In place of the sliding magazine tube, though, Oliver F. Winchester proposed that the tube have an open slot at its rear which could be exposed by a sliding metal fore end[14]. To load the magazine, the catch that secured the fore end to the magazine tube was released and the fore end moved forward to expose the loading aperture. As in Briggs' design, a stud on the inner surface of the fore end catch extended into the magazine tube to serve as a cartridge detent

Top: Plate 26

George W. Briggs sample .44 caliber carbine, serial number 1. Winchester Arms Collection (Inv. No. W257), Cody Firearms Museum. Olin Corporation photograph.

Bottom: Plate 27

Detail of the Briggs carbine illustrated in Plate 26. Olin Corporation photograph.

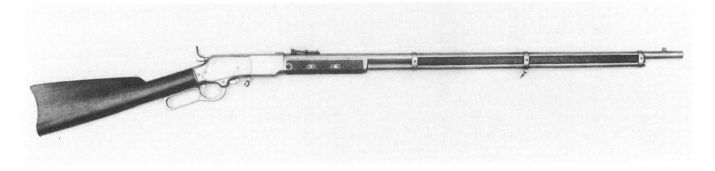

when the fore end was in its forward loading position.

The earliest sample of this design is a .44 rimfire caliber musket (Winchester Arms Collection, Inv. No. W255, Plates 29-31)[15] having a 34-inch barrel and an overall length of 54 inches. Similar to the Smith sample discussed above, Winchester's has detachable side-plates, a pivoted finger lever catch, trigger safety and an improved bolt, firing pin as well as extractor. To allow its use as a single-shot weapon, a hinged lug is attached to the lower surface of the receiver immediately forward of the finger. When this lug is moved into its forward position, it does not interfere with the movement of the finger lever. However, when the lug is moved rearward, the travel of the lever is restricted to the extent that the cartridge carrier is raised just sufficiently to eject a spent cartridge, but not so far as to bring a new round from the magazine into position for chambering. Based upon a surviving elevation drawing of this musket (Plate 32), it was specifically designed to conform in length to the Swiss Model 1863 rifle[16].

The carbine version of this design (Plates 33-35) differs from the musket only in the reduced size of the receiver, shorter barrel length, butt form, the use of a Henry-style finger lever catch and the deletion of the cartridge cutoff device.

Though the exact date of this design's development cannot be fixed with the same degree of certainty as its

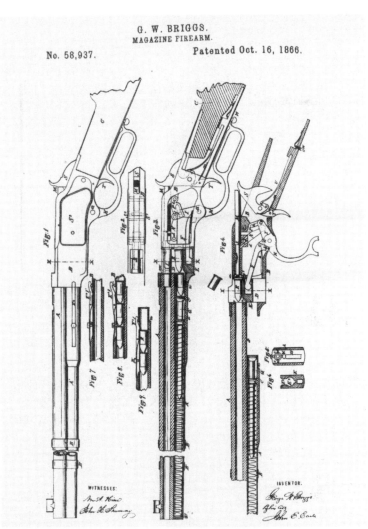

Top: Plate 28

*S*pecification drawings enrolled with George W. Briggs' U.S. Patent Number 58937 issued Oct. 16, 1866. Winchester Arms Collection Archives, Cody Firearms Museum.

Bottom: Plate 29

*O*liver F. Winchester's sample .44 caliber musket, made in September or early October 1865, and submitted to the Swiss Federal Rifle Trials prior to Nov. 1, 1865. Winchester Arms Collection (Inv. No. W255), Cody Firearms Museum. Olin Corporation photograph.

After the end of the Civil War, virtually all the major American firearms manufacturers realized that their survival depended upon the cultivation of foreign markets for their products as the rapidly diminishing domestic sales threatened to idle the factories they had built or enlarged to satisfy wartime needs. Among the first to actively seek out foreign customers was Oliver F. Winchester, who traveled extensively to Europe in 1865 and 1866. The novelty and usefulness of his repeating rifles were immediately recognized there, and his endeavors were rewarded with a number of contracts issued by a variety of foreign states. These purchases not only ensured the survival of the Winchester Arms Company, but also allowed it to expand and flourish in an era when many other companies failed.

predecessors, it was prior to the middle of October 1865, as Winchester took samples of it, together with those of the Smith and Briggs designs, with him to Europe at the time[17].

After a brief stop in England, where he gave his London patent agent, William Clark, a full set of drawings and a sample of each design so that an application for British patents could be filed[18], Winchester proceeded directly to Switzerland. There he submitted samples of the designs together with a standard Henry rifle for comparison, to the Swiss Federal Rifle Commission

meeting in Aarau, prior to Nov. 1[19]. Winchester then went to Paris, where he met with M. de Suzanne to demonstrate the three revised designs of the Henry rifle, the development of which had been discussed the previous April[20]. Upon completion of a variety of tests, de Suzanne authorized the purchase of 1,000 carbines having Winchester's improvements to the magazine at a fixed price of $34 per arm with fifty percent of the price to be paid immediately and the balance upon their shipment from New York to Havana, Cuba[21].

Top: Plate 30

*D*etail of the Winchester musket illustrated in Plate 29. Olin Corporation photograph.

Bottom: Plate 31

*D*etail of the Winchester musket illustrated in Plate 29 with the fore end moved forward for loading. Olin Corporation photograph.

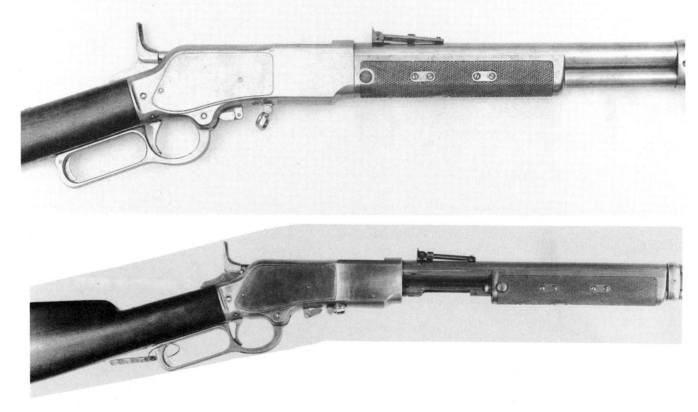

36

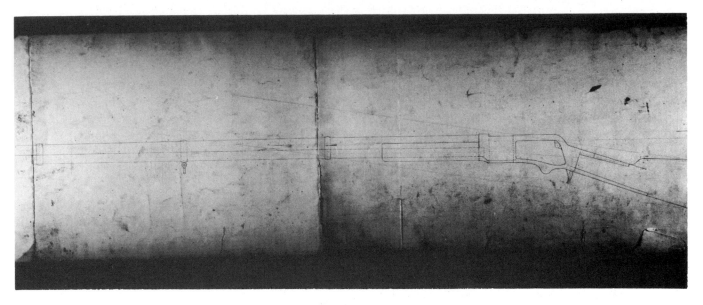

Top: Plate 32

F*ull length design drawing of the Winchester musket illustrated in Plate 29. The reverse of this drawing illustrates a Swiss Model 1863 Sharpshooter's rifle. Winchester Arms Collection Archives, Cody Firearms Museum.*

Bottom: Plate 33

O*liver F. Winchester's sample .44 caliber carbine, made in September or early October 1865, and submitted to the Swiss Federal Rifle Trials prior to Nov. 1, 1865. Winchester Arms Collection (Inv. No. W256), Cody Firearms Museum.*

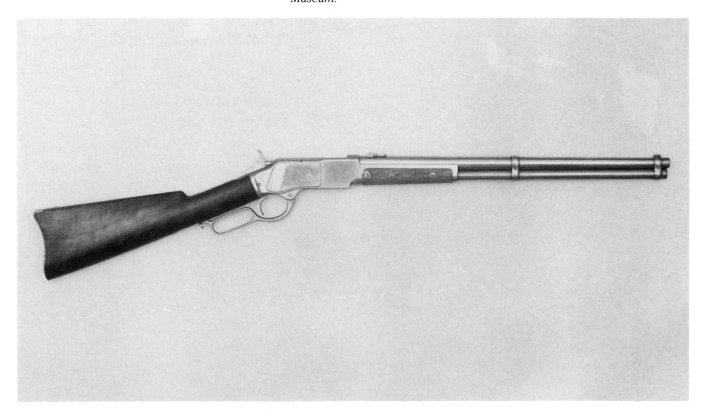

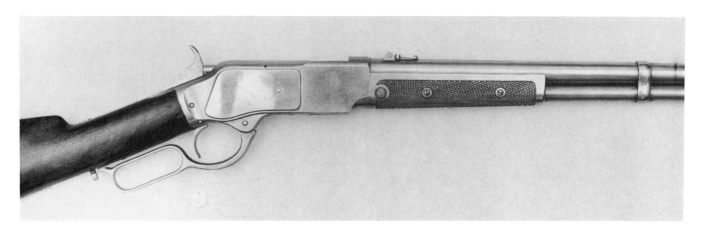

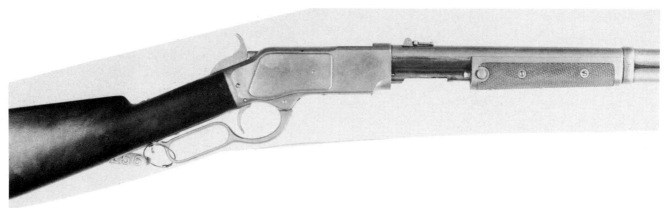

Top: Plate 34

*D*etail of the Winchester carbine illustrated in Plate 33. Olin Corporation photograph.

Middle: Plate 35

*D*etail of the Winchester carbine illustrated in Plate 33 with the fore end moved forward for loading. Olin Corporation photograph.

Bottom: Plate 36

*W*inchester's Improvement .44 caliber carbine of the type manufactured by the Winchester Arms Company from December 1865 through the early spring of 1866, for Maximilian I of Mexico. Winchester Arms Collection (Inv. No. W242), Cody Firearms Museum. Olin Corporation photograph.

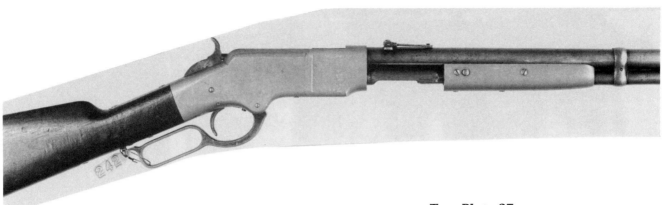

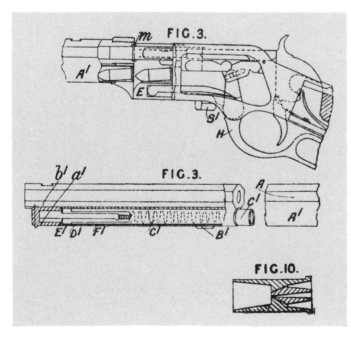

Top: Plate 37

*D*etail of the Winchester's Improvement carbine illustrated in Plate 36 with the fore end moved forward for loading. Olin Corporation.

Middle/Below: Plate 38

*S*pecification drawings illustrating Smith's, Briggs' and Winchester's Improvements published with the abridged patent specifications for William Clark's (on behalf of O.F. Winchester) English Patent Number 3284, issued Dec. 19, 1865.

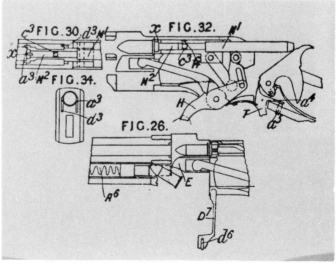

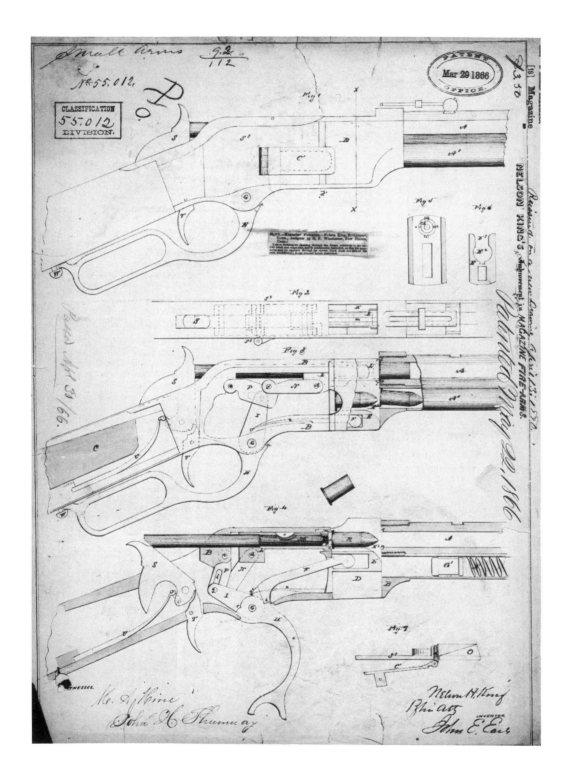

Plate 39

Original specification drawing for Nelson King's U.S. Patent Number 55012 issued May 22, 1866. Record Group 241, National Archives of the United States, Washington, D.C. Photograph courtesy of the National Archives.

By the close of November, Winchester was again in New Haven, and at that time or shortly thereafter, the Bridgeport factory began work on modifying the existing machinery there to produce the new carbine. To facilitate production, it was decided to retain the Henry-style receiver, for which tooling existed, and to substitute a pressed brass fore end (Plate 36 and 37) in place of the machined steel version used in the samples.

Although this design was never patented in the United States, it was protected by the English patent that William Clark had applied for on Winchester's behalf, which was granted on Dec. 19, 1865 (Number 3284, Plate 38)[22]. The lack of any application for American patent protection strongly suggests that Winchester never intended to market arms of this design in the United States.

Actual production of the improved carbine evidently began almost immediately, as an export receipt from J.P. Moore & Son indicate that 150 carbines were shipped by Winchester from New York to Cuba on Jan. 12, 1866[23]. While the majority of the arms of this pattern were produced for the French contract, some apparently were sold commercially, despite the lack of patent protection. A leaf from the Winchester company's sales register for 1866 indicates that on March 5, an "improved Carbine" and an "improved Rifle" were both sold to Philip Wilson & Company and William Golcher for a total of $72 ($40 for the carbine plus $50 for the rifle less a twenty percent discount)[24].

The total production of this model, including both military and civilian examples, is estimated to be in excess of 700 units, based upon the serial numbers of surviving arms and the fact that the balance due on the French contract after the fall of Maximilian I of Mexico was satisfied by a shipment of 300 Model 1866 carbines sent to France in 1867[25].

As the fortunes of the Winchester Arms Company improved, those of the New Haven Arms Company declined. During the autumn of 1865, the company witnessed a substantial reduction in orders and, as a result, a radical loss in income. In consequence, its work force was systematically reduced from a peak of fifty-five persons as of July 8, 1865, to 25 as of Nov. 25[26].

Recognizing that the time had arrived to take over the New Haven Arms Company, Winchester and John M. Davies called an extraordinary meeting of the company's stock holders for Dec. 31[27].

Plate 40

Nelson King sample .44 caliber demonstration model made in early 1866. Winchester Arms Collection (Inv. No. W1257), Cody Firearms Museum. Olin Corporation photograph.

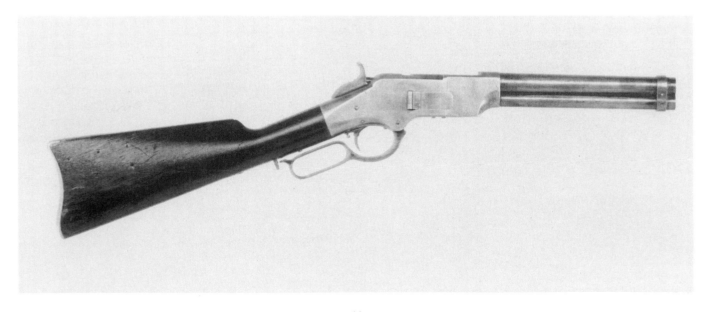

At that meeting, Winchester offered to assume all the credits and liabilities of the firm either by the outright purchase of its existing stock or through an exchange of such stock for that to be issued by a new corporation he would form. The terms of the offer also stipulated that it had to be accepted or rejected "35 days hence"[28], that being one day after the next regularly scheduled meeting of the company's officers and stock holders[29].

Perhaps realizing that any influence he might have had with respect to the New Haven Arms Company's future operations was rapidly disappearing, Benjamin Tyler Henry attempted to forestall the takeover by filing suit against the company in January 1866, alleging that it had not fully honored his 1859 contract and that he was due further compensation for his 1860 invention[30].

While Henry's suit was intended to delay adoption of Winchester's offer, in all likelihood it probably had quite the opposite effect. Faced with the reality that the New Haven Arms Company was failing, and that any investment in it might not be recoverable, especially if Henry's claims proved valid, the majority of its stock holders voted to accept Winchester's offer at their meeting held on Feb. 3, 1866[31]. Having secured their approval, Winchester then petitioned the Connecticut State Legislature to modify the firm's 1865 charter to reflect the change of ownership[32].

Work then began in New Haven on the completion of all outstanding orders for both arms and ammunition, and the gradual dismantling of the factory's machinery so that it could be shipped to Bridgeport[33]. The transfer was completed by the beginning of July, and on July 7, 1866, the New Haven Arms Company's payroll book was formally closed[34].

Although those carbines and rifles having Oliver F. Winchester's magazine system, which were primarily produced for the French government in early 1866, must be regarded as the first, true production Winchester firearms, the ultimate prosperity of the Winchester Arms Company and its later successor, the Winchester Repeating Arms Company, was not to be the result of their manufacture. Rather, it was to be due to the introduction of a fifth modification of the Henry rifle designed by Nelson King, the superintendent of the Bridgeport factory.

By altering the construction of the cartridge carrier so that a cartridge could pass through its lower section directly into the magazine when the action was closed, King demonstrated that loading could be accomplished through an aperture located in either the right or left side of the receiver. The major benefits of this arrangement were that it reduced the number of movements necessary for loading in comparison with either the Briggs or Winchester systems, and did not render an arm unusable for any protracted

Plate 41
Nelson King sample .45 caliber musket made in early 1866. Winchester Arms Collection (Inv. No. W252), Cody Firearms Museum. Olin Corporation photograph.

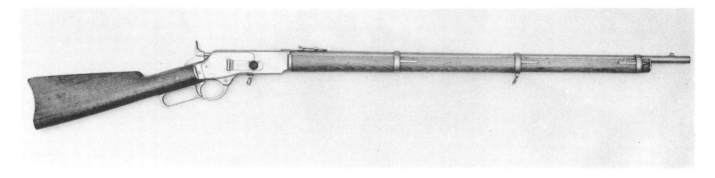

period of time as was the case in all the loading methods tried previously. In addition, since access to the magazine tube's most vulnerable section, its rear, was no longer necessary, it could be protected from damage by being enclosed in a wood fore end. Furthermore, by using a loading aperture with a greatly reduced area than that found in the Briggs or Winchester systems, the likelihood of foreign matter being introduced into the magazine or action during loading that might impair an arm's function was significantly reduced.

Although it is not precisely known when King conceived this idea, it appears that it occurred in late December 1865 or early January 1866. Certainly, by the end of the second week of January in 1866, the design had reached an advanced state since a detailed elevation sketch of the loading aperture cover was drawn on the 14th[35].

In its original form, as illustrated in the drawing mentioned above and those submitted with his patent application in March 1866 (Plate 39)[36], King's improvement consisted of a twelve- piece unit comprising the following: cartridge carrier; sideplate; loading aperture cover; cover hinge pin; cover lockingcatch; locking catch pin; locking catch spring; cover open-

■ Nelson King

Ironically, little is known about the man whose modification of the Henry Rifle revolutionized the design of lever-action rifles made by the Winchester company. Other than the fact that he entered the service of Oliver F. Winchester in 1864, and left to become superintendent of the Sharps Rifle Company in 1875, no record of his life appears to have survived.

ing stud; opening stud spring; opening spring set screw; cartridge guide; and cartridge guide bolt.

The primary elements of the design, however, were the modified sideplate having a rectangular aperture cut in it; an angled block bolted to the interior surface of the sideplate to guide cartridges into the carrier block; and the modified carrier block itself. When the action was closed with the carrier block in the lowered position, the axis of the magazine tube came into alignment with the cartridge channel drilled in the carrier as well as the loading aperture in the sideplate so that cartridges could be inserted successively into the carrier and then the magazine. To prevent the cartridge in the carrier from moving rearward under pressure from those in front of it, the receiver was constructed so that a shallow shoulder projected partially into the axis of the carrier

Plate 42
Detail of the King musket illustrated in Plate 41. Olin Corporation photograph.

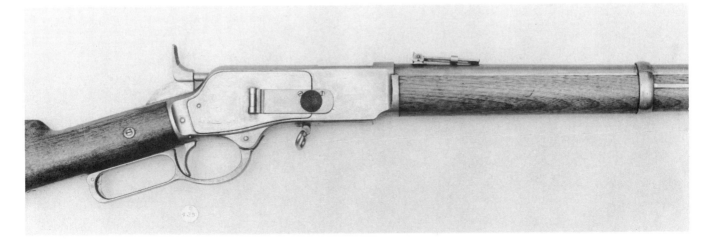

block channel to catch the left rim of the cartridge that had been inserted into the channel. When the magazine was filled, or the desired number of cartridges fed in to it, a more positive cartridge stop was provided by a buttress machined on the inner surface of the loading port cover's leading edge. As the cover was closed, the buttress moved into a position directly behind the carrier block channel thereby, in effect, becoming an extension of the receiver's inner wall to seal the opening at the rear of the carrier. To insure that the loading port cover remained closed during use, it was fitted with a vertically mounted spring catch set within the receiver. When pressure was applied to the visible section of the catch located immediately in front of the finger lever pivot point, the catch disengaged from a notch in the cover. The cover then automatically opened under pressure from a spring-loaded mount in the cartridge guide block that operated through a hole cut in the sideplate just forward of the cover's hinge. At some point after the patent specification drawings and the first samples made (Plates 40-43 and Color Plate 5), the dual locking and release system was replaced by a single exterior sliding cover latch similar to that used by James D. Smith.

While the total number of samples made to demonstrate the first and second styles of King's improvement is,

unfortunately, unknown, it is estimated to have been at least nine since a sample musket having the sliding loading port cover latch and bearing the serial number 9 is preserved in the Winchester Arms Collection (Inv. No. W252)[37].

Based upon design, it is believed that Luke Wheelock submitted the rifle illustrated in Plate 44 (Winchester Arms Collection, Inv. No. W258)[38] to Oliver F. Winchester for consideration at about this time. Though closely resembling and clearly adapted from the King system discussed above, Wheelock's differed in two ways. Instead of having the loading port located to the rear of the cartridge carrier, Wheelock situated it directly to the side of the carrier so that the latter need only have an opening cut

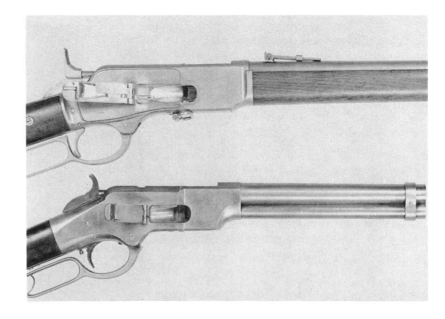

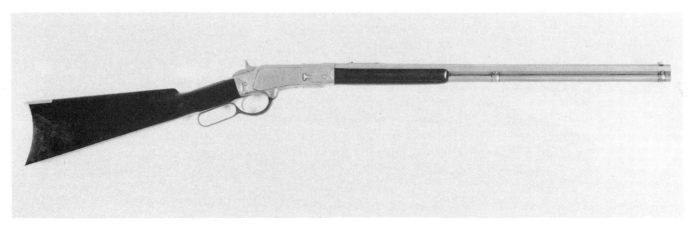

in its side rather than being bored through with a cartridge channel. In loading, the first cartridge fed into the aperture was pressed back into the cartridge carrier by the pressure of the magazine spring, and subsequent cartridges entered the magazine tube itself passing over the bullet of the rearmost cartridge in the carrier. Despite some advantages that this system may have provided (by reducing the action's exposure to dirt by the relocation of the loading port and the solid rear wall of the carrier), they were not evidently sufficient to warrant further work on the design, and it was abandoned after this sample was completed.

In the late spring or early summer of 1866, King drastically revised his design. The exterior hinged loading port cover and the shaped interior cartridge guide were replaced by a single spring steel plate mounted on the inside of the sideplate. This plate, which somewhat resembled a square bladed paddle, was attached solely at its rearmost point by one or two screws to the sideplate so that its free forward end could pivot inward when pressure was applied to it. Loading, consequently, could be accomplished simply by pressing a cartridge against the plate until it had moved sufficiently inward to allow the cartridge to slide forward into the carrier block. As soon as pressure was withdrawn from the plate, it returned to the closed position under its own tension, and a buttress on its forward edge blocked the rear of the cartridge channel in the carrier.

Apart from the simplicity of its operation, King's revised loading port design had a distinct advantage over its immediate predecessors. In contrast to the maximum of twelve parts used in the first design, the revised version only consisted of five components (the cartridge carrier, sideplate, spring plate and two retaining screws).

In recognition of the design's merits, Oliver F. Winchester authorized the conversion of the Bridgeport plant's tooling and machinery for its manufacture in July 1866, after all the New Haven factory's equipment had been transferred there[39].

The decision to manufacture King's improvement arms with bronze alloy receivers having dovetailed sideplates rather than with iron receivers of the more modern design with detachable sideplates, was probably purely pragmatic. Although there were distinct benefits to be gained by using the new style of receiver both from the viewpoint of strength and the ease with which the action could be uncovered for cleaning, its adoption would have involved both a considerable expense due to retooling and a substantial delay before arms of the pattern could be marketed. The efficiency of King's design, however, allowed it to be used with equal ease in receivers of the type employed for the Henry rifle. More importantly, the use of that pattern did not necessitate any substantial retooling since only a minimal number of jigs and milling machines needed to be altered to accommodate production of the King's system[40]. It should be noted also that it was to Winchester's advantage to press for the rapid introduction of the new model. In February 1866, he and four associates had petitioned the Connecticut State Legislature to remodify the original charter of the New Haven Arms Company so that it could operate as a corporation under the name of the Winchester Fire Arms Company[41]. Since the potential investors needed to make that corporation a reality had to have good cause to invest their monies, it was essential that the company be in production of a successful and profitable model.

To stimulate public interest in the new model and hopefully guarantee a positive public reception of it, Winchester circulated printed descriptions, together with drawings, to a number of authors and newspaper editors during the late summer of 1866. While the reaction to this publicity campaign varied from one area to another, notices of the new model were published in various parts of the country as well as abroad[42]. One of the more exuberant reports was written by Horace W.S. Cleveland in his piece titled "Breechloading Arms" published in the Sept. 6 issue of the New York World. After noting its pedigree and competitors, Cleveland pronounced the new rifle as being "unsurpassed in simplicity and efficiency by any repeating gun yet produced"[43], precisely the reaction Winchester had hoped for.

Although considerable controversy has surrounded the date when production of the King's Improvement or Model 1866 began[44], it may be unequivocally stated to have commenced in August 1866, with the first completed arms shipped on Sept. 15. While evidence for this assertion has always existed in George Walker's production notes for the Model 1866[45] preserved in the archives of the Winchester company, it has been either ignored or dismissed as apocryphal by a succession of arms historians[46]. Instead, the date has been assigned to 1867 for a variety of reasons[47]. The validity of Walker's accounts are, however, supported by a number of disparate contemporary sources, both American and foreign. Chief among these are a series of entries in the daily journal maintained by John M. Davies during 1866, which records the meetings he had with vari-

Sept 6
- In New York Saw O and Chapin off

Sept 8
- Mr. Seymour arrived in afternoon Has received advice from Keller that Henry will pursue a claim. S optimistic Wrote O

Sept 12
- Rec new rifle from Mr King Handsome piece. 10 to be sent to Europe

Sept 20
- Mr here. Gave him new rifle

Sept 23
- Telgd King to send rifles to Cooper & Pond

Oct 1
- Mr King reports last week's production 212 rifles All for Chile

Oct 9
- King here 241 last week

Oct 10
- O in Berne

ous individuals associated with the Winchester Arms Company and other events while Oliver F. Winchester was in Europe in September and October. In chronological order, the relevant entries are as follows[48]:

The importance of these notes lies not only in that they substantiate Walker's later account, but that they provide concrete evidence of the Bridgeport plant's production capacity during the initial phase of the Model 1866's manufacture. Based upon the figures quoted in the entries for Oct. 1 and 9, it can be estimated that approximately 900 arms were made during the second month of the new rifle's production. Davies' notes also demonstrate that examples of the new model were made available to at least one retail agency shortly after manufacture began.

The availability of arms incorporating King's improvement in the autumn of 1866 is further confirmed by the cor-

Mr. O. F. Winchester
a Berne

My Dear Mr. Winchester

I am in receipt of the new Henry rifle which Mr. Lawrence delivered at your request. I shot it in the Woods this morning and it functioned superbly. The door on the right side is much better situated than before and the rifle [is] pleasant to use. Marshal Canrobert was particularly impressed with its application to cavalry and has requested some be sent for test.

Thank you for your kindness. Awaiting your presence and orders I remain yours very truly.

F. de Suzanne
2d October 1866

Plate 45
Receiver detail of a First Variation Winchester Model 1866 carbine, serial number 13534, produced in late 1866, which was rebarreled later in its working life. Olin Corporation photograph.

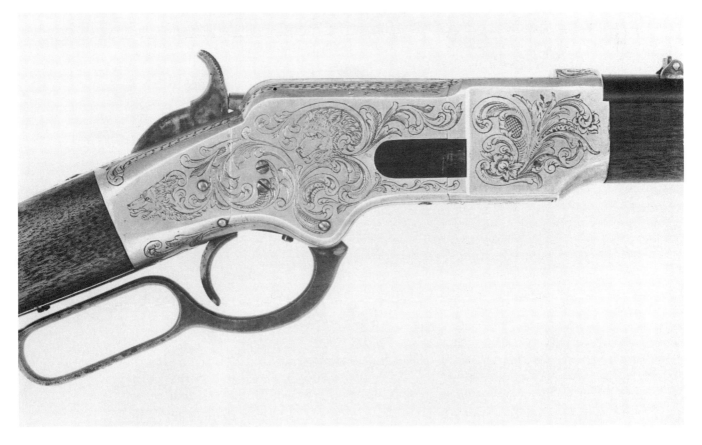

respondence of F. de Suzanne. The letter on the preceeding page can be found on page 286 of the latter's letter press book [49].

Despite the statement that the rifle received was a Henry, there can be no doubt whatsoever that it was either a sample or production Model 1866, as only that model had a loading "door on the right side" at that time. Whether the reference to the "door" being "Much better situated than before" refers to the James D. Smith sample which de Suzanne had examined in November 1865 or one of the other samples tested then cannot be determined, though the Smith comparison would be the most apt. Marshal Canrobert's request was fulfilled in early 1867 when 100 carbines were sold to the French Ministry of War for field trials[50].

Of even greater importance in establishing not only that production occurred in 1866, but the degree of that production, is a manuscript summation of the Winchester Arms Company and Winchester Repeating Arms Company's yearly sales for the period of 1866 to 1870, written by Oliver F. Winchester[51]. For the year 1866, Winchester recorded that the total sales amounted to $192,411.12. The magnitude of this amount reveals a level of operations never suspected before. Discounting the money received from the French government for the arms and ammunition shipped to Cuba for Mexico and a sizeable allocation of the receipts as having been realized for the sale of ammunition elsewhere, the balance indicates that approximately 4,500 Model 1866s were made and sold between Sept. 15, 1866 and Jan. 31,

Top: Plate 46

First Variation Winchester Model 1866 carbine, serial number 14838, made in 1867. Olin Corporation photograph.

Bottom: Plate 47

Left side view of the Model 1866 carbine illustrated in Plate 46. Olin Corporation photograph.

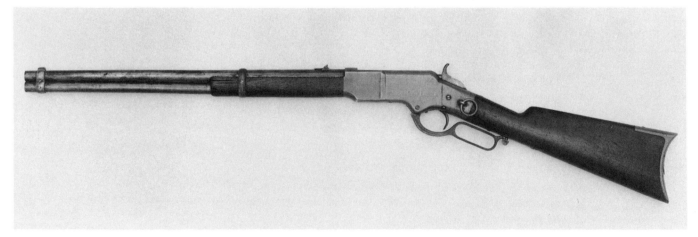

1867[52]. Interestingly, this reveals that the production figures given by Nelson King to John M. Davies in October only negligibly increased over the first months of the model's manufacture.

With respect to the configuration of the Model 1866 arms made during the first three and a half months of its production (Plates 45-48), all had bronze alloy receivers similar in form to those used in the Henry rifle. Their profile, however, was altered somewhat by the extension and deepening of the receiver's forward section to allow for the positioning of the magazine and the insertion of the fore end's rear tenon. The spring steel plates used to seal the loading aperture in the right sideplate were all of flat construction and had two vertically positioned retaining screws. Based upon surviving examples and known orders, it would appear that the Model 1866 was only made in carbine form when first introduced[53]. However, by November 1866, other versions of it were available since Major General William B. Franklin noted in his aide-memoir on Nov. 6 that Winchester visited him "with new models & c of the Henry gun."[54] Both the rifle and carbine originally were fitted with buttstocks identical to those used for the Henry rifle. The carbine forend, though, was secured by a screw retained barrel band, while the rifle's was held in place by a transverse screw. Actual production of rifle and musket versions of the Model 1866, during this period other than as samples, is extremely questionable since it would have involved addi-

Plate 48

Detail of the Winchester Model 1866 carbine illustrated in Plate 46. Olin Corporation photograph.

tional tooling at the factory and the diversion of hands from the contracts in process of manufacture.

One aspect of the Model 1866's production history that has aroused considerable discussion is the matter of its serial numbering. Many enthusiasts firmly believe that the model was numbered in sequence to the Henry rifle, while others, including this author, have argued that it had its own distinct serial numbers beginning with 1[55]. The reasons advanced for the model being sequentially serial numbered to the Henry rifle are as follows: the assumption that the model did not enter production at Bridgeport until 1867, after the Winchester Repeating Arms Company had been organized; the fact that the Winchester Repeating Arms Company's Board of Directors only approved the production of 5,000 arms of the pattern at their meeting held on March 4, 1867; the inclusion of Oliver F. Winchester's article titled "The Coming Gun" in the 1867 sales catalog; the fact that the model was marketed as an "improvement"; and the scarcity of examples having serial numbers below 13,000[56].

However, when these arguments are critically examined, they are not sustainable. As demonstrated earlier in this chapter, production of the Model 1866 began in August 1866 and was well established by October. The board meeting directive, which has been often cited as "proof positive," unfortunately does not refer to the Model 1866, but, as will be shown shortly, is concerned with the manufacture of the Model 1867 Swiss Contract rifle.

"The Coming Gun" article appeared repeatedly in Winchester catalogs. Its title cannot be used as a priority, evidence that when published, the model it referred to was yet to be manufactured. Rather, the word "Coming" only meant that the model was destined to make all other arms obsolete[57]. That

the Model 1866 was marketed as an "improvement" of the Henry rifle could suggest that a sequential serial numbering was a viable option, but this is invalidated by the fact that all the other "improvements" manufactured or developed by the Winchester Arms Company were assigned their own serial number ranges beginning with 1[58]. Furthermore, it should be noted the Winchester Arms Company was not a successor in business to the New Haven Arms/Henry Repeating Rifle Company, but rather was their purchaser, technically speaking. Therefore, the assumption of a serial numbering system from the firm purchased would be incongruous as it would have implied a relationship between the companies that exceeded what really existed. The final point taken, that being the scarcity of surviving examples of the model numbered below 13,000, equally is not supportable. The existence of specimens bearing four-digit serial numbers has been known for years, however they have been regarded as anomalies by those who advance the 1867 date of production commencement[59]. The reasoning for this lies in the assumption that more examples would exist had they been produced. The probability, though, that the majority of the Model 1866's pro-

Perhaps no other competition to select a cartridge rifle for military service was more closely watched than that conducted by the Swiss government in 1865 and 1866. The wide variety of entrants combined with the rigorous test procedures applied made the Swiss Trials an ideal proving ground for new designs. As the Trials proceeded, reports were published in virtually every industrialized country in the world, thereby giving the Winchester rifle an unparalleled exposure which was capitalized upon by Winchester in his advertising. Although ultimately the Swiss decided to adopt another rifle, the success of the Winchester rifle in their Trials resulted in a significant number of orders from countries such as France, Siam, Chile and elsewhere.

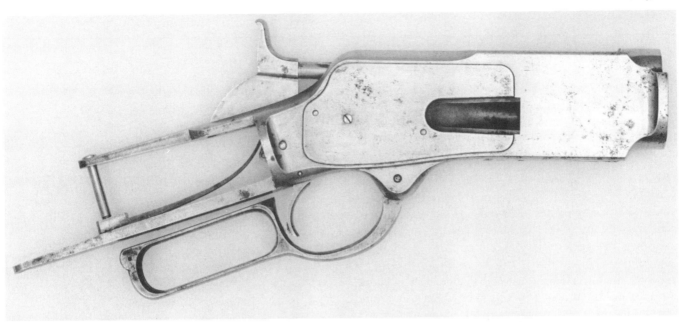

duction was made for export (as is shown in Davies' diary and elsewhere) provides an explanation for the low survival rate in this country, as well as abroad. Arms destined for foreign military service, especially in areas of conflict during this period, had limited survival rates, and few have survived to be imported back into this country. For example, of the 1,000 Model 1866 carbines known to have been made for the government of Chile in 1866, only one is currently known to exist, and no example has been found of the 5,000 Model 1866s made for Japan in 1867[60]. On a far grander scale, it should be noted that exceedingly few of the 711,612 American firearms sent to France during 1870 and 1871 are known to survive today[61].

The most telling evidence that the Model 1866 was serial numbered from 1 on is provided by testimony given by Oliver F. Winchester himself in 1874. At that time, he testified that 140,000 firearms incorporating Benjamin Tyler Henry's 1860 improvement to Smith & Wesson's 1854 patent had been made[62]. This number cannot be reconciled with known production data unless the

Model 1866 production began with serial number 1.

Although Oliver F. Winchester had authorized the commercial production of King's Improvement Rifles with bronze alloy receivers having dovetailed sideplates, he had not totally abandoned the idea of manufacturing arms with iron receivers and screw retained sideplates. Indeed, during the late summer of 1866, the sample rifle muskets being prepared for the second Swiss Federal Rifle Trials were made with receivers of that design. The importance of this series of rifles is that they incorporated, from their very inception, a number of technical improvements that were only used on commercial arms at a much later date.

The earliest surviving Swiss Trials sample is a near complete model receiver bearing the serial number 1 (Plates 49- 52)[63]. Originally made with flat sides that extended without any change in width to their forward edge, this receiver was subsequently modified to incorporate a forward flange into which the forestock tenon could be set. To accomplish this, the receiver's face was partially cut away and a sepa-

Plate 49

Winchester Model 1866 Swiss Contract musket sample receiver, serial number 1, made in the late summer of 1866. R.C. Romanella Collection, Geneva, Switzerland.

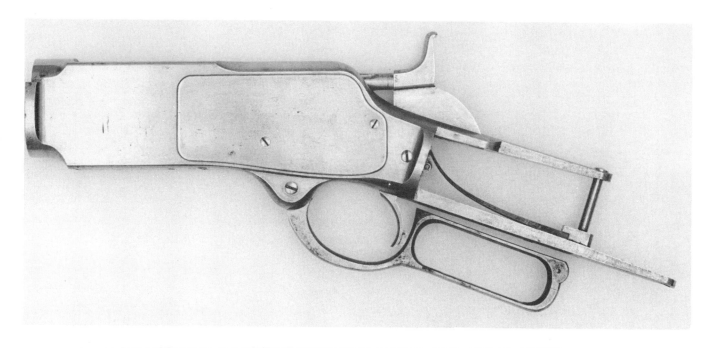

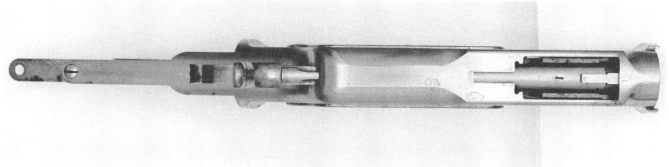

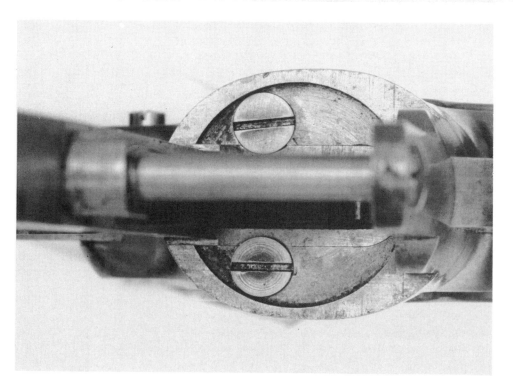

Top: Plate 50

*L*eft side view of the sample receiver illustrated in Plate 49.

Middle: Plate 51

*T*op view of the sample receiver illustrated in Plate 49.

Bottom: Plate 52

*D*etail of the screws securing the vertical flange of the lower tang to the rear face of the sample receiver illustrated in Plate 49.

Plate 53

Detail of the screws and pins securing the flanged section added to the forward face of the sample receiver illustrated in Plate 49.

rate flange was inserted and secured by two screws and a pair of pins (Plate 53).

The form of this receiver's ejection port also differs from the commercial models in that its rear section is cut with cartridge rim guides to facilitate the use of the action as a single shot rifle. In all other respects, save the use of the internally mounted King's Improvement loading gate, the form of the receiver is identical to those found on the Smith and early King samples.

In common with the King Patent sample rifle musket, the cartridge carrier used in this receiver has its lower bearing surface reduced in size to alleviate any problems which might arise from dirt entering the action. To achieve this, the sides of the carrier are cut with relieved panels so that the bearing surface within the receiver mortise is limited to the four corners of the carrier and a rear extension (Plate 54).

Technically, the most interesting features of this receiver are the construction of its firing pin and extractor (Color Plate 6). The firing pin itself fits within and is held in place by a detachable face plate of the bolt. The rear end of the pin is partially cut away so that it fits loosely over a mating cut on the grooved striker that extends longitudinally through the bolt and rear receiver wall. To limit the movement of the striker so that its forward tip does not come out of alignment with the firing pin, the lower forward section of the striker is cut with a slot to accommo-

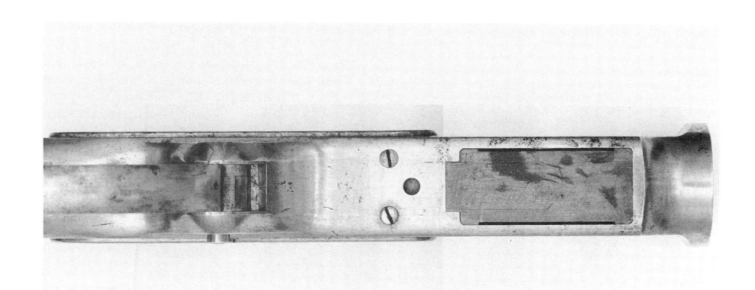

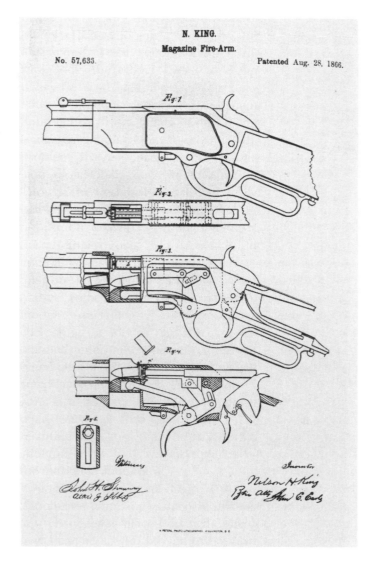

N. KING.
Magazine Fire-Arm.

No. 57,633.

Patented Aug. 28, 1866.

Top: Plate 54

Lower surface view of the cartridge carrier fitted to the sample receiver illustrated in Plate 49.

Left: Plate 55

Specification drawings enrolled with Nelson King's U.S. Patent Number 57633 issued Aug. 28, 1866. Winchester Arms Collection Archives, Cody Firearms Museum.

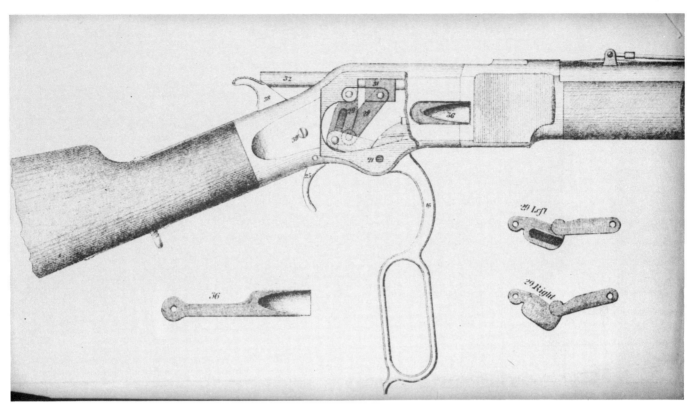

date the head of a set screw that is located in the body of the bolt. The extractor is formed as a collar that can slide over a recessed portion of the bolt head and is based upon the design patented by Nelson King on Aug. 28, 1866 (U.S. Patent Number 57633, Plate 55). The detachable bolt face is held in place by a single set screw that bears upon its rear collar. One other feature that should be noted is the form of the loading gate. Rather than being flat-faced, it is deeply and broadly chamfered to ease loading. Commercial King's Improvement Rifles were fitted with gates of this style only some six months later (Plate 56)[64].

Based upon the serial numbers of surviving Swiss Trials samples or components built with this type of firing pin mechanism and extractor, it appears that in excess of twenty-five were made in July and August 1866[65].

Concurrently, a parallel developmental program was underway in which a slightly modified firing pin mechanism was tried. In the second series of samples, the firing pin had a needle-nosed shape and a flat rear section that was hit by the striker (Color Plate 7). In addition, the pin was fitted with a spring so that it was automatically retracted when the hammer was at half or full cock. Another improvement found in the second series of trial samples is that the striker is enclosed with a hollow guide that screws into the rear of the bolt. In place of the set screw arrangement used to limit the striker's movement as used in the first series, the strikers of the second series have a collar machined on their forward section that is of greater diameter than the guide aperture. The benefit of this arrangement is that the firing pin can be simply replaced by merely unscrewing the guide and allowing the striker, pin and pin spring to be withdrawn by the force of gravity. An additional advantage to this revised construction is that, by placing the striker within a

Plate 56

*I*llustration of the Model 1866's receiver and lockwork demonstrating the sharply angled loading gate indentation introduced in mid-1867. **Winchester's Repeating Fire Arms** (Winchester Repeating Arms Company; New Haven, CT: 1867). Private Collection.

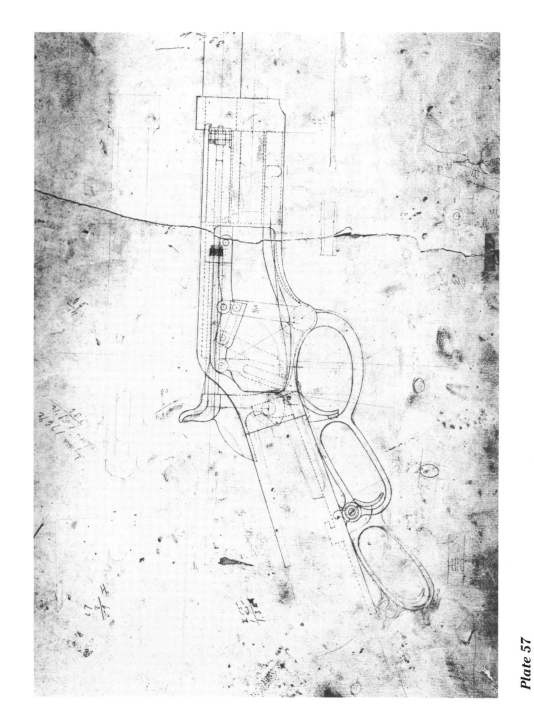

Plate 57

Design drawing for the Model 1866 Swiss Contract musket illustrating the trigger safety extension and finger lever locking device. R.C. Romanella Collection, Geneva, Switzerland.

guide tube, it is less likely to be bent during the use of the arm.

While the initial prototype for these samples used the collar extractor, the arms submitted to the Swiss had bar extractors fitted to the upper part of the bolt[66]. One other difference between the two series is the form of the finger lever latch. While those of the first type had latches identical to those found on the Smith and King patent samples, the second series have a substantially different variant. The latch is formed as a pivot piece within the upper rear bow of the lever. The upper portion of this pivot is hooked and enters a slot cut in the receiver's lower tang, while the lower section closely resembles a trigger, which stands proud of the rear lever bow (Plate 57). The only apparent advantage of this system over its predecessor is that the release for the lever could be quickly effected by the rearward movement of the fingers in the lever rather than by a separate movement requiring the fingers to be removed from the lever and the locking catch released by thumb pressure as is necessary in the first arrangement.

Production of the second series of samples (Plates 58 and 59), estimated to have been approximately twenty-five, were made with their own separate serial number sequence[67].

Samples of both the first and second type were submitted to the Swiss Federal Rifle Trials by Oliver F. Winchester on or about Oct. 1, 1866[68]. Throughout the trials, the Winchester rifle muskets performed flawlessly and easily surpassed their rivals. For example, in accuracy tests against the standard Swiss infantry rifle, the Winchester was able to consistently deliver a tighter hit radius on targets from 300 to 1000 paces. Similarly, when tested for accuracy under rapid-fire conditions, the

Top: Plate 58

Winchester Model 1866 Swiss Contract musket .45 caliber sample made in the early autumn of 1866. Winchester Arms Collection (Inv. No. W261), Cody Firearms Museum. Olin Corporation photograph.

Bottom: Plate 59

Detail of the sample Model 1866 Swiss Contract musket illustrated in Plate 58. Olin Corporation photograph.

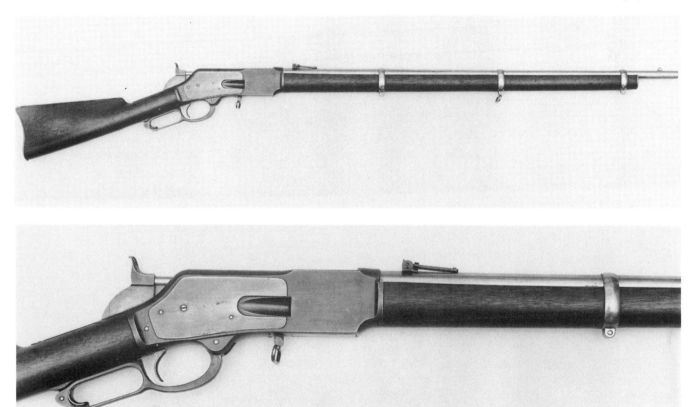

Winchester rifles averaged 14.5 hits at 300 paces, each 43 seconds. None of the other competing arms (Howard, Martini-Peabody, Remington, Spencer or Chassepot) were able to even approach that success rate[69].

Though the Trials Commission had recommended against the introduction of breech-loading rifles after their first set of trials in January 1866, due to the cost of the Winchester Improvement that had won that competition[70], Oliver Winchester's offer to sell the Swiss government rifles at the same price as the standard infantry rifle convinced the reconvened commission to approve the adoption of repeating arms[71]. In their final report of Nov. 28, 1866, the Commission wholeheartedly recommended the adoption of Winchester rifles for use by sharpshooters, provided that the following changes in the design were made[72]:

- The bore to be of Swiss caliber.
- Powder chamber adequate to the new uniform cartridge.
- The sight in conformity with the order of 1863.
- Bayonet in conformity with the order of 1863.
- For the sharpshooters, the sword-bayonet and contrivance for fastening it.
- Room in the magazine for at least thirteen cartridges.

- Barrel and arm a little shorter, if in consequence of the tests about to be proceeded to, it shall be deemed possible in a technical point of view.
- Inclination of the gun stock in conformity with the order of 1863.

Shortly after the above report was made, the Swiss government contracted with Winchester for 200 rifles incorporating the above-mentioned changes[73]. These arms, identified as the Swiss Model 1866 Sharpshooters Rifle, were made jointly in the United States and Switzerland. The receivers and lockworks were built in Bridgeport, and then sent to Weber-Ruesch in Zurich for mounting with barrels and stocks (Plate 60)[74].

The rifles sold to Switzerland differed from the samples not only in their caliber, but also in the form of their finger lever locking latch. In lieu of the large trigger type release found on the second series of samples and the original recessed release, a modified version combining features of both was used. Production models also were fitted with a safety designed by Luke Wheelock. To prevent the premature release of the hammer from the full cock position, an independent secondary sear was fitted to the lockwork (Plate 61). To release this sear, the finger lever had to

Plate 60

Winchester Model 1866 Swiss Sharpshooters rifle, serial number 419, made jointly by Winchester (the receiver and lockwork) and Weber-Ruesch (barrel and stock) of Zurich, Switzerland, in late 1866 or early 1867. Lloyd Bender Collection photograph, Winchester Arms Collection Archives, Cody Firearms Museum.

be fully drawn up against the lower tang so that a pin machined in the upper surface of the lever bow could pass through the tang and force the secondary sear out of alignment with the hammer notch. The exact date when this safety was devised is not known, but its presence on the second pattern Trials sample serial number 25 suggests that an October or November 1866, date is plausible[75].

Production of the Swiss Model 1866 Sharpshooters Rifle exceeded the 200 units called for under government contract as examples are known with serial numbers above 400[76].

Shortly after the conclusion of the Swiss Trials, Oliver Winchester returned to the United States. On the 30th of October, 1866, he met with Major General William B. Franklin, General Manager of the Colt's Patent Fire Arms Manufacturing Company in Hartford, Connecticut, to discuss the possible manufacture of the Model 1866 Swiss Sharpshooters Rifle at Colt[77]. Winchester's decision to approach the Colt company can only be explained if the Bridgeport factory was running to capacity at that time. Otherwise, it is doubtful whether Winchester would have even considered subcontracting production of the Swiss rifles as such an arrangement substantially reduced the margin of profit for Winchester. One plausible explanation is that the commercial Model 1866 rifles then being made in Bridgeport were not for South American as Davies wrote, but rather were part of the 1,000 arm contract known to have been shipped to Benito Jaurez in November or early December of that year.

While all the various references to this sale refer to the arms as Henry rifles, it is likely, given the date and known production of the Bridgeport plant, that they were Model 1866s. Further evidence supporting this supposition is to be found in Thomas Addis'

account of his trip to Mexico to deliver these arms. In the typescript copy of this story prepared by Addis before 1906, he refers to the arms as "Winchester rifles," not Henry's[78]. Later versions, however, changed that identification to Henry rifles presumably because it was thought the Model 1866 was not in production at that time[79]. Another potential reason for Winchester's discussion with Franklin probably was the pending contract with Chile for 1,000 arms that would tie up the Bridgeport factory's machinery

Plate 61

Specification drawings enrolled with Luke Wheelock's U.S. Patent Number 84598 issued Dec. 1, 1868.

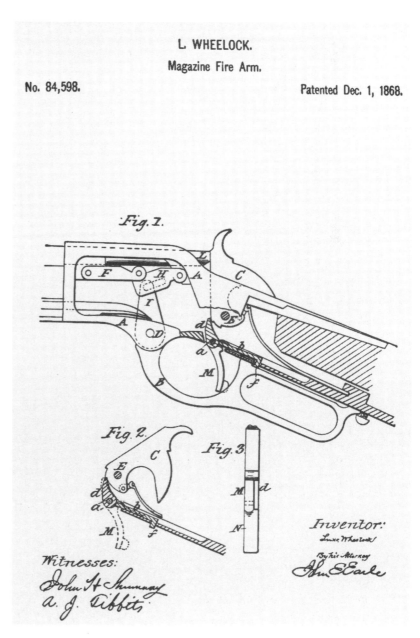

59

for at least a month[80]. The Chilean contract was fulfilled prior to March 1867, and its timing was such that production of those arms was evidently accomplished in sequence to those destined for Mexico.

Whatever the reason for Winchester's approach of the Colt company, negotiations continued into November, though no commitments were made at that time.

By the beginning of December 1866, it was clear to Winchester that the fortunes of his company were sufficiently advanced to begin incorporation proceedings for the Winchester Repeating Arms Company. In accordance with the provisions of the new firm's charter, as amended the previous May, a meeting was called on Dec. 3 to begin its capitalization. The surviving first page of that meeting's minutes is preserved in the Winchester Arms Collection Archives of the Cody Firearms Museum and reads as follows[81]:

1866
Dec 3d New Haven
Winchester Fire arms Co.
• At a meeting held at the offices of Mess Winchester
and Davies New Haven
Present O F Winchester
John M. Davies Mr. King Sup
I A Bishop
James Willson
Mr. & Mrs. Tyler
Wm E Trendwald
Bench
Ed. Mitchell}
Chas English}
W B Pasdue Exn John English
Sheldon
Henry Hickes
Geo G Bishop

• Meeting called to order by O F Winchester and on motion of I A Bishop W B Pasdue was elected Secty. Protem On motion of [entry deleted] O F Winchester the books for the new Subscription was opened for Subscribers

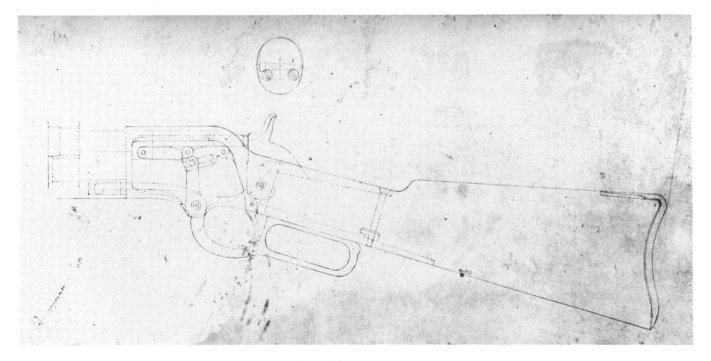

Plate 62
Design drawing illustrating the receiver, lockwork and butt of a Winchester Model 1867 carbine. R.C. Romanella Collection, Geneva, Switzerland.

The capitalization of the new company, set at $400,000 by its charter, was partially achieved through the exchange of shares in the New Haven Arms/Henry Repeating Rifle Company for new stock at the fixed rate of $100 per share[82]. New funds, however, were generated by subscriptions made by Davies, English and others, which exceeded $100,000[83]. Winchester and Davies also were to receive at some future date stock equal in value to their capital investment in the machinery and tooling at the Bridgeport plant[84]. By this maneuver, both men were able to convert a depreciating asset into one which held considerable promise of appreciation. As subsequent events indicate, Winchester maintained ownership of all the patents which he had secured from the collapse of the Volcanic Repeating Arms company and those issued subsequently, so that they effectively had absolute control over their use and the production of arms made under their license.

As full capitalization of the new company was not achieved at this meeting, its articles of incorporation could not be submitted to the Connecticut State Legislature for approval. Consequently, the Bridgeport plant continued to operate under the aegis of the privately owned Winchester Arms Company. It

would appear, though, that after this date, the profits of the Winchester Arms Company accrued not only to Winchester and Davies, but those other investors would had subscribed to stock in the new concern[85].

As 1867 dawned, Oliver Winchester's faith in the efficiency and marketability of the King's Improvement repeating rifle was being handsomely rewarded. The sales of that model to Mexico and South America were about to enrich his firm's treasury by $115,000. In addition, the prospect of substantial sales to Switzerland also promised further profit. One other potential avenue to increase sales, which was explored early in 1867, was the manufacture of two different breech-loading muskets under the patents owned by Henry Burton in England and Benjamin S. Roberts in the United States[86]. Despite successful trials of both systems, it appears that the level of profit margin was not sufficient to warrant significant investment, and Winchester's interest waned rather quickly.

In early February 1867, Winchester received notification from M. de Suzanne that the French government wished the 312 arms still outstanding on their order for Maximilian I of Mexico to be shipped to LeHavre. In addition, de Suzanne ordered 250 iron frame rifles to be used for field tests[87]. According to a letter sent by Henry Chapin to John Davies, all of these arms had been received in Paris by March 30[88]. The content of Chapin's letter does not indicate whether or not the 312 rifles from the Mexico order were of the pattern contracted for (i.e., the Winchester Improvement) or standard commercial Model 1866s. However, due to the date of shipment and other factors mentioned previously in the discussion of the Winchester Improvement Rifle, it is most likely that the arms supplied to France in conjunction with the completion of the Mexican order were standard Model 1866 carbines. With respect to the order for 250 iron frame rifles, it is believed that they were of the improved or Model 1867 Swiss Contract type. These improved rifles differed from the earlier year's model only in the substitution of a one-piece spring-loaded firing pin in place of the two-piece version originally fitted, and a new lever latch (Plates 62-64). Although by this date Winchester had supplied machinery to Weber-Ruesch to manufacture the Model 1867, it does not appear that the contract for these trial rifles was subcontracted to that firm since a surviving example from the contract (serial number 189) bears no manufacturer's markings

other than its serial number whereas Weber-Ruesch arms always are identified as such[89].

Beginning in late February 1867, Winchester initiated a series of stockholders meetings to bring about the formal establishment of the Winchester Repeating Arms company. On Feb. 25 and March 4, Winchester and Davies secured sufficient new investors to complete the company's capitalization of $400,000[90]. Winchester, Davies, and Pasdue then submitted a report to the Connecticut State Legislature stating that the articles of incorporation had been complied with and requested authorization to commence operations as a duly accredited corporation. This authorization was received shortly thereafter, and on April 1, 1867, the Winchester Repeating Arms Company was formally established (Plate 65)[91]. The first act of the new corporation was the issuance of a financial statement that commingled the assets and liabilities of the two original concerns (i.e., the New Haven Arms/Henry Repeating Rifle Company and the Winchester Arms Company). The original copy of this financial report is preserved in the Winchester Repeating Arms Company Archives of Olin Corporation and reads as follows[92]:

Plate 64
Detail of the Model 1867 carbine illustrated in Plate 63. Olin Corporation photograph.

Winchester Repeating Arms Company

New Haven, Connecticut

April 1, 1867

Current Assets

Cash$1,374.65

Accounts Receivable from New Haven Arms Company	182,234.20
Inventory	72,447.74
Chilean-Peruvian Assets	57,000.00
Stock Subscription Receivable (payable April 1 to December 1, 1867)	82,936.99
	$395,993.58

Current Liabilities

Accounts Payable from New Haven Arms Company	$188,493.58
Due Stockholders of New Haven Arms Company	136,500.00
	$324993.58

Net Working Capital	$71,000.00
Fixed Assets	
Value of New Haven Arms Company Plant	$150,000.00

Other Assets

Burnside Rifle Claim	$21,000.00
Mexican Matter	58,000.00
Patent Rights	150,000.00
	$379,000.00

Net Worth	$450,000.00

In his business dealings, Oliver F. Winchester was a ruthless competitor who never failed to take advantage of situations that might benefit the growth of the companies he owned. When, in 1865, he learned that Isaac Hartshorn, the India Rubber magnate, was filing a patent suit against the Burnside Rifle Company, a manufacturer of the Spencer Repeating Rifle, the Henry Rifle's chief rival, Winchester secretly purchased Hartshorn's patent while the suit was in progress. With pure Machiavellian foresight, Winchester knew that if the matter was decided in Hartshorn's favor, Winchester could then, by proxy, dictate the terms of settlement. After Hartshorn's claim was determined to be valid in 1866, Winchester requested payment of damages to be made in machinery, thus forcing the Burnside Rifle Company out of the firearms business.

THE
Winchester Repeating Rifle,

TWO SHOTS A SECOND.

This splendid weapon is a great improvement on the celebrated "Henry" Rifle. These improvements removing all the objections to that Arm; it is lighter and more simple in its construction, less liable to get out of order, and in every respect a better and more perfect weapon, which for power, accuracy and rapidity of fire, exceeds any other weapon ever made and used with a corresponding charge. It is of the same caliber and length of barrel as the Henry Rifle, and carries two charges more, or seventeen shots in the magazine, and one in the barrel.

For Indian, Bear, or Buffalo hunting, it is unrivalled ; and as a war weapon is as much superior to the Prussian Needle Gun, or any single Breech Loader, as they are to the old muzzle loading arm, not only in rapidity, but in accuracy and power.

The great advantage of this Rifle over all others does not consist solely in being able to deliver eighteen shots in nine seconds, but in the moral effect it has, (either upon an army or an individual,) for if there is any thing that will make a party of men, or one single man stand up and fight to the last moment, it is the knowledge that he has a gun in his hands that will not fail to do its duty just at the time when it is most wanted.

The first thought connected with fast firing is, a great waste of ammunition—but this is in reality quite the contrary ; as it is not necessary to commence firing at the enemy when five or six hundred yards off, (for fear of being unable to load up again before he gets right on you), but the fire can be reserved until he is within one hundred, or even fifty yards (with the assurance that before he can get up to you, you can deliver either eighteen or fourteen shots as the case may be, whether you have a Rifle or Carbine), and consequently there is so much greater chance of being able to make every shot count.

The advantage that this Gun possesses over all others for *single individuals* traveling through a wild country, where there is reason to expect a sudden attack either from *robbers or Indians*, cannot be *over-estimated*, as it is well known to all who have used a gun to any extent (especially in close quarters), that there is a *little* uncertainty of its going off ; but with this Gun there can be no such feeling, because even though a Cartridge should miss fire, it is drawn from the barrel with *unfailing certainty*, and another placed in its stead, and fired in just *half a second*, thereby giving two chances, even though the enemy should be within twenty feet at the firing of the first shot, which is something that no other Rifle yet built is capable of doing.

For those living in a country where there is reason to expect an attack from *Indians*, (and as it is at times necessary for all the men to be away from home, consequently leaving their wives and children to fight for themselves), this Gun is what has long been wanted ; it is so simple in its construction, that a child ten years old can with half an hours instruction, load and fire it with perfect safety, it being impossible to get a cartridge into it otherwise than right.

Another great advantage that it has over all other Rifles is, that it can be loaded and fired as a Single Breech Loader as fast as any other Breech Loading Gun that is built, either in this country or Europe, at the same time having in the magazine in reserve *sixteen shots* that can be used in an emergency as before stated ; this last advantage places it far ahead of any other Rifle yet made, whether it is Repeating or Single Loading. With regard to penetration, it is fully equal to any other Rifle that is made, having the same length of barrel, charge of powder and caliber, or bore.

The greatest care is taken in making the barrels, (which are all of steel) ; the straightening of them is done by the best workmen that can be found ; the rifling is also done by experienced men, and with the most improved machinery, consequently with regard to *accuracy* they are equal to the best Target Rifles.

At present but two sizes are made, namely, a rifle with an octagon barrel, twenty-four inches long, and weighing nine and a half pounds, and carrying seventeen shots in the magazine, and one in the barrel, or eighteen shots in all, all of which can be fired by an expert in nine seconds, or at the rate of two shots per second. Also a carbine with a round barrel, twenty inches long, carrying thirteen shots in the magazine, and one in the barrel, or fourteen shots in all, weighing seven and a half pounds ; this is especially adapted to the use of cavalry, as for hunting on the western plains. Both these guns use the same charge, or cartridge as is used in the old model Henry Rifle ⚘. None are genuine without the letter H or W raised in the end of the copper cartridge.

To the following price list the cost of packing will be added in all cases. Box for single guns seventy-five cents. Cases for ten guns $2.50. Lining boxes with tin for shipment holding ten guns, $3.50 each extra.

Rifles with varnished Stocks and Slings,	$50.00
Carbines with oiled Stocks without Slings,	40.00
Cartridges, per 1000,	20 00
Slings for Carbines,	2.50
Leather Cases,	6.00 to 7.50
Extra finish with plating and engraving will cost from	60 00 to 100.00

CAUTION.

As much of the accuracy and power of any good Rifle depends upon the *care* and accuracy with which the ammunition is made, and the quality of the material. We have paid, and still pay great attention to keeping up the quality of our Cartridges, and none are genuine, or of our make, except those that have the letter H or the letter W raised in the metal on the head of the copper shell. All manufacturers are cautioned against using or copying this trade mark. All our arms that have gun metal frames and mountings, use the catridges with the letter H. All cartridges with the letter W, are adapted to the new models, with Iron Frames and mounting, designed expressly for army use.

All buyers who want a reliable article are cautioned against buying any of the poor trash in the market, some of which is offered at one to three, or even five dollars per 1000 less than a good article can be sold for. Sold by all the principal gun dealers in the country.

MANUFACTURED BY THE
WINCHESTER REPEATING ARMS CO.,
New Haven, Conn.

O. P. DAVIS, Sec'y.   O. F. WINCHESTER, Pres't.

Plate 65

Advertising broadside distributed by the Winchester Repeating Arms Company after April 1, 1867. Olin Corporation photograph.

A note attached to this financial statement indicates that the "Accounts Receivable from New Haven Arms Company" consisted of "Sales Receipts Due" of $8,915 and "Recompense for Machinery and Real Estate" of $173,319.20. The "Accounts Payable from New Haven Arms Company" are noted on the same document as being made up of the following amounts: "Winchester & Davies Mortgage $150,000"; "Salaries unpaid $4,510"; and "Sundries $33,983.58."[93] In light of this second explanatory statement, it appears that Winchester and Davies converted their mortgage on the New Haven Arms/Henry Repeating Rifle Company"s machinery for capital stock in the Winchester Repeating Arms Company because the value of that machinery is noted as a fixed asset without encumbrance. Likewise, the absence of the Bridgeport's machinery being listed as an asset indicates that Winchester and Davies continued to hold it in their own names.

While John E. Parsons stated in **The First Winchester: The Story of the 1866 Repeating Rifle** [94] that a meeting of the Winchester Repeating Arms Company's board of directors that took place on March 3, 1867 authorized the production of 5,000 rifles for the coming fiscal year, no evidence for that meeting ever having taken place has been found in either the company's archives at the Cody Firearms Museum

or at the Olin Corporation. There is, however, evidence that a board meeting took place on April 4, 1867, during which Winchester was given approval to continue his negotiations with the Colt company regarding the production there of rifles for Switzerland[95]. It is likely, therefore, that Parson's reference actually refers to the latter meeting.

On June 20, 1867, Winchester again met with General Franklin in Hartford to discuss Colt's participation in the Swiss contract[96]. However, with the passing of each month, the likelihood of the Swiss contract ever being issued to the Winchester company became more and more remote due to lobbying by Friedrich Vetterli in Switzerland to have his bolt-action rifle adopted for service[97]. Despite the ascendence of the Vetterli rifle, private orders and one government contract for 100 Model 1867 rifles were received by Weber-Ruesch[98]. Whether these arms were made totally in Bridgeport or were assembled in Zurich is not known, but circumstantial evidence suggests the latter[99].

Despite the delay in receiving the Swiss contract, increased sales of the standard Model 1866 buoyed the Winchester company's fortunes. In July, the company received an order for 1,000 carbines and 250,000 rounds of ammunition from Emperor Pedro II of Brazil,[100] and in early September 5,000

Plate 66

Winchester Model 1868 musket, no serial number. Winchester Arms Collection (Inv. No. W262), Cody Firearms Museum. Olin Corporation photograph.

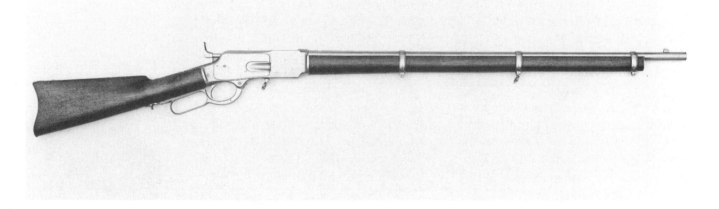

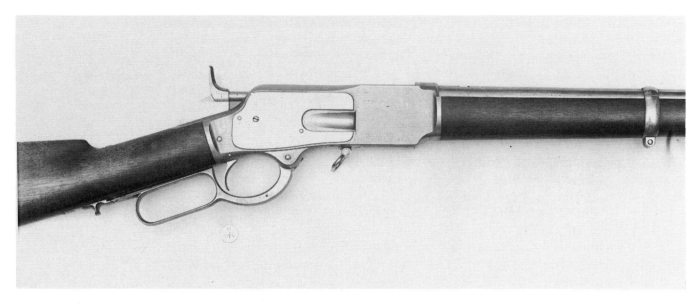

carbines were purchased by a French trading house for shipment to Japan[101]. Thus, by the close of the fiscal year, the Winchester Repeating Arms Company was able to report gross sales amounting to \$223,736.69[102]. Though substantial, this figure demonstrates that the company's sales had yet to reach the full manufacturing capacity of the concern.

During 1868, the company continued to consolidate its position within the North and South American arms' markets. In addition, it also began to view the Far East as a potentially lucrative market. The combination of growing domestic and foreign sales increased the firm's gross by approximately twenty percent to \$271,984.35 during that fiscal year[103].

The increased prosperity of the Winchester company did have some unforeseen side effects. In July 1868, Henry Hicks began to press a claim against the Winchester Repeating Arms Company for royalties on the cartridge extractors used on the company's rifles[104]. Hicks based his claim on a patent issued to him on March 10, 1857 (Patent Number 16797), which protected a prong extractor designed for use in Volcanic arms. Although the Hicks extractor was never made com-

mercially and was not intended for use with metallic cartridges having rims, Winchester took the claim seriously, and after refusing to pay royalties, began proceedings against Hicks to disprove the latter's assertions. Ultimately, six years were to pass before this matter was to be resolved in the Winchester company's favor[105].

Though the Model 1866 remained the company's primary product, work continued during 1868 on iron frame rifles. With the loss of the Swiss contract on March 6[106], the company decided to begin the development of a successor to the Model 1867. The first modification in the design was the elimination of the pivoted locking catch in the rear bow of the finger lever and the substitution for it of a simple sliding stud mounted on the lower tang that, when moved forward, engaged a flat extension on the lever's upper section (Plates 66-69). The use of a steel cartridge carrier was experimented with on some examples, and the lines of the receiver itself were slightly modified. An unknown number of Model 1868 rifles and carbines were also fitted with an internally mounted safety sear, developed by Luke Wheelock, that was subsequently patented on Dec. 1, 1868[107].

Plate 67

Detail of the Model 1868 musket illustrated in Plate 66. Olin Corporation photograph.

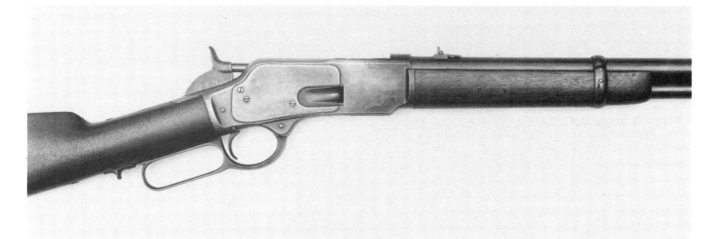

In place of the stud release machined in the upper surface of the finger lever, Wheelock mounted a pin release within the lower tang that only released the secondary sear when the lever was fully drawn up against the lower tang. This eliminated any problems which might be associated with the lever coming out of alignment with the stud aperture due to improper use or damage that evidently had been encountered in the first design. The most noteworthy feature of the Model 1868 is that some were fitted with barrels having a rifling system designed by Oliver Winchester (for example, the carbine illustrated in Plates 68 and 69). To reduce fouling and increase muzzle velocity, Winchester proposed that the first ten or twelve inches of the barrel be free or smooth bored before the rifling commenced. While this system was not patented in the United States until June 25, 1872

(Patent Number 128,446), it was patented in England on April 17, 1869 (Patent Number 1184).

In October 1868, one musket of the revised design was submitted for trial in England (Plates 70 and 71),[108] and a series of carbines, together with rifles of the Model 1868 pattern, were sent to France for examination[109].

Though the Model 1868 Winchester rifle performed well in all the English trial tests except when exposed to sand, the Trial Committee did not recommend its adoption[110]. The reasons for its rejection were its complicated mechanism, the use of a sliding bolt, its weight when loaded, and the fact that the committee did not see any advantages to be gained from the adoption of a repeating rifle for general service[111].

When Oliver F. Winchester received a copy of the committee's printed report, he wrote a detailed rebuttal of the pub-

Top: Plate 68

*W*inchester Model 1868 carbine, serial number 10. R.C. Romanella Collection, Geneva, Switzerland.

Bottom: Plate 69

*D*etail of the Model 1868 carbine illustrated in Plate 68.

lished findings to Edward Cardwell, the Secretary of State for War in London, England[112]. In particular, Winchester questioned the Committee's definition of those characteristics which exemplarized a satisfactory military arm: strength, lightness, safety, flatness of trajectory and accuracy. Through quotes of the committee's queries and comments, Winchester demonstrated that they had determined these factors before any evidence was taken in testimony. He also discussed various aspects of ballistics and the problems associated with fouling. In a critical comment on the cartridge adopted for British service, Winchester noted that it was "a dose for an adult elephant." In closing, Winchester repeated that the Prussian Army had demonstrated the efficiency of repeating rifles just three years earlier and that their use did not generate an undo expenditure of ammunition as the committee feared would happen if multi-shot weapons were issued. The text of this letter was later privately printed by Winchester in pamphlet form under the title "The First Requisite of a Military Rifle."[113] It was also incorporated into later catalogs of the Winchester company[114].

Upon learning of Oliver F. Winchester's purchase of his chief competitor, the American Repeating Rifle Company (the owner of the former Spencer Repeating Rifle Company) in 1869, one New Englander wrote with typical understatement that "he made a good thing of it."

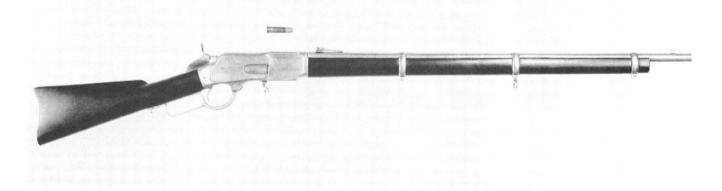

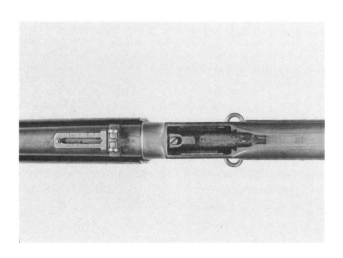

Above: Plate 70

Winchester Model 1868 musket, .455 caliber, serial number 15. Submitted to the English Rifle Trials of 1868. Winchester Arms Collection (Inv. No. W254), Cody Firearms Museum. Olin Corporation photograph.

Left: Plate 71

View of the ejection port of the Model 1868 musket illustrated in Plate 70. Olin Corporation photograph.

While the Winchester company had prospered during the post- Civil War period, a large number of its competitors had not. In November 1868, the company learned that one of its primary competitors, the Spencer Repeating Rifle Company, was in serious financial difficulty and that its principals wished to sell it. At a special meeting of the Winchester board of directors held on Nov. 16, Oliver F. Winchester and two other directors were authorized to explore the possibility of the Winchester company purchasing the Spencer company[115]. After reviewing the assets and liabilities of Spencer, the officers of the Winchester company declined to purchase it[116]. Approximately one month later, the Fogarty Repeating Rifle Company of Boston bought the Spencer concern[117].

The wisdom of the Winchester company's deferral in acquiring the Spencer Repeating Rifle Company became evident less than nine months later, when the American Repeating Rifle Company (the corporation founded on April 20, 1869, consolidating the Fogarty and Spencer firms) declared bankruptcy in August 1869[118]. The Winchester Repeating Arms Company then purchased the combined assets of the Fogarty-Spencer firms, including all machinery, completed arms, work in progress and patents, for $200,000[119]. Little over a month later, on Sept. 28, Winchester sold all the machinery at public auction in Boston for approximately $138,000[120]. As a result, the company was able to secure the patent rights for the firms and a substantial number of arms for $62,000. The number of arms involved in this purchase is perhaps best demonstrated by an advertisement placed by the Winchester company in the Dec. 11 issue of The Scientific American, which reads in part as follows[121]:

For Sale, viz.-

2,000 Spencer Repeating Muskets
30,000 Spencer Repeating Carbines
500 Spencer Repeating Sporting Rifles

While the sales of arms slowed somewhat during 1869, they still amounted to $323,511.50 for the fiscal year[122].

During early 1870, Luke Wheelock explored the possibilities of using some of the features contained in the Fogarty and Spencer patents acquired the previous year. Specifically, his research centered upon the combination of the Winchester lever-action system with the rotating Spencer breechblock to effect a more positive locking of the breech. The advantages of developing such a system was that a positive locking of the bolt face to the barrel breech would allow more powerful cartridges to be used[123]. Eventually, these experiments were to lead Wheelock to

Plate 72
Luke Wheelock sample .40 caliber musket made in 1870. Winchester Arms Collection (Inv. No. W248), Cody Firearms Museum. Olin Corporation photograph.

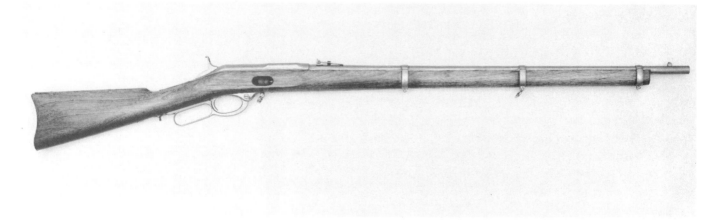

develop a locking bar that engaged a slot cut in the sides of the breech bolt and a notch in the upper receiver wall. By modifying the construction of the finger lever pivot, Wheelock was able to adjust its travel so that after the bolt had been fully closed, the final closing action of the finger lever caused the locking bar to be raised into alignment with the bolt sides and receiver notch. Similarly, the modified pivot allowed the retraction of the locking bar before any rearward movement of the bolt began when the finger lever was opened. Another major feature of Wheelock's design was that he fitted the bolt with a cammed operating rod rather than the jointed toggle links used previously. To improve loading, the cartridge carrier was dispensed with and a simple pivoted lifting platform was employed. To prevent the escape of cartridges from the magazine, the lifter was spring-loaded so that it remained out of alignment with the loading port during the normal operation of the arm. However, when cartridges were loaded, they caused the lifter to be depressed into a shallow relief cut in the receiver base so that the cartridges could easily pass over the lifter and into the magazine. Visually, the most striking feature of the new design was that the receiver was enclosed within the stock with only its upper surface exposed (Plate 72). Ultimately, this design was to be patented on Jan. 31, 1871 (U.S. Patent Number 111,500, Plates 73-76).

The three single events which drastically affected the fortunes of the Winchester Repeating Rifle Company during 1870 were the decision to relocate the factory to New Haven, the Franco-Prussian War and the receipt from the Ottoman Empire of an order for 20,000 arms.

Evidently, sometime in late 1869, the previously cordial relationship between Oliver F. Winchester, Nathaniel Wheeler and James Wilson began to deteriorate. The exact reasons bringing about the animosity are unknown, but one contemporary account states that it was based upon Wheeler and Wilson's determination to raise the lease on the Bridgeport factory[124]. Whatever the cause, by early 1870, Winchester was proposing that the company relocate its factory to New Haven. The suggestion was tabled at the Feb. 14, 1870, board of directors meeting[125]. By midsummer, however, Winchester had convinced the board that a move was necessary, and on Aug. 27, a decision to

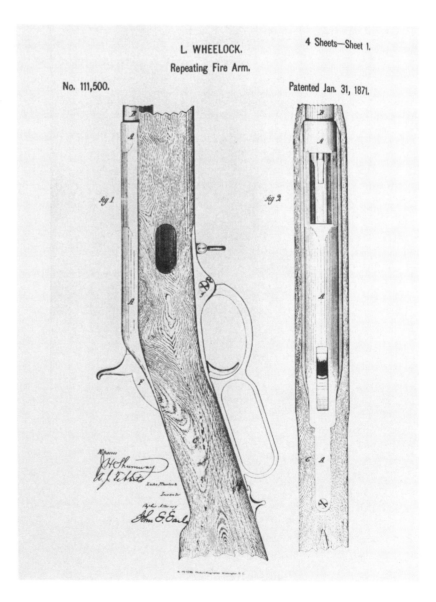

purchase land from Winchester in New Haven and to construct a new plant was approved, with Wheeler and Wilson dissenting[126].

In many respects, the timing of the relocation could not have been better, for in September 1870, the company received a substantial order for arms from the government of France. Napoleon III's ill-fated adventure against Germany, which started on Aug. 2, had, by Sept. 2, resulted in the greater part of the French Army being defeated, interned or rendered useless. After Napoleon III's forced abdication, the Provisional Government of France for its National Defense hurriedly began purchasing whatever munitions of war they could procure in England and the United States. Through the agency of E. Remington & Sons, the Winchester company sold its entire stock of Spencer carbines and rifles to France, together with 4,406 Model 1866 carbines and muskets[127]. An additional 1,594 Model 1866s originally intended for that country were never delivered due to the cessation of hostilities[128].

The second event that made the occupation of a larger plant facility a necessity was the receipt in November of an order from the Imperial Ottoman Empire for 15,000 Model 1866 muskets and 5,000 Model 1866 carbines (Plates 77-79)[129]. The result of overtures began in late 1866[130], the Ottoman order was worth in excess of $550,000, including the accompanying ammunition. The date of its receipt, though, was just prior to the first efforts to begin the relocation of the factory. Consequently, the company had to devise a means by which the contract could be fulfilled while machinery was transferred.

A memorandum, believed to have been written by an employee who worked in the Barrel Shop at the time, best describes what happened[131]:

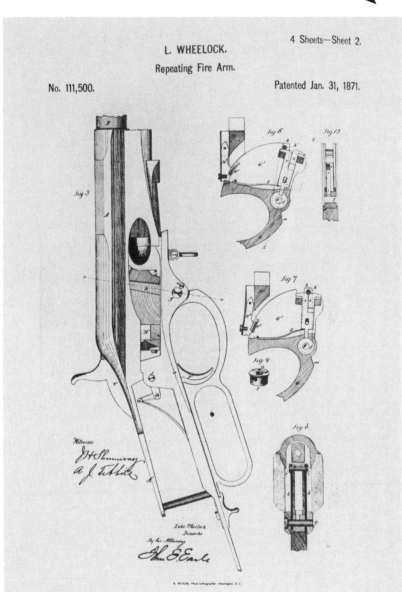

Plate 74

*S*heet 2 of the patent specification drawings for Luke Wheelock's Jan. 31, 1871, patent.

"In the Winter of 1870, the Shop was running on the Turkish Contract on 1866 Model. There was a big drive and most Contracts were running two set of hands, ten hours each. The limit on the Barrel Job was 350 per day. During this period the works was moved to their new shop in New Haven. Such was the hurry for work that no machine was stoped [sic] untill [sic] trams were ready to transport to depot. In one case at least the last machine on the Bbl [sic] job was in use till 12 Oclock. The belt was cut and the machine was in new shop next morning. But not withstanding this drive, no machine could be place in new shop untill [sic] it was taken down, cleaned and painted."

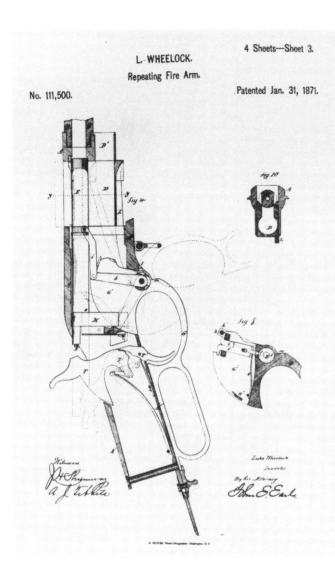

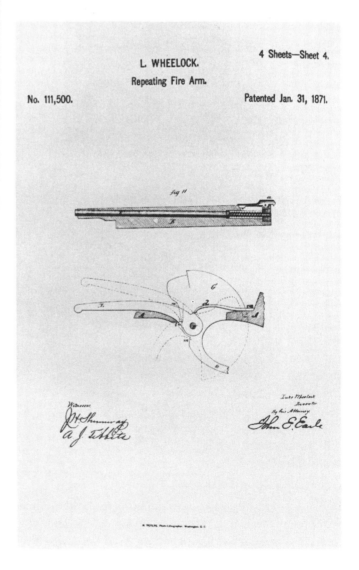

Left: *Plate 75*

*S*heet 3 of the patent specification drawings illustrated in Plates 73 and 74.

Bottom: *Plate 76*

*S*heet 4 of the patent specification drawings illustrated in Plates 73, 74 and 75.

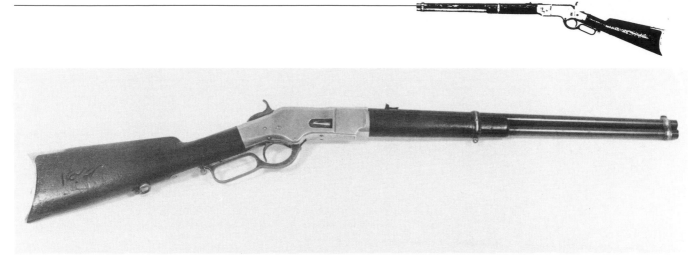

While the French and Ottoman orders were the largest received in 1870, other smaller government orders, such as one for 600 Model 1866 carbines from Peru[132], also helped to swell the company's gross arms sales to $809,393.64 even though the full receipts for the Ottoman contract were not to be completely realized until 1871[133].

By April 1871, the transfer of the Winchester company's holdings in Bridgeport to the New Haven factory had been completed. According to George Walker's notes, the last part of the plant to be moved was the cartridge department. Its transfer was delayed until all the ammunition called for in the Ottoman contract had been made[134].

Technically, the year 1871 witnessed only two significant developments in firearm's design. Early in the year, George R. Stetson proposed an enclosed lever action (Plate 80) as an alternative to Wheelock's. In place of

the rising bolt lock used by Wheelock, Stetson employed a rocking collar on the bolt to effect the locking of the bolt. The final movement of the finger lever first closed the bolt and then caused a collar pivoted to the sides of the bolt to rise up into a recess cut in the upper receiver. Stetson's design, unlike all pervious Winchester rifles, had an enclosed upper receiver and an ejection port located to the right of the bolt. As with Wheelock's design, Stetson used a cartridge lifter rather than a carrier. Though the loading aperture was located in the same position as Wheelock's, it was fitted with a sliding cover that automatically closed after the last round was fed into the magazine.

The second design to be developed that year was Baron von Nolken's hammerless version of the Model 1866. Von Nolken, the Winchester company's travelling representative in the German speaking states of Europe[135], rede-

Top: Plate 77
Turkish Contract Winchester Model 1866 carbine, serial number 48694. The butt stamped with possession and issuance marks. Norman McWilliams Collection.

Bottom: Plate 78
Left side view of the Model 1866 Turkish Contract carbine illustrated in Plate 77.

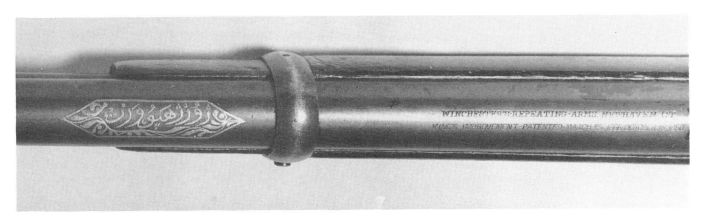

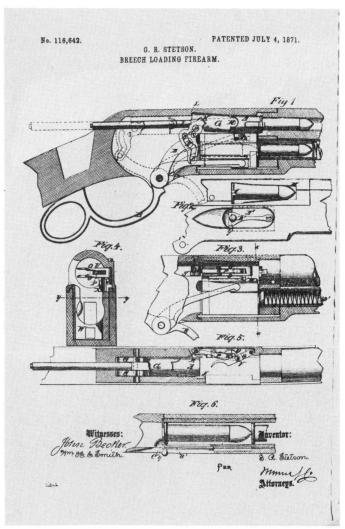

No. 116,642.   PATENTED JULY 4, 1871.

G. R. STETSON.
BREECH LOADING FIREARM.

Fig 1

Fig.2

Fig.4.

Fig.3.

Fig.5.

Fig. 6.

Witnesses: Inventor:

John Becker.   G. R. Stetson.

Wm. H. L. Smith.

Per

Attorneys.

Top: **Plate 79**

Detail of the barrel inscriptions found in the Turkish Contract Model 1866 carbine illustrated in Plate 77.

Left: **Plate 80**

Specification drawings enrolled with George R. Stetson's U.S. Patent Number 116642 issued July 4, 1871. Winchester Arms Collection Archives, Cody Firearms Museum.

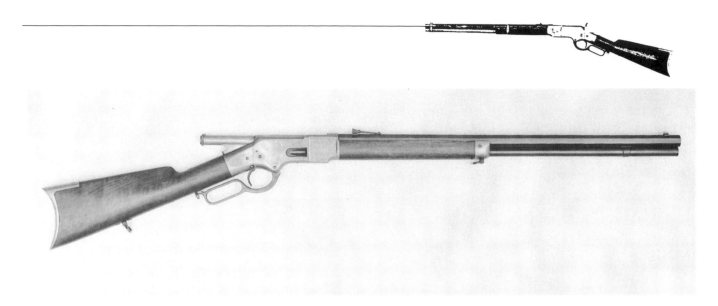

signed the Model 1866's bolt so that it had an internal combination striker-firing pin that could be released by a sear mounted within the receiver much like later bolt-action rifles (Plate 81). To reduce the possibility of this striker-firing pin mechanism becoming fouled, he attached a tubular shroud to the rear of the receiver. While the design had some merit, it was never seriously considered for manufacture.

On Aug. 19, 1871, the New Haven plant was given its first opportunity to demonstrate its full capabilities. The receipt of an order that day for 30,000 Model 1866 muskets from the Imperial Ottoman government caused the factory to be put on double shift and overtime status[136]. The production facilities proved to have been laid out for optimum use, and the contract was filled within six weeks.

In all, domestic and foreign sales during 1871 raised the Winchester company's gross to $1,015,652.00, its most lucrative year to that point[137].

Plate 81

*B*aron von Nolken's enclosed striker Model 1866 sporting rifle. No serial number. Winchester Arms Collection, (Inv. No. W244), Cody Firearms Museum. Olin Corporation photograph.

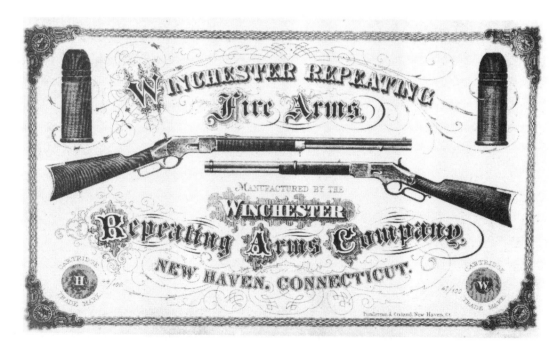

Plate 82

Cover of the Winchester Repeating Arms Company's 1870 catalog, illustrating the .44 caliber rimfire cartridge on the left and O.F. Winchester's centerfire .47 caliber cartridge on the right. Private Collection.

Endnotes

1. Davies Diary, op. cit., entry dated July 1, 1865.

2. Ibid.

3. James D. Smith's appointment as assistant superintendent at the Bridgeport factory is recorded in Davies Diary, op. cit., entry for July 1, 1865.

4. See Figure 26 of the specification drawings enrolled with William Clark's (for O.F. Winchester) English Patent Number 3284 issued Dec. 19, 1865, and Figures 3 and 4 of the specification drawings enrolled with Smith's United States Patent Number 52934 issued Feb. 27, 1866.

5. For the construction of the lower tang, see Plate 52.

6. James D. Smith, United States Patent Number 52934, issued Feb. 27, 1866, specifications, pages 1-3.

7. Winchester Firearms Reference Collection, op. cit., page 49.

8. Hank Wieand Bowman, **Famous Guns From the Smithsonian Collection** (Fawcett Publications, Inc.; Greenwich, CT: 1966), pages 108-109.

9. See Note 6 above.

10. Specifically, the major concern voiced about this design was the manner in which it was loaded (i.e., with the action open) and that this arrangement necessitated the cycling of the action twice before a cartridge could be chambered if one were not manually put in the chamber.

11. Briggs' leave from the New Haven Arms Company during September 1865 is confirmed by his absence from the firm's payroll (New Haven Arms Company Payroll Book, op. cit., August, September and October 1865). The September design date is confirmed by a dated design drawing preserved in a private collection. As Oliver F. Winchester was president of the New Haven Arms Company, the matter of releasing Briggs from his duties with that company so that he could work for the Winchester Arms Company in Bridgeport was in all likelihood authorized by Winchester himself.

12. See Inventory Number W243, Winchester Firearms Reference Collection, op. cit., page 47.

13. Ibid, page 50.

14. Winchester's authorship of this design is confirmed in Weber-Ruesch op. cit., pages 4 and 5.

15. Winchester Firearms Reference Collection, op. cit., page 50.

16. Undated design drawing, Winchester Arms Collection Archives, Cody Firearms Museum, loc. cit.

17. The exact of O.F. Winchester's departure for Europe is unknown. A letter from Winchester dated Oct. 21, 1865, postmarked London, is preserved in the Davies Family Papers.

18. William Clark (for Oliver F. Winchester), Patent Number 3284, issued Dec. 19, 1865. **Patents For Inventions. Abridgements of Specifications. Class 119, Small-Arms. Period-A.D. 1855-1866** (H.M.S.O.; London: 1905), pages 195 and 196.

19. For a complete account of the Swiss Federal Rifle Trials, see Franz von Erlach, "Der Henry-Stutzen," **Allgemeine Schweizerische Militar-Zeitung** (Basel, Switzerland), Volume 11, Number 45 (Nov. 9, 1866), pages 373-385, 409-412 and 415-420 (pages 415-420 translated and published verbatim

in Winchester catalogs from 1867 forward); and Wilhelm von Ploennies, **Neue Hinterladungs-Gewehre** (Edward Zernin; Darmstadt and Leipzig: 1867), pages 137-168. Confirmation that the Winchester Improvement was submitted to the Trials is found on pages 144 of Ploennies.

20. See Introduction.

21. The full text of the agreement is as follows:

Paris

6e, Novr 1865

Mr. Oliver F. Winchester of New Haven, Connecticut, United States of America, agrees to make One Thousand Henry rifles having the approved improvements for [Blank] at the price of Thirty Four U.S. Dollars Gold per rifle with Sundry parts and implements delivered to New York City. Deliveries to commence Two Months forward from this date. In receipt and acceptance whereof, Mr. Winchester acknowledges payment this day of Seventeen Thousand U.S. Dollars Gold.

| Witnessed | F. deSuzanne |
| Georges Chasteau | O.F. Winchester |

(de Suzanne Letter Press Book, op. cit., pages 211-212.)

The specification that these arms were to be shipped to Havana, Cuba was probably due to apprehensions on the part of the French goverment that the United States might place an export embargo on arms being shipped directly to Mexico. Since Cuba was not involved in the Mexican conflict, arms shipped there would not have aroused any suspicion on the part of American port authorities.

22. English Patent Abridgements, op. cit., page 195 (Figures 13, 15, 19 and 21).

23. Receipt from J.P. Moore & Son, New York, dated Jan. 12, 1865. Photocopy in New Haven Arms Company File, Winchester Arms Collection Archives, Cody Firearms Museum.

24. Verso of Item 13, File 2, Documents Relating to the Volcanic Repeating Arms Company, etc., Winchester Arms Collection Archives, Cody Firearms Museum.

25. George Walker's Production Notes for the Model 1866. Winchester Arms Collection Archives, Cody Firearms Museum.

26. New Haven Arms Company Payroll Book, op. cit., July 8, 1865 to Nov. 25, 1865.

27. Davies Diary, op. cit., entry dated Dec. 31, 1865.

28. Ibid.

29. The date of the meeting being Feb. 3, 1866.

30. References to a suit being filed "In Equity" are to be found in both Walker's Model 1866 Production Notes, op. cit., and Davies Diary under various dates. A manuscript title page, evidently for this action, reads "Benjamin Tyler Henry vs The Henry Repeating Rifle Company In Equity, Southern District of Connecticut. January, 1866." Winchester Repeating Arms Company Legal Documents, Winchester Arms Collection Archives, Cody Firearms Museum.

31. Davies Diary, op. cit., entry dated Dec. 3, 1866.

32. Application for special legislation to accomplish the modification of the Henry Repeating Rifle Company's 1865 Charter was apparently filed in February 1866.

33. Walker's Model 1866 Production Notes, op. cit.

34. New Haven Arms Company Payroll Book, op. cit., July 7, 1866.

35. Pen and ink design drawing of the loading aperture cover (vertical and horizontal elevations) dated at the lower left edge Jan 14. 1866. Private Collection.

36. The original specification drawing enrolled with Nelson King's United States Patent Number 55012, issued May 22, 1866, is stamped with the Patent Office's receipt mark bearing the date March 29, 1866. National Archives, Record Group 241, Washington, D.C.

37. Winchester Firearms Reference Collection, op. cit., page 49.

38. Ibid, page 50.

39. Walker's Model 1866 Production Notes, op. cit.

40. Essentially, only the right receiver, right sideplate and carrier milling machine needed to be altered.

41. The application was subsequently modified again in order to change the corporate name to the Winchester Repeating Arms Company.

42. A list attached to the Cleveland article indicates that notices were published in Leslie's Magazine and newspapers located in the following cities: Boston, Chicago, London, Louisville, New Orleans, New York, Paris, San Francisco, St. Petersburg (Russia) and Washington. Model 1866 Production File, Winchester Arms Collection Archives, Cody Firearms Museum.

43. New York World, Sept. 6, 1866.

44. For a detailed discussion of this controversy see: H.G. Houze, "A Reevaluation of the Henry and Model 1866 Serial Numbering," **Man at Arms**, Volume 13, Number 4 (July/August 1991), page 10-17, and W. Sword, "Winchester Model 1866 Serial Numbers – Another Perspective," **Man at Arms**, Volume 14, Number 1 (January/February 1992), pages 8,9 and 42 (with a rebuttal by Houze.)

45. Walker's Model 1866 Production Notes, op. cit.

46. Williamson, op. cit., page 49, and Sword, op. cit.,

pages 8-9.

47. See Note 44.

48. Davies Diary, op. cit., entries dated Sept. 6, 8, 12, 20, 23, Oct. 1, 9, and 10, 1866.

49. de Suzanne Letter Press Book, op. cit., Letters - 4, page 286.

50. Walker's Model 1866 Production Notes, op. cit.

51. Manuscript account written by Oliver F. Winchester and initialed in his hand OFW. Winchester Repeating Arms Company Archives, Olin Corporation, Stanford, Connecticut.

52. This number was arrived at by allowing an average price of $32.50 per Model 1866 sold.

53. Walker's Model 1866 Production Notes, op. cit.

54. Major General William B. Franklin, manuscript Aide-Memoire (Nov. 15, 1865 to Dec. 31, 1867), entry dated Nov. 6, 1866, page 116. Record Group 103. Records of the Colt's Patent Fire Arms Manufacturing Company, Connecticut State Library, Hartford, Connecticut.

55. See Note 44 above.

56. Ibid.

57. The word "coming" is a synonym for "promising," and it is in that context the word was most commonly used during the nineteenth century.

58. For example, the Smith, Briggs, Winchester and Swiss Contract sample arms all are serial numbered separately beginning with serial number 1.

59. Correspondence to Edwin Pugsley concerning four-digit serial numbered Model 1866s exists from the 1920s and '30s (noted in Houze, "Reevaluation," op. cit., notes 35 and 36, page 17). These low number arms are attributed by some as originating in special orders (Sword, op. cit., page 9) so as to not jeopardize their belief in the 1867 commencement of production.

60. Mention of the Chilean and Japanese contracts is found in Walker's Model 1866 Production Notes, op. cit.

61. Pierre Lorain and Jean Boudriot, **Les Armes Americanines De La Defense Nationale 1870-1871** (Les Presses de l'Emancipatrice; Paris: 1970), pages 90 and 91.

62. Henry Patent Extension, op. cit., page 3.

63. R.C. Romanella Collection, Geneva, Switzerland.

64. Production of commercial Model 1866 carbines and rifles having this modification began in 1867 (Walker's Model 1866 Production Notes, op. cit.).

65. The highest serial presently known for arms of this type is 29.

66. See Color Plate 5 and serial number 1 in the Winchester Arms Collection (Inv. No. W261), Cody Firearms Museum.

67. Serial number 1 and 25 are preserved in the Winchester Arms Collection (Inv. No's W261 and W264), Cody Firearms Museum.

68. The trials involving the Winchester samples began on Oct. 1 and continued through Oct. 13, 1866 (Karl von Elgger, **Die Kriegsfeuerwaffen der Gegenwart** [n.p. Leipzig: 1868], pages 163-166, and **Winchester's Repeating Fire Arms** [Winchester Repeating Arms Co.; New Haven, CT: 1867], pages 22-28.

69. Ibid.

70. Erlach, op. cit., page 418.

71. Ibid.

72. Ibid, page 420.

73. Ibid, page 385. H. von Yobell in **Des Zundnadelgewehrs Geschichte und Konkurrenten** (E.G. Mittler & Son; Berlin: 1867) notes on page 98 that an order for 8,000 Winchester rifle muskets was to be placed by the Swiss government.

74. Erlach, op. cit., page 385, and; Weber-Ruesch, op. cit., pages 5 and 6.

75. There is a possibility that this safety could have been developed as late as March 1867, when work stopped on the Swiss Contract.

76. The highest recorded serial numbers presently known are 406 (Swiss Private Collection) and 419 (formerly in Lloyd Bender's Collection).

77. Franklin, Aide-Memoire, op. cit., entry dated Oct. 30, 1866, page 113.

78. Thomas Addis, typescript autobiography, page 2. Addis File, Winchester Arms Collection Archives, Cody Firearms Museum.

79. Williamson, op. cit., pages 52-53 is non-committal and only mentions "rifles"; Parsons, op. cit., page 49, identifies the arms as "Henrys."

80. The Chilean contract was fulfilled in 1867 (Walker's Model 1866 Production Notes, op. cit.).

81. Minutes of the Winchester Fire Arms Company organization meeting held on Dec. 3, 1866. Item 13, File 2, Documents Relating to the Volcanic Repeating Arms Company, etc., Winchester Arms Collection Archives, Cody Firearms Museum.

82. Davies Diary, op. cit., entry dated Dec. 3, 1866.

83. Ibid.

84. Ibid.

85. This is suggested by Winchester's manuscript account of the total sales from 1866 to 1870, cited in Note 51 above.

86. James Henry Burton, English Patent Number 850, issued March 22, 1866 and Patent Number 69, issued Jan. 9, 1867. Benjamin Stone Roberts, United States Patent Number 52887, issued Feb. 27, 1866, and Patent Number 65607, issued June 11, 1867. Winchester's interest in both inventors' work is noted in a June 21, 1926, letter from Edwin Pugsley to L.D. Satterlee (Pugsley Correspondence, Winchester Arms Collection Archives, Cody Firearms Museum, loc. cit.). Further, Franklin noted in his Aide-Memoire on Jan. 25, 1867, that Luke Wheelock (then employed by Winchester) had visited him regarding the production of Roberts' rifles (Franklin, Aide-Memoire, op. cit., entry dated Jan. 25, 1867, page 131).

87. de Suzanne Letter Press Book, op. cit., Letters - 5, page 15 (letter dated Jan. 14 or 15, 1867).

88. John M. Davies, Manuscript Diary for the period Jan. 1, 1867 to Dec. 30, 1868. Entry dated April 27, 1867. Davies Family Papers, loc. cit.

89. For example the Weber-Ruesch rifle serial number 419 formerly in the Lloyd Bender Collection.

90. Williamson, op. cit., page 47, and; Davies Diary, op. cit., entry dated March 4, 1867.

91. Historical Summation of the Winchester Repeating Arms Company, page 1. Papers Relative to the Bankruptcy of the Winchester Repeating Arms Company (1930), Winchester Arms Collection Archives, Cody Firearms Museum. The formal establishment of the new corporation, election of officers and the appointment of a board of directors took place on February 25, 1867.

92. Winchester Repeating Arms Company Archives, Olin Corporation. The Burnisde Rifle Claim listed under Other Assets represents the discounted value of Winchester's rights in a patent suit filed by Isaac Hartshorn against the Burnside Rifle Company. Winchester purchased Hartshorn's

patent while the suit was in progress in an effort to remove the Burnside company from the arms buisness if Hartshorn's claim was found to be valid (which it was in 1866).

93. Ibid.

94. John E. Parsons, The First Winchester: The Story of the 1866 Repeating Rifle (Winchester Press; New York: 1969), page 58.

95. Davies Diary, op. cit., entry dated April 5, 1867.

96. Franklin, Aide-Memoire, op. cit., entry dated June 20, 1867, page 173.

97. Hugo Schneider, Michael am Rhyn, Oskar Krebs, Christian Reinhart and Robert Schiess. **Bewaffnung und Ausrustung der Schweizer Armee seit 1817: Handfeuerwaffen System Vetterli** (Stocker-Schmid; Zurich: 1970), pages 13 and 18.

98. Weber-Ruesch, op. cit., pages 6-7.

99. A number of Winchester pattern arms with receivers slightly unlike those made in New Haven are known. This difference in construction strongly suggests that they were totally made by Weber-Ruesch whose name they bear in the receiver.

100. Walker's Model 1866 Production Notes, op. cit.

101. Ibid. Also, the early use of Model 1866 Winchester carbines in Japan is noted in the catalog titled **Japanese Firearms: An Outline of the Yoshioka Collection** published in conjunction with an exhibition of that collection at Osaka Castle in March 1983, page 39.

102. O.F. Winchester's 1866-1870 Sales Account, op. cit.

103. Ibid.

104. The pending dispute is first indicated in a letter from Smith & Wesson to O.F. Winchester dated July 25, 1868. Smith & Wesson Correspondence, Winchester Arms Collection Archives, Cody Firearms Museum, loc. cit.

105. The last letter between Smith & Wesson and Winchester regarding this matter is dated June 10, 1873 (Smith & Wesson Correspondence, op. cit.). A full record of the proceedings was published in two volumes (Defendant's Record and Complainant's Record) under the title **United States Circuit Court, Southern District of New York. In Equity. E.S. Renwick, W.C. Hicks, Horace Smith and D.B. Wesson vs. Charles H. Pond** (Evening Journal; Jersey City, NJ: 1871).

106. Hugo Schneider, et al., op. cit., page 10.

107. Luke Wheelock, United States Patent Number 84598 issued Dec. 1, 1868.

108. **Reports of a Special Committee in Breech-Loading Rifles; together with Minutes of Evidence** (Queen's Printer; London: 1869), page xxviii.

109. Walker's Model 1866 Production Notes, op. cit., misidentifies this order as being standard production Model 1866 Rifles.

110. Special Committee Report, op. cit., page xxix.

111. Ibid.

112. O.F. Winchester to the Right Honorable Edward Cardwell, M.P., Secretary of State for War, dated Aug. 2, 1869.

113. O.F. Winchester, **The First Requisite of a Military Rifle** (Winchester Repeating Arms Company; New Haven, CT: 1870).

114. **Winchester's Repeating Fire Arms** (Winchester Repeating Arms Company; New Haven, CT: 1871), pages 1-16.

115. Roy M. Marcot, **Spencer Repeating Firearms** (Northwood Heritage Press; Irvine, CA: 1990), page 153.

116. Ibid.

117. Ibid.

118. Ibid, page 155.

119. Ibid, and Records of the R.G. Dun Company, Connecticut, Volume 40, page 558.

120. Marcot, op. cit., page 155.

121. Reproduced in Marcot, op. cit., page 156. Cf. Note 127 below.

122. O.F. Winchester 1866-1870 Sales Account, op. cit.

123. Two models are preserved in the Winchester Arms Collection (Inv. No's W471 and W472) and are illustrated in Marcot, op. cit., page 307.

124. Davies Diary, op. cit., entry dated Dec. 15, 1868.

125. Williamson, op. cit., page 59.

126. Ibid.

127. Walker's Model 1866 Production Notes, op. cit., and Lorain and Boudriot, op. cit., pages 60-64 and 90-91. In addition, the Winchester company sold the French government the stock of 2,000 Joslyn carbines advertised in the Dec. 11, 1869, issue of **The Scientific American**.

128. Ibid. Walker cites the total order as 6,000 arms while Lorain and Boudriot record the delivery of only 4,406.

129. Walker's Model 1866 Production Notes, op. cit., and Williamson, op. cit., page 56.

130. Williamson, op. cit., page 56 (based upon depositions taken in the matter of Christophus Oscanyon vs. the Winchester Repeating Arms Company).

131. Unsigned and undated "Memorandum", Item 1, File 4, Documents Relating to the Volcanic Repeating Arms Company, etc., op. cit.

132. Walker's Model 1866 Production Notes, op. cit.

133. Records of the R.G. Dun Company, Connecticut, Volume 40, page 558, and Winchester Repeating Arms Company Financial Statement for 1870, Winchester Repeating Arms Company Archives, Olin Corporation.

134. Walker's Model 1866 Production Notes, op. cit.

135. Baron A. von Nolcken represented the Winchester company unofficially during the 1870s and '80s. He had Lebeda of Prague build a similar hammerless rifle, circa 1875, which is now in the Cody Firearms Museum.

136. Williamson, op. cit., page 56.

137. Records of the R.G. Dun Company, Connecticut, Volume 40, page 266, and Winchester Repeating Arms Company Financial Statement for 1871, Winchester Repeating Arms Company Archives, Olin Corporation.

CHAPTER 2

THE WINCHESTER REPEATING ARMS COMPANY'S SEARCH FOR NEW MARKETS: 1872-1883

Recognizing that the continued growth of the Winchester Repeating Arms Company depended upon the expansion and modernization of its product line, Oliver F. Winchester launched an ambitious development program in 1872. The initial goals of this program were the development of a new rifle and cartridge to replace the model 1866, whose design and .44 rimfire cartridge were rapidly becoming outdated[1].

To accomplish these aims, Luke Wheelock was asked to continue the refinement of his enclosed action rifle, while George H. Dupee and George R. Stetson were assigned the task of perfecting a new cartridge.

Wheelock's modification of his 1871 design consisted of a substitution of a simpler locking mechanism for that originally proposed (Plates 83 and 84)[2]. The revised locking bar was a broad L-shaped piece of steel suspended vertically within the rear wall of the receiver. By adding an extension to the finger lever pivot, the locking bar could be raised up into alignment with a cut in the lower surface of the bolt when the finger lever was closed. A hook on the rear pivot extension rode over the bottom of the locking bar so that when the lever was lowered, the bar was forced downward out of engagement

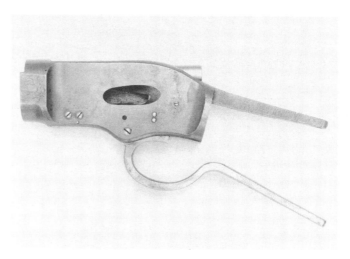

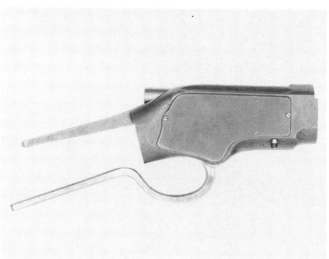

Top: Plate 83

Sample receiver fitted with Luke Wheelock's vertical bolt lock. Winchester Arms Collection (Inv. No. W705), Cody Firearms Museum.

Bottom: Plate 84

Right side view of the sample receiver illustrated in Plate 83.

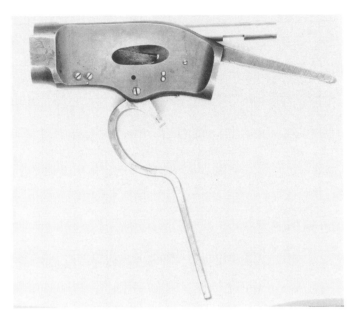

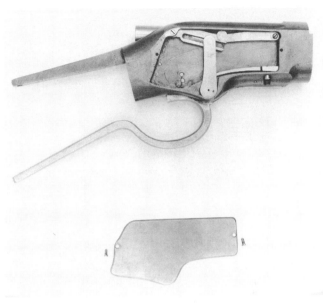

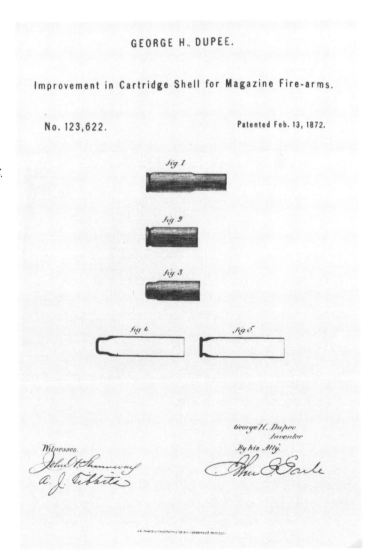

Top Left: Plate 85

*W*heelock sample receiver with the bolt in open position showing the locking recess in the bottom of the bolt and notched lower end of the locking bar.

Top Right: Plate 86

*R*ight side of the Wheelock sample receiver illustrated in Plate 83 with the sideplate removed to expose the bolt linkage.

Bottom Right: Plate 87

*S*pecification drawings enrolled with George H. Dupee's U.S. Patent Number 123622 issued Feb. 13, 1872. Winchester Arms Collection Archives, Cody Firearms Museum.

GEORGE H. DUPEE.

Improvement in Cartridge Shell for Magazine Fire-arms.

No. 123,622.   Patented Feb. 13, 1872.

fig 1

fig 2

fig 3

fig 4   *fig 5*

George H. Dupee
Inventor
By his Atty.

Witnesses.

with the bolt before the latter could start its rearward movement (Plate 85).

The major problem with this design was that the position of the locking bar prevented the use of the cam operating linkage developed by Wheelock, as well as the normal toggle links first designed by Smith & Wesson in 1854. The novel solution to this dilemma that Wheelock devised was the installation of a single set of links connected to the side of the bolt which were set within a recess cut in the exterior wall of the receiver that could be covered by a detachable sideplate (Plate 86). Although this arrangement did work, the thinness of the links made the design somewhat problematic since they could not withstand any great pressure before becoming deformed or binding[3]. Thus, if a rifle using this type of action became fouled with dirt or any other foreign matter, it was likely to become inoperable rather quickly. As a result, Wheelock totally redesigned the lockwork of his rifle for a third time. Though the revised design superficially resembled its predecessors, internally it was quite different. The locking bar was totally abandoned and normal toggle links were used to move the bolt.

By the time Wheelock had completed work on his final design, Dupee and Stetson had perfected a new series of full and semi- bottle neck cartridges based largely upon Dupee's Feb. 13, 1872, United States Patent Number 123,622 (Plate 87). Consequently, the third series of Wheelock samples built during the second half of 1872 were chambered for the new ammunition[4].

In June 1872, the second phase of O.F. Winchester's development program was begun when William W. Wetmore of Springfield, Massachusetts, was hired to establish and oversee a Model Room at the New Haven factory. In a deposition given some twenty-five years later, Wetmore stated that he was hired[5]:

"After leaving Smith & Wesson I entered the employ of the Winchester Repeating Arms Company to develop a revolver for them."

Accompanying Wetmore from Springfield was Charles S. Wells, another former employee of the Smith & Wesson Company[6]. Together, Wetmore and Wells spent the autumn developing a rudimentary design for a single-action revolver incorporating a manually operated ejector mounted to the rear of the loading aperture (Plate 88). The forward edge of this extractor fit within a groove cut in the rear surface of the cylinder so that it could ride under the rims of any chambered cartridges. Extraction was accomplished by draw-

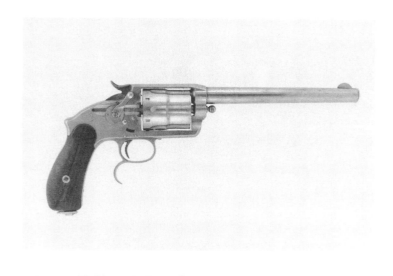

Top: Plate 88

W*inchester-Wetmore-Wells .38 caliber sample revolver made during the autumn of 1872. Winchester Arms Collection (Inv. No. W1783), Cody Firearms Museum.*

Bottom: Plate 89

D*etail of the Winchester-Wetmore-Wells sample revolver illustrated in Plate 88, with the manual extractor in the forward position.*

ing back the extractor when a shell was in line with the loading port (Plate 89)[7].

By the close of the year, Winchester's broad-based development program had yielded concrete results in Wheelock's third series of sample rifles (Plates 90-93 and Color Plates 8 and 9), the Wetmore-Wells revolver and a new type of center fire cartridge.

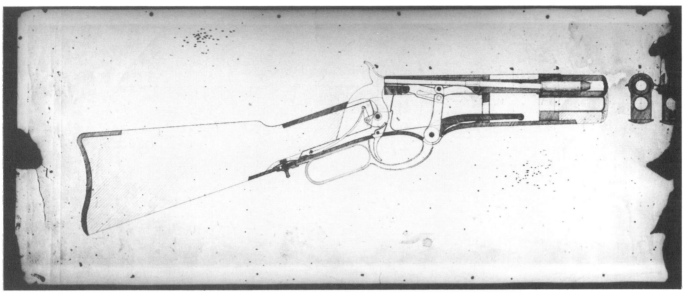

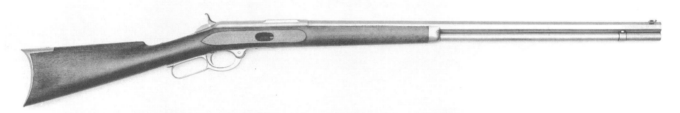

Unfortunately, in 1873, it was found that the Wheelock rifle, despite its aesthetically appealing lines and simple action, had serious faults. In trials held by the U.S. Army Board of Ordnance during February (Plates 94 and 95), the sloped-shaped design of the Wheelock bolt displayed a tendency to bind, especially when the action was fouled[8]. Additionally, the enclosed action weakened the stock so that it cracked (Plate 96) when the rifle was exposed to rigorous use[9]. In light of these failings, work on the design and the tooling necessary to manufacture it was suspended. The Model Room was then instructed to commence work on an alternative design.

Wetmore decided that the best course of action was to revive the Model 1868 iron frame program. To reduce tooling costs, however, he chose to modify the Model 1866 receiver so that it could be manufactured in iron and be fitted with detach-

able sideplates[10]. The original model for this design demonstrates that the Model 1866 receiver was lengthened slightly to accommodate the new .44-40 cartridge developed by Wells and its side walls reshaped so that a screw retained sideplate could be fitted (Plate 97). As the resulting design differed from its proven predecessors only cosmetically, no operational problems were encountered. Interestingly, Wetmore decided against the use of the shrouded firing pin design developed for the Model 1867 and 1868 rifles and instead adopted an exposed striker-firing pin. By late March 1873, the final configuration of the receiver had been set and work began on the construction of tooling to manufacture it[11].

Concurrently, Winchester authorized a major expansion of the company's ammunition works. In addition to the manufacture of rimfire ammunition and the new .44-40 cartridge, the firm

Top: Plate 90

*D*esign drawing for Luke Wheelock's revised lockwork configuration developed in 1872. Winchester Arms Collection Archives, Cody Firearms Museum.

Bottom: Plate 91

*W*heelock .40 Dupee caliber sample sporting rifle made in late 1872. Winchester Arms Collection (Inv. No. W249), Cody Firearms Museum. Olin Corporation photograph.

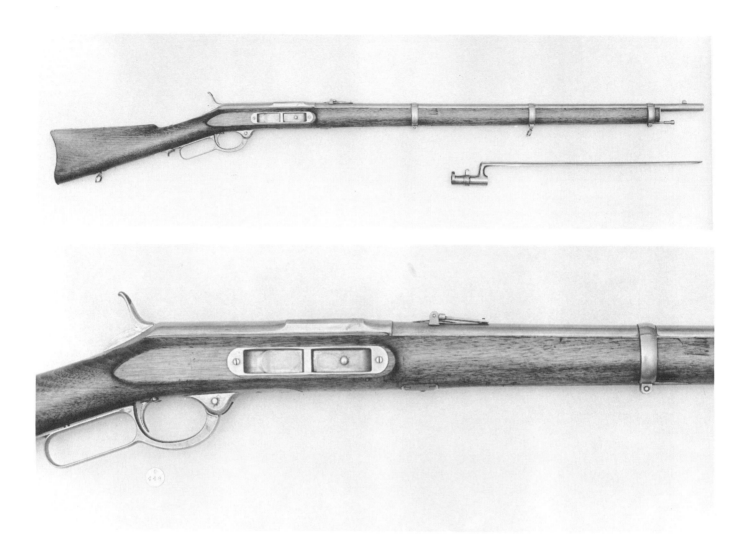

was about to enter broader ammunition markets[12].

Although the Model 1873 (Plates 98 and 99) proved to be a slow seller during the first few months after its introduction in September 1873, sales began to increase by the close of the year. Despite the extensive costs of tooling for the new model, the losses incurred in the development of the Wheelock rifle and expansion of the ammunition department, the Winchester company still managed to turn a profit of $132,326.10 that year[13].

Almost immediately after the introduction of the Model 1873, work began on a larger scale version. The initial efforts in this direction were prompted by a request from M. de Suzanne[14]. While the first samples delivered to him

for testing by the French government were special Model 1873s, later samples built during 1874 were chambered for a series of new cartridges designed by Wells. The new ammunition used large diameter short cases necked to .38, .40, .42, and .44 caliber. These experimental rounds were also used in the Wetmore-Wells sample revolvers produced at the same time[15]. Though this gives the appearance that the two development programs were associated, they were in fact totally independent ventures sharing only a common ammunition. Throughout 1874, work continued on these projects as well as the perfection of the shot shells the company intended to introduce. At least three different frame sized sample rifles were built for de Suzanne during

Top: Plate 92
Wheelock .50 caliber sample musket, serial number 3, made in late 1872. Winchester Arms Collection (Inv. No. W251), Cody Firearms Museum. Olin Corporation photograph.

Bottom: Plate 93
Detail of the Wheelock sample musket illustrated in Plate 92. Olin Corporation photograph.

Above: Plate 94

*D*etail of the Wheelock .45-70 caliber sample musket, serial number 2, submitted for trials by the U.S. Army Ordnance Department in February 1873. Winchester Arms Collection (Inv. No. W250), Cody Firearms Museum. Olin Corporation photograph.

Below: Plate 95

*D*etail of the U.S. Army Ordnance Department Trials' Wheelock sample musket with the loading port over in the open position. Olin Corporation photograph.

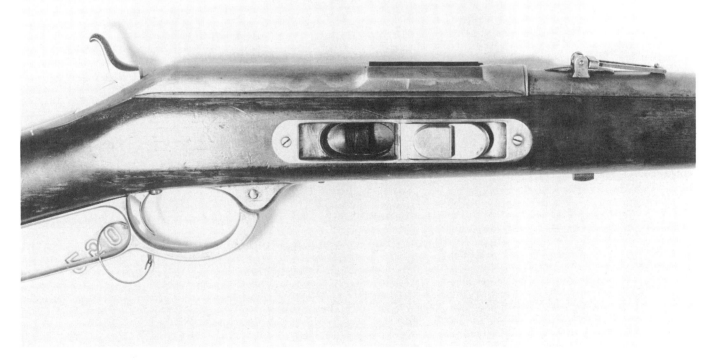

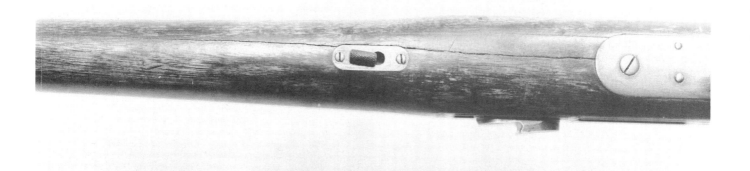

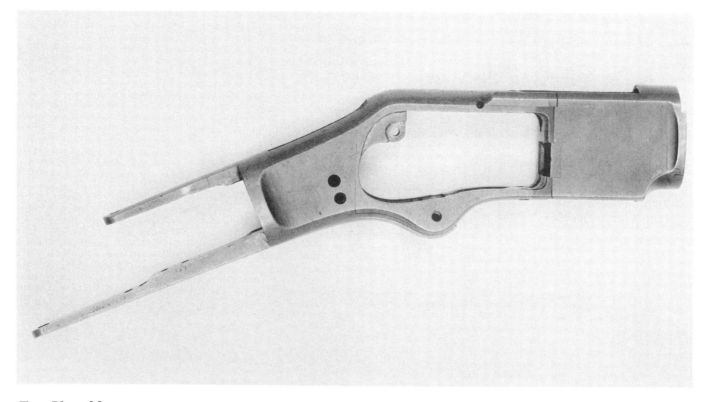

Top: Plate 96

Detail of the U.S. Army Ordnance Department Trials' Wheelock sample musket illustrating the crack in the fore end, which developed during its test. Olin Corporation photograph.

Bottom: Plate 97

Winchester Model 1866 receiver modified to serve as a sample pattern for the proposed Model 1873. Winchester Arms Collection (Inv. No. W3481), Cody Firearms Museum.

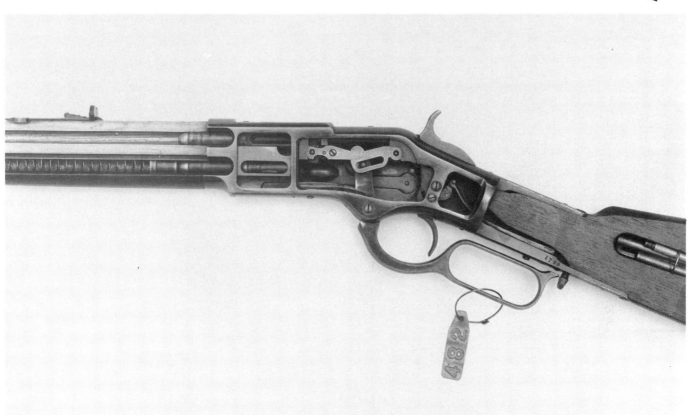

Top: Plate 98

*S*keletonized Winchester Model 1873 sporting rifle, serial number 13966. Winchester Arms Collection (Inv. No. W482), Cody Firearms Museum. Olin Corporation photograph.

Bottom: Plate 99

*D*etail of a Winchester Model 1873 Deluxe sporting rifle, circa 1874-1875. Olin Corporation photograph.

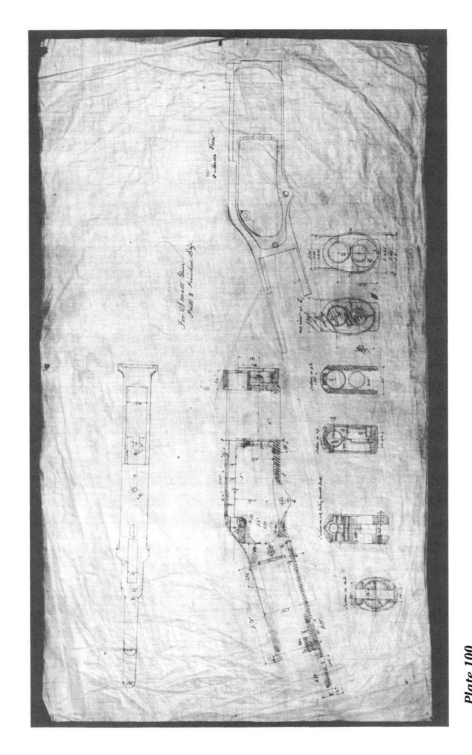

Plate 100

*D*esign drawing for the de Suzanne "Small Gun" receiver, circa 1874. Winchester Arms Collection Archives, Cody Firearms Museum.

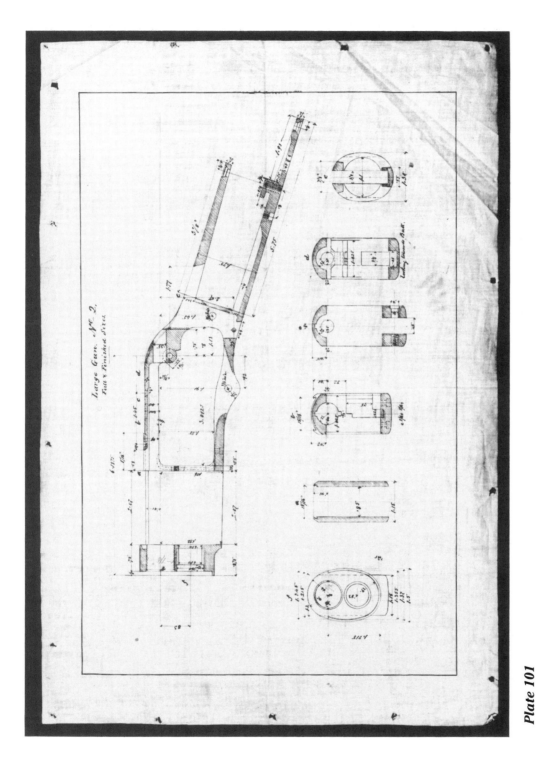

Plate 101

Design drawing for the de Suzanne "Large Gun No. 2" receiver, circa 1874. Winchester Arms Collection Archives, Cody Firearms Museum.

the year (Plates 100 and 101). In addition, the Wetmore-Wells revolver design was modified for use with an automatic ejector based upon Wells patent of Dec. 10, 1872 (U.S. Patent Number 133,732, Plate 102)[16]. The design of this ejector allowed spent shells to be ejected rearward from the cylinder as the cylinder was turned.

By 1875, the de Suzanne samples had been refined sufficiently to be assigned the designation Model /75[17]. While it is known that they no longer were under consideration by the French government, it is believed that their development was in response to inquiries the company had received from the Spanish government. Whatever the case, the Model /75 samples (Plates 103-109 and Color Plate 10) were produced in a wide range of calibers from .50-.38 to .58-.45. The advantages of the new design in its

Right: Plate 102

S*pecification drawings enrolled with Charles S. Wells' U.S. Patent Number 133732 issued Dec. 10, 1872. Winchester Arms Collection Archives, Cody Firearms Museum.*

Bottom: Plate 103

S*ample receiver made for a Model /75 carbine in late 1874 or early 1875. Winchester Arms Collection (Inv. No. not assigned), Cody Firearms Museum.*

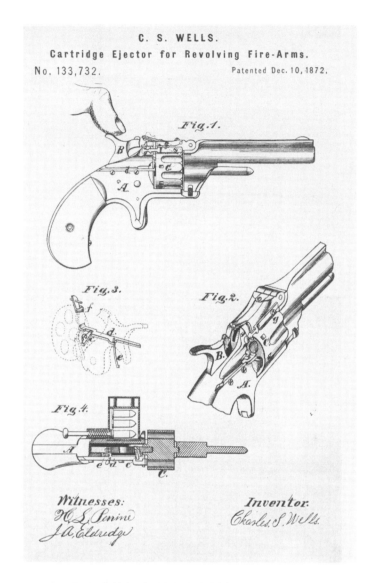

C. S. WELLS.
Cartridge Ejector for Revolving Fire-Arms.
No. 133,732.   Patented Dec. 10, 1872.

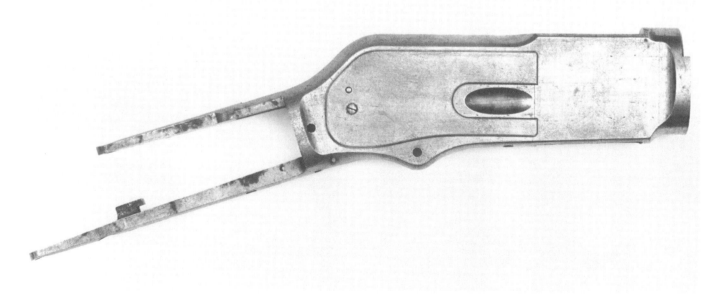

adaptability to a variety of high-velocity cartridges was not lost upon the Winchester company. Indeed, they saw in its design the answer to criticisms which had been received about the Model 1873[18]. Specifically, the consumer complaints about the Model 1873 centered upon its caliber. The .44-.40 cartridge was insufficient for heavy game except at close quarters. To remedy this situation, it was necessary to either rechamber the Model 1873 or introduce a new model that could handle larger bore cartridges. The versatility of the Model /75's action made the latter course a realizable goal. Consequently, the design was modified several times in late 1875 and early 1876 to accommodate larger and larger cartridges[19].

Meanwhile, work continued on the Wetmore-Wells revolver, even though its design was proving to be increasingly mettlesome. The major problem with the design was that neither the manual nor the automatic ejector could be relied upon to function properly at all times. This notwithstanding, the Winchester company persisted in work on the design[20]. Indeed, drawings and samples of the Wetmore-Wells revolver were exhibited at the Centennial Exhibition held in Philadelphia, Pennsylvania, in 1876 (Plates 110-112).

In 1875, the Winchester company faced its first true financial test when the heirs of John Davies requested payment of the $90,000 Davies had held in mortgages against the firm[21]. This amount was paid by Oliver F. Winchester in the form of a loan to the company against its expected profits[22]. When at the close of the year the company showed a net profit of $358,323.04, Winchester was repaid in full[23]. Interestingly, the company's profits for that

Plate 104

Design drawing for the Model /75 No. 3 carbine prepared in early 1875. Winchester Arms Collection Archives, Cody Firearms Museum.

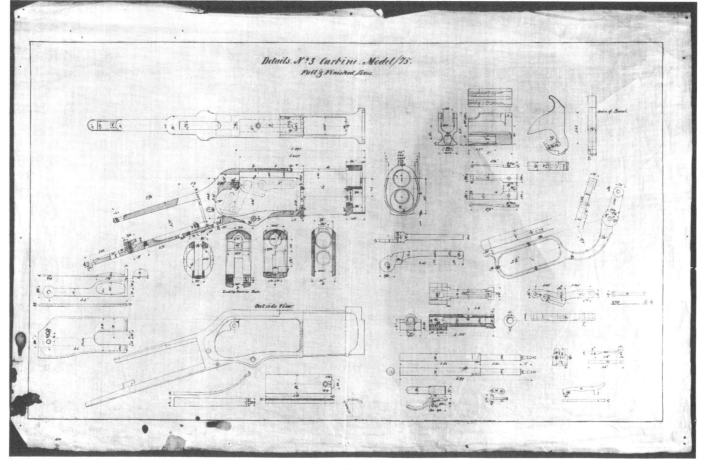

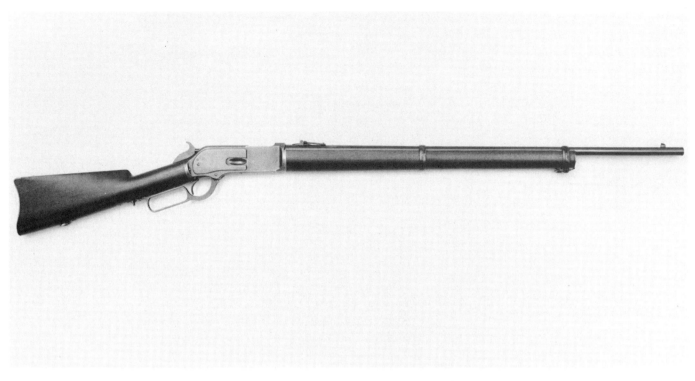

Above: Plate 105

*W*inchester sample Model /75 .40 carbine fitted with a 30-inch barrel and saddle ring. Winchester Arms Collection (Inv. No. W259), Cody Firearms Museum.

Below: Plate 106

*L*eft side view of the 30-inch barrel sample Model /75 carbine illustrated in Plate 105.

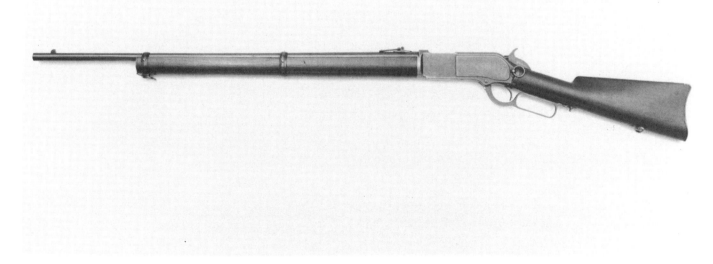

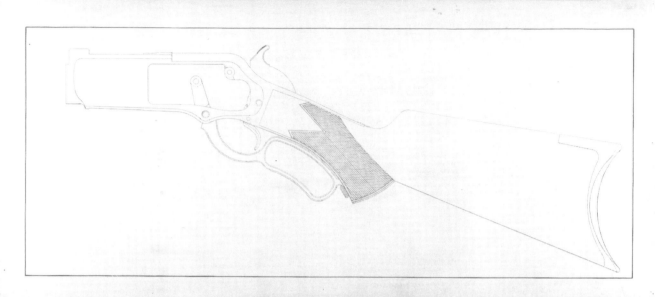

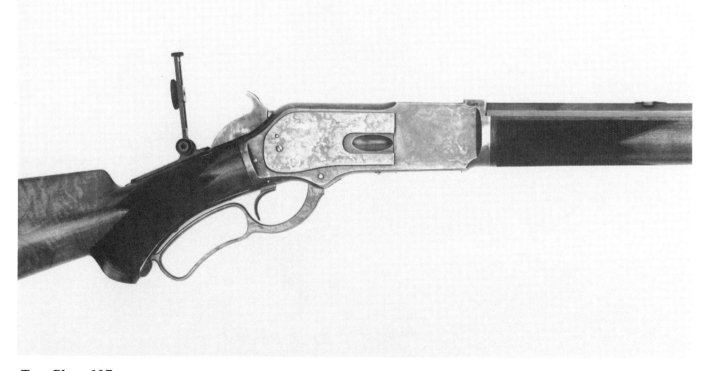

Top: Plate 107

Design drawing for the receiver and butt stock of a Model /75 sporting rifle prepared in late 1875. Private Collection.

Bottom: Plate 108

Winchester Sample Model /75 .42 caliber sporting rifle exhibited as the "Centennial Model Rifle" at the International Exhibition held in Philadelphia in 1876. The cyanide case-hardening colors on the receiver were described as "Centennial Finish" in Winchester records of the period. Winchester Arms Collection (Inv. No. W132), Cody Firearms Museum.

Sometime in 1874 or early 1875, William F. Cody, better known as Buffalo Bill, wrote the Winchester company a letter containing the following comments about a Model 1873 rifle he had purchased: "I have been using and have thoroughly tested your latest improved rifle...and for general hunting, or Indian fighting, I pronounce your improved Winchester the Boss."

year were not the result of arms sales, but rather, represented the results of an aggressive marketing of ammunition, particularly to foreign governments[24]. Even though arms sales had slackened, one contemporary commentator noted that the Winchester factory was manufacturing an average of seventy-five rifles a day that year[25].

While the samples of the Model /75, rechristened the Centennial or Model 1876, displayed at the Exhibition were enthusiastically received, the revolvers were little noted[26]. The Centennial Exhibition proved to be worthwhile to the company for several unforeseen reasons. The construction and efficiency of its ammunition was recognized by the presentation of a bronze medal (Plates 113 and 114), an award capitalized upon by the company in later advertising. Also, it was at the Exhibition that O.F. Winchester first met Benjamin B. Hotchkiss and examined the bolt-action rifle he had designed[27]. Ultimately, this meeting was to result in the production of Hotchkiss rifles by the Winchester company.

Whether it was at the Exhibition or elsewhere, it was at this time that Wetmore came into contact with Stephen W. Wood[28]. Just as the Winchester-Hotchkiss association was to prove fruitful, the Wetmore-Wood relationship was to result in the development of a marketable revolver.

Wood's improvement consisted of the construction of a cylinder mounted on a yoke, which could be rotated out of alignment with the revolver frame, and a plunger-actuated extractor that pushed all chambered cartridges rearward out of the cylinder when pressure was applied to the plunger (Plates 115-117)[29]. Based upon surviving evidence, it appears that the collaboration of Wetmore and Wood to produce a revolver incorporating these features began in July 1876[30]. The simplicity of the design and its assured extraction of cartridges immediately marked the Wetmore-Wood revolver as a viable replacement to the Wetmore-Wells. Therefore, work on that design ceased in August 1876[31]. During the autumn of 1876, work on the design had progressed to the point that samples were submitted for testing to the United States Navy Ordnance Bureau (Plate 118) and the Ottoman government[32]. Although no contract was to be forthcoming from the first submission, the second was to have immediate results. Upon receipt of the sample, the Sultan of Turkey approved the adoption of the revolver for his army, and a contract for 30,000 was issued in June 1877[33].

Plate 109

Design drawings for the Winchester Model /75 musket prepared in late 1875. Winchester Arms Collection Archives (Gift of Alexander Acevedo), Cody Firearms Museum.

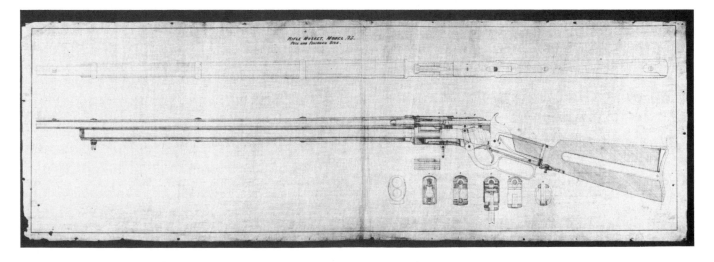

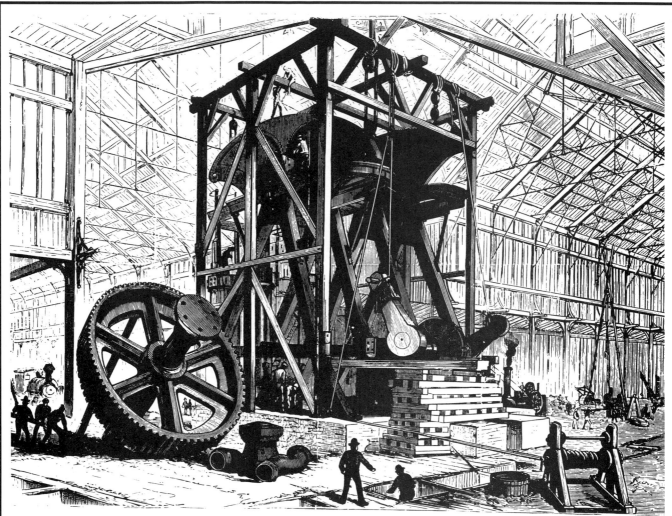

ERECTING THE CORLISS ENGINES IN THE SOUTH TRANSEPT OF MACHINERY HALL.

When the Centennial Exhibition of the United States opened in Philadelphia on May 15, 1876, the Corliss steam engine was viewed by many visitors as the absolute embodiment of the United States' rise to industrial power. Its sheer size mirrored the country's new self-confidence at home and abroad. Fifty days later, that self-confidence and sense of moral superiority was to be severely shaken when the news was published that Col. George Armstrong Custer and a significant number of men under his command had been slaughtered on June 25 at the Battle of the Little Big Horn some 2,000 miles to the west in the Montana Territory. That single action reminded Americans that despite their technological power and growth, their country was yet to be fully civilized and that a modern army could be defeated by any hostile force that was fighting for what they believed.

Paul Fees

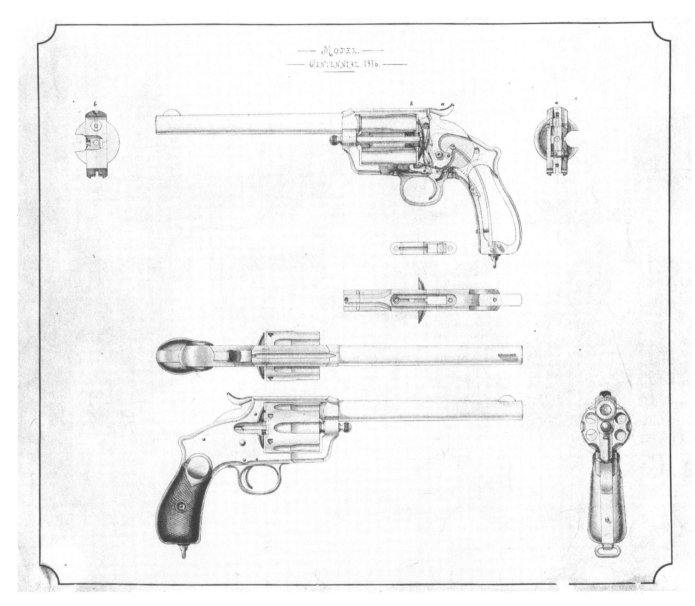

Plate 110

*D*esign drawings for the Winchester-Wetmore-Wells "Centennial 1876"
revolver, exhibited at the International Exhibition held in Philadelphia. Winchester Arms Collection Archives, Cody Firearms Museum.

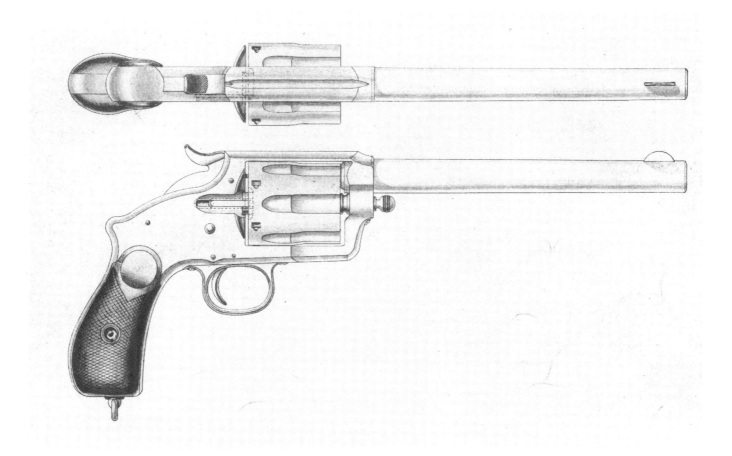

Plate 113

*R*ecto of the bronze medal awarded to the Winchester Repeating Arms Company for the excellence of its ammunition at the *International Exhibition of 1876 held in Philadelphia. Winchester Arms Collection Archives, Cody Firearms Museum.*

Plate 114

*V*erso of the prize medal illustrated in Plate 113.

Right: Plate 115

*W*inchester-Wetmore-Wood sample revolver made in 1876. Winchester Arms Collection (Inv. No. W646), Cody Firearms Museum.

Below: Plate 116

*L*eft side view of the Winchester-Wetmore-Wood sample revolver illustrated in Plate 115.

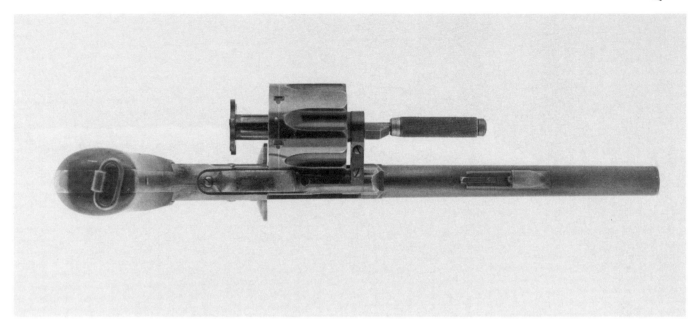

Above: Plate 117

*D*etail of the Winchester-Wetmore-Wood sample revolver illustrated in Plate 115 with the cylinder in open loading position.

Left: Plate 118

*W*inchester-Wetmore-Wood sample revolver submitted to the United States Navy Ordnance Bureau in December 1876. Private Collection.

Swelled by substantial sales of ammunition to the Ottoman Empire and ever-increasing arms sales, the Winchester company made a net profit $444,479.54, in 1876, on sales of $1,066,994.91[34].

In many respects, 1877 was to be a banner year for the Winchester Repeating Arms Company. Not only did the company finally begin to realize a profit from the revolver development program, but also on Feb. 14, the firm's board of directors authorized the purchase of Benjamin B. Hotchkiss's patents and a further expansion of the cartridge works to include the manufacture of shot shells[35]. The year also witnessed the introduction of the Model 1876 (Plate 119), whose manufacture had been delayed by the press to produce tooling for the Wetmore-Wood revolver[36].

Company records indicate that work on perfecting the Hotchkiss rifle began immediately after the patent rights were purchased. Initially, these efforts were directed toward the development of a sleeved receiver version, which allowed the use of a two-piece stock (Plate 120) instead of the one-piece version originally used by Hotchkiss[37].

The reasons behind this course of action probably stemmed from the problems the company had encountered with the Wheelock one-piece stock design in 1873. This avenue of design, however, was quickly set aside and the original stock construction readapted (Plate 121)[38]. One of the major features of the Hotchkiss, which the Model Room addressed, was the form of the cartridge cut-off that allowed the rifle to be used as a single-shot. Hotchkiss's design was replaced by a more positive-acting version created by Wetmore (Plates 122 and 123)[39]. In addition, every major component of the Hotchkiss was examined for durability and ease of function during 1877, with problem parts being reformed and replaced. In the late autumn, the magazine system was adapted for use in the Russian Berdan Rifle (Plate 124) at the request of the Imperial Russian Ministry of War[40].

Refinement of the Wetmore-Wood revolver also took place in 1877, and the resulting revolver was designated the Model 1877 (Plate 125)[41]. The revised version differed from earlier examples only in the use of a detachable left sideplate. The main purpose of this sideplate was that it allowed quick and easy access to the lockwork when cleaning was necessary. All the revolv-

Plate 119

Winchester Model 1876 sporting rifle. Olin Corporation photograph.

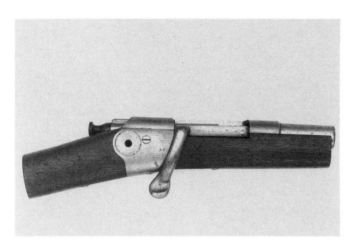

Plate 120

*S*ample receiver model for the full receiver, or sleeved action, Hotchkiss magazine rifle made in 1877. Winchester Arms Collection (Inv. No. W602), Cody Firearms Museum.

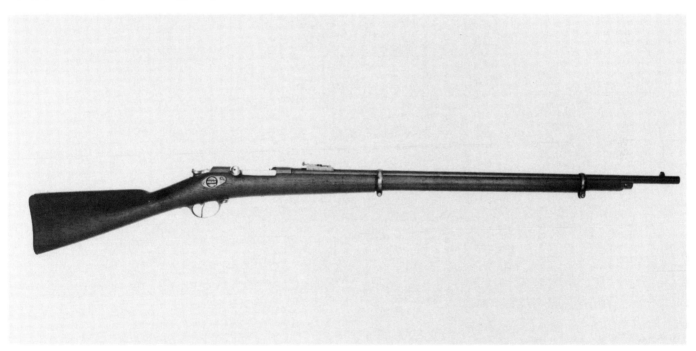

Plate 121

*S*ample Winchester Hotchkiss magazine rifle, .45-70 caliber, made in 1877. Winchester Arms Collection (Inv. No. W548), Cody Firearms Museum.

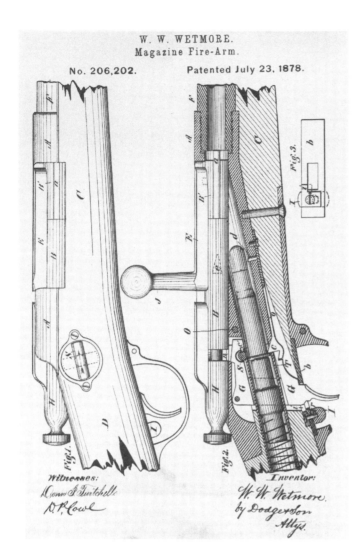

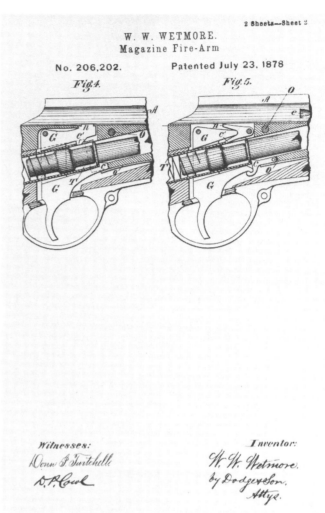

Above Left: Plate 122

*S*pecification drawings enrolled with William W. Wetmore's U.S. Patent Number 206202 issued July 23, 1878. Winchester Arms Museum Archives, Cody Firearms Museum.

Above Right: Plate 123

*S*heet 2 of the patent specifications drawings illustrated in Plate 122.

Below: Plate 124

*W*inchester Russian Model .42 caliber Hotchkiss magazine rifle made in 1877. Winchester Arms Collection (Inv. No. W552), Cody Firearms Museum.

ers delivered to the Ottoman government were of this style[42].

In many respects, the most far-reaching decision made by the company in 1877 was the expansion of its ammunition line[43]. By authorizing the development and introduction of shot shells, the firm's officers began a program which was to have long-lasting and extremely profitable benefits to the company's financial well-being.

As a result of the Ottoman contract for both Model 1877 revolvers and a substantial amount of ammunition in a variety of calibers, the Winchester Repeating Arms Company's gross sales for the year ending Dec. 31, 1877, were $2,802,564.16, and their net profit for the same period was $668,381.35[44].

In March 1878, the Winchester company began preparations for the submission of sample Hotchkiss rifles to the U.S. Army Board of Ordnance Trials that had been convened in Springfield, Massachusetts. In all, a total of five Hotchkiss rifles incorporating minor differences were tested along with one example of the ill-fated Model 1878 lever-action rifle[45]. The latter piece, of which only the receiver now survives (Plates 126 and 127), was an enlarged version of the Model 1876 designed for use with the .45-70 U.S. Army service cartridge. Although it performed reasonably well during the preliminary tests, during the supplementary tests it was withdrawn from consideration after seizing when immersed in the saline solution to simulate rusting[46]. Despite mechanical problems with four of the Hotchkiss samples, which brought about their withdrawal, sample number 5 (Test Docket Number 19) performed flawlessly[47]. In recognition of it merits, the Trial Board recommended that the Hotchkiss system (Plate 128) be adopted for the U.S. Army on Sept. 28, 1878[48].

To promote the company's firearms and ammunition, it was decided in 1878

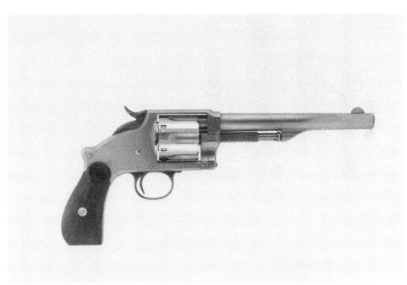

to open a retail store in New York City. As its first manager, O.F. Winchester selected Charles L. Mitchell, a director of the company and close personal friend[49]. Apart from Winchester products, the sales agency stocked arms and sporting equipment made by other manufacturers. Thus, single-shot rifles by Sharps and revolvers by Colt, Remington and so forth were displayed along with Model 1866, 1873, and 1876 and sample Hotchkiss rifles[50]. Among the new products prominently featured at the agency were the brass and paper shot shells which the company introduced in August of that year. The potential of the agency to generate increased income for the company was quickly realized, and O.F. Winchester began to examine a number of options that would further those sales even more.

By late May 1879, production of the Hotchkiss Rifle had begun in earnest, and deliveries could begin on the U.S. government contract[51]. Shortly after the first arms were delivered, the U.S. Navy authorized the purchase of 2,500 Hotchkiss rifles for extensive field trials[52]. Combined with the Army and civilian sales, this swelled orders for the Hotchkiss to approximately 4,000 units for immediate delivery.

Plate 125

Winchester-Wetmore-Wood Model 1877 revolver. Winchester Arms Collection (Inv. No. W1781), Cody Firearms Museum.

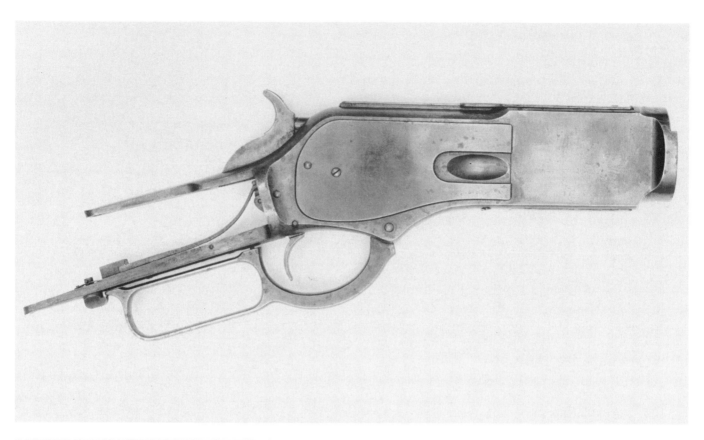

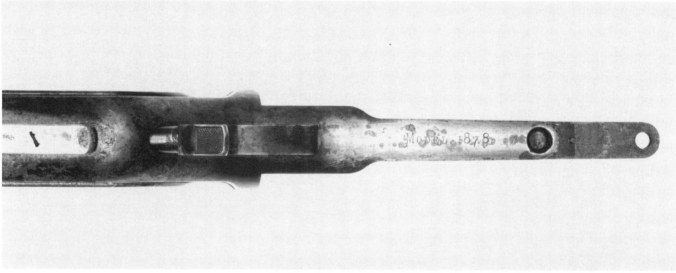

Top: Plate 126

*Winchester Model 1878 musket receiver serial number 1, .45-70 caliber.
Winchester Arms Collection (Inv. No. W260), Cody Firearms Museum.*

Bottom: Plate 127

Detail of the upper tang inscription on the Model 1878 musket receiver illustrated in Plate 126.

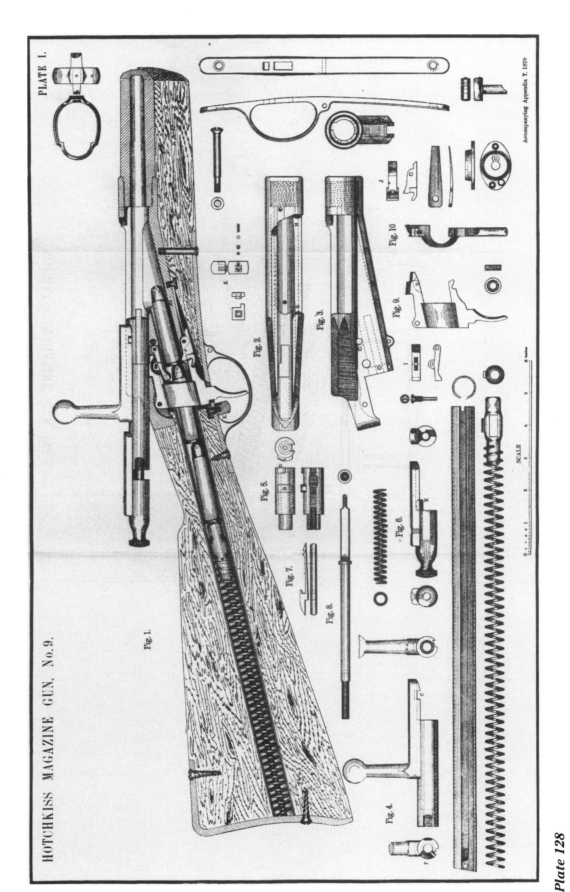

Plate 128

Illustration of the Hotchkiss magazine rifle system published as Plate 1, **Report of the Board of Ordnance Officers Convened in Pursuance of the Act of Congress Approved November 21, 1877, to Select a Magazine Gun for the U.S. Military Service** *(U.S. Government Printing Office; Washington, D.C.: 1878).*

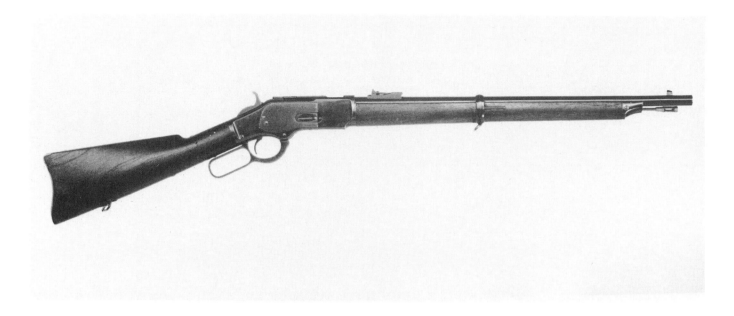

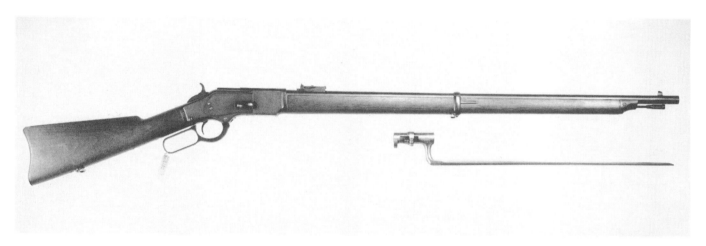

The corporate health of the Winchester Repeating Arms Company at this time is perhaps best demonstrated by the fact that its capitalization was increased to $1 million in 1879, and that the new shares regularly sold for over $130 each, providing a real capitalization in excess of $1,300,000[53].

The company's steady expansion into overseas markets during 1878 and 1879 is demonstrated by a number of large sales that occurred then. Apart from the Ottoman government, Chile, Haiti, Morocco, Peru, and Spain purchased significant amounts of both arms and ammunition (Plates 129-130)[54]. The growing importance of the Far Eastern market was recognized by the Winchester company in 1878, when Thomas Addis was sent to Shanghai, China[55], to open a sales agency there (Plate 131). Over the next several years, the value of the agency was to be well demonstrated through the sale of a considerable volume of firearms[56]. In 1878, the Japanese government contracted with the Winchester Repeating Arms Company to produce the tools and fixtures necessary to manufacture the single-shot bolt-action rifle designed by Murata Tsuneyoshi, which had been adopted for their armed services (Color Plate 12 and Plate 132)[57]. Delivery of that machinery evidently took place in 1879, as the Murata Rifle entered service in 1880[58].

Top: Plate 129

Winchester Model 1873 Spanish Contract carbine, serial number 33904. Winchester Arms Collection (Inv. No. W276), Cody Firearms Museum. Olin Corporation photograph.

Bottom: Plate 130

Winchester Model 1873 Spanish Contract musket, serial number 33903. Winchester Arms Collection (Inv. No. P2460), Cody Firearms Museum. Olin Corporation photograph.

■ Thomas Emmett Addis

Born Thomas O'Connor, Addis adopted his name at a relatively young age for reasons that are now unknown. First employed by the New Haven Arms Company, he worked for his entire life for Oliver F. Winchester and the companies he established. Beginning in the mid-1860s, Addis began traversing the world in search of new markets for Winchester rifles. Described as a quiet spoken and distinguished-looking gentleman, Addis built his reputation upon honesty and absolute integrity. That these traits were appreciated by his clients is best demonstrated by the fact that foreign sales of Winchester products increased several thousand percent while Addis was employed. An even greater memorial to his demeanor is shown by the fact that his name is still reverently referred to in some parts of the Far East where Addis lived and worked for over ten years in the 1880s and 1890s.

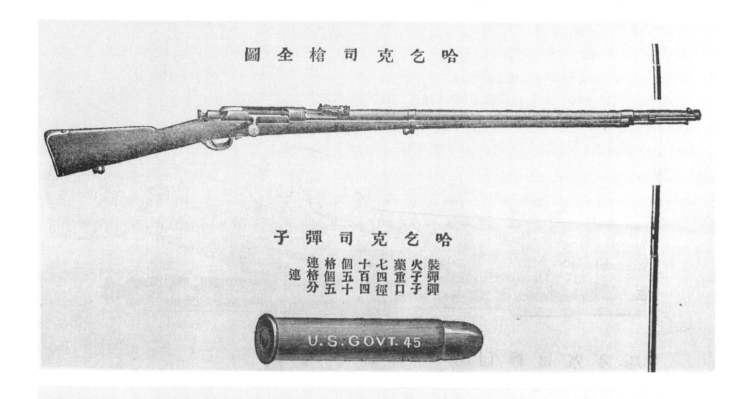

圖全槍司克乞哈

彈子司克乞哈

裝彈彈 火子彈 藥重口徑 七百四十 個五百十五 格個五十 連分五十

U.S.GOVT.45

When Charles L. Mitchell announced that he was going to retire as manager of the New York Sales Agency in December 1879, Winchester selected Major General William F. Smith to be his replacement[59]. Though Mitchell had been a capable administrator, he was not a native New Yorker and, therefore, did not have a wide circle of friends or contacts there. As this was essential to building a clientele, Smith's selection was ideal. A Corps Commander in the Army of the Potomac during the Civil War, Smith had later served as president of the International Ocean Telegraph Company, commissioner of the New York City Police and most lately as the president of the Police Board[60]. His reputation and credentials were impeccable.

After accessing the New York market, Smith advised Winchester that there would be ready sales for inexpensive good-quality double barrel shotguns[61]. In consequence of this suggestion, the Winchester company contracted with Christopher G. Bonehill of Birmingham, England to produce double barrel shotguns bearing the Winchester name (Plate 133)[62]. Available in five styles priced from $40 to $85, the Bonehill-Winchester guns were enthusiastically received with the first 500 delivered

Plate 131

Illustration of the Hotchkiss magazine rifle published in the Winchester Repeating Arms Company's 1878 Shanghai, China, catalog. Winchester Arms Collection Archives, Cody Firearms Museum.

Plate 132

Winchester manufactured Murata Model 1880 single-shot rifle, serial number 1, made in 1879. Cody Firearms Museum.

being sold within three months[63]. Immediately thereafter, another order for 500 was given to Bonehill, with the same sales results when they were received[64]. The general increased sales of the agency, and his acumen in recommending the stocking of shotguns verified Winchester's faith in Smith as the ideal person to manage the New York agency. Sadly, though, this was to be one of the last corporate decisions to be made by Oliver F. Winchester.

Although concerns had been voiced during the preceding decade that the financial stability of the Winchester Repeating Arms Company could be jeopardized by the death of its founder[65], they were to prove unfounded when Oliver F. Winchester died on Dec. 10, 1880. The size of the company and its operations worldwide were so great that even if his executors had liquidated his holdings, the company could have met the resulting obligations. As it was, Winchester's will was written in such a way that his death did not have any effect upon the company. Prepared on June 6, 1878, the will reads as follows[66]:

"I Oliver F. Winchester of the city of New Haven do make publish and declare the following as my last will.

――――

First – I direct that my just debts and funeral expenses be paid.

――――

Second – I give and bequeath to my wife Jane Ellen Winchester all my household furniture of every name and description and also the pair of horses and the two carriages which she is in the habit of using to be hers absolutely without inventory or appraisement.

――――

Third – I give and bequeath to my son William W. Winchester the horses and carriages not given to

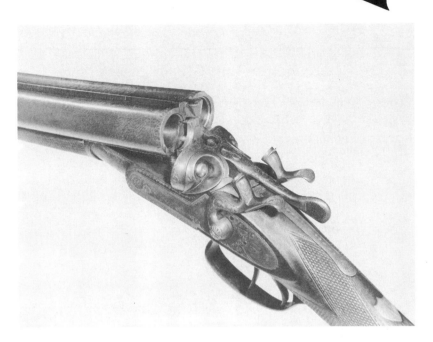

my said wife, to be his absolutely without inventory or appraisement.

――――

Fourth – I give and bequeath to my executors hereinafter named the sum of fifty thousand dollars upon the following trust:

To appropriate so much of the net income thereof as may be necessary for the education maintenance and support of my grandson Oliver W. Dye until he shall arrive at the age of thirty years, and then to pay over to him the principal of said sum to be his absolutely. The surplus income, if any, accruing during the existence of said trust is to be added to the principal and made part thereof.

If my said grandson should die before arriving at the age of thirty years leaving a child or children surviving him, then I direct said Trustees to pay over said principal to said child or children in equal proportions.

If my said grandson should die before arriving at the age of thirty years leaving a child or children

Plate 133

Winchester-Bonehill 12 gauge double barrel match gun made in 1880. Winchester Arms Collection (Inv. No. W1352), Cody Firearms Museum. Olin Corporation photograph.

surviving him, then I direct said Trustees to pay over said principal to the "Trustees of the Winchester Observatory" to be applied by said corporation for the uses and purposed set forth in their articles of association bearing the date July 17, 1871.

———

Fifth – All the rest and residue of my estate of every name and nature I give bequest and bequeath to William W. Winchester, Thomas G. Bennett and William W. Converse all of the City of New Haven and to the survivors and survivor of them To Have and To Hold the same as joint tenets and in fee simple, in trust to pay over the new annual income thereof to my said wife Jane Ellen Winchester during her natural life – and this bequest to her is in line of owner – and attend upon the decease of my said wife said trust shall terminate and I give devise and bequeath said rest and residue to my son William W. Winchester and my Daughter Hannah Jane Bennett and their legal representatives in equal portions that is one half thereof to each.

———

Sixth – I here by authorize and empower said Trustees to sell and dispose of any part of said trust estate at their discretion, to make good and sufficient titles thereto, to invest the avails in such manner as they may deem expedient, and to vary investments from time to time at their discretion.

———

Seventh – I appoint the said William W. Winchester, Thomas G. Bennett, and William W. Converse Executors hereof and direct that no

bond be required of them either as executors or as trustees.

———

In witness whereof I have hereto placed my hand and seal this sixth day of June A.C. 1878.

O.F. Winchester"

On Dec. 20, 1880, the Probate Court for the District of New Haven received an Inventory of the Estate of Oliver F. Winchester prepared by Luzon B. Morris and John P. Little, the court appointed appraisers. Winchester's assets were listed as follows[67]:

1 Lot and buildings thereon on west side Prospect St 300ft Northerly 1073ft Easterly 300ft Southerly 1030ft

$100,000.00

1 Parcel on West side Whitney Ave 126ft Northerly Highland St 634ft Westerly St Ronan St 1100ft Southerly Canner 521ft

50,000.00

1 Lot & buildings thereon on South Side Court St 65ft 9in, East 134ft 6in, Southerly 66ft Westerly 134-6

6,500.00

1 Lot & buildings thereon East side Winchester Ave 268ft 4, Southerly 477ft, Easterly Mansfield St 262 ft, Chas U Shepard 74ft Northerly 603ft 6in

11,000.00

1 Lot East side Winchester Ave 272ft Southerly Albert G Bristol, Easterly Mansfield St 200ft Northerly West Drive 407ft & W B Bristol 330ft

9,500.00

1 Lot bounded by Shelton Ave on West 206ft on North Thompson 150ft on East NH&N RR 325ft on South Division St 325ft less lot on NW Corner Shelton Ave and Division St, 100ft on Shelton Ave 150ft on Division St occupied by City New Haven for school purposes.

3,000.00

1 Lot on W Side Mansfield St 193ft North H.A. Munson 394ft West Drive 196ft South W Drive 364ft

2,900.00

1 Lot bounded easterly Canal St 145ft Southerly by Compton St extended westerly by NH&N RR Northerly by A B Todd 100ft

1,500.00

———

$184,400.00

4000 shares WRACo stock 100 @ 100	400,000.00
34 " New Haven Water Co 50 @ 75	2,550.00
15 " Yale Nat Bank 100 @ 116	1,740.00
50 " Adams Ex Co 100 @ 117	5,950.00
100 " Cleveland & Pittsburg 50 @ 63	6,350.00
50 " P. F W & Chicago 100 @ 125	6,250.00
125 " L Candee & Co 25 @ 37	4,625.00
40 " Whitney Ave HRR 25 @ 1	40.00
11 Bonds " " " " 100	1,100.00
5 " Brooklyn Flatbush & Coney Is RR 1,000	5,000.00
Bills Rec C I Mersick & Co & Jas English	10,000.00
" "Chas L. Mitchell	10,000.00
Household Furniture 500	500.00
Horses & Carriages 500	500.00
	————
	$478,605.00
Total	$663,005.00

Although William W. Winchester was immediately appointed acting president of the Winchester Repeating Arms Company, his own ill health forced him to relinquish the actual duties of the presidency to his cousin, William W. Converse. As William W. Winchester's condition worsened, an orderly corporate succession was arranged by Converse's election as president on March 2, 1881[68], five days before William Wirt Winchester's death[69]. Thomas G. Bennett subsequently was appointed treasurer of the Winchester company on March 26[70]. Since both Converse and Bennett were members of the Winchester family and major beneficiaries of the estate, there was to be little change in the firm's management style. For the most part, programs initiated by Oliver F. Winchester were continued and supported much as he would have done.

Converse was a cautious man, and when he feared that a recession might adversely effect the Winchester company's fortunes, he canceled work on several development projects (most notably an internal hammer double barrel shotgun being considered for manufacture that year)[71]. However, when it became clear that the recession was not about to worsen, Converse met with Bennett to plan new development projects[72]. It was as a result of these meetings that the company was to secure the services of one of the nineteenth century's greatest firearms designer, William Mason (Plate 136)[73].

Mason, then a designer with the Colt company in Hartford, had begun his career working with single-shot muzzle loading percussion arms and had rapidly turned his inventive mind to the perfecting of cartridge arms[74].

A quiet, unassuming man, Mason already had sixteen patents to his credit when he joined the Winchester company in early 1882[75]. Among the projects he was immediately involved with were the improvement of the Hotchkiss rifle, the development of a

Plate 134

Obverse and reverse of the silver prize medal awarded to the Winchester Repeating Arms Company at the International Exhibition held in Sydney, Australia, in 1879. Winchester Arms Collection Archives, Cody Firearms Museum.

Plate 135

Obverse and reverse of the gold medal awarded to the Winchester company at the International Exhibition held in Melbourne, Australia, in 1880. Winchester Arms Collection Archives, Cody Firearms Museum.

double barrel shotgun, single-shot rifle and box magazine rifle[76].

By the end of May 1882, he and Wetmore had redesigned the Hotchkiss so that it had an exposed receiver and used a two-piece stock[77]. Mason also solved one of the Hotchkiss' most vexing problems by modifying the construction of the cartridge cut-off[78]. While his work on the Hotchkiss resulted in a speedy correction of its previous faults and led, within a short period of time, to the Model 1883 Hotchkiss (Plates 137 and 138), the other design initiatives he addressed were more problematic.

Although Mason demonstrated that the multi-caliber single-shot bolt-action rifle was a feasible endeavor, he also pointed out that due to the necessary variations in its bolt design to allow the use of various cartridges, the resulting product would be cost prohibitive[79]. Similarly, he recommended that work on the double barrel shotgun be halted as its construction would be excessively complicated in order to evade his own previous patents assigned to the Colt company[80]. Consequently, for the greater part of 1882, Mason and Wetmore directed their attentions to the perfection of the Model 1883 Hotchkiss and the tooling needed to manufacture it[81].

As noted earlier, beginning in 1880, General Smith had begun selling imported English shotguns at the New York City Sales Agency. By 1882, the sale of these shotguns had seriously eroded the shotgun sales of the Colt company. Indeed, it could be successfully argued that by 1882, the Winchester company had managed to monopolize the New York shotgun market. To counter Winchester's competition, the Colt company retaliated by beginning the development of a lever-action rifle based on the designs of Andrew Burgess and R.L. Brewer[82]. In response, the Winchester company imported 600 P. Webley & Sons double-action revolvers (Plate 139) for sale in New York[83]. As these revolvers could be sold at a substantial discount over the Colt Model 1878 double-action, Winchester's intention was to flood the market and thereby demonstrate that it could, just as it had done with the shotguns, control the New York market.

The effectiveness of this campaign can be best demonstrated by the fact that the Colt company began pressuring its "allies" (i.e., long-standing retailers of its products) to begin publicly complaining about the Winchester company's practice of selling imported arms in New York at prices well below those of American- made arms[84].

Left: Plate 136

Photograph of William Mason taken about the time of his retirement in 1906. Winchester Arms Collection Archives, Cody Firearms Museum. Olin Corporation photograph.

Middle: Plate 137

Engraved Winchester Model 1883 Hotchkiss magazine sporting rifle, .45-70 caliber, serial number 52706. Winchester Arms Collection (Inv. No. W135), Cody Firearms Museum. Olin Corporation photograph.

Bottom: Plate 138

Detail of a Winchester Model 1883 Hotchkiss magazine rifle with the action open. Olin Corporation photograph.

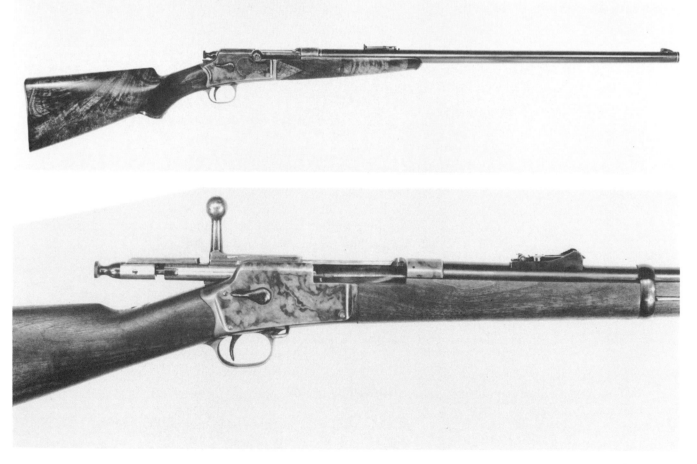

One of the unfortunate casualties of the increasing rivalry between Colt and Winchester was General Smith. Due to his friendship with Major General William B. Franklin, the general manager and vice president of the Colt's Patent Fire Arms Manufacturing Company, that dated back to the Civil War, Smith resigned his position effective Dec. 31, 1882[85]. As his replacement, the company selected Philip G. Sandford who had known protectionist sentiments. Though this choice had the appearance of indicating a policy change by the Winchester company, another event of late 1882 demonstrates that it was a ruse.

Stung by Colt's planned incursion into Winchester's prime markets through the development of a lever-action rifle, Thomas G. Bennett set in motion a plan to not only destroy Colt's shotgun markets but also their sales of any new long arms. Preliminary work on this plan was set in motion on Nov. 2, 1882, when Mason was authorized by Bennett to begin designing a single-action revolver and a slide-action rifle[86]. Work was to continue on these projects throughout 1883, at the same time as Sandford publicly voiced his support of the American arms industry in New York, thereby allaying Colt's concerns about Winchester's intentions[87].

As the Winchester company went ahead with plans to secure an even larger share of the United States and foreign firearms market, they also proceeded with plans to increase cartridge production. In preparation for the introduction of loaded shot shells to the firm's product line, a felt factory and brass mill were built in 1882 at the New Haven works[88]. The construction of the brass mill also eliminated any dependence the company had on outside suppliers for raw brass stock needed to manufacture ammunition of all types. With the addition of this mill, the company was, therefore, able to completely control its output for the first time.

Plate 139

P. Webley & Son .44 caliber British Bull Dog revolver, serial number 88463, imported by the Winchester company's New York City Sales Depot in 1882. Winchester Arms Collection (Inv. No. W1975), Cody Firearms Museum.

Endnotes

1. The increasing popularity of reloadable center fire cartridges and their ballistic superiority over rimfire rounds had long been recognized by Winchester. Indeed, the Model 1866 to 1868 series of iron frame rifles had been chambered for that type of ammunition. Consequently, it was only a matter of time before the Winchester company introduced a commercial centerfire rifle.

2. The sample receiver for this design is preserved in the Winchester Arms Collection (Inv. No. W705), Cody Firearms Museum; and Winchester Firearms Reference Collection, op. cit., page 114.

3. The linkage in the sample receiver exhibits evidence of having been deformed due to excessive pressure having been applied to it during the cycling of the bolt.

4. The sporting rifle from this series (Inv. No. W249, Winchester Arms Collection, Cody Firearms Museum) is chambered for a modified .40 caliber Dupee cartridge; and Winchester Firearms Reference Collection, op. cit., page 48.

5. Typescript copy of a deposition taken by Frederic C. Earle, Standing Examiner, on Oct. 16, 1896, in the matter of Francis Bannerman against Philip G. Sandford, Circuit Court of the United States for the Southern District of New York, page 1. Bannerman- Sandford File, Winchester Arms Collection Archives, Cody Firearms Museum.

6. Winchester Repeating Arms Company, Payroll Book (April 1871-May 3, 1873), Payroll Number 4 for the period ending July 13, 1872. Winchester Arms Collection Archives, Cody Firearms Museum.

7. For a detailed description of the Winchester-Wetmore-Wells revolvers see: H.G. Houze, "Fact & Fancy: A Critical Reassessment of the Origins, Development and Purpose of the Experimental Revolvers Produced by the Winchester Repeating Arms Company During the 1870's," **ARMAX**, Volume IV, Number 1 (1992), pages 13-47.

8. **Ordnance Memoranda No. 15. Report of the Board of Officers Appointed in Pursuance of the Act of Congress Approved June 6, 1872, for the Purpose of Selecting a Breech-System for the Muskets and Carbines of the Military Service** (U.S. Government Printing Office, Washington, D.C.: 1873), page 96.

9. Ibid., page 79.

10. The sample receiver modified to accept sideplates is preserved in the Winchester Arms Collection (Inv. No. W3481), Cody Firearms Museum, and; Winchester Firearms Reference Collection, op. cit.,page 480.

11. The earliest engineering drawings for the Model 1873 tools and fixtures bear dates from March 27 to April 6, 1873. Winchester Arms Collection Archives, Cody Firearms Museum.

12. Production of a broader range of ammunition began in 1874.

13. Winchester Repeating Arms Company Financial Statement for 1873. Winchester Repeating Arms Company Archives, Olin Corporation.

14. Although no correspondence exists to verify this, the original design drawings for these arms all are inscribed "de Suzanne." Winchester Arms Collection Archives, Cody Firearms Museum.

15. For a physical description of these cartridges see: Paul Foster, "Winchester's 'Forgotten' Cartridges, 1866-1900," **Gun Digest Treasury** (Gun Digest Company; Chicago, IL: 1956), page 283.

16. Houze, "Fact & Fancy," op. cit., pages 34-36.

17. The designation "Model/75" first appears on a modified tracing of the receiver for the "de Suzanne Small Gun." Winchester Arms Collection Archives, Cody Firearms Museum.

18. Comments had been received from the very introduction of the Model 1873 that it was unsuitable for use against heavy game and that its limited range was objectionable. The fact that the .44-40 cartridge essentially was a pistol round was amply demonstrated when Colt, as well as the Merwin & Hulbert companies, introduced revolvers chambered for the cartridge.

19. These changes are documented in a series of design drawings for the Models/75 and 76, preserved in the Winchester Arms Collection, Cody Firearms Museum.

20. Houze, "Fact & Fancy," op. cit., pages 34-36.

21. Records of the R.G. Dun Company, Connecticut, Volume 41, page 106.

22. Ibid.

23. Winchester Repeating Arms Company Financial Statement for 1875. Winchester Repeating Arms Company Archives, Olin Corporation, and; Records of the R.G. Dun Company, Connecticut, Volume 41, page 206.

24. Major purchasers of ammunition during 1875, included Egypt and the Ottoman Empire.

25. Records of the R.G. Dun Company, Connecticut, Volume 41, page106.

26. No mention of the revolvers is to be found in any of the published accounts regarding the Exhibition or its exhibitors.

27. Hotchkiss first exhibited his bolt-action rifle at the Philadelphia Exhibition and won a bronze medal for its design. B.B. Hotchkiss Biography, Hotchkiss Library, Sharon, Connecticut.

28. Houze, "Fact & Fancy," op. cit., pages 47-50.

29. Ibid.

30. Ibid.

31. Ibid, page 22.

32. For the full text of the letter accompanying the Winchester- Wetmore-Wood revolver submitted to the U.S. Navy, see: Ibid, page 91, Note 4. Mention of the revolvers sent to the Ottoman government is made in the correspondence of the Colt company to its London agent, Baron von Oppen. On March 23, 1877, Maj. Gen. William B. Franklin, General Manager of the Colt works, wrote as follows:

Your letter of the 10ist. has been received. It appears Winchester has sent a pistol to Turkey which takes his central fire .44 cal. cartridge. It seems to have made a good impression, & we hear that he has been offered a contract for 30,000. Now we can chamber our pistol to take that cartridge & will do so at once & send it to you. But in the meantime it will be well for you to be able to write your correspondent what the real rival of our pistol is. Winchester's pistol is a six shot revolver. This thing seems of importance. I was told that the Winchester model had been turned over to the Sultan. How much that means I do not know.

(Reproduced in C. Kenneth Moore, **Colt Single Action Army Revolvers and the London Agency** [Andrew Mowbray, Publishers; Lincoln, RI: 1990], page 126).

33. Some controversy surrounds this contract as it cannot be confirmed by any Winchester corporate documents. Evidence does exist, however, which indicates that some revolvers were made in New Haven for the Ottoman Empire and that machinery was supplied (Houze, "Fact & Fancy," op. cit., pages 86-87 and 94).

34. Winchester Repeating Arms Company Financial Statement for 1876. Winchester Repeating Arms Company Archives, Olin Corporation.

35. Minutes of the Feb. 14, 1877 Board of Directors Meeting. Winchester Repeating Arms Company Archives, Olin Corporation.

36. Winchester Repeating Arms Company, Model 1876 Serial Number Register Volume 1. Winchester Arms Collection Archives, Cody Firearms Museum.

37. H.G. Houze, "The Designs, Development and Initial Production of the Hotchkiss Magazine Rifle 1876-1879," **ARMAX**, Volume III, Number 2 (1991), pages 25-29.

38. Work on the revised design evidently began in November 1877. Ibid., page 27.

39. William W. Wetmore, United States Patent Number 219886, issued Sept. 23, 1879. See also: Houze, "Hotchkiss," op. cit., pages 30-33, for the earlier versions of the cartridge detente.

40. Roy M. Marcot, **Civil War Chief of Sharpshooters Hiram Berdan Military Commander and Firearms Inventor** (Northwood Heritage Press; Irvine, CA: 1989), pages 262-265.

41. Houze, "Fact & Fancy," op. cit., pages 53 and 72-77.

42. Ibid, pages 72-77.

43. Thomas C. Johnson, "A Brief History of the Paper Shot Shells Manufactured by the Winchester Repeating Arms Co. June 1st, 1912. Dedicated to George Dudley Seymour, New Haven, Conn. June 1st, 1912." pages 1-3. Winchester Arms Collection Archives, Cody Firearms Museum.

44. Winchester Repeating Arms Company Financial Statement for 1877. Winchester Repeating Arms Company Archives, Olin Corporation, loc. cit.

45. Inventory Number W260, Winchester Firearms Reference Collection, op. cit., page 51. This receiver exhibits evidence of having been burned at some time.

46. **Report of the Board of Ordnance Officers Convened In Pursuance of the Act of Congress Approved November 21, 1877, To Select a Magazine Gun for the U.S. Military Service** (U.S. Government Printing Office; Washington, D.C.: 1878), Rifle Docket Number 13, pages 494-496.

47. Ibid, pages 32-33.

48. Ibid, page 2.

49. George Walker, Synopsis of New York Sales Depot's Operations 1878-1884, page 1. Winchester Arms Museum Archives, Cody Firearms Museum.

50. Ibid.

51. Winchester Repeating Arms Company. Hotchkiss Magazine Rifle Serial Number Registers, Volume 1, and; Houze, Hotchkiss Design and Development, op. cit., page 55.

52. Houze, Hotchkiss Design and Development, op. cit., page 57.

53. Records of the R.G. Dun Company, Connecticut, Volume 41, page 357.

54. George Walker, Model 1866, 1873 and Hotchkiss Production Notes, op. cit. Winchester Arms Collection Archives, Cody Firearms Museum.

55. Addis Autobiography, op. cit., page 5. Winchester Arms Collection Archives, Cody Firearms Museum.

56. In particular, sales of Hotchkiss Rifles beginning in 1880.

57. Houze, "Fact & Fancy," op. cit., pages 86 and 94.

58. Yoshioka Collection, op. cit., page 40.

59. Walker, New York Depot Synopsis, op. cit., page 1.

60. James H. Wilson, **Life and Services of William Farrar Smith** (John M. Rogers Press; Wilmington, DE: 1904), pages 26-28; and Walker, New York Depot Synopsis, op. cit., page 1.

61. Thomas C. Johnson, "History of Repeating Firearms and the Winchester Repeating Arms Company Dedicated to George Dudley Seymour," page 17. Winchester Arms Collection Archives, Cody Firearms Museum.

62. Walker, New York Depot Synopsis, op. cit., pages 1-2.

63. Ibid, page 2.

64. Ibid.

65. Records of the R.G. Dun Company, Connecticut, Volume 41, page 206.

66. Estate of Oliver F. Winchester. Probate Court Records, New Haven, 1880-Number 29,155. Will. Photocopy in Winchester Arms Collection Archives, Cody Firearms Museum.

67. Estate of Oliver F. Winchester. Probate Court Records, New Haven, 1880-Number 29, 155. Inventory. Photocopy in Winchester Arms Collection Archives, Cody Firearms Museum.

68. Winchester Repeating Arms Company Board of Directors Meeting Minutes, March 2, 1881. Winchester Repeating Arms Company Archives, Olin Corporation.

69. Winchester Repeating Arms Company Miscellaneous Notes for 1881. Winchester Repeating Arms Company Archives, Olin Corporation.

70. Ibid.

71. Thomas G. Bennett, manuscript Aide-Memoire (Jan. 1, 1880- Dec. 29, 1883), entry dated March 4, 1881.

72. Ibid, entry dated Dec. 19, 1881.

73. Ibid, entry dated Dec. 20, 1881.

74. R.Q. Sutherland and R.L. Wilson, **The Book of Colt Firearms** (R.Q. Sutherland; Kansas City, MO: 1971), pages 222-223, 317, 321, 483- 490. For a list of Mason's patents see Frank M. Sellers, **American Gunsmiths** (The Gun Room Press; Highland Park, NJ: 1983), page 202.

75. Sellers, ibid.

76. The exact date this work began is unknown. However, a design drawing dated May 24, 1882, of a modified Hotchkiss Magazine rifle, demonstrates that he had been at work on the project for some time. Likewise, the date at which the other programs were abandoned (see Notes 79 and 80 below) further substantiates a lengthy involvement in their design.

77. Winchester Repeating Arms Company Design Drawing dated May 24, 1882. Private Collection.

78. This particular part had caused innumerable problems for the Model Room since work on the Hotchkiss had begun in 1877, and it was not until Mason's design was adopted that a truly satisfactory and reliable cartridge cut-off was fitted to the Hotchkiss.

79. Bennett Aide-Memoire, op. cit., entry dated June 10, 1882.

80. Ibid.

81. This is based upon design drawings for Hotchkiss components and, especially, tooling, preserved in the Winchester Arms Collection Archives, Cody Firearms Museum.

82. Sutherland & Wilson, op. cit., pages 491-492.

83. Johnson, Winchester History, op. cit., page 18; and Walker, New York Depot Synopsis, op. cit., page 3.

84. Johnson, ibid, page 18.

85. Ibid.

86. Bennett, Aide-Memoire, op. cit., entry dated Nov. 2, 1882.

87. Johnson, Winchester History, op. cit., page 18.

88. Records of the R.G. Dun Company, Connecticut, Volume 41, page 512.

CHAPTER 3

THE WINCHESTER REPEATING ARMS COMPANY COMES OF AGE: 1883-1900

For a company manufacturing a limited product line, the Winchester Repeating Arms company had, by the close of 1882, achieved an enviable position within the American arms industry. In size it ranked third in the production of firearms, and in ammunition, second[1]. This level of success had been achieved not only due to the business acumen of its founder, but the willingness of he and his successors to adapt to changing consumer needs. Thus, the Winchester company survived and thrived while some of its competitors foundered. To further consolidate its position, the company, in late 1882, decided to assert its power relative to a new potential rival, the Colt's Patent Fire Arms Manufacturing Company.

Stung by the inroads the Winchester company had made with their Model 1877 Wetmore-Wood revolver into foreign pistol markets and, more importantly, Winchester's monopolization of shotgun sales in New York, Colt retaliated in 1882 by developing a .44 caliber lever action rifle designed specifically to compete with the Winchester Model 1873[2]. The serious consequences of this challenge were not lost on William Converse (Plate 140) and T.G. Bennett (Plate 141), for they both realized that the extensive network of Colt dealers

and salesmen could generate substantial sales for the new model to the detriment of the Model 1873. To counter this, Bennett implemented a long-range plan designed to thwart Colt's intentions in late 1882. The first phase of Bennett's scheme was, as previously

Plate 140

William W. Converse, president of the Winchester Repeating Arms Company from 1881 to 1889. Olin Corporation photograph.

mentioned in Chapter Two, the development by the Winchester company of a slide-action rifle designed to compete directly with the Colt Lightning magazine rifle, which was then about to enter production, and a single-action revolver similar in style to the Colt Model 1873 single-action Army. With the completion of the sample slide-action rifle (Plates 142 and 143) and revolver (Plate 144) in the late summer or early autumn of 1883[3], Bennett set about to create an elaborate subterfuge designed to convince the Colt company of Winchester's plans to produce the two arms. On Bennett's order, the Design Department was instructed to begin work on detailed drawings with full specifications for the tooling and fixtures needed to manufacture the Mason rifle and revolver[4]. By Christmas, the Colt company was aware of Winchester's activity and had stepped up work on the Lightning rifle to speed its introduction so that Colt might maintain an edge in the marketplace[5]. Bennett, however, still had not completely played his hand. At the Feb. 14, 1884 meeting of the Winchester Repeating Arms Company's board of directors, Bennett received authorization to put the final three phases of this plan into effect[6]. First, the company publicly announced, ostensibly at the request of Philip Sandford, that English shotguns would no longer be imported into the United States for resale at the New York City Sales Depot. Secondly, in a closed session Bennett received permission to dispose of the existing stock of shotguns in any manner he saw fit[7], and finally, he was given authority to deal with the Colt problem in whatever way he wished, even if it resulted in a financial loss to the Winchester company.

The announcement regarding the vexing problem of the English shotguns probably was met with relief by the Colt company as it indicated that Winchester was about to abandon that

field. Therefore, the futures of both the Colt Model 1878 and 1883 Shotguns looked bright. What Colt did not know was that Bennett planned to saturate the New York market with the English shotguns that were held in reserve by the company. In early May, Bennett quietly made arrangements with J.P. Moore & Son of New York to purchase the entire stock of English shotguns then held by Winchester at a price amounting to 67¢ on the dollar[8]. Simultaneously, Bennett wrote to Major General Franklin and requested a meeting to discuss the Winchester company's plans to market slide-action rifles and

Plate 141

Thomas G. Bennett, vice president of the Winchester Repeating Arms Company from 1882 to 1889, and president from 1889 to 1921. Olin Corporation photograph.

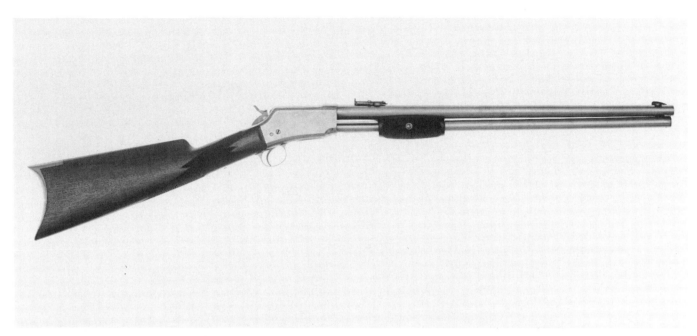

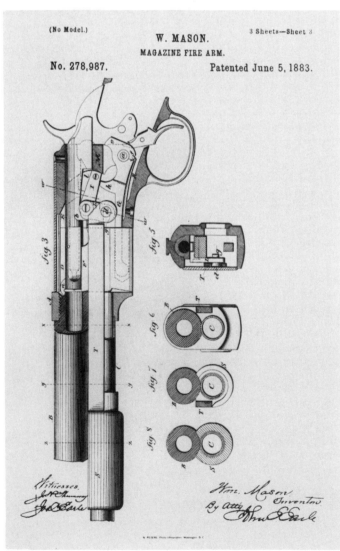

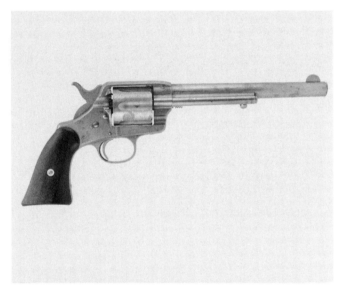

Top: Plate 142

Sample .44 caliber slide-action carbine made by William Mason in 1883. Winchester Arms Collection (Inv. No. W113), Cody Firearms Museum. Olin Corporation photograph.

Left: Plate 143

Sheet 3 of the specification drawings enrolled with William Mason's U.S. Patent Number 278987 issued June 5, 1883. Winchester Arms Collection Archives, Cody Firearms Museum.

Right: Plate 144

Sample .44 caliber single-action revolver made by William Mason in 1883. Winchester Arms Collection Archives (Inv. No. W648), Cody Firearms Museum. Olin Corporation photograph.

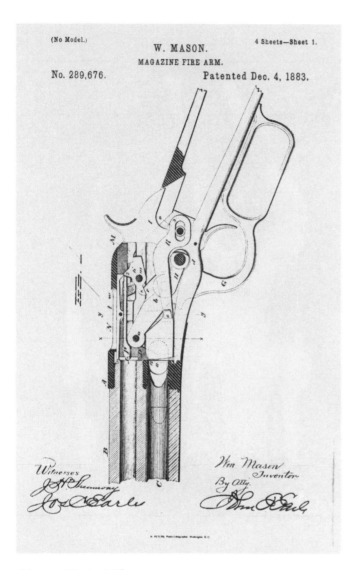

Above: Plate 145

Sheet 1 of the specification drawings enrolled with William Mason's U.S. Patent Number 289676 issued Dec. 4, 1883. Winchester Arms Collection Archives, Cody Firearms Museum.

Right: Plate 146

Sheet 2 of the specification drawings for William Mason's Dec. 4, 1883, patent.

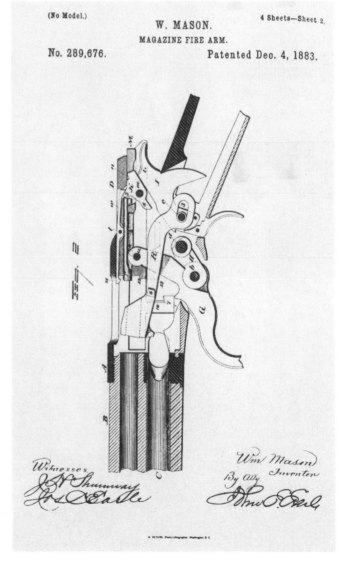

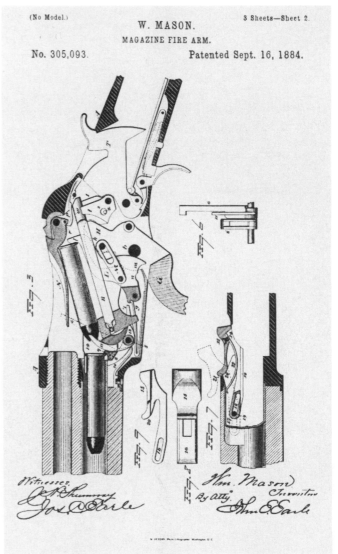

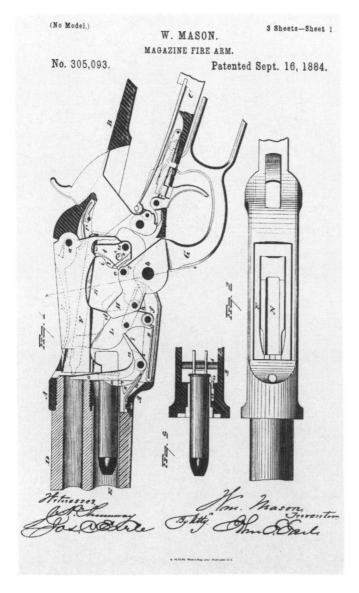

single action revolvers. By the time that this meeting took place on June 1, 1884[9], Bennett's arrangement with J.P. Moore & Son had become public knowledge and its effect already realized by the Colt company. By selling 1,356 shotguns[10] at a discounted price, which was well below their actual cost, the Winchester company had effectively destroyed Colt's New York shotgun market for that year and most likely the following one. Coupled with Bennett's announcement that the Winchester company was ready and willing to openly compete with Colt in the sale of revolvers and slide-action rifles, the Colt company realized that they might be about to enter into a period of financially ruinous intercene corporate warfare. Consequently, when Bennett and Franklin met, a rapprochement was reached between the two firms. As Bennett succinctly wrote in his diary, they agreed "not to interfere in each other's Markets"[11]. Interestingly, this gentleman's agreement, whereby the Colt company withdrew from the production of lever- action rifles and the Winchester company likewise did not pursue the manufacture of pistols, was to be honored throughout the rest of the Winchester Repeating Arms Company's history.

The Winchester company's willingness to play hardball with an established and powerful competitor demonstrates the level of confidence the firm had achieved by 1883/1884. To gain its ends, losses could be sustained and tolerated so long as the final results benefited the company. The firm's dealings with the Colt company also demonstrated that it would not brook opposition, no matter what the source. In a broader sense, it could be said that the Winchester company had finally come of age.

This maturation manifested itself in other ways. Beginning in 1883, the company began a multi-faceted design program to develop a number of new models. In response to the success of the Marlin Fire Arms Company's Model 1881 rifle, which was chambered for the .45-70 caliber cartridge, William Mason was assigned the task of developing a new lever-action rifle to meet the Marlin challenge. The first practical design to be developed by Mason was rather unusual. In place of a sliding breech bolt, he proposed using a pivoted breech block that could be lowered and raised by a finger lever (Plates 145 and 146) somewhat like that invented some sixteen years earlier by Friedrich von Martini[12]. The major benefit of this design[13] was that the action could not be forced open by the firing of a defec-

Plate 149
P*ortrait of John M. Browning, circa 1910-1915. Browning Collection, Ogden Union Station, Ogden, Utah.*

tive or overloaded cartridge. In contrast to the horizontally sliding bolt, where extreme chamber pressures could force the cartridge case rearward against the bolt face to the extent that the bolt began to open, the vertical orientation of Mason's action insured that no such case movement could take place no matter what degree of pressure was generated. The disadvantage of the system, however, was that if a case head separated from the shell body or a primer ruptured or blew back at ignition, the clearance needed to lower the breechblock would be reduced to such an extent that the block could not be moved. This potential failing, therefore, prevented the design from ever being considered for production.

Mason then examined ways of modifying the conventional Winchester action to allow its use with high-pressure cartridges. In a series of samples made in 1883[14], he fitted a succession of pivoted bolt locks to standard action rifles. These bolt locks operated in such a way as to cam up into the upper rear wall of the receiver when the breech bolt was closed so that it could not move rearward until the finger lever was lowered (Plates 147 and 148). In some samples a secondary locking system was supplied by the use of a redesigned finger lever, which had an extension that served as the operating bar for the breech bolt. In arms

equipped with this design, movement of the breech bolt could not be brought about until the finger lever had been partially lowered so as to move the operating bar out of alignment with the cartridge carrier lever. Although this design was theoretically sound and rather simple to manufacture, it depended upon the maintenance of extremely close tolerances within the action so that all the necessary locking components cammed together properly, insuring positive lock-up. For all practical purposes, this was an impossibility as the wear to the bearing surfaces brought about by a rifle's normal use would rather quickly reduce the necessary tolerances to an unacceptable level. Consequently, in 1884, this design approach was also discarded.

While it was not recognized at the time, one event in 1883 would provide the solution to the Winchester company's problems in the development of a high-velocity rifle. In March or April of that year, Charles Benton, a traveling salesman for the company, visited the Browning Brothers shop in Ogden, Utah. While there, Benton found that the Brownings were making a cartridge reloading tool, which appeared to be an infringement upon V.A. King's U.S. Patent Number 232189 (issued Sept. 14, 1880) owned by the Winchester company[15]. This event became the catalyst that brought John M. Browning (Plate 149) to the notice of the Win-

Plate 150

B*rowning Brother's .38 caliber single-shot sporting rifle, purchased by Charles Benton for Thomas G. Bennett in June 1883. Winchester Arms Collection (Inv. No. W502), Cody Firearms Museum.*

chester company. Upon returning east, Benton turned over the reloading tool to the company's patent attorneys, who quickly determined that it was indeed an infringement. The company, however, elected to deal lightly with the Brownings in contrast to their previous treatment of patent infringers[16]. The reason for this leniency was due to the fact that Benton had evidently informed Bennett and Converse that John M. Browning had developed a practical single-shot rifle, which was highly regarded[17]. As one of the company's development goals at that time was the creation of a single-shot rifle which could take advantage of the market brought about by the failure of the Sharps Rifle Company[18], the possibility that Browning's design could be secured meant that some tact had to be used. Bennett authorized Benton to purchase an example of the Browning rifle (Plate 150) upon his return to the West and to ship it to New Haven for examination[19]. Instead of immediately beginning negotiations with Browning after the rifle came to hand in June 1883[20], its features, protected by Browning's U.S. Patent Number 220271 (issued Oct. 7, 1879, Plate 151), were apparently analyzed. Bennett then asked Mason to develop a similar rifle which did not infringe upon the Browning design[21]. Only when this proved to be impossible (Plate 152), did the Winchester company approach Browning about purchasing his patent. The acquisition of the patent on Dec. 12, 1883[22] was to mark the beginning of a relationship between John M. Browning and the Winchester company, which was to last sixteen years.

As work continued through 1884, on the refinement of the Browning single-shot rifle so that it could be quickly added to the company's product line, the matter of a .45-70 caliber lever-action rifle was not forgotten. Ultimately, John M. Browning was to pro-

vide an easy solution to the problem of insuring a positively locked bolt. By using twin locking bars connected to the finger lever in such a way that they vertically rode up into mortises cut in the sides of the bolt as well as the receiver walls when the finger lever was raised, (Plates 153-154) Browning was able to totally lock the bolt in its forward position. This positive lock-up prevented any movement of the breech bolt except by the movement of the finger lever because the unlocking motion was vertical instead of horizontal and could only be accomplished by moving the finger lever substantially downward. Thus, excessive chamber pressures had no effect other than more securely locking the bolt by pushing it

Plate 151

Specification drawings enrolled with John M. Browning's U.S. Patent Number 220271 issued Oct. 7, 1879. Browning Collection, Ogden Union Station, Ogden, Utah.

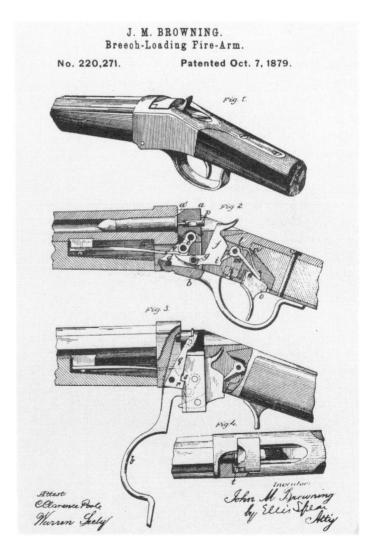

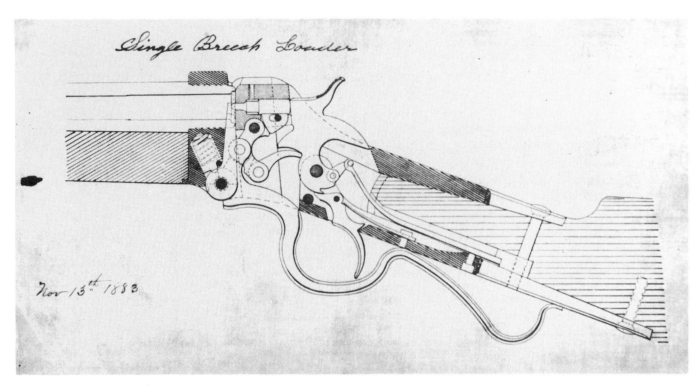

Single Breech Loader

Nov 13th 1883

back against the locking bars. Realizing the benefits of this design, the Winchester company purchased the rights to it and also entered into an agreement with Browning to buy any other rifle designs he might develop. This collaboration between Browning and the Winchester company eventually resulted in the development of eight new models in addition to the Model 1885 single-shot rifle (Plate 155), which were based primarily upon Browning's designs[23] (Lower Right).

In most instances, however, the company's designers had to perfect the basic idea supplied by Browning. Consequently, many of the production models are based not only upon Browning's patents, but also, those awarded to William Mason (Plate 163) or T.G. Bennett[24].

The importance of the Browning-Winchester alliance is that it allowed the company to considerably expand its consumer base through the introduction of a broad spectrum of models. In this manner the company was able to cater to virtually every segment of the longarm market, from single-shot .22 caliber boy's rifles, medium and large caliber sporting or hunting rifles to repeating shotguns.

In 1887, the Winchester company further consolidated its position within the ammunition market by introducing a full line of loaded shot shells[25]. Produced in sizes ranging from 4 to 20 gauge, a total of seven new lines were

Plate 152

Design drawings dated Nov. 13, 1883, illustrating the single-shot rifle action developed by William Mason between late September and early November 1883. Winchester Arms Collection Archives, Cody Firearms Museum.

Model 1886 (U.S. Patent Number 306577 issued Oct. 14, 1884, Plate 156)

Model 1887 (U.S. Patent Number 336287 issued Feb. 16, 1886, Plate 157)

Model 1890 (U.S. Patent Number 385238 issued June 26, 1888, Plate 158 and 159)

Model 1892 (U.S. Patent Number 465339 issued Dec. 15, 1891)

Model 1893 (U.S. Patent Number 441390 issued Nov. 25, 1890, Plate 160)

Model 1894 (U.S. Patent Number 524702 issued Aug. 21, 1894)

Model 1895 (U.S. Patent Number 549345 issued Nov. 5, 1895, Plates 161 and 162)

Model 1899 (U.S. Patent Number 632094 issued Aug. 29, 1899)

offered: First and Second Quality; Star; XX; Rival; and Leader. The success of this venture is illustrated by the fact that between 1887 and 1898, a total of 41,972,700 loaded shot shells were sold[26]. In addition, the company continued to sell unloaded shells at a rate of approximately 4.75 million per year[27].

The position of the Winchester Repeating Arms Company as the largest manufacturer of rifles and shotguns in the United States was ensured by two unexpected events in 1888. In January of that year, the executors of Eli Whitney's estate decided to liquidate the Whitney Arms Company by selling its plant and leasing all rights to manufac-

ture the rifles and pistols it held patents for. On Feb. 15, the Winchester company's board of directors agreed to purchase the Whitney plant and also to lease its patent rights, thereby removing a competitor from the market[28]. Winchester then retooled the Whitney facilities so that they could be used to produce components for Winchester products. In addition, under the aegis of the Whitney Arms Company, Winchester began to dispose of the former's stock of completed firearms and parts[29]. Winchester did not, however, elect to use any of the Whitney patents, even though they cost the company $10,000 per year to lease. After leasing

Left: Plate 153

Sheet 1 of the specification drawings enrolled with John M. Browning's U.S. Patent Number 306577 issued Oct. 14, 1884. Winchester Arms Collection Archives, Cody Firearms Museum.

Right: Plate 154

Sheet 2 of the specification drawings for John M. Browning's Oct. 14, 1884, patent.

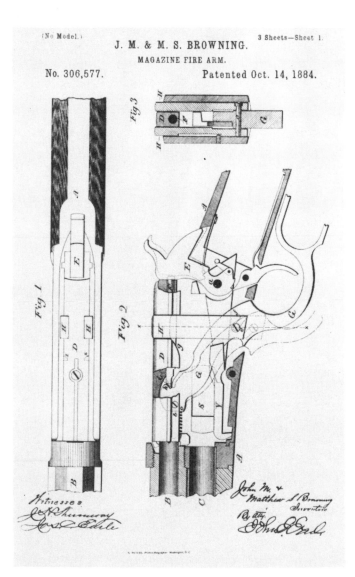

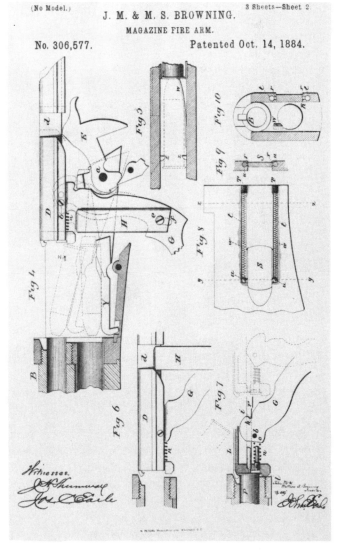

The Bartlett Family

During the 1880s and 1890s, some of the most popular performers at circuses and wild west shows were trick shooters. Able to hit coins tossed in the air or shatter glass balls thrown above them, both commoners and kings delighted at their unerring accuracy. While some, like Annie Oakley, are well known today, many others are only remembered due to cabinet photographs such as the one illustrated here.

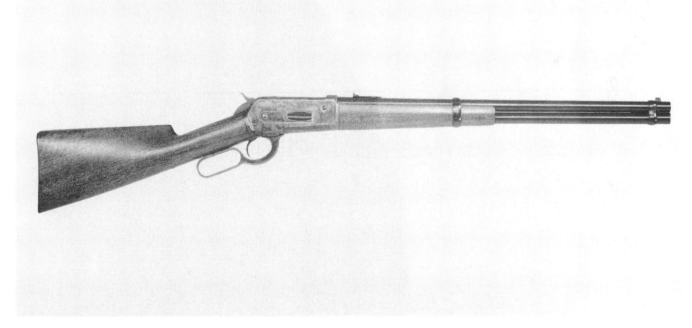

Top: Plate 155

*L*eft receiver detail of a skeletonized Winchester Model 1885 single-shot
rifle. Olin Corporation photograph.

Bottom: Plate 156

*W*inchester Model 1886 Carbine. Olin Corporation photograph.

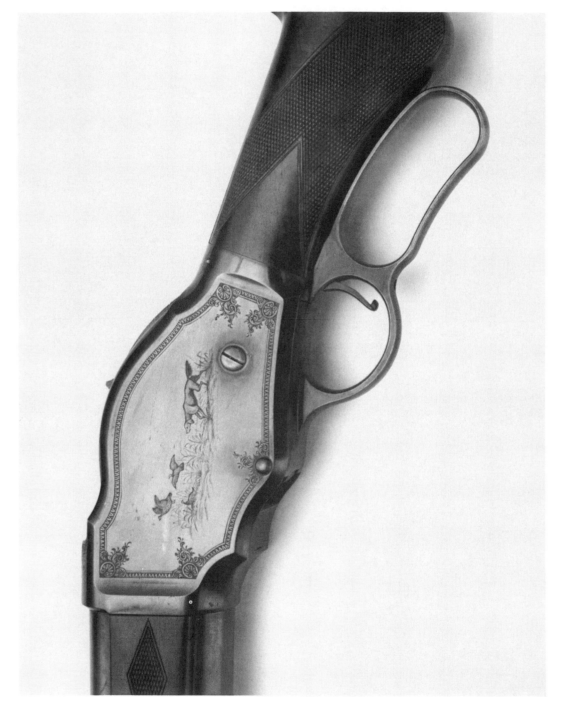

Plate 157
Left receiver detail of the Winchester Model 1887 shotgun serial number 1 originally owned by Henry Ford and subsequently given by him to Harvey Firestone. Cody Firearms Museum.

the patents for four years, the Winchester company renegotiated its arrangement with the Whitney executors[30]. In exchange for purchasing Eli Whitney and W.C. Scharf's Dec. 21, 1886 patent (Number 354757, Plate 164)[31], the Whitney executors released the Winchester company from their obligation to continue the lease for the remaining two years of the contract. As only the Whitney-Scharf patent was of any practical use, the Winchester company had effectively reduced the worth of the other patents so far as their lease value might have been to any competitor.

The second advantageous event of 1888 was the acquisition of a fifty per-

Right: Plate 158

Sheet 1 of the specification drawings enrolled with John M. Browning's U.S. Patent Number 436965 issued Sept. 23, 1890. Winchester Arms Collection Archives, Cody Firearms Museum.

Below: Plate 159

Receiver detail of a Winchester Model 1890 sporting rifle, serial number 449006, engraved by John Gough. Olin Corporation photograph.

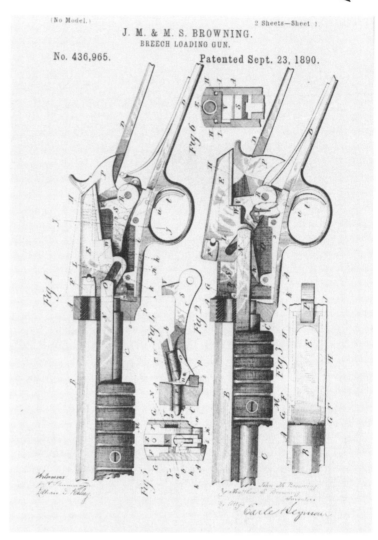

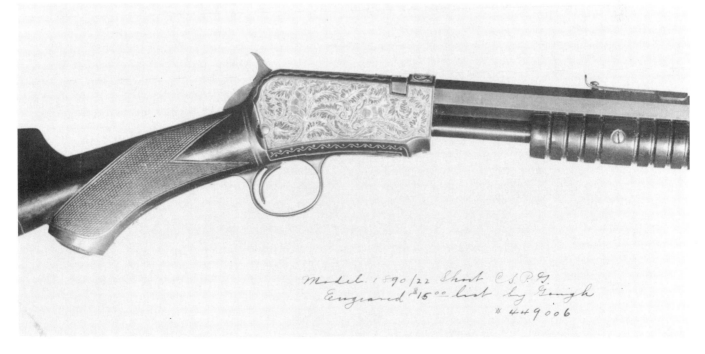

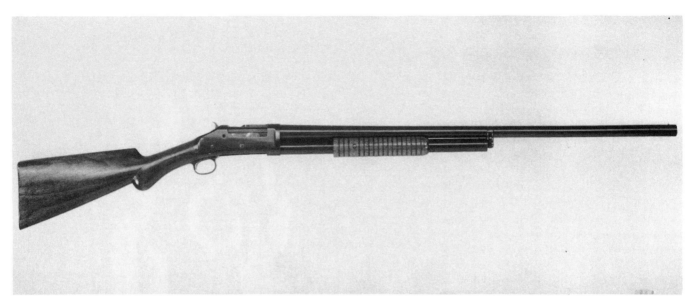

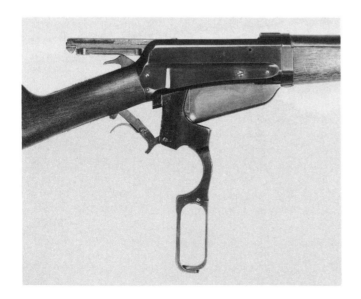

Top: Plate 160

*W*inchester Model 1893 shotgun. Olin Corporation photograph.

Middle: Plate 161

*W*inchester Model 1895 sporting rifle. Olin Corporation photograph.

Left: Plate 162

*D*etail of a Winchester Model 1895 sporting rifle with the action open. Olin Corporation photograph.

cent interest in E. Remington & Sons[32]. Shortly after Remington had sold its typewriter division in 1886, the company was forced into receivership by its creditors. Subsequently, A. N. Russell and A. Brill had tried to save Remington, but ever-increasing losses were incurred. In 1888, Marcellus Hartley, owner of Hartley & Graham in New York, Remington's most important sales agent, and the Winchester company jointly purchased the Ilion, New York, concern. The decision of the Winchester company to become involved in the acquisition of Remington as a partner and not sole owner was purely economic. As a partner, it could control Remington's future without a large outlay of capital and at the same time effec-

Right: Plate 163

Sheet 1 of the specification drawings enrolled with William Mason's U.S. Patent Number 306630 issued Oct. 14, 1884, protecting improvements to Browning's patent Number 306577. Winchester Arms Collection Archives, Cody Firearms Museum.

Below: Plate 164

Whitney-Scharf sporting rifle made in 1887. Olin Corporation photograph.

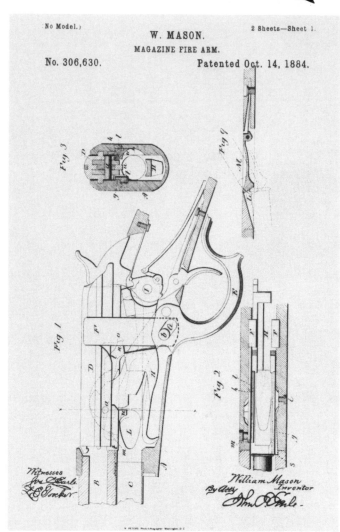

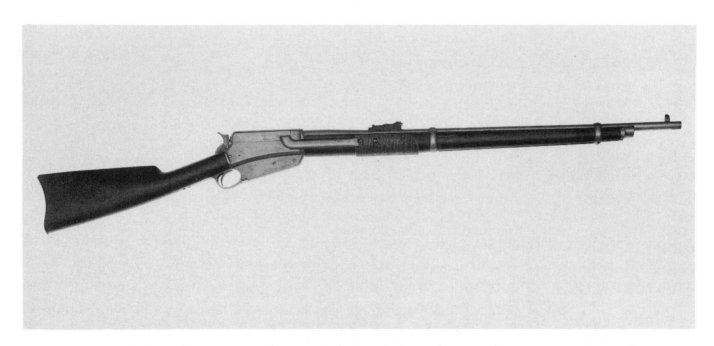

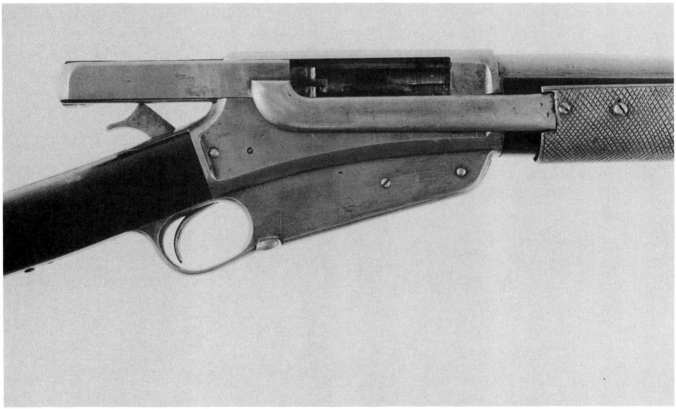

Top: Plate 165

Sample .30 caliber slide-action rifle incorporating design features protected by John M. Browning's U.S. Patent Number 545672 issued Sept. 3, 1895. Winchester Arms Collection (Inv. No. W51), Cody Firearms Museum. Olin Corporation photograph.

Bottom: Plate 166

Detail of the sample Browning rifle illustrated in Plate 165.

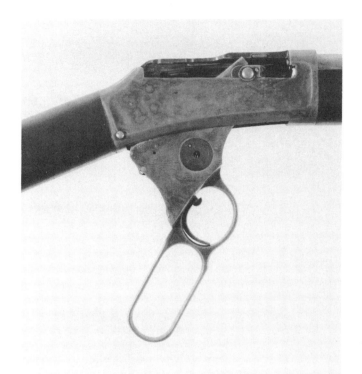

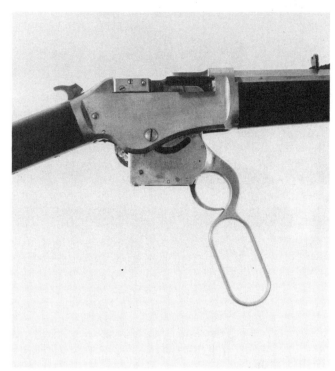

Above: Plate 167

*D*etail of a sample .44 caliber lever-action musket incorporating design features protected by John M. Browning's U.S. Patent Number 376576 issued Jan. 17, 1888. Winchester Arms Collection (Inv. No. W293), Cody Firearms Museum. Olin Corporation photograph.

Below: Plate 168

*S*ample .44 caliber lever-action rifle incorporating design features protected by John M. Browning's U.S. Patent Number 428887 issued May 27, 1890. Winchester Arms Collection (Inv. No. W232), Cody Firearms Museum. Olin Corporation photograph.

Top Right: Plate 169

*D*etail of the sample Browning rifle illustrated in Plate 168.

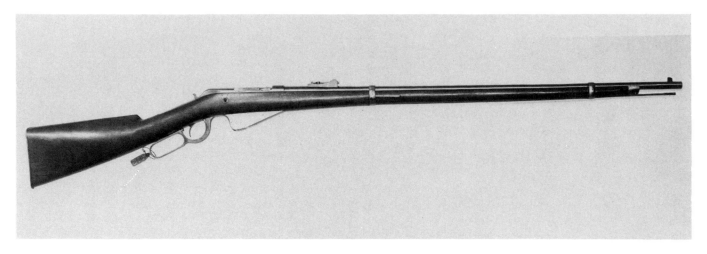

Above: Plate 170

*S*ample .30 caliber lever-action rifle incorporating design features protected by John M. Browning's U.S. Patent Number 486272 issued Nov. 15, 1892. Winchester Arms Collection (Inv. No. W205), Cody Firearms Museum. Olin Corporation photograph.

Left: Plate 171

*D*etail of the sample Browning rifle illustrated in Plate 170.

Right: Plate 172

*S*ample .236 caliber lever action rifle incorporating design features protected by John M. Browning's U.S. Patent Number 599595 issued Feb. 22, 1898. Winchester Arms Collection (Inv. No. W231), Cody Firearms Museum. Olin Corporation photograph.

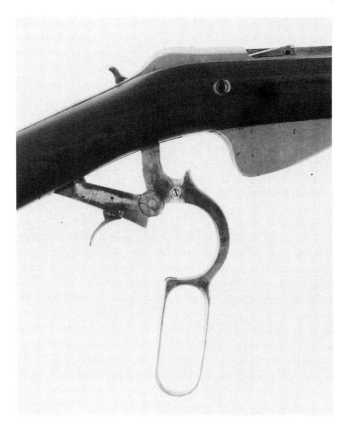

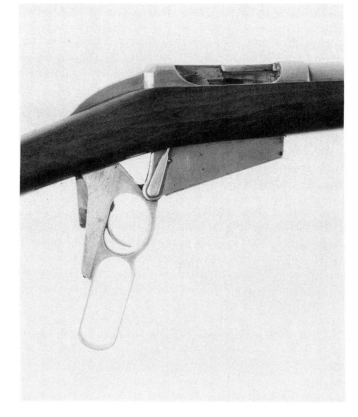

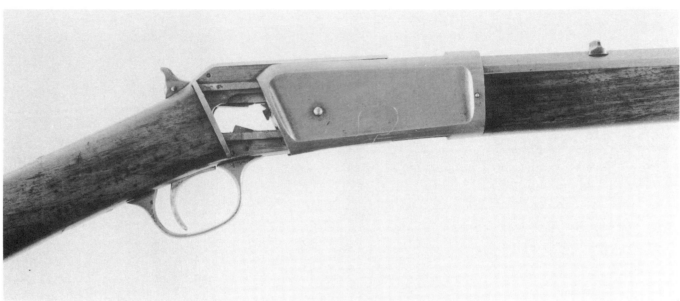

tively increase its arms' market share. Among the first acts of the Hartley-Winchester partnership were the discontinuance of Remington's production of ammunition, the sale of its sewing machine patents as well as sewing machine production machinery and the cancellation of any further work on repeating rifles. The removal of Remington from the ammunition trade benefited both Hartley and Winchester, as both were involved in the same business. The sale of the sewing machine division was purely economically motivated. As one of the company's most profitable components, its sale generated a substantial amount of money and, thus, allowed the partners to recoup a large portion of their original investment. From the Winchester company's standpoint, their partnership in the Remington company was beneficial since it allowed Winchester access to and the use of the Remington company's agents overseas, particularly in South America and the Far East. Over the six years of the Hartley-Winchester partnership, the Winchester company carefully cultivated those agents so that when the partnership was dissolved, many contin-

ued to be joint agents rather than be bound to one or the other company.

Although the Browning-Winchester arrangement resulted in nine new models for the company, the terms of the agreement obliged the firm to purchase a total of thirty-three other designs, which never went into production. Some of these were quite practical (e.g., the slide-action shotguns), but others, such as the pull-apart actions, bordered on pure whimsy. They all, however, represented a significant expense to the company. Apart from their initial purchase price, the firm also incurred costs attendant to the building of samples, perfection of design, preparation of patent drawings and, finally, the cost of the patent procedure itself. It was believed, though, that as long as Browning submitted designs that could be financially beneficial to the company, the cost of developing and patenting other unusable inventions would be more than compensated. Thus, between 1886 and 1899, the following patents were applied for by the Winchester Repeating Arms Company on behalf of John M. Browning[33]:

Plate 173

Sample .22 caliber pull-apart action rifle incorporating design features protected by John M. Browning's U.S. Patent Number 465340 issued Dec. 15, 1891. Winchester Arms Collection (Inv. No. W199), Cody Firearms Museum. Olin Corporation photograph.

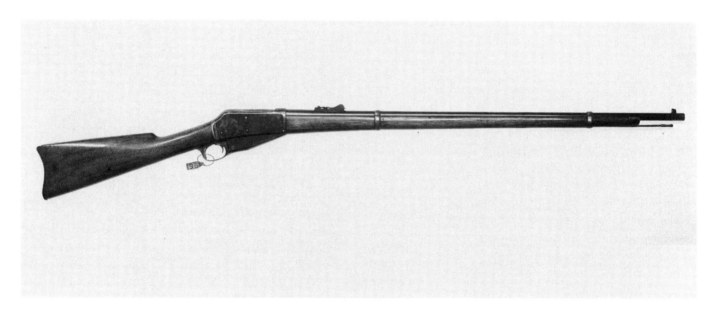

Plate 174

Sample .30 caliber pull-apart action rifle incorporating design features protected by John M. Browning's U.S. Patent Number 486273 issued Nov. 15, 1892. Winchester Arms Collection (Inv. No. W196), Cody Firearms Museum. Olin Corporation photograph.

Slide-Action Shotguns:

Number 345881 issued July 20, 1886

Number 345882 issued July 20, 1886

Number 356271 issued Jan. 18, 1887

Number 385238 issued June 26, 1888

Number 409600 issued Aug. 20, 1889

Number 421663 issued Feb. 18, 1890

Number 550778 issued Dec. 3, 1895

Number 552864 issued Jan. 7, 1896

Number 577281 issued Feb. 16, 1897

Slide-Action Rifles:

Number 367336 issued July 26, 1887

Number 436965 issued Sept. 23, 1890

Number 545672 issued Sept. 3, 1895 (Plates 165 and 166)

Lever-Action Shotguns:

Number 346021 issued July 20, 1886

Lever-Action Rifles:

Number 324296 issued Aug. 11, 1885

Number 324297 issued Aug. 11, 1885

Number 376576 issued Jan. 17, 1888 (Plate 167)

Number 428887 issued May 27, 1890 (Plates 168 and 169)

Number 486272 issued Nov. 15, 1892 (Plates 170 and 171)

Number 492459 issued Feb. 28, 1892

Number 545671 issued Sept. 3, 1895

Number 599595 issued Feb. 22, 1898 (Plate 172)

Number 619132 issued Feb. 7, 1899

Pull-Apart Actions:

Number 465340 issued Dec. 15, 1891 (Plate 173)

Number 486273 issued Nov. 15, 1892 (Plates 174 and 175)

Number 487659 issued Dec. 6, 1892 (Plates 176 and 177)

Number 499005 issued June 6, 1893

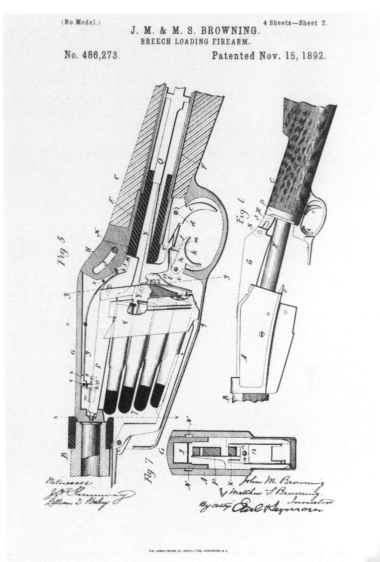

Single-Shot Rifles:

Number 359917 issued March 22, 1887

Number 511677 issued Dec. 26, 1893

Miscellaneous Rifles:

Number 499007 issued June 6, 1893 (Plate 178)

Component Designs:

Number 486274 issued Nov. 15, 1892

Number 487660 issued Dec. 6, 1892

Number 499005 issued June 6, 1893

Number 547986 issued Oct. 15, 1895

Plate 175

Sheet 2 of the specifications drawings enrolled with John M. Browning's U.S. Patent Number 486273 issued Nov. 15, 1892. Winchester Arms Collection Archives, Cody Firearms Museum.

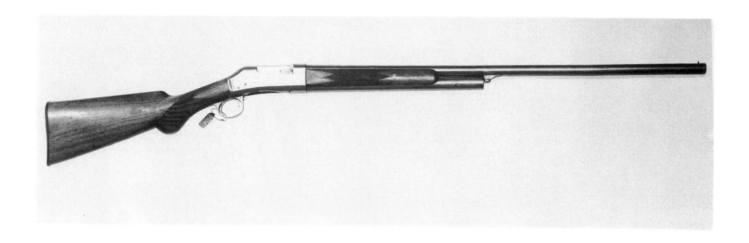

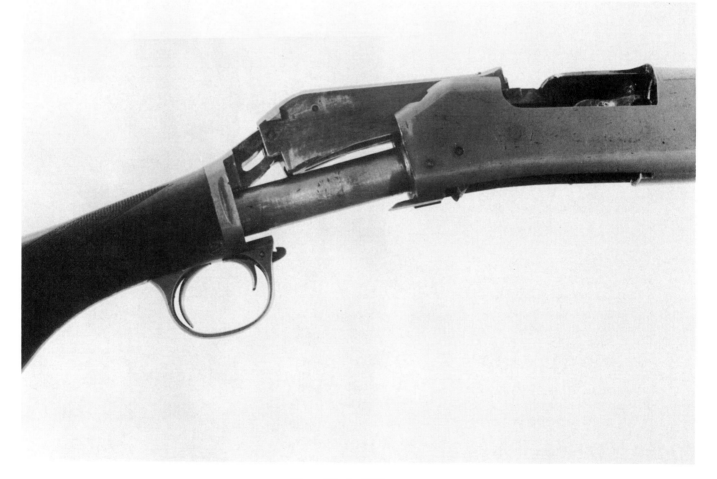

Top: Plate 176

Sample 12 gauge pull-apart action shotgun incorporating design features protected by John M. Browning's U.S. Patent Number 487659 issued Dec. 6, 1892. Winchester Arms Collection (Inv. No. W534), Cody Firearms Museum. Olin Corporation photograph.

Bottom: Plate 177

Detail of the sample Browning shotgun illustrated in Plate 176.

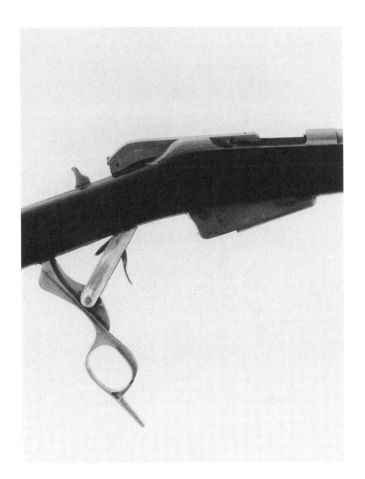

Left: Plate 178

Detail of the sample .30 swinging guard action rifle incorporating design features protected by John M. Browning's U.S. Patent Number 499007 issued June 6, 1893. Winchester Arms Collection (Inv. No. W228), Cody Firearms Museum. Olin Corporation photograph.

Below: Plate 179

Sample 12 gauge slide-action shotgun incorporating design features protected by John M. Browning's U.S. Patent Number 577281 issued Feb. 16, 1897. Winchester Arms Collection (Inv. No. W6), Cody Firearms Museum. Olin Corporation photograph.

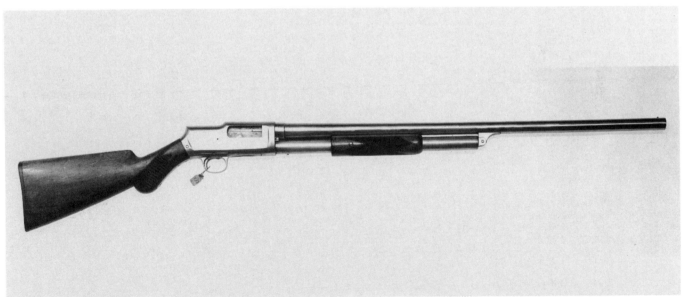

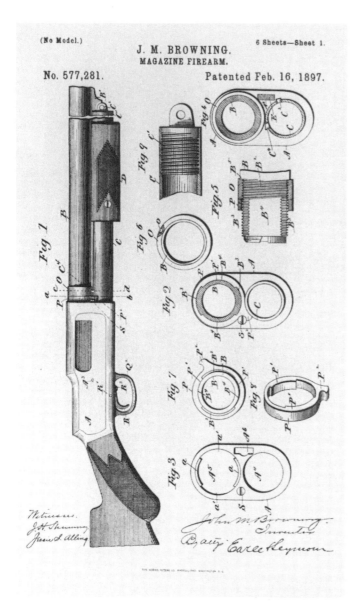

Plate 180

*S*heet 1 of the specification drawings enrolled with John M. Browning's U.S. Patent Number 577281 issued Feb. 16, 1897. Winchester Arms Collection Archives, Cody Firearms Museum.

Plate 181

*S*heet 2 of the specification drawings for John M. Browning's Feb. 16, 1897, patent.

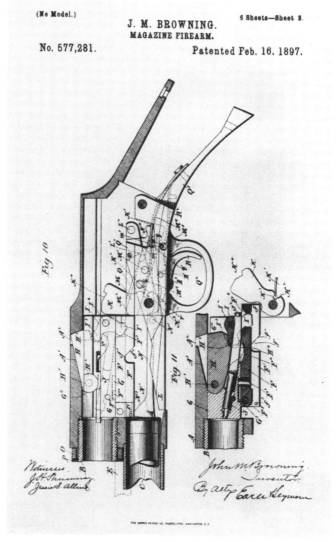

Top: Plate 182
Winchester Model 1897 Shotgun. Olin Corporation photograph.

Middle: Plate 183
Winchester Lee .236 caliber U.S. Navy Rifle. Olin Corporation photograph.

Bottom: Plate 184
Winchester Lee sporting rifle. Olin Corporation photograph.

While a total of forty-one patents were secured for either John M. Browning alone, or in association with his brother Mathew between 1884 and 1899, it is important not to overestimate his importance to the Winchester company. Certainly, he was a prime source of design ideas, but he was not the only one. For example, during the same fifteen-year period, William Mason was awarded sixty-one patents (primarily for firearms) and Thomas G. Bennett, the Winchester company's president from 1889 onward, received twenty-nine patents, again, primarily for firearms[34].

The first evidence of any strain in the Browning-Winchester relationship appeared in 1895, when the company began to receive complaints about the Model 1893 shotgun[35]. Due to the absence of a positive bolt and operating slide lock, the Model 1893 had a tendency to blow open under certain operating conditions. When the company approached Browning about developing a design modification to correct the problem, his response was the submission of a totally new shotgun action. Though the design (Plates 179-181) was beautifully conceived, the company did not want to take up its production due to the attendant costs[36]. In particular, the company was loathe to lose its investment in the Model 1893's tooling, which had yet to be paid for by the sale of the model. Consequently, the problem of correcting the Model 1893's design was handled internally. Through the combined efforts of Thomas G. Bennett, William Mason and William W. Wetmore, a revised action and receiver were developed between 1895 and 1897[37]. The resulting arm, known as the Model 1897 shotgun (Plate 182), was first placed on the market in June 1897[38].

As Browning's relationship with the Winchester company worsened, increasing reliance was placed upon the firm's own designers, who proved to be more

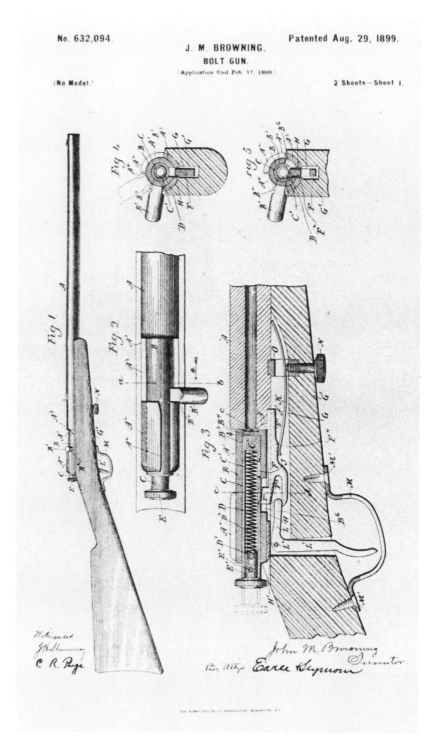

Plate 185

Sheet 1 of the specification drawings enrolled with John M. Browning's U.S. Patent Number 632094 issued Aug. 29, 1899. Winchester Arms Collection Archives, Cody Firearms Museum.

than capable of handling any task assigned to them. In addition, independent designers were also courted by the company. Chief among these was James Paris Lee, who the firm had come into contact with during their involvement with the Remington company. In November 1895, the Winchester company purchased the rights to manufacture Lee's straight pull bolt-action rifle[39]. Manufactured under six patents granted to Lee and two subsequent patents awarded to Thomas C. Johnson and William Mason, the Winchester-Lee Rifle (Plates 183 and 184) entered production in September 1896. Although 15,000 were sold to the U.S. Navy, the model never proved popular, and its manufacture was ended in 1900, after fewer than 20,000 had been built[40].

At approximately this time, Mrs. Thomas G. Bennett provided the final footnote to the history of the New Haven Arms Company, when she presented fifty Volcanic carbines to the Calvary Baptist Church Boys' Brigade. Organized on March 13, 1893, the Brigade was later known as the Calvary Navy Reserves during World War I. Throughout its history, the carbines were used for drill purposes until the Brigade was disbanded in

about 1920. At that time, the carbines were distributed to the organization's members by its last commander, Hawley Lincoln, Sr.[41]

Although the final Browning design to be purchased and manufactured by the Winchester company was that for the Model 1900 single-shot rifle (Plate 185)[42], the firm was heavily involved in the work concerned with the perfection of Browning's self-loading shotgun during 1899 and 1900[43]. Indeed, all the perfected samples, patent specifications and patent drawings for that arm were prepared in New Haven[44]. Unfortunately, this work was to prove a loss to the company as the company could not come to any agreement with the Browning Brothers regarding its manufacture. Their request for a royalty arrangement instead of an outright sale of the design, as had been their previous practice, was rejected by the company, and they decided to market their designs elsewhere. Evidently, there was some rancor on the part of Matthew Browning regarding the collapse of the Browning-Winchester association, as the company felt the need in 1903 to circulate the following letter to its dealers and agents in order to clarify the matter[45].

WINCHESTER REPEATING ARMS COMPANY
New Haven, Conn., U.S.A.

Aug. 21, 1903.

MISSIONARIES & SALESMEN

Dear Sir:...

In reply to a question put by one of our missionaries we have written as follows. Thinking that perhaps you might have the same questions asked you we send the matter as written for your information:

Where it becomes worth while to talk about inventions, you can say as to the Automatic that it is the invention of Thomas C. Johnson, who is one of our employes [sic]. Of course the Winchester company, as a company, cannot invent anything. The people who are employed for that purpose are the real inventors.

For a number of years it seemed best to us to employ the Messrs. Browning Bros. We bought everything which they invented which had merit, whether we used it or not. It seemed to us at the end that they had become rather high-priced, and we let them go to Colt's. They had got to feel that they were the only people who could invent guns, that our suggestions as to what was needed by the public were of no value, and that they were really the "whole thing". Mr. John Browning was a very nice man, and we were sorry to part with him because he was in many respects a genius. His younger brother, Mr. Matthew Browning, was a more difficult proposition. We understood he was not the inventor, but that Mr. John Browning was the inventor.

None of the things invented by them were made by us exactly as presented. They were all worked over by the people in our employ to get them into such shape that they could be manufactured successfully. For instance, the Model 1886 gun is more largely the invention of our Mr. Mason than it is of the Browning Bros.; the Brownings having supplied us with the locking features only.

We shall be perfectly able to get along without the Brownings, and shall probably be better off without them than with them. The .22 Automatic is a sample. On the other hand, we do not believe they will get along as well without us as they did with us. There is room for both. We should not like to have you say anything that would look as though we were inimical, but if there is any suggestion of their claiming that they are the "whole thing" and there is nothing left, the .22 Automatic gun is our answer; and we shall within a little while have other answers of the same kind to such argument.

Yours respectfully,

Winchester Repeating Arms Co.

Endnotes

1. The two largest manufacturers of firearms in the early 1880s were the Colt Patent Fire Arms Manufacturing Company of Hartford, Connecticut, and, E. Remington & Sons of Ilion, New York. The largest American ammunition maker was the United Metallic Cartridge Company of Bridgeport, Connecticut.

2. Sutherland and Wilson, op. cit., pages 491-492.

3. It is evident that William Mason had completed work on both the slide-action rifle and the single-action revolver by Sept. 15, 1883, as complete design drawings for both arms exist (in the Winchester Arms Collection Archives, Cody Firearms Museum) bearing dates in late September of that year.

4. The earliest tooling drawings for the Mason revolver are dated Oct. 1 and 2, 1883 (Winchester Arms Collection Archives, Cody Firearms Museum).

5. Photocopy of a letter written by Major General William B. Franklin to Messrs. Hartley & Graham dated Dec. 28 (?), 1883. Hartley & Graham Archives, Cody Firearms Museum.

6. Minutes of the Winchester Repeating Arms Company Board of Directors Meeting, Feb. 14, 1884. Winchester Repeating Arms Company Archives, Olin Corporation.

7. Bennett, Aide-Memoire, op. cit., entry dated Feb. 14, 1884.

8. Walker, New York Depot Synopsis, op. cit., page 2.

9. Bennett, Aide-Memoire, op. cit., entry dated June 1, 1884.

10. Johnson, Winchester History, op. cit., page 18.

11. Bennett, Aide-Memoire, op. cit., entry dated June 1, 1884.

12. Herbert Woodend, **British Rifles: A catalogue of the Enfield Pattern Room** (H.M.S.O.; London: 1981), page 18.

13. William Mason's United States Patent Number 305093 issued Sept. 16, 1884 (application filed Feb. 26, 1883).

14. Drawings for this series of rifles are preserved in the Winchester Arms Collection Archives, Cody Firearms Museum.

15. Due to John M. Browning's later reputation and his Horatio Alger-like life, a mythology has developed concerning the circumstances associated with his first contact with the Winchester Repeating Arms Company, as well as the Winchester company's purchase of his 1879 patent. In some accounts the Winchester representative who visited the Browning shop is identified as Andrew McAusland (Richard Rattenbury, **The Browning Connection** [Buffalo Bill Historical Center; Cody, WY: 1982], page 6), while others state that the Brownings came to the Winchester company's attention through the New York firm of Schovering and Daly (William West, **Browning Arms & History** [W.West; Santa Fe Springs, CA: 1972], pages 3-13). All agree, however, that T.G. Bennett, upon learning of the Browning rifle, immediately traveled to Utah to secure the patent rights (Rattenbury, page 6 and West, pages 3-13). Unfortunately, no record can be found in any contemporary records of the Winchester company of an Andrew McAusland ever having been employed by the firm. An A.D. McAusland of Miles City, Montana was an authorized Winchester dealer from shortly after his arrival in Montana on Dec. 24, 1879 until his retirement in 1918. (Gerald R. Mayberry, "The Sharps Rifle in Frontier Montana", **ARMAX**, Volume IV, Number 2 [1993], pages 24-25). It is possible that A. (for Alexander) D. McAusland served as model for the fictitious Andrew McAusland. More compelling evidence regarding the matter is provided by Thomas G. Bennett's Aide-Memoire. In it, Charles

Benton is identified as the Winchester representative who first visited the Brownings and who purchased a single-shot rifle from them for Bennett (entries dated May 18, June 20, 1883, etc.). Furthermore, no evidence is to be found in the Aide-Memoire supporting the statement that Bennett journeyed to Ogden in 1883 or 1884, even though Bennett scrupulously recorded trips elsewhere.

16. The text of the Winchester-Browning agreement is reproduced in Houze, To The Dreams of Youth: Winchester .22 caliber Single Shot Rifles (Krause Publications, Inc.; Iola WI: 1993), Note 2, page 13.

17. Bennett, Aide-Memoire, op. cit., entry dated May 18, 1883.

18. Frank Sellers, **Sharps Firearms** (Beinfeld Publishing, Inc.; North Hollywood, CA: 1978), pages 259-261.

19. Bennett Aide-Memoire, op. cit., entry dated May 18, 1883.

20. Ibid, entry dated June 20, 1883.

21. Ibid, entry dated Sept. 26, 1883.

22. Ibid, entry dated Dec. 12, 1883.

23. Extracted from U.S. Patent Files, Winchester Arms Collection Archives, Cody Firearms Museum.

24. For example, a number of patents concerned with various features of the Models 1886, 1887 and 1895 were issued to T.G. Bennett, William Mason and William Wetmore, before or shortly after those arms entered production. In addition, design drawings for all the Browning production models exhibit refinements which can only be attributed to the previously mentioned individuals (in particular, Mason).

25. Johnson, History of Shot Shells, op. cit., page 1.

26. Ibid, page 2.

27. Ibid.

28. Winchester Repeating Arms Company Board of Directors Meeting Minutes, Feb. 15, 1888. Winchester Repeating Arms Company Archives, Olin Corporation. Cf., Johnson, Winchester History, op. cit., pages 22 and 23.

29. This is confirmed by correspondence between the Winchester company and Hartley & Graham Company of New York. Hartley & Graham Archives, Cody Firearms Museum.

30. Winchester Repeating Arms Company Board of Directors Meeting Minutes, Feb. 14, 1892. Winchester Repeating Arms Company Archives, Olin Corporation.

31. Patents Owned by the Winchester Repeating Arms Company, Volume 1. Winchester Arms Collection Archives, Cody Firearms Museum.

32. Johnson, Winchester History, op. cit., page 18c.

33. Extracted from the United States Patent Files, Winchester Arms Collection Archives, Cody Firearms Museum.

34. Ibid.

35. Records of the complaints are contained in two manuscript notebooks maintained by T.C. Johnson, now in the Winchester Arms Collection Archives, Cody Firearms Museum.

36. A comparison prepared in 1896, of the number parts and operations needed to make them between the Model 1893 and the proposed Browning replacement, indicates the following:

Model 1893 Browning

Number of Component Parts 8488

Number of Operations 407395

Number of Parts in Browning the same as Winchester 26

Number of New Parts 62

Number of Operations Requiring New Tools and Fixtures 349

37. T.G. Bennett, U.S. Patent Number 564420 issued July 21, 1896

T.G. Bennett, U.S. Patent Number 564421 issued July 21, 1896

T.G. Bennett and W. Mason, U.S. Patent Number 599587 issued Feb. 22, 1898

W. Mason, U.S. Patent Number 564440 issued July 21, 1896

W. Mason, U.S. Patent Number 565767 issued Aug. 11, 1896

W. Mason, U.S. Patent Number 585392 issued June 29, 1897

W. Mason, U.S. Patent Number 586856 issued July 20, 1897

W. Wetmore, U.S. Patent Number 548410 issued Oct. 22, 1895

38. H.B. Dow, Model 1897 Production Notes. Winchester Arms Collection Archives, Cody Firearms Museum.

39. Johnson, Winchester History, op. cit., pages 30-31.

40. Ibid, page 31.

41. History of Volcanic Carbine, Serial No. 5. Documents Relating to the Volcanic Repeating Arms Company, File 2, unnumbered. Winchester Arms Collection Archives, Cody Firearms Museum.

42. John M. Browning's United States Patent Number 632094 issued Aug. 29, 1899.

43. Approximately six designs for the action of the Browning self-loading shotgun are preserved in the Winchester Arms Collection Archives, Cody Firearms Museum. These drawings are dated from July 1899 through May 1900.

44. The patent for the Browning shotgun (Number 689283, issued Dec. 17, 1901) was filed by the Winchester company's patent attorneys Seymour and Earle.

45. Letter from the Winchester Repeating Arms Company to Missionaries & Salesmen dated Aug. 21, 1903. Browning File, Winchester Arms Collection Archives, Cody Firearms Museum.

CHAPTER 4

THE NEW CENTURY: 1901-1913

As the twentieth century began, the United States was undergoing a radical change. Electrification lit cities, towns and even some villages; automobiles had begun to be more frequent companions to horses on American streets; and wonders, such as the telephone which had been merely a scientific curiosity in 1876, were commonplace. The country's population, too, was changing. Rural communities began to remain static in size as urban, industrialized centers grew. Society in general became more aware that they lived in an era of change and promise. Fair labor laws, the increased availability of education and the relative prosperity of the period all contributed to an increased optimism about the country's future.

Plate 186

Design Drawing Number 7097 dated Dec. 22, 1899, illustrating William Mason's 12 gauge self-loading shotgun. Winchester Arms Collection Archives, Cody Firearms Museum.

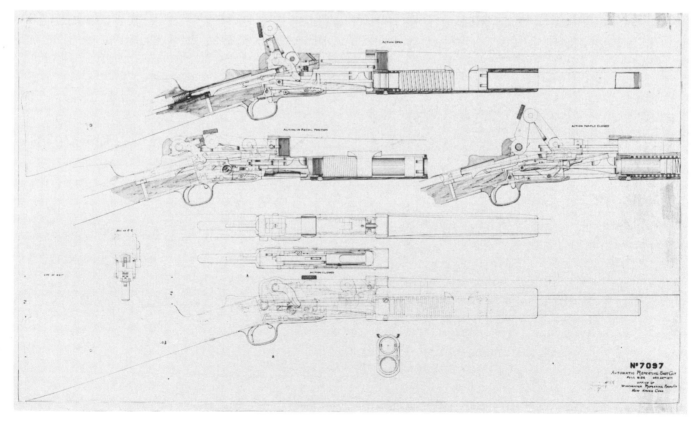

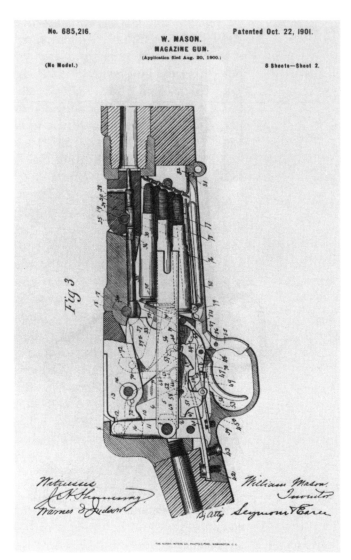

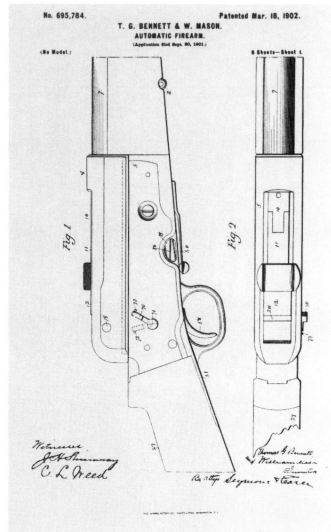

Left: Plate 187

*S*heet 2 of the specification drawings enrolled with William Mason's U.S. Patent Number 685216 issued Dec. 22, 1901. Winchester Arms Collection Archives, Cody Firearms Museum.

Right: Plate 188

*S*heet 1 of the specification drawings enrolled with Thomas G. Bennett and William Mason's U.S. Patent Number 695784 issued March 18, 1902. Winchester Arms Collection Archives, Cody Firearms Museum.

While some American arms companies had not anticipated the changes which would be wrought in society during the last decade and a half of the previous century, others, such as the Colt and Winchester companies, had recognized that the country was rapidly developing. As early as 1883, both firms had instituted development programs designed to produce products that would meet the needs of an increasingly sophisticated public.[1] To its advantage, the Winchester Repeating Arms Company during that period could rely upon two of the nineteenth century's greatest designers, John M. Browning and William Mason. The company, therefore, was confident that it

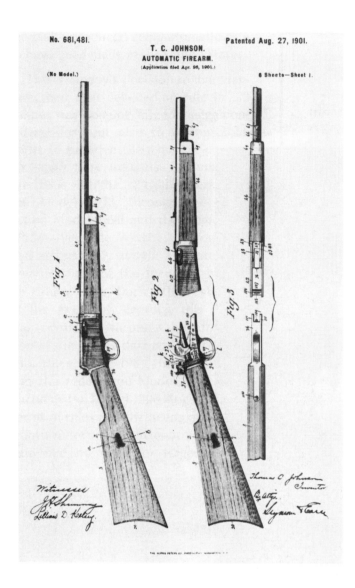

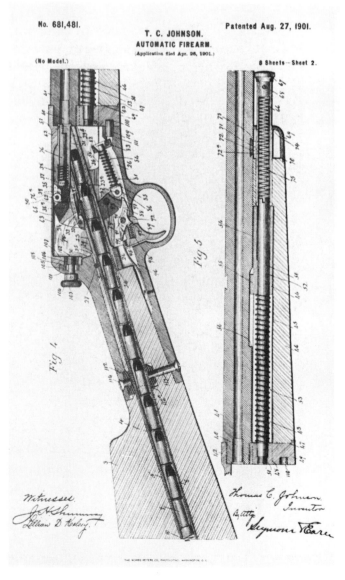

Plate 194

*S*heet 1 of the specification drawings enrolled with Thomas C. Johnson's U.S. Patent Number 681481 issued Aug. 27, 1901. Winchester Arms Collection Archives, Cody Firearms Museum.

Plate 195

*S*heet 2 of the specification drawings for Thomas C. Johnson's Aug. 27, 1901 patent.

Plate 196

*W*inchester Model 1903 self-loading .22 caliber rifle. Olin Corporation photograph.

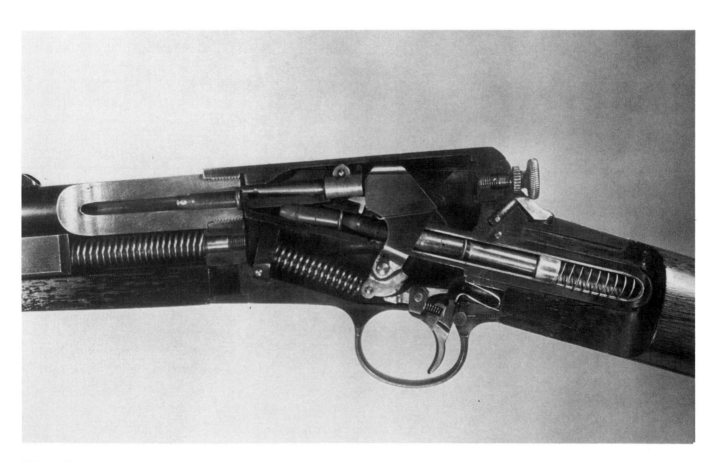

Plate 197

*L*eft receiver detail of a skeletonized Winchester Model 1903 self-loading rifle. Olin Corporation photograph.

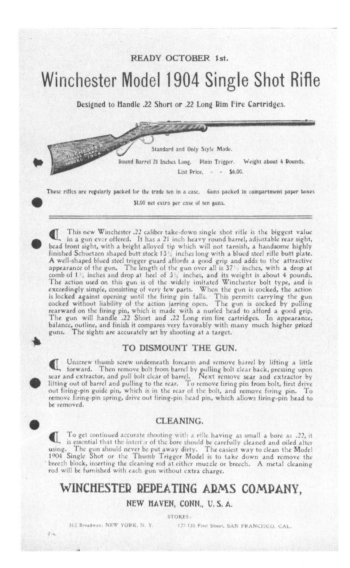

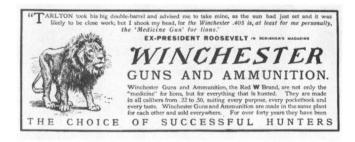

customer for a Winchester centerfire rifle or shotgun[10].

By 1904, Johnson had developed balanced bolt designs for a series of centerfire rifles utilizing .32, .35 and .40 short case cartridges derived from the .44 caliber semi-rimless pattern used in the Mason semiautomatic carbine[11]. Ultimately, this work was to result in the Model 1905, 1907 and 1910 (Plate 201) series of Winchester self-loading rifles, which were again the first of their type to be manufactured in the United States.

While the Winchester Repeating Arms Company had managed to secure a substantial competitive edge in manufacturing and marketing self-loading

Left: Plate: 198

Brochure circulated on July 15, 1904, announcing the forthcoming introduction of the Winchester Model 1904 single-shot rifle. Private Collection.

Top Right: Plate 199

Winchester definitive proofmark adopted for use on centerfire rifle and shotgun barrels as of July 17, 1905 and for all arms as of Oct. 12, 1908. Olin Corporation photograph.

Bottom Right: Plate 200

Proof print of a Winchester advertizement published circa 1910. Private Collection.

■ The Winchester Fire Brigade

Founded in 1872, the Winchester Fire Brigade was an essential part of the New Haven factory's work force until just prior to World War I, when motorized fire equipment was introduced. An elite group upon whom the safety of the company's employees depended should fire break out, the brigade was particularly proud of its reputation that it had not allowed any lives or buildings to be lost during the period of its existence. Although this photograph was taken in 1904, the uniform of the Brigade changed little over the years, and it is probable that the original members would have had little trouble identifying their successors as members of the Winchester fire department.

rifles, that success was not achieved with respect to shotguns. Instead, the Remington Arms Company achieved the distinction of introducing the first semiautomatic shotgun when it began production of the Browning autoloader in 1905[12]. Ironically, much of the initial design work on that shotgun had been carried out at the Winchester plant prior to Browning's dissolution of his association with the company.

To counter Browning, T.C. Johnson began work on a recoil-operated shotgun in early 1903[13]. By 1905, Johnson had developed an action which divided the recoil caused by a shot shell being fired. The initial and strongest portion of the recoil was absorbed by a spiral spring mounted below the barrel, which was compressed against the

Right: Plate 201

Advertisement for the Winchester Model 1910 self-loading .401 caliber rifle, circa 1910-1911. Private Collection.

Bottom: Plate 202

Winchester Model 1911 Deluxe self-loading 12 gauge shotgun. Olin Corporation photograph.

It Hits Like the Hammer of Thor, the

WINCHESTER

.401 CALIBER

Model 1910 Self-Loading Rifle

This repeater, which is the latest Winchester product, has speed and power plus. It's speedy because, being reloaded by the recoil of the fired cartridge, it can be shot as fast as the trigger can be pulled. It's powerful because it handles a cartridge of the most modern type—one that strikes a blow of 2038 foot pounds. The knock-down, shocking power of this cartridge, with its heavy bullet of large diameter, driven with high velocity, is tremendous; and the combination of such power with the rapidity of fire which this rifle is capable of, makes it unusually desirable for hunting the biggest of big game. There is no rifle made which will deliver five as powerful blows in as few seconds as the Winchester Model 1910.

Ask your dealer to show you one, or send for circular fully describing this rifle.

WINCHESTER REPEATING ARMS CO., - NEW HAVEN, CONN.

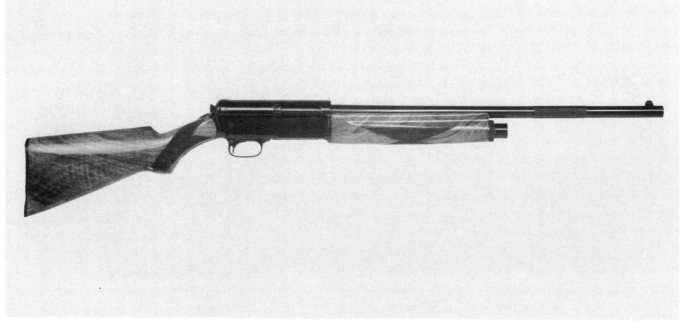

receiver as the barrel assembly moved rearward. The residual recoil was then absorbed by the movement of the bolt and, if need be, a buffer located at the rear of the receiver. As with the self-loading rifles, the forward motion of the bolt was caused by the reverse pressure of the two buffer springs. Although the mechanics of the action were established by early 1905[14], the production and introduction of the shotgun were to be delayed almost six years due to problems associated with the feeding and extraction of paper hulled shot shells. Eventually, these problems were overcome through the installation of an improved cartridge lifter and the lengthening of the bolt's travel so that a larger ejection port could be milled in

the receiver. Despite its clean lines and smooth action, the Model 1911 self-loading shotgun (Plate 202) never achieved the acceptance that the Browning had, despite an energetic promotional campaign that emphasized its advantages over the Browning.

Although the Winchester company's efforts to maintain and enlarge its mar-

Top: Plate 203

Blueprint of Design Drawing Number 7667 dated Nov. 6, 1901, illustrating a single-shot bolt-action shotgun with an index finger hole stock designed by C.H. Griffin or T.C. Johnson. Winchester Arms Collection Archives, Cody Firearms Museum.

Bottom: Plate 204

Blueprint of Design Drawing Number 7308 dated Dec. 14, 1900, illustrating a self-loading shotgun developed by T.C. Johnson. Winchester Arms Collection Archives, Cody Firearms Museum.

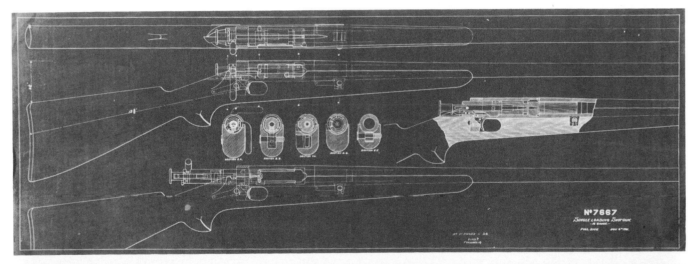

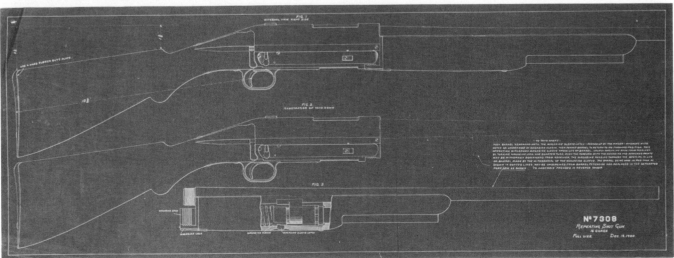

kets were primarily centered upon self-loading arms during this period, a myriad of other firearms designs were also developed from 1901 to 1910. Chief among these were a series of single-shot shotguns, one of which by William Mason was of surprisingly modern design (Plate 203), rising bolt lever-action rifles patterned after the Model 1890 action and a series of single-shot .22 caliber rifles[15]. In addition, as previously mentioned, William Mason continued to work on various types of gas and recoil-operated self-loading rifles and shotguns (Plates 204 and 205) up to his retirement. While none of these designs ever was selected for production, some of their component features were to prove of use in the development of later production models.

During the first decade of the century, the only major contribution made

by the company, in the design of ammunition, was its development of a special bullet alloy for small-bore rifle cartridges. The advantage of this alloy was that it dispensed with the coating of grease previously applied to bullets of this type, thereby eliminating the deterioration of the smokeless powder the cartridges were loaded with and the fouling of the rifle bores caused by grease residue. A major benefit arising from the use of greaseless cartridges was that accuracy was improved. Introduced in 1902[16], with little fanfare, the greaseless cartridge was to achieve a dominant share of the small bore ammunition market by 1904 (Color Plate 17), and its manufacture contributed substantial revenues to the company throughout its production life.

Beginning in 1905, the Winchester Repeating Arms Company began to

Top: Plate 205
Blueprint of Design Drawing Number 7362 dated April 2, 1901, illustrating a 16 gauge self-loading shotgun designed by William Mason. Winchester Arms Collection Archives, Cody Firearms Museum.

Bottom: Plate 206
Winchester Model 12 Shotgun. Olin Corporation photograph.

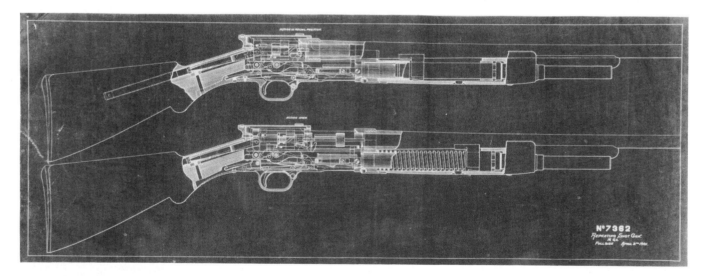

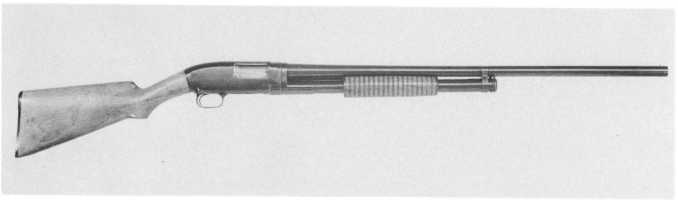

receive requests from sportsmen world-wide for a light-weight hammerless repeating shotgun[17]. By 1909, the demand had reached the level that T.G. Bennett requested that the work begin on such a design. Throughout that year and the two following, T.C. Johnson drew up the plans for an entirely new shotgun that met the requirements set by consumers[18]. The resulting design, put into production as the Model 1912 (Plates 206 and 207), surpassed all expectations and was to prove one of the most popular arms ever made by the company.

The company's interest in shotgun development reflected the change that had occurred within consumer markets over the previous decade. No longer were centerfire rifles the chief product of the firm; rather, rimfire rifles and shotguns had achieved supremacy. Fire-arms increasingly used for shooting sports and big game hunting was declin-ing as the population became ever increasingly urbanized. The demo-graphics of this change is best illus-trated by a comparison of firearms sales from 1904 (the first year for which fig-ures are available by model) to 1913[19].

In 1909, a number of rumors began to circulate that the Winchester company was about to begin the manufacture of automobiles. Fueled in part because of Henry Ford's visit to the factory and the fact that it was known that the company had entered negotiations with Hotchkiss & Cie of Paris to produce their cars under license, the reports peaked during the summer when **The Motor Age** announced that new facilities were being constructed at the New Haven plant solely for automobile production. Unfortunately, the Winchester-Hotchkiss negotiations failed, and the company declined to pursue the matter any further, thus ending any speculation that it would enter the burgeoning car market.

Plate 207

Illustration of an engraved Winchester Model 12 shotgun originally intended for publication in the **1914 Winchester Highly Embellished Arms Cata-logue***, which was never printed. Private Collection.*

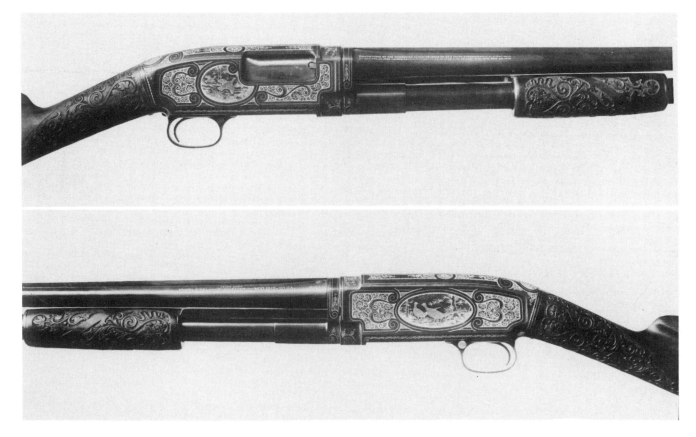

WINCHESTER

AFRICA

"MY rifles were an Army Springfield, 30-calibre, stocked and sighted to suit myself; a **Winchester** 405; and a double-barrelled 500-450 Holland, a beautiful weapon presented to me by English friends. Kermit's battery was of the same type, except that instead of a Springfield he had another **Winchester,** shooting the army ammunition, and his double barrel was a Rigby."

EX-PRESIDENT ROOSEVELT IN THE OCTOBER SCRIBNER

Winchester

Winchester Rifles and Winchester Ammunition are the invariable choice of experience-taught and discriminating big game hunters.

Sold everywhere. Ask for

THE RED **W** BRAND

TRUTH WILL OUT

■ The Reticent Endorser

While Theodore Roosevelt had used Winchester rifles from the 1880s onward, after he became President, he expressly forbade the company from using any of the comments he had made in his correspondence to the company in their advertising. Even after he left the presidency, Roosevelt continued to refuse the company to use his name in their promotional material. Thus, when an article he wrote for Colliers Magazine specifically mentioned that he and his son had used Winchester rifles while on safari, the company immediately jumped at the chance to use quotes from this public statement in their advertising.

RIMFIRE RIFLES

	1904	1913
Model 1885	1505	393
Model 1890	34219	27331
Model 1902	32979	28260
Model 1903	6944	7907
Model 1904	3321	13377
Thumb Trigger	10891	2036
Model 1906	-	54600
SUB TOTAL	89859	133904

CENTERFIRE RIFLES

Model 1873	15550	5922
Model 1885	282	772
Model 1886	3347	989
Model 1892	34622	47878
Model 1894	37881	54163
Model 1895	3290	3840
Lee Rifle	108	30
Model 1905	-	957
Model 1907	-	1883
Model 1910	-	1775
SUB TOTAL	124690	118209

SHOTGUNS

Model 1897	37373	30900
Model 1901	3	597
Model 1911	-	9018
Model 1912	-	27115
SUB TOTAL	37376	67630
TOTAL ALL ARMS	**251925**	**319743**

As the above table demonstrates, rimfire and shotgun sales increased by the close of 1913, to 149.02 percent and 180.95 percent of their 1904 levels. Centerfire rifle sales, however, decreased to 94.80 percent of their 1904 level over the same period. The cumulative totals for the period also indicated that firearms sales were increasing at an exceedingly low rate, approximately three percent per annum. Fortunately, though, the Winchester company's sales of ammunition were increasing at a rate of better than fifteen percent per annum, thereby offsetting any decline in arms sales[20].

The shift away from centerfire rifles in the American consumer market is even more pronounced when foreign sales are examined. For example, in 1910, G. Amsinck & Company purchased approximately 2,500 Model 1892 rifles and carbines together with approximately one million rounds of ammunition for export to Brazil[21]. This one company, thus, accounted for almost four percent of the Model 1892's production for that year[22].

In many respects, the least recognized accomplishment of the Winchester Repeating Arms Company during the 1901 to 1913 period is the expansion of its dealer network. Within the United States, the company had established preferential purchase agreements (due to their bulk purchases of arms and ammunition) with the following firms by 1912[23]:

The Arizona Copper Company
Babbitt Brothers
Baker & Hamilton
Basche-Sage Hardware Company
California Hardware Company
Coeur d'Alene Hardware Company
Dunham, Carrigan & Hayden Company
Dyas-Cline Company
Failing McCalman Company
Golcher Brothers
Harper & Reynolds Company
Samuel Hill Hardware Company
The William H. Hoegee Company
Holley-Mason Hardware Company
The H. T. Hudson Arms Company
Jensen-King-Byrd Company
Kimball Gun Store, Inc.
Kimball-Upson Company
E. H. Ladd
Lewald & Schlueter
The McCormick-Saeltzer Company
Marshall-Wells Hardware Company

Morse Hardware Company
Northern Commercial Company
Pacific Hardware & Steel Company
Phelps, Dodge & Company
John Philipson
Pinney & Robinson
The Shaw-Batcher Company
W. F. Sheard
F. Schilling & Son
A. & B. Schuster Company
Schwabacher Hardware Company
Seattle Hardware Company
Shreve & Barber Company
The Smith Sporting Goods Company
Albert Steinfeld & Company Ltd.
The Thomson-Diggs Company
Tufts-Lyon Arms Company
Union Hardware & Metal Company
Walther-Williams Hardware Company
Ware Brothers Company
Western Metal Supply Company
Whiton Hardware Company

Perhaps even more impressive was the expansion of the company's contacts overseas. By 1912, catalogs and sales brochures were regularly distributed to agents, dealers and jobbers in the following forty-eight countries, territories and colonies[24]:

Austria
Belgium
Denmark
England
France
Germany
Greece
Holland
Italy
Norway
Portugal
Russia
Sweden

Australia
Fiji
New Caledonia
New Guinea
New Zealand
Tasmania
Philippine Islands
Siam
Straits Settlements
Sumatra
British Guinea
British Honduras
British West Indies

Ceylon
China
India
Japan
Java
Korea
Argentina
Bolivia
Canal Zone
Trinidad
Chile
Costa Rica
Panama

East Africa
North Africa
South Africa
West Africa
Canada
Newfoundland
Arabia
Turkey
Peru
Mexico
Switzerland

While it must be noted that the company had only a single retail outlet in some of the above-listed areas, in others there could be as many as a dozen or more. Due to potential large volume sales, the Winchester company also maintained permanent sales agents in Buenes Aires (Argentina), Rio de Janeiro (Brazil), Shanghai (China), London (England), Tokyo (Japan), Mexico City (Mexico), and Singapore (Straits Settlements)[25].

The sales generated by these foreign retailers varied considerably. Some ordered less than $100 of goods per year, while others exceeded $100,000[26]. In addition, the company regularly processed wholesale and government orders placed by the following seven international trading houses having their headquarters or offices in New York[27]:

Hammacher, Delius & Company
M. Hartley Company
Market & Company
Edward Mauer

Melchior Armstrong & Dessau
Oliver Brothers
H. W. Peabody & Company

Cumulatively, therefore, foreign sales amounted to a significant proportion of the Winchester company's income by 1913, and very shortly to provide even more.

Plate 208

Interior view of the Winchester factory in 1912, showing Model 1894 receivers being drilled. Olin Corporation photograph.

Plate 209
Interior view of the Winchester factory in 1912, illustrating milling machines. Olin Corporation photograph.

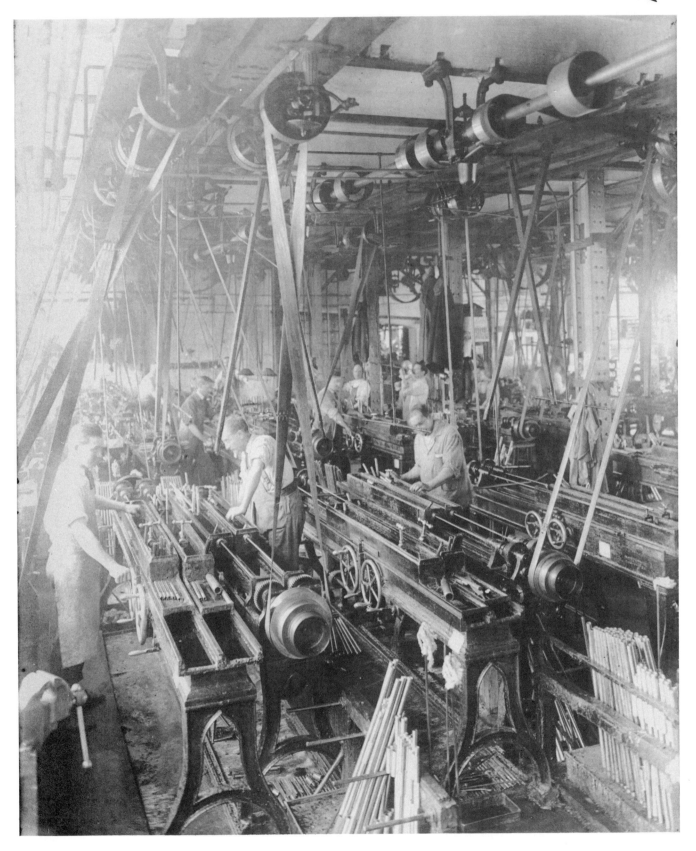

Plate 210
Interior view of the Winchester factory in 1912, illustrating the barrel boring shop. Olin Corporation photograph.

Plate 211

Lithograph of the Winchester Repeating Arms Company factory in 1914. Olin Corporation photograph.

Endnotes

1. The most dramatic change in American society, which had taken place by the early 1880s, was the closing of the frontier. This substantially reduced the call for arms in that area and made both Colt, as well as, Winchester more dependent on sales generated on the East Coast where shotguns, small bore rifles and pocket revolvers were popular.

2. For a detailed discussion of Mason's earliest attempts to design a gas-operated rifle, see Ned Schwing, **Winchester Slide-Action Rifles, Volume I: Model 1890 & Model 1906** (Krause Publications; Iola, WI: 1992), pages 192-194.

3. A 12 gauge Mason toggle link self-loading shotgun is illustrated in Drawing Number 7259 dated Aug. 16, 1900, preserved in the Winchester Arms Collection Archives, Cody Firearms Museum. For centerfire rifle versions of this design, see Drawing Numbers 6977 (Aug. 15, 1899), 7073 (Oct. 23, 1899), etc., loc. cit. Samples for these designs, as well as those discussed below, are preserved in the Winchester Arms Collection.

4. For an illustration of the short case .44 caliber cartridge, see Plate 189.

5. The threat of Borchardt pursuing action against the Winchester Repeating Arms Company is mentioned in a letter dated Aug. 15, 1900, from Seymour & Earle of New Haven, to the Browning Brothers Company. Miscellaneous Correspondence Relating to the Browning Brothers. Winchester Arms Collection Archives, Cody Firearms Museum.

6. William Mason, United States Patent Number 685216, issued Oct. 22, 1901. Winchester Arms Collection Archives, Cody Firearms Museum.

7. The date of William Mason's retirement is variously recorded as having occurred in June or September 1907, in various Winchester company documents.

8. Drawing Number 7256, which can be positively dated to August 1900, illustrates an early design for Johnson's balanced bolt system in .22 caliber. Varying versions of this drawing (as amended up to mid-1901) exist in the collection of Ned Schwing and the Winchester Arms Collection Archives, Cody Firearms Museum.

9. Preparation of the final design drawings for use in the production of tooling and fixtures began in April 1902.

10. A virtually complete record of the Winchester Repeating Arms Company's letters and brochures circulated to salesmen from 1898 to 1905 is preserved in H.S. Leonard's Correspondence File Number 1, Winchester Arms Collection Archives, Cody Firearms Museum.

11. Preliminary design drawings for this series of rifles are preserved in the Winchester Arms Collection Archives, Cody Firearms Museum.

12. Alden Hatch, **Remington Arms In American History** (Remington Arms Co.; Ilion, NY: 1972), pages 199-201 and 342.

13. The earliest design drawing for what was to become the Model 1911 is Number 8490 dated March 27, 1903. Winchester Arms Collection Archives, Cody Firearms Museum.

14. For example, see the copies of Design Drawing 9543 dated Dec. 17, 1904 and Jan. 24, 1905. Winchester Arms Collection Archives, Cody Firearms Museum.

15. A large number of firearms' design drawings dating from 1901 to 1910, are preserved in the Winchester Arms Collection Archives, Cody Firearms Museum. The numbering sequence for drawings prepared during this period ranges from 7300 to approximately 13000.

16. Memorandum from George R. Watrous to Edwin Pugsley dated Dec. 1, 1947. Pugsley Miscellaneous File, Winchester Arms Collection Archives, Cody Firearms Museum.

17. Johnson, Winchester History, op. cit., page 26.

18. Ibid.

19. These figures are extracted from George R. Watrous' **Sales of Winchester Arms from 1904-1945**, typescript. Winchester Arms Collection Archives, Cody Firearms Museum.

20. Ibid.

21. Summary of Sales to G. Amsinck & Company (1910). Export File, World War I, Winchester Arms Collection Archives, Cody Firearms Museum.

22. This percentage is based upon a comparison of the amounts listed in Note 21 above and Watrous, op. cit.

23. List of firms receiving preferential treatment, dated May 16, 1912. Private Collection.

24. List of Foreign Countries Being Supplied with Catalogues and Sales Literature dated March 1, 1912. Overseas Exports Miscellaneous Correspondence File, Winchester Arms Collection Archives, Cody Firearms Museum.

25. Ibid.

26. Letter from H.F. Brewer to W. Sherer, Jr., dated May 18, 1910. Foreign Trade and Discounts File, Winchester Arms Collection Archives, Cody Firearms Museum.

27. List of New York Export Houses dated Jan. 31, 1908. Foreign Trade, Commissions and Discounts File, Winchester Arms Collection Archives, Cody Firearms Museum.

CHAPTER 5

WORLD WAR I: 1914-1919

On June 28, 1914, the assassination of Archduke Francis Ferdinand of Austria-Hungary and his wife at Sarajevo in Bosnia set in motion a series of political events which were to shatter peace in Europe.

Convinced that Serbia was responsible for the outrage, the Austo-Hungarian Empire demanded concessions from that country. Although Serbia tried to mollify Austria and agreed to many of the terms, it refused to comply with them fully. Consequently, on July 28, Austria declared war on Serbia. This war might have remained localized had not Serbia had a political alliance with Russia. Despite attempts by Kaiser Wilhelm II of Germany to dissuade the Russians from assisting Serbia, Czar Nicholas II mobilized his armies on July 30. Germany then was bound by its agreements with Austria to provide military assistance if that country was in peril of attack. In compliance with those treaties, Germany declared war on Russia on Aug. 1. When France indicated it would honor defense agreements with Russia, Germany declared war on it two days later. The domino effect widening the war continued when Germany invaded France through Belgium, whose neutrality was guaranteed by Great Britain under a treaty

> ### ■ The War to End All Wars
> Sensing that the war that had been declared that day against Germany and the Austro-Hungarian Empire was not going to be over quickly, the British Foreign Secretary, Edward, Viscount Grey of Fallodan, commented to his aide that evening that "the lights are going out all over Europe, we shall not see them lit again in our lifetime."

signed in 1831. Thus, on Aug. 4, Great Britain was drawn into the war.

The speed with which these events occurred caught virtually all the combatants off guard. While the major powers had built up considerable reserves of war material, it was realized that these could be expended rather rapidly if the war continued much beyond the autumn 1914. As a result, contingency plans were made immediately to ensure that war supplies could be secured. When the outbreak of war seemed imminent, the British government contracted with the Winchester Repeating Arms Company for 60,000,000 rounds of .303 ammunition. The receipt of this order by the Winchester company on Aug. 4, the day Britain declared war on Germany, made it the first contract the firm was to receive as a result of the European conflict[1].

Though many did not expect the war to continue for any protracted period, by the conclusion of the First Battle of the Marne (Sept. 6-9), it had become evident that there was not going to be any speedy end to it. This assessment became even more painfully clear after the First Battle of Ypres, which lasted from mid-October through mid-November. The severe losses of men and material during that engagement demonstrated what the costs of the war were likely to be. In consequence of these two actions, both Britain and France began contracting for supplies in the United States.

The second war contract received by the Winchester company was placed by the Republic of France. On Sept. 22, an order was placed for 15,000 Model 1894 carbines and 1,500,000 rounds of .30WCF ammunition[2]. The odd nature of this order has given rise to speculation as to its ultimate destination. One researcher suggested, in 1948, that the rifles were intended for use in the French Colonies so that standard Lebel rifles stored there could be released for use in Europe[3]. A letter from the contracting agent the Remington-UMC Company, however, makes it clear that they were to be used in arming the French merchant marine[4]. Deliveries under this contract began on Oct. 13,

1914 and were completed by April 6, 1915, at a total cost of $347,300[5].

In November 1914, the British government, through the agency of the J.P. Morgan & Company in New York, approached both the Remington and Winchester companies to determine whether or not both or either would be interested in manufacturing the new .303 Pattern 1914 service rifle. Both agreed, and on Nov. 24, the Winchester company entered into an agreement to produce 200,000 Pattern 1914 rifles[6]. Under the provisions of the contract, the purchase price was set at $32.50 per rifle plus an additional 15¢ per arm to cover alterations in design[7].

Immediately after the contract was signed, the company's designers evaluated the rifle and began work on modifying its construction. The modified version was accepted for production by the British War Department on Jan. 7, 1915, and an initial advance against the contract of $1,625,000 was paid to the Winchester company on Jan. 27[8]. Using the modified sample and blueprints supplied by the Royal Small Arms Factory at Enfield, work then began on the design and construction of the machinery needed to produce the rifle. Due to a series of changes made in the rifle's design at the request of the British government, actual pro-

Plate 212

Winchester .303 caliber Pattern 14 British Service rifle. Olin Corporation photograph.

duction was delayed until February 1916[9]. Deliveries under this contract continued from Feb. 8 until Oct. 24, when a total of 50,423 had been shipped[10]. At that point, a contract negotiated between J.P. Morgan & Company and Winchester, on March 16, 1915, went into effect, and further deliveries were charged at a rate of $30.15 per rifle[11]. A total of 185,085 Pattern 14s(Plate 212) were delivered between Nov. 4, 1916 and July 11, 1917, under the second agreement[12]. The gross value of these two orders was $7,226,623.70[13].

While the British and French orders were essentially for supplementary supplies, those received from Russia in late 1914 were not. A series of disastrous battles with the Germans along the eastern front had severely depleted Russia's supply of service weapons. Consequently, on Nov. 13, it ordered 100,000 Model 1895 rifle muskets in 7.62mm caliber at a cost of $27.00 per rifle[14]. Deliveries on this contract were to begin by early January 1915.

As the war in Europe continued, the pace of orders to the Winchester company for small arms, ammunition and other supplies such as cannon shells increased. On Feb. 4, 1915, the British government ordered 20 million rounds of .303 caliber ammunition and a further 23 million rounds on the 10th of the same month[15]. On July 2, the French government ordered two million rounds of .32ACP ammunition[16]. Russia, on the 10th of the same month,

Plate 213

Winchester .351 caliber Model 1907 self-loading rifle adapted for use in airplanes by the addition of a spent cartridge casing collector and a larger operating rod terminal. Olin Corporation photograph.

■ The Model 1895 In Action

Many of the Winchester Model 1895 rifle muskets supplied to the Czar between 1915 and 1917 later were used by Vladimir Lenin's troops against the British Expeditionary Force sent to North Russia in 1919. One British officer attached with that force later recalled that "at times the campaigns in North Russia resembled actions that might have occurred in the American West. The Bolsheviks would attack our lines charging wildly on horseback firing their lever action Winchester rifles, just like the Indians had done." (Lt. Col. L.M. Collins)

ordered 200 million rounds of 7.62mm ammunition at a cost of $36.50 per thousand rounds[17]. Their order for Model 1895 rifle muskets was expanded on Aug. 27 to include an additional 200,000 arms[18].

The most unusual arms orders to be processed at this time were for Model 1907 self-loading rifles. Both Britain and France purchased a considerable number of these weapons beginning in 1915. A total of 120 were shipped to England and 3,300 went to France, along with 2,700,000 rounds of .351 caliber ammunition[19]. Though the Model 1907s sent to England were destined for use by the Royal Flying Corps (Plate 213), only a limited number from the French purchase were destined for aerial use. The balance were to be used in trench warfare, and a substantial number were altered so that they were capable of "volley fire" or full automatic operation[20]. In addition to the Model 1907s, France evidently had privately purchased a supply of .401 caliber Model 1901 self-loading rifles as orders for spare magazines and 25,000 rounds of ammunition were received by the Winchester company in September and October 1915[21].

In addition to the contracts it accepted, the Winchester company received over one hundred requests to produce arms and ammunition, which it declined. Among these were the following orders[22]:

Portugal - 6.5mm Model 1904 Rifles (Nov. 23, 1914)

Romania - 6.5mm ammunition (Dec. 23, 1914)

France - 8mm Lebel ammunition (Jan. 18, 1915)

Greece - 7.65mm ammunition (March 6, 1915)

Italy - 10.35mm Vetterli ammunition (April 16, 1915)

Romania - 6.5mm Model 1893 Rifles (July 10, 1916)

While some of these contracts were not picked up due to the costs associated with them, others arrived when the Winchester works were fully committed to other projects.

Despite the volume to foreign war orders, the Winchester company maintained all its sporting production line intact as the following sales figures for 1914 to 1916 demonstrate[23]:

	1914	1915	1916
RIMFIRE RIFLES			
Model 1885	727	1539	1460
Model 1890	24083	20271	19207
Model 1902	21406	19628	15745
Model 1903	5044	2787	2585
Model 1904	7054	10368	6936
Model 1906	40812	31146	29925
CENTERFIRE RIFLES			
Model 1873	2479	1932	5606
Model 1885	504	617	255
Model 1886	891	566	501
Model 1892	28768	33246	25420
Model 1894	82374	86488	20741
Model 1895	5678	4786*	2786*
Lee Rifle	535	20	13
Model 1905	551	451	349
Model 1907	1265	1400**	3943**
Model 1910	824	922	555
SHOTGUNS			
Model 1897	17519	14941	16865
Model 1901	438	307	261
Model 1911	3428	3179	2107
Model 1912	47347	29750	26896
TOTAL ARMS PER YEAR	291727	264344	182156

* Does not include the 104,404 Model 1895s shipped to Russia in 1915, or the 189,414 shipped in 1916.

** Includes Model 1907s shipped to Great Britain and France in 1915 and 1916.

Throughout this period, the company also maintained a rigorous advertising policy designed to increase the sales of its more popular models. Particular attention was paid to the promotion of the Model 1912 and its adaptability to all different kinds of the shooting sports. Rimfire rifles were also actively advertised due to the increase in interest in target shooting that had been brought about both by the Boy Scout movement in the United States and reports of the European war[24]. Indeed, it was in 1915 that the first mention was made of possibly creating a Winchester-sponsored shooting organization[25]. Some two years later, this suggestion was to result in the establishment of the Winchester Junior Rifle Corps.

Foreign war orders also did not disrupt the development of new sporting arms designs. On the contrary, the company's work on the Pattern 1914 service rifle for Great Britain actually prompted the speeding up of work on one design.

In the late summer of 1914, T.C. Johnson had developed a hybrid Mauser-type bolt-action sporting rifle chambered for the .30-06 cartridge. After the company had expressed interest in producing rifles for Great Britain, the Model A (Plates 214-216), as it had been designated, was given serious consideration as an alternative rifle should the Pattern 14 prove to be difficult to manufacture[26]. When that did not turn out to be the case, the Model A continued to be developed as a poten-

Top: Plate 214

Winchester Model A bolt-action military rifle in .30-06 caliber made in 1914 or early 1915. Winchester Arms Collection (Inv. No. W905), Cody Firearms Museum.

Bottom: Plate 215

Left-hand view of the Model A military rifle illustrated in Plate 214.

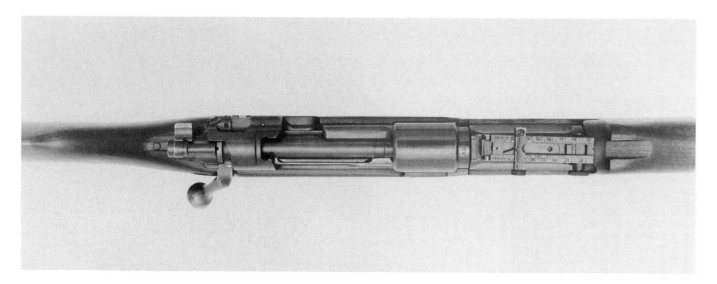

tial new sporting rifle. In 1915, the number of changes in the design were sufficient to warrant a change in model designation to Model B (Plate 217)[27].

The major identifying characteristics of both rifles were the use of takedown barrel and fore end assemblies, and barrels which had multiple stepped-down diameters instead of tapering. Johnson continued to modify the design throughout 1915 and 1916, and it was successively known as the Model C (Plate 218) then Model D[28]. The principal changes in the design were related to the construction of the extractor and sear. In November 1916, ten Model D rifles in 7.62mm were taken to Russia for trial testing by the Russian Artillery Commission[29]. Examples were also made for testing by the British govern-

ment in .303 caliber, 6.5mm caliber for Portugal and 7mm for Spain and several other countries[30]. A number of sample Model D rifles were made in .30-06 caliber for review by the United States Army Board of Ordnance. Throughout the development program, however, the company's primary aim was the design of a sporting arm capable of competing with centerfire bolt-action rifles manufactured by its competitors.

The other major task assigned to the Design Department during this period was the development of a low-cost double barrel shotgun[31]. In addition, several variations of the Model 1885 were made for foreign governments interested in purchasing arms for marksmanship training[32].

Top: Plate 216

Receiver top detail of the Model A military rifle illustrated in Plate 214.

Bottom: Plate 217

Winchester Model B bolt-action military rifle made in 1915. Winchester Arms Collection (Inv. No. W907), Cody Firearms Museum.

There is also evidence strongly suggesting that the Winchester company was involved in the development of a light machine gun in 7.65mm caliber for the Argentine Navy[33]. The company's contacts with the Argentine Navy were long-standing, and as recently as 1914, it had fulfilled a contract for five million rounds of ammunition for it[34]. The

Top: Plate 218

Winchester Model C bolt-action sporting rifle (top) and military rifle (bottom), both in .30-06 caliber made in late 1916. Winchester Arms Collection (Inv. Nos. W908 and W909), Cody Firearms Museum.

Bottom: Plate 219

Sample of Frank F. Burton's .345 selective fire aerial use and infantry assault rifle made in 1917. Winchester Arms Collection (Inv. No. W967), Cody Firearms Museum. Olin Corporation photograph.

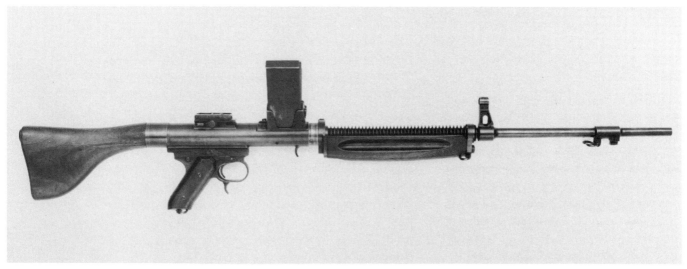

drawings that survive for this automatic weapon indicate that it was to have a combination recoiling barrel and piston operating mechanism of a type which had never been used before. The feed mechanism, too, was of novel design in that it could accommodate both clips and belts. That samples of this design were made and tested cannot be disputed, since one drawing has pencilled notations in Spanish listing changes to be made based upon failures noted during tests[35].

The ultimate fate of this arm was probably determined by the entry of the United States into World War I and the company's decision then to terminate any new foreign contracts, as the drawing mentioned above is dated Feb. 1(?), 1917. The designer of this machine gun is identified on another of the drawings as Grant Hammond[36]. Hammond's association with the Winchester company was somewhat informal since he never became an employee of the firm. Rather, he would submit designs to the company for their consideration, and if interest was expressed, would work in the Experimental Department on their development. Between 1914 and 1925, he offered the company approximately six designs for a wide variety of arms ranging from the machine gun noted here to self-loading shotguns and rifles[37]. He also used the Experimental Department to build the samples for his .45 caliber semiautomatic pistol for which he is best known[38].

The most interesting arm to be developed "early in the war"[39] was Frank Burton's solid bolt self-loading rifle[40]. Designed for use in airplanes or by switching the barrel assembly for ground troops (Plate 219), Burton's rifle had a fixed firing pin on the face of the bolt and a selective fire mechanism allowing it to be used either as single-shot rifle or a fully automatic weapon.

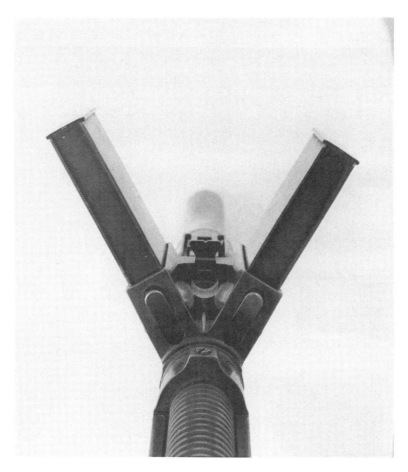

To accomplish this, a dual trigger system was employed. When the trigger located within the triggerguard was pulled, the arm functioned as a regular semiautomatic rifle firing from an open bolt. By depressing the secondary trigger located beneath the triggerguard bow, the rifle's sear was disengaged and the arm functioned as a fully automatic weapon. Several other features of the Burton rifle were unique for its time. In place of a single magazine, he used a tandem set of magazines (Plate 220) set up in such a way that the right magazine had to be empty before the left one began feeding the action. Burton also located the operating spring and bolt buffer mechanism within the buttstock. The cartridge adopted to this weapon also is of interest in that it was a high-velocity short-cased round of .345-inch diameter quite unlike anything ever considered for military use

Plate 220

Detail of the magazine housing employed in Burton's .345 caliber selective fire rifle illustrated in Plate 219.

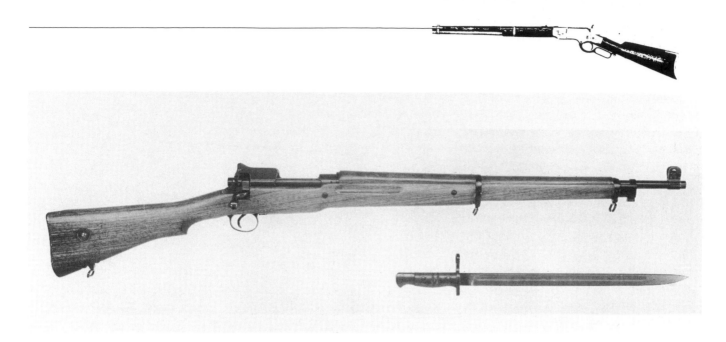

up to then. In its configuration, selective fire capability and chambering, the Burton rifle was some thirty years ahead of its time, and it must be accorded the distinction of being the first true assault rifle ever to be made. Though its characteristics would be recognized much later as being ideal for an infantry weapon, they were considered too radical when the first samples were built, and the rifle was never adopted for production.

By April 6, 1917, the Winchester Repeating Arms Company had manufactured an immense amount of arms and ammunition for the Allied Powers.

Under the seven major contracts, a total of 535,517 rifles, 273,483,500 rounds of ammunition and 1,965,000 British 18 Pounder shell casings plus 7,604,600 primers for the same size shell cases[41]. When these figures are combined with the company's civilian production during the same period (discussed earlier), the true magnitude of the firm's capabilities and size is evident.

In early 1917, the deteriorating relationship between the United States and Germany prompted the Winchester company to approach the U.S. Army Board of Ordnance to discuss its needs

Top: Plate 221

Winchester Model 1917 U.S. rifle in .30-06 caliber. Olin Corporation photograph.

Bottom: Plate 222

Winchester Model 1918 Browning automatic rifle in .30-06 caliber. Olin Corporation photograph.

should war break out. As a result of this meeting, a series of thirteen Model D rifles in .30-06 caliber were submitted to the Ordnance Department for examination and trial[42]. Though these rifles were well accepted and passed all the tests they were submitted to, the Ordnance Department expressed concerns regarding the speed with which they could be manufactured should the political situation worsen quickly, since the company would have to tool up for their production. The declaration of war by the United States on April 23, 1917, made this issue critical, and the company responded by submitting a modified Pattern 14 rifle in .30-06 caliber to the Ordnance Department at a meeting held on April 30 in New York[43].

Recognizing that this rifle could be quickly made not only by Winchester, but also the Remington company, the government approved its design and two additional samples were sent to the Springfield Armory on May 7[44]. After rigorous tests there, the modified Pattern 14 rifle was approved for government service as the U.S. Model 1917 Enfield rifle (Plate 221).

Upon its adoption, the Winchester company received an order for 225,000 and immediately set about altering the Pattern 14 machinery for production of the new model[45]. Deliveries under this first contract began in July 1917. The speed with which the company completed retooling and began production was to be later credited as one of the significant factors in allowing U.S. troops to be speedily sent to Europe since there were no delays in training recruits in the use of the new rifle arising out of postponed or late rifle deliveries[46].

Above: Plate 223

Skeletonized Colt Model 1911 semiautomatic pistol given by the Colt's Patent Fire Arms Manufacturing Company to the Winchester Repeating Arms Company when the latter received a Model 1911 production contract in 1918. Winchester Arms Collection, Cody Firearms Museum. Olin Corporation photograph.

Below: Plate 224

Sample of Edwin Pugsley's .50 caliber bolt-action antitank rifle made in late 1918. Olin Corporation photograph.

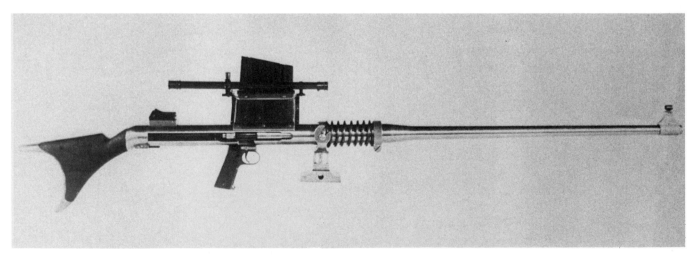

Over the next seventeen months, the volume of war orders steadily increased until the cessation of hostilities on Nov. 11, 1918. At that time, all outstanding contracts were reviewed by the government, and work on those considered necessary to national defense was continued and all others were suspended. In all, the Winchester Repeating Arms Company produced the following under a total of 292 U.S. government contracts between May 1, 1917 and June 1, 1919[47](below):

In addition to the above, the Winchester company carried out experimental work on the .50 Browning machine gun cartridge and developed a bolt-action .50 caliber anti-tank rifle for the government[48]. The anti-tank rifle (Plate 224), designed in 1918 by Edwin Pugsley (Plate 225), is of note more for its outlandish appearance than its mechanics. The company also fulfilled several foreign military orders while working on the U.S. government con-

U.S. Model 1917 Rifles	545,566
U.S. Model 1917 Sniper Rifles	288
Browning Automatic Rifles (Plate 222)	47,129
Colt Model 1911 Pistols (Plate 223)	50
Winchester Model 1885 single-shot Rifles	8,289
Winchester Model 1903 Self-Loading Rifles	601
Winchester Model 1890 Rifles	365
Winchester Model 1894 Rifles	1,800
Winchester Model 1897 Shotguns	1,473
Winchester Model 1897 Riot Shotguns	17,820
Winchester Model 1911 Shotguns	100
Winchester Model 1912 Shotguns	177
Winchester Model 1912 Riot Shotguns	600
Telescopic Sights	3,800
Other Sights	8,200
.30-06 Cartridges	485,040,000
.30-06 Blank Cartridges	11,603,660
.30-06 Tracer Cartridges	1,167,300
.30-06 Special Ball Cartridges	455
.30-06 Primed Cases	6,551,000
.30-06 Bullets	50,000
.45ACP Cartridges	58,000,000
Other Ammunition (12,500,000 12 gauge, 5,000,000 .22 caliber 1,200,000 other calibers)	18,700,000
Stokes 3" Mortar Shells	3,059,900
Cannon Shell Cases	448,500
Cannon Shell Primers	310,200,000

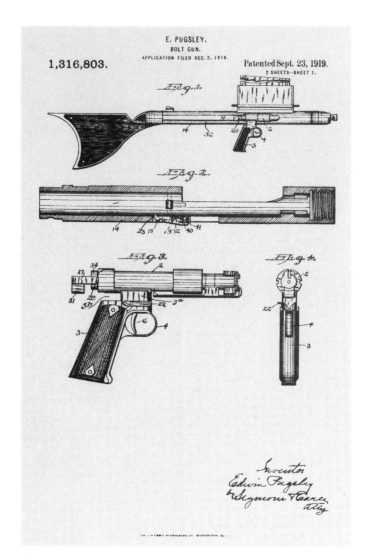

Plate 225

*S*heet 1 of the specification drawings enrolled with Edwin Pugsley's U.S. Patent Number 1316803 issued Sept. 23, 1919. In this design, the bolt and pistol grip are made in one piece. To operate the weapon (see Plate 224), the grip is rotated counter-clockwise 90° and then drawn rearward to extract a fired cartridge casing. Reversing the motion chambers a new round, and after the grip is lowered, allows the piece to be fired. Winchester Arms Collection Archives, Cody Firearms Museum.

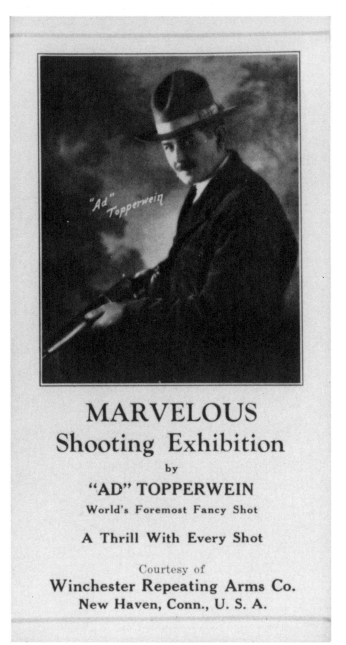

Plate 226

*B*rochure publicizing Adolph Topperwein exhibition shooting circulated by the Winchester company in 1917. Winchester Arms Collection Archives, Cody Firearms Museum.

tracts. In 1918, it delivered 350 Model 1907 self-loading rifles to France along with 1,200,000 rounds of .351 ammunition and 400,000 rounds of .401 caliber ammunition[49]. The same year, Great Britain purchased 550 Model 1903 self-loading rifles and an undisclosed amount of ammunition for use by its Territorial Army[50].

Throughout the war, the company's most efficient department was the cartridge works managed by George R. Watrous. It consistently exceeded production quotas and set two records which were not to be equalled until World War II.

On March 30, 1917, it produced a total of 2,201,126 centerfire cartridges (1,826,400 in 7.62mm Russian and 374,726 in other calibers[51]). That record was subsequently passed on Dec. 18, 1917, when 2,204,919 rounds of centerfire ammunition were made

(1,827,917 in .30-06 caliber and 377,002 in other sizes[52]).

The total value of all war work completed by the Winchester Repeating Arms Company between 1914 and 1919 amounted to $97,576,882 ($59,973,882 from the United States and $37,603,000 from France, Great Britain and Russia[53]).

As it had while working on the British and Russian military contracts, the Winchester company continued to produce sporting arms and ammunition after the United States entered the war. By February 1918, however, the press for war work had reduced the amount of equipment used for civilian arms to a level of thirty percent of that used in April 1917[54]. The dual production system and increasing allocation of machinery to government contracts resulted in equipment scheduling problems as the manufacture of sporting

Left: Plate 227

*P*roof print of an advertisement published in 1917, promoting the Winchester Junior Rifle Corps. Private Collection.

Right: Plate 228

*P*roof print of an advertisement published in 1917, promoting the Winchester Model 1904 and 1906 .22 caliber rifles. Private Collection.

arms had to be carried out on a diminishing number of machines. To accomplish this, multiple models were produced on the same machines with tooling and fixtures changed when one particular model was about to commence on another[55]. The irregularity of steel deliveries not allocated for government use played havoc with this system, and at times the sporting arms lines were idled due to the lack of raw materials before planned fixture changes were set to take place[56].

Despite these problems, Winchester still managed to produce 191,340 rimfire rifles, 114,111 centerfire rifles and 98,938 shotguns during 1917 and 1918[57].

Winchester's decision to maintain the production of civilian arms had one unforeseen side effect. In mid-1918, the War Trade Board placed an embargo on the company's exports of sporting arms and ammunition in response to complaints that work on civilian products was interfering with military production[58]. The company lodged a formal protest, and after the matter was reviewed, the board found the complaint to be without basis. Immediately thereafter, Winchester requested that the government inspector who was responsible for the embargo be transferred to another post[59].

One of the major problems the company encountered in late 1917 was the restriction of the working week to fifty-five hours by the federal government[60]. Though designed to conserve fuel during the forthcoming winter months, the law would have reduced the company's production levels by nearly fifty percent since it was running double shifts at all times. The firm's management consequently petitioned Washington for an exemption from the act. Supported by the War Department, Winchester, along with all other manufacturers of war material, were

Left: Plate 229

Proof print of an advertisement published in 1917, promoting the Winchester Model 1892, 1894, 1895 and 1910 centerfire rifles. Private Collection.

Right: Plate 230

Brochure published in 1917, by the Winchester company to announce the Model 1906 "Expert" .22 caliber rifle. Private Collection.

Plate 231

Sample .22 caliber Page-Sorrow single-shot rifle made in 1917. Winchester Arms Collection (Inv. No. W933), Cody Firearms Museum.

immediately granted permission to continue their operations as before[61].

A more serious threat to the maintenance of production were strikes and sabotage. Though strikes had been a problem in some war plants prior to the United States' entry into the war[62], the posting of the penalties in work areas, which strikers would incur if government contracts were interrupted, limited protests to the clandestine circulation of political and radical labor tracts. This was tolerated to a limited degree by the Winchester company's officers so long as it did not adversely affect morale[63]. To prevent sabotage, the company maintained extremely tight security and a substantial guard force[64]. As a result, there were no accidents or other events at the plant which could be attributed to enemy action.

The growth of the Winchester company during World War I is perhaps best illustrated by the fact that its average monthly expenses exceeded what its total annual sales had been not that many years before. For example, in August 1917, the estimated and actual operating costs were as follows[65](right):

Payments	Estimated	Actual
Fuel Oil	$9,000.00	$6,870.43
Gun Lumber	13,000.00	24.34
Copper	250,000.00	207,210.23
Spelter		
Steel	150,000.00	23,956.71
Coal	40,000.00	10,565.91
Lead	0.00	97,647.93
Miscellaneous Debits	50,000.00	64,798.40
Miscellaneous Material	150,000.00	164,987.57
P.S.S. Components	70,000.00	22,419.79
Freight	9,000.00	10,519.00
Missionaries & Shooters	17,000.00	17,485.53
Crucibles	10,400.00	6,745.58
Purchased Service	86,000.00	36,860.21
Explosives	160,000.00	123,550.00
Other Lumber	16,000.00	19,452.99
Packing Cases Purchased	15,000.00	6,349.89
Insurance & Taxes	297,000.00	110,225.53
Interest	422,200.00	397,950.00
Payrolls	1,200,000.00	1,042,868.98
New Machinery & Equipment	0.00	11,183.74
	2,964,600.00	2,381,674.22

One of the expenses listed above, "Missionaries & Shooter," demonstrates the firm's commitment to maintaining and increasing its civilian sales. Substantial amounts of money were spent throughout the war on the distribution of advertising by its staff of nearly 100 salesmen operating nationwide, and in supplying the five to seven exhibition shooters (Plate 226) who demonstrated the company's products[66].

A weekly newsletter was also circulated across the country, and sales contests were continually held. As might be expected, due to the changed demographics of the nation, the largest volume of sales were always generated from rural areas. However, when the Winchester Junior Rifle Corps plan was introduced in mid-1917 (Plate 227)[67], ever-increasing sales were stimulated in urban centers.

In July 1917, Winchester began a major sales campaign with the distribution of a pamphlet titled "Important Development in Arms and Ammunition Business."[68] Among the sales points stressed in it were the increase in hunting licenses being issued, the increased popularity of trapshooting and the growth of marksmanship courses, all of which would stimulate sales[69]. It also stated that[70](right):

The development in the international situation that has forced America into war has made every man realize the need of knowing how to handle firearms intelligently.

American preparedness may avert further international complications that would otherwise arise, and the knowledge by every householder of how to use firearms is the first step in preparedness.

Salesmen were also provided with a series of promotional kits to be given to their prime customers. Included in these were[71]:

- Leader Shot Shell Cutouts
- Repeater Shot Shell Cutouts
- New Rival Shot Shell Cutouts
- Nublack Shot Shell Cutouts
- Nublack Shot Shell folders
- Hunter and Dog Cutouts
- Deer Cutouts
- Bird Cutouts
- Goat Cutouts
- Musket Hangers
- Trapshooting Booklets
- Musket Folders
- Rifle Shotgun Catalogues
- Model 1912 Shotgun Folders
- Loaded Shotgun Shell Booklets
- Game Law Booklets
- Air Rifle Shot Cards
- Trapshooter's Rules
- Model 1912 20 Gauge Cutout (man, dog, bird)
- Winchester Junior Rifle Corps Hangers
- Winchester Junior Rifle Corps Medal Contest Hangers
- Ask Dad Booklets
- How to Handle Booklets
- Winchester Junior Rifle Corps Targets

■ Memories of a Junior Rifle Corps Member

"At our summer home on Braddock Heights near Frederick, Maryland, my father set up a post about 50 ft. from our front porch on which he mounted an iron shooting gallery target about 12 on. in diameter with a 3/4 in. hole in the center behind which was a bell-like piece of metal which rang loudly if the bullseye was hit. This rest became also a place for W.J.R.C. targets...When we had guests, the men would gather in their rocking chairs and bang away at the Iron target, with whoops of joy when the bell rang."

M.J. Urner

At the same time, the company launched a comprehensive advertising campaign in the popular press[72]. Full and half-page ads were placed in all national magazines starting in August (Plates 228 and 229). This program continued well into the autumn and was only terminated after Christmas.

One of the key selling points which the company stressed in 1917 and again in 1918, was the fact that Winchester sporting arms sold for less money than their production cost[73]. In reality, for the most part of 1917 and the first months of 1918, they did not, as the steel used in their manufacture had been purchased prior to the United States' entry into the war. However, when those stocks were exhausted, the company began to use new steel, which cost significantly more. Only then did production costs exceed sales prices. This development was of concern to the company, and by September 1918, sample rifles were being prepared with lower grades of finish to reduce manufacturing costs[74]. Certain categories of arms, particularly rimfire rifles, were subsequently made with lower quality finishes and the practice was continued through 1920, despite the public's poor reception of the altered models[75].

The development of new sporting models was also not neglected during 1917 and 1918. A revised version of the Model 1906 slide-action .22 caliber rifle was perfected and introduced on May 28, 1918, as the Model 1906 "Expert" (Plate 230)[76]. Work also continued on a low to intermediately priced double barrel shotgun and a single barrel shotgun[77].

The most important project, though, was the construction of a bolt-action detachable box magazine .22 caliber rifle. Intended, like the Model 1906 "Expert," to capitalize upon the general interest in marksmanship, the design and production of this rifle was a priority for Winchester. Evolving from the Page-Sorrow single-shot bolt-action rifle (Plate 231) developed in 1917[78], the new arm incorporated a refined lockwork and trigger mechanism designed by T.C. Johnson. As it became clear that the U.S. Army was committed to replacing both the Springfield and Winchester .22 caliber rifles then in use with another model, the company began a spirited campaign to promote their new rifle. Due to problems encountered by Johnson with the design of the magazine, the initial samples were of single-shot construction. By mid-April 1919, the magazine had been perfected, and a modified sample was taken to Washington by Captain Laudensack to be viewed by Colonel Townsend Whelen and Major LaGarde of the U.S. Army General Staff, General Phillips of the National Rifle Association and the editor of *Arms & The Man*.

Plate 232
Sample Winchester Model 52 target rifle made for exhibition at the Caldwell International Small Bore Rifle Match held in September 1919. Olin Corporation photograph.

■ Henry Ford

In 1908 or 1909, Henry Ford visited the Winchester factory in New Haven to study the gauging process used to ensure that all firearm components were absolutely interchangeable in an effort to design a similar system for use in the production of his Model T automobile. While there, he evidently purchased two rifles, a Model 1885 single-shot and 1903 self-loader. He also test fired a Model 1907 self-loading rifle as shown on the previous page, which was taken at the time. Sometime later he added another Winchester to his collection, a deluxe special order Model 1894 rifle which he was photographed firing at his Maine hunting camp in 1919.

The positive reaction elicited by the Johnson rifle is demonstrated by Henry Brewer's report written on April 24 to Johnson[79]:

"The gun received very favorable comment. There was not an essential feature of the gun which received adverse criticism. They all thought that the general style of the gun, the balance, the weight, the magazine, trigger pull, sight, etc., were exceedingly good. They were very much pleased with the accurate and the uniform way in which the gun handled the ammunition either as a single loader or a magazine loader. The pistol grip met with their universal approval. Each one, after feeling the gun, remarked that they liked the feel of the grip. They all expressed approval of the excellent trigger pull.

The following suggestions were made which were thought might possibly benefit the gun:-

Major LaGarde suggested that the barrel should be 2" or 4" shorter to make it nearer the length of the Springfield rifle for drill purposes. He admitted that the loss in velocity would mitigate against the long range out-of-door shooting which is now becoming popular and he suggested that we put it out in two lengths of barrel. Col. Whelen felt that the present length was satisfactory and that one length barrel would fill all the requirements. I recommend that we make no change in barrel length.

Both Major LaGarde and Col. Whelen felt that the stock should be about 1/2" longer. The Army has come to the conclusion that the Springfield rifle has too short a stock and they are seriously

Plate 233

Detail of the sample Model 52 target rifle illustrated in Plate 232.

considering increasing the length of the Springfield stock a half inch. They both admitted that the present length of stock is better for boys and that it might be better, if we are going to manufacture only one length of stock, to stick to the present length. I think we should stick to the present length which has the sanction of the Springfield Arsenal.

It was suggested that we should have a battle sight similar to the Springfield. This would be merely for military purposes. This could be added for a small expense but I think it should be extra and not on the regular rifle.

It was suggested that the stock should be made up with an oil finish instead of varnish because the oil finish is adopted on practically all military arms. I think the sporting trade would prefer the varnish and if we adopted the oil finish, it might be well to feature it in our advertising as being the military finish, thus forestalling any criticism from the sporting fraternities.

It was suggested that the forearm should run the full length of the barrel, simply because the military men are accustomed to this length forearm. It was admitted that it would not improve the shooting qualities of the gun. This suggestion came from LaGarde and was not endorsed by Whelan. I would suggest that we make no change.

Col. Whelen suggested that the trigger should be roughened, that in handling greased cartridges the fingers become greasy and are liable to slip on the trigger. I would recommend that we make no change but adopt the roughened trigger later if occasion demands.

On none of these suggestions were they at all insistent. They were merely things which occurred to them as being possible improvements. They stated frankly that the gun was so nearly perfect that they had little to suggest."

Subsequently, Whelen independently wrote Thomas A. Davis and Henry Brewer to express his opinions concerning the Winchester rifle[80].

Plate 234

P*hotograph of Lt. Col. Townsend Whelen of the U.S. Army General Staff, reproduced on page 1 of the January 1923 issue of the **Winchester Junior Rifle Corps News**, Volume 7, Number 1. Winchester Arms Collection Archives, Cody Firearms Museum.*

April 28, 1919.

Thomas A. Davis, Esq.
72 Columbia Heights.
Brooklyn, N.Y.

My dear Davis:

I am in receipt of our letter of the 26th instant relative to probable demand for the Winchester .22 caliber Bolt Action repeating rifle. In the regular army we have at present under consideration the doing away of the .22 caliber Springfield rifle, and substituting therefore .30 caliber reduced loads for gallery practice. This would really act in favor of the sale of your rifle instead of against it, because it will probably mean a discontinuance of the manufacture of the .22 caliber Springfield rifle.

While some of the National Guard and School organizations may wish to use our .30 caliber reduced loads for gallery practice, I believe that the bulk of such organization will desire to continue to use .22 caliber ammunition owning to their using 25 yard indoor galleries for practice, which are hardly adapted to the .30 caliber reduced load. I would be very much in favor of the abandonment of the .22 caliber Springfield, and of the Government purchase of such numbers of Winchester .22 caliber bolt-action rifles as are needed for these organizations.

Your rifle is so efficient and so suitable for the purpose that in my opinion it is bound to become at once the standard rifle for gallery practice in the National Guard, Schools, Colleges, and Civilian Rifle Clubs. Whether the Government takes up the purchase of these rifles for this purpose or not, you are bound to sell so many direct that I believe that it will certainly pay to place this rifle on the market. You have a most excellent chance now to advertise it at the National Matches. You know that small bore matches are to be included there this year. Put 50 rifles on the grounds for use, and have another 100 there for sale. The efficiency of these rifles will thus be spread broadcast throughout all Government, State, School, and College teams, and among the civilian riflemen attending. Rifles purchased will be carried to all parts of the country to halp [sic] with the advertising, and by the time that November comes around and small bore work has started, your rifle should be thoroughly known, and a large demand for it created. This will allow you until November to get up your production in quantity.

It seems to me that you should be able to count on selling at least 10,000 of these rifles the first year, and if we succeed in getting the rifle designated as a regular article of supply by the Ordnance Department, then this should add another 10,000 to the number the first year. I think it would be a grave misfortune if you did not put this rifle out. It is just what we have been wanting for many years. I would like to have you enter my order for one of the first you turn out.

Yours very truly,

Townsend Whelen.
Lt.Colonel, General Staff.

Plate 235

*D*esign drawing of the proposed Winchester Model G20P .22 caliber single-shot target pistol. R.C. Romanella Collection. Geneva, Switzerland.

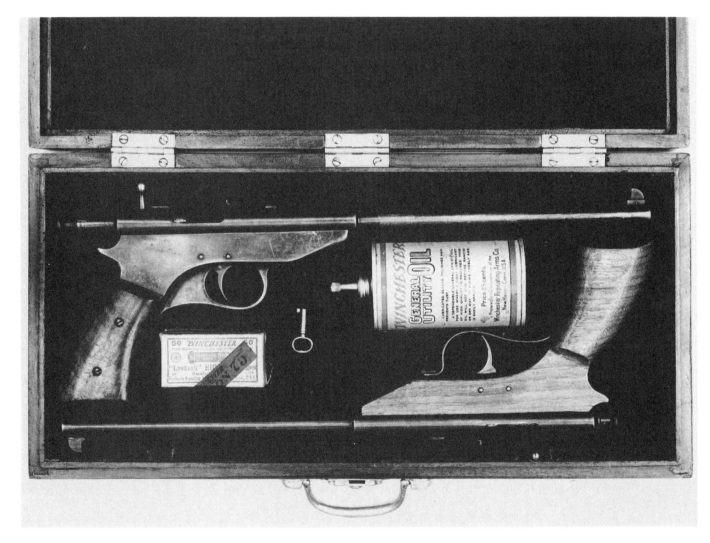

Plate 236

*S*ample Model 20 single-shot target pistols
cased for exhibition at the 1919 Caldwell
Match. Winchester Arms Collection (Inv. Nos.
P2067 and P2068), Cody Firearms Museum.

June 23, 1919

Henry Brewer, Esq, Vice President.
The Winchester Repeating Arms Co.
New Haven, Conn.

My dear Mr. Brewer:

I am in receipt of your letter of the 20th instant relative to the abandonment of the .22 gallery practice rifle in the Regular Army in favor of an accurate .30 caliber reduced gallery load to be used in the Springfield rifle.

This course was arrived at for several reasons. We have on hand very few .22 caliber Springfield gallery practice rifles, and it will cost us as much to resume with this system as to institute the system of .30 caliber reduced loads. The .22 caliber system was never satisfactory because it involved shooting the .22 caliber short cartridge from a holder instead of from a regular chamber, which was inaccurate in principle and practice. These .22 caliber rifles took the most expert care to maintain them in condition, and in practice they did not receive this care, and there was constant deterioration. *It is a better policy to have the recruit do his gallery work with the same rifle he will shoot on the outdoor range and in battle*, because he thereby becomes used to the trigger pull, bolt-action, etc., of his own rifle.

Please note that the adoption of this ammunition *concerns only the regular army*. Practically all the gallery work in the regular army is done outdoors on miniature ranges which are easily made safe for this ammunition.

In my opinion *this move creates even more of a market for your .22* caliber bolt-action rifles than would be the case were we to have continued with the .22 caliber Springfield gallery rifle. The *.30 caliber reduced load is not suitable for indoor gallery use in the National Guard and Civilian Rifle Clubs*, nor in the various schools and colleges. These organizations will be able to obtain *very few* .22 caliber Springfield gallery rifles for their use. They *must* have something of the kind, and will *naturally turn to your most perfect weapon*. I think that funds appropriated for civilian rifle practice are available right now to furnish such rifles to civilian rifle clubs and to schools and colleges. In addition many organizations will purchase them from private funds. It may also be that in the future the Ordnance Department, realizing the need for .22 caliber gallery rifles in certain spheres of military training, will arrange for the purchase of such rifles of private make in preference to again going to the expense of resuming manufacture of their old .22 caliber gallery practice rifle which has already been declared unsatisfactory. *I feel sure that were the matter put up to the equipment branch of the General Staff, they would concur enthusiastically on the suitability of your rifle for indoor gallery practice.*

Perhaps I may be a little optimistic, but it does look to me as though there was *a splendid future for your .22 caliber bolt action rifle*, although of course *much demends [sic] upon the price* at which you are able to place it on the market, and to the continuance here in Washington of those who fully understand these matters.

In this connection I have just been appointed Team Captain of the American Small Bore Team who are to compete with the English team in an international competition at Caldwell, N.J. in the middle of August. I have already approached your Mr. Davis on the subject of getting these Winchester .22 caliber bolt action rifles for this team. I feel very keenly the importance of this subject. I do not know of any rifle that will answer the requirements half as well. I know that the National Board for the Promotion of Rifle Practice would greatly appreciate it if the Winchester Repeating Arms Company could extend help in this *direction by turning out rifles and ammunition for the team*. Also I think that you will also appreciate the advertising value of having this team win the match with your new .22 caliber bolt action rifle and Winchester ammunition. The team will be composed of twenty men. *Rifles and ammunition should be available at Caldwell, N.J. by August 6, 1919.* Of course it may be that if justice to other manufactures some sort of competition as to rifles and ammunition used may be necessary, but I have no doubt whatever as to your produce winning out easily. This is a new matter just sprung on me day before yesterday, and I have no further information on it other than this. I will keep Mr. Davis informed of all developments...

Lt. Col. Townsend Whelen

Buoyed by the enthusiasm generated, the Winchester company rapidly began the production of the tooling for the Model 52, as it was designated on May 1, 1919[81]. In preparation for the public introduction of the Model 52 at the Caldwell International Small Bore Rifle Match in August 1919, a series of fifteen additional samples (Plates 232 and 233) were built in the Model Room[82]. As Whelan (Plate 234) had predicted, the Model 52 was an immediate success, unlike a single-shot .22 caliber target pistol (Plates 235 and 236) probably designed by Edwin Pugsley that was also publicly debuted there[83].

Given the profits which had been realized on its European and non-cost-plus American war contracts, together with the technical virtuosity of its designers, the Winchester Repeating Arms Company was in the strongest position it had ever enjoyed by mid-1919. Yet, while fame and fortune had both smiled upon Oliver F. Winchester's heirs, the seeds of his company's destruction had already been sown.

Plate 237

John E. Otterson, president of the Winchester Repeating Arms Company from 1919-1924. Olin Corporation photograph.

Endnotes

1. Contract Summations and Production Schedule for .303 British Cartridges, Contract of Aug. 4, 1914. Foreign Orders–World War I. Winchester Arms Collection Archives, Cody Firearms Museum.

2. Contract Summations, Republic of France Purchase File. Foreign Orders–World War I. Winchester Arms Collection Archives, Cody Firearms Museum.

3. Letter from John E. Parsons to Edwin Pugsley dated Jan. 14, 1948. Pugsley Correspondence File 3. Winchester Arms Collection, Cody Firearms Museum.

4. Republic of France Purchase File, op. cit.

5. Ibid.

6. First Pattern 14 Rifle Contract, Pattern 14 Rifle File Number 1. Winchester Arms Collection Archives, Cody Firearms Museum.

7. Ibid.

8. Second Pattern 14 Rifle Contract, Pattern 14 Rifle File Number 1, op. cit.

9. Pattern 14 Production Summary. Foreign Orders–World War I. Winchester Arms Collection Archives, Cody Firearms Museum.

10. Ibid.

11. Ibid.

12. Ibid.

13. Ibid.

14. M.95 7.62 Russian Muskets Contract Summations and Production Summary. Foreign Orders–World War I. Winchester Arms Collection Archives, Cody Firearms Museum.

15. .303 british Cartridge Contract Summations, op. cit.

16. Contract Summations, Republic of France, op. cit.

17. 7.62mm Russian Cartridge Contracts Summation and Production Schedule. Foreign Orders–World War I. Winchester Arms Collection Archives, Cody Firearms Museum.

18. M.95 7.62 Russian Muskets Contract Summations, op. cit.

19. Contract and Delivery Summations. Model 1907-World War I Foreign Orders. Winchester Arms Collection Archives, Cody Firearms Museum.

20. Ibid.

21. Contract and Delivery Summations. Model 1910 and .401 Cartridge Foreign Orders–World War I. Winchester Arms Collection Archives, Cody Firearms Museum.

22. Summation of Foreign Order Requests Received–World War I, pages 1-3. Winchester Arms Collection Archives, Cody Firearms Museum.

23. Watrous, op. cit.

24. Houze, Dreams of Youth, op. cit., pages 99-101.

25. Memorandum written by Henry Brewer to Winchester Bennett dated February [blank], 1915. Miscellaneous Correspondence–World War I. Winchester Arms Collection Archives, Cody Firearms Museum.

26. The initial design work on the Model A rifle is believed to have begun in late 1913.

27. Redesignation of the model identification took place November 1914 (per design drawings for Order No. 25840, Winchester Arms Collection Archives, Cody Firearms Museum).

28. The designation Model C was assigned in April 1916, and Model D in August 1916 (per design drawings for Box Magazine Rifle 93 and No. 27007, Winchester Arms Collection Archives, Cody Firearms Museum).

29. Report on the Winchester Commission to Russia, page 3. European Trip–World War I. Winchester Arms Collection Archives, Cody Firearms Museum.

30. See the sample Model D Rifles, Inv. Nos. W910, W911, W913, W915, W916, W918, W919, W920, W926, W927, W928, and W929 in the Winchester Arms Collection, Cody Firearms Museum. Cf. Winchester Firearms Reference Collection, op. cit., pages 140-141.

31. Work on double barrel shotgun designs had begun in 1911. Cf. Ned Schwing, **Winchester's Finest The Model 21** (Krause Publications; Iola, WI: 1990), pages 14-17.

32. Houze, Dreams of Youth, op. cit., pages 115-118.

33. The documentation for this statement consists of five design drawings preserved in the Winchester Arms Collection Archives, Cody Firearms Museum.

34. Summation of Foreign Order Requests Received, op. cit., page 3.

35. Ibid, Drawing Number 3.

36. Ibid, Drawing Number 4 (endorsed "With changes approved by Grant Hammond 3.6.17").

37. For example, a two-shot self-loading shotgun formerly Inv. No. W2124 in the Winchester Firearms Reference Collection, op. cit., page 313.

38. An undated manuscript note written by Edwin Pugsley confirms that the Grant Hammond pistols were made at the Winchester factory (Miscellaneous Arms File, Winchester Arms Collection Archives, Cody Firearms Museum). In addition, a number of unfinished and finished Grant Hammond pistol components are preserved in the Winchester Arms Collection, Cody Firearms Museum. For a detailed study of Grant Hammond pistols, see Roger Marsh, **The Automatic Weapons Design Series Number 2: The Grant Hammond, Savage and Schouboe .45 Automatic Pistols** (Roger Marsh; Hudson, OH: 1945), pages 2-13.

39. Memorandum from Henry Brewer to J.E. Otterson dated Aug. 2, 1919. Miscellaneous Arms–World War I. Winchester Arms Collection Archives, Cody Firearms Museum.

40. The term used for the bolt in the memorandum cited above was "solid breech bolt." Cf. Winchester Firearms Reference Collection, op. cit., Inv. No. W2663, page 385.

41. War Orders Contract Summation dated April 1, 1919. Winchester Exports–World War I. Winchester Arms Collection Archives, Cody Firearms Museum.

42. Winchester Firearms Reference Collection, op. cit., Inv. No. W931, page 142.

43. Ibid, Inv. No. W2343, page 340.

44. Ibid, Inv. No. W2342, page 339.

45. U.S. Model 1917 Rifle Contract Number 1. Model 1917 Contract Files. Winchester Arms Collection Archives, Cody Firearms Museum.

46. Letter from Major H.J. Smith, Army Inspector of Ordnance, to J.E. Otterson dated Nov. 29, 1919. Miscellaneous Correspondence Concerning World War I Production & Related Matters (1917-1919). Winchester Arms Collection Archives, Cody Firearms Museum.

47. Memoranda from B. Holmes to F.H. Madden dated April 4, 1919, and F.A. Hall to Mr. Schirmer dated July 1, 1921. Exports–World War I. Winchester Arms Collection Archives, Cody Firearms Museum.

48. Hall-Schirmer memorandum op. cit.

49. Model 1907 World War I File, op. cit.

50. Contract and Delivery Summations. Model 1903-World War I Foreign Orders. Winchester Arms Collection Archives, Cody Firearms Museum.

51. Memorandum from G.R. Watrous to J.E. Otterson dated Dec. 21, 1917. Factory Production–Miscellaneous Reports (World War I). Winchester Arms Collection Archives, Cody Firearms Museum.

52. Ibid.

53. Memoranda from F.A. Hall dated Dec. 22, 1919, and B.E. Holmes dated Feb. 19, 1919. Winchester Exports–World War I. Winchester Arms Collection Archives, Cody Firearms Museum.

54. Memorandum from G.H. Barber to Henry Brewer dated Feb. 19, 1918. General Contract File–World War I. Winchester Arms Collection Archives, Cody Firearms Museum.

55. Ibid.

56. See the Minutes of Production Committee Meetings Number 58 forward in Miscellaneous Correspondence Concerning World War I Production, op. cit.

57. Watrous, op. cit.

58. Notice of this embargo is contained in an unsigned and unaddressed memorandum dated March 1, 1919. Miscellaneous Arms–World War I. Winchester Arms Collection Archives, Cody Firearms Museum.

59. This matter is fully discussed in a series of letters and memoranda in U.S. Inspectors File Number 1–World War I. Winchester Arms Collection Archives, Cody Firearms Museum.

60. Memorandum from Henry Brewer to Maxson, Watrous, Rosien and Jewettun dated (in reference to conference of Sept. 21, 1918). Miscellaneous Correspondence Concerning World War I Production, op. cit.

61. Ibid, attachment.

62. Letter from Col. O.B. Mitcham to Chief of Ordnance, U.S. Army dated July 28, 1917. Strikes and Labor Disruptions–World War I. Winchester Arms Collection Archives, Cody Firearms Museum.

63. Memorandum from J.E. Otterson to Division Superintendents, dated May 1, 1917. Strikes and Labor Disruptions, op. cit.

64. Undated circular advertising the Model 11 and 12 riot guns, as well as the Model 94 rifle, for use in plant protection. Page 2 has an illustration of the Winchester company's security force. This circular was distributed in Feb. 12, 1918, per an attachment. Miscellaneous Correspondence With Salesmen (1917-1919). Winchester Arms Collection Archives, Cody Firearms Museum.

65. August 1917, Expense Sheet. Miscellaneous Financial Matters (1917-1919). Winchester Arms Collection Archives, Cody Firearms Museum.

66. The importance of the exhibition shooting program is demonstrated by various documents in the Topperwein File, Winchester Arms Collection Archives, Cody Firearms Museum.

67. Houze, Dreams of Youth, op. cit., pages 129 ff.; Sales Department Bulletin Number 84 dated July 10, 1917 (Sales Department Correspondence July 2-Nov. 27, 1917. Winchester Arms Collection Archives, Cody Firearms Museum).

68. Important Development, op. cit.

69. Ibid, pages 2-4.

70. Ibid, page 1.

71. Sales Department Bulletin No. 114 dated Aug. 2, 1917, page 2. Sales Department Correspondence July 2 -Nov. 27, 1917, op. cit.

72. See Plates 227-229.

73. Winchester Sales and Advertising Campaign for 1917, page 2. Miscellaneous Correspondence With Salesmen (1917-1919), op. cit.

74. Memorandum from Henry Brewer to Edwin Pugsley dated Sept. 28, 1918. Miscellaneous Arms--World War I. Winchester Arms Collection Archives, Cody Firearms Museum.

75. Houze, Dreams of Youth, op. cit., pages 78, 93, and 94.

76. Circular distributed in May 29, 1918. Miscellaneous Correspondence With Salesmen (1917-1919), op. cit.

77. Minutes of Production Committee Meetings Number 58 forward, op. cit.

78. Houze, Dreams of Youth, op. cit., pages 117-119.

79. Memorandum from Henry Brewer to T.C. Johnson dated April 24, 1919. Miscellaneous Arms-World War I, op. cit.

80. Letter from Townsend Whelen to Thomas A. Davis dated April 28, 1919; and Letter from Townsend Whelan to Henry Brewer dated June 23, 1919. Miscellaneous Arms-World War I, op. cit.

81. Model 52 Production File. Winchester Arms Collection Archives, Cody Firearms Museum.

82. Memorandum from Henry Brewer to Mr. Hawkins dated July 28, 1919. Miscellaneous Arms–World War I, op. cit.

83. Houze, Dreams of Youth, op. cit., pages 128-129.

CHAPTER 6

REORGANIZATION, COLLAPSE AND RESURRECTION 1919-1939

The good fortune of the Winchester Repeating Arms Company during World War I did, however, have its darker side. To manufacture the quantities of arms and ammunition called for in its wartime contracts, the company had extensively expanded its production facilities beginning in 1915, financing these building programs through short term loans[1]. The maturity date of these notes in 1919[2] became a concern to the firm's officers during the third quarter of 1918, when economists forecast a period of hyper-inflation and decreased consumer buying following the end of the war[3]. This prediction, more than anything else, caused the company to develop a plan whereby its debt could be restructured. Essentially, the plan that was adopted was the formation of a working partnership with a banking house so that, as money was needed, it could be advanced by the bank in exchange for either common or preferred shares in the new company[4]. While in theory this plan had the advantage of allowing the firm immediate access to financing, its disadvantages were the implicit partnership it created and the real possibility that through the advance system, the bank could gain control of the firm by virtue of its stock holdings. The benefits, though, were evidently believed to outweigh any liabilities, and in late 1918, reorganization plans on this model were set in motion. While some shareholders vehemently opposed the restructuring[5], a majority, acting upon the recommendations of Thomas G. Bennett, approved[6]. Consequently, on April 16, 1919, a new corporation simply known as the Winchester Company, was brought into being with Kidder, Peabody & Company of New York as its financial backer[7]. Under the agreements covering its incorporation, the stock of the new firm was distributed as follows[8](below).

Although the former Winchester Repeating Arms Company had established its reputation and wealth by the

- $1,000,000 Common Shares to Kidder, Peabody & Company

- $7,254,700 First Preferred Shares to stockholders of the old Winchester Repeating Arms Company

- $2,500,000 First Preferred Shares to Kidder, Peabody & Company

- $2,000,000 Second Preferred Shares to Kidder, Peabody & Company

production of arms and ammunition, the management of the new company decided to diversify the firm's product line in order to lessen any potential loss of business due to the anticipated unstable economy. This diversification would also allow the company to utilize the extensive production facilities that would be idled by the cancellation of military contracts. To accomplish this goal, the Winchester Company began an aggressive acquisition program, financed chiefly by Kidder, Peabody & Company, in 1919. Over the next two years, the following firms were to be purchased[9].

1919: Barney & Berry Incorporated
       Eagle Pocket Knife Company
       E.W. Edwards
       A.B. Hendryx Company
       Labanon Machine Company

       Mack Axe Company
       Morrill Target Company
       Napanoch Knife Company
       Page Storm Company
1920: Walden Knife Company
1921: William Read & Sons, Company

By these purchases, the Winchester Company immediately established itself as a major manufacturer and retailer of all types of sporting goods. The new product line included athletic supplies (jerseys, bats, baseballs, helmets, footballs, etc.), fishing equipment (rods, reels, lures, etc.), ice and roller skates, axes, pocket knives, arms, and ammunition (Plates 238-243). It also established retail stores in the following cities[10]: Boston, Massachusetts (the William Read & Sons facility); Springfield, Massachusetts; Providence, Rhode Island; Troy, New York; and New

Left: Plate 238

1925 Winchester basketball equipment advertisement published on page 24 of the July/August 1924 issue of the **Winchester Herald.** *Private Collection.*

Right: Plate 239

1925 Winchester basketball equipment advertisement published on page 25 of the July/August 1924 issue of the **Winchester Herald**. *Private Collection.*

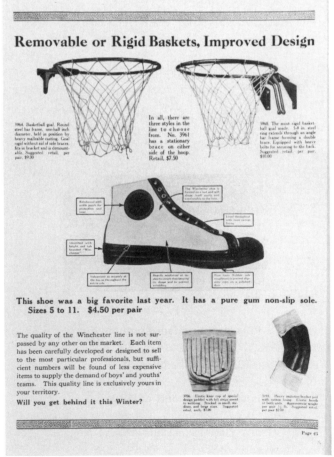

Plate 240

*W*inchester saw advertisement published on page 34 of the July/August 1924 issue of the **Winchester Herald**. Private Collection.

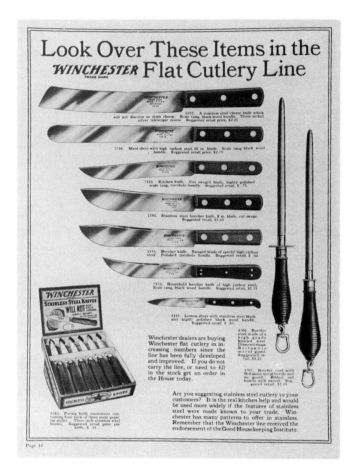

Plate 241

*W*inchester knife advertisement published on page 42 of the July/August 1924, issue of the **Winchester Herald**. Private Collection.

York City at a new, more fashionable, address (Fifth Avenue and 42nd Street).

Had the company been satisfied with this measure of growth, it might have survived, but on Aug. 22, 1922, it merged with the Associated Simmons Hardware Companies to become the Winchester- Simmons Company[11]. The amalgamation of these two companies not only provided the Winchester Company with access to an established retail network, but also, further enlarged the firm's product line to include all types of hardware. Unfortu-

nately, it continued the practice the company had begun in 1919, of enlarging its operations to increase gross income so that debts could be paid. By 1924, the losses incurred by the Winchester-Simmons Company caused it to cut back its operations. The stores set up in Boston, Springfield, Providence, New Haven, Troy and New York were all closed at a total loss of $2,350,152.20[12]. The seriousness of the situation is clearly evident in the company's year end balance report[13]:

Net Sales	$12,758,034.79
Amounts Received from Shareholders of Subsidiaries	$159,404.03
Cost of Sales	$10,270,150.14
Selling and General Expense Including Depreciation	$3,086,192.95
Interest on Floating Debt	$502,889.91
Interest on Twenty Year Gold Bonds	$526,606.00
Losses Brought About by Closing Selling Agencies	$2,350,152.20
Miscellaneous Deductions	$374,591.87
Reserve for Inventories Considered Obsolete or Excessive	$1,537,857.90

The net result of the year's operations was a loss totalling $6,147,608.38. The book value of the company was, however, $39,500,392.29, so the loss did not arouse much concern[14]. Also, much of the loss could be attributed to one-time events such as the sale of the retail stores and the liquidation of obsolete inventories (including the tools, fixtures and parts for the Models 1873 and 1885[15]).

The affection the Winchester Company and subsequently the Winchester-Simmons Company had for new products is perhaps best illustrated by the patents they secured. During the 1920s, the ratio of non-firearm-related patents to those covering firearms and ammunition averaged about 10 to 1[16]. As the decade progressed, the ratio worsened since what little financing available for research and development was directed increasingly toward the company's electrical division. Despite this, arms and ammunition continued to be a major contributor to the firm's gross sales, as the following shipment totals demonstrate[17](lower right):

The only model of significance to be introduced during this period was the Model 54 (Plates 244 and 245), which had been developed from the Model D bolt-action rifle designed during World War I[18]. With the exception of the .22 caliber single-shot boy's rifles, the other models first offered between 1922 and 1929 all proved to be less than stellar products. For example, the Model 20, 36 and 41 shotguns all had gross sales prior to their cancellation which did not even cover their development and tooling costs[19]. Similarly, the Model 53 and 55 lever-action rifles patterned after the Model 1892 and 1894 never achieved much commercial success[20]. Though research and development funds were severely limited, the firearms division continued work on a double-barrel shotgun first proposed in 1919, at a slow pace[21]. Modest advances were also made in ammunition design. The experimental .27 caliber cartridge developed for the Model D was introduced in 1925 as the .270 Winchester centerfire. This round has the distinction of having been the first commercially made cartridge to have had a muzzle velocity of over 3,100 feet per second[22]. The popularity of this

	RIMFIRE RIFLES	CENTERFIRE RIFLES	SHOTGUNS	TOTAL
1921	17,872	19,670	32,634	70,176
1922	37,103	25,832	60,152	123,087
1923	55,989	28,071	68,242	153,302
1924	48,070	27,682	57,280	133,032
1925	56,821	31,253	56,297	144,371
1926	68,942	34,947	59,022	162,911
1927	66,468	39,979	78,682	185,129
1928	75,695	44,827	63,184	183,706
1929	63,348	43,514	58,884	165,746
1930	42,524	23,875	32,744	99,143
1931	130,521	22,786	45,975	199,282

Sales Service Merchandising Plans

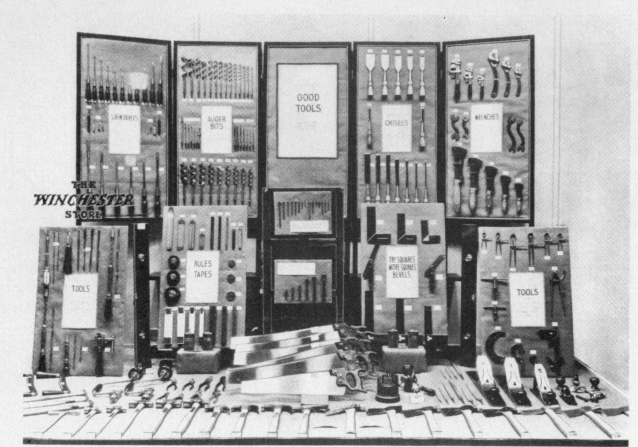

A window display of tools that will sell goods. Every item is priced. A catalog display of this kind takes time to make, but will bring big results. Use emerald green decorative paper to cover the floor and panels

round contributed heavily to the success of the Model 54 and much later the other Winchester bolt-action rifles chambered for it.

In late 1926, the Winchester-Simmons Company decided, despite continued operating losses, to acquire another firm, the George W. Dunham Corporation, a manufacturer of washing machines, in order to again enlarge its production and market base[23]. Renamed The Whirldry Corporation (Color Plate 19) on Jan. 25, 1927, this division was to prove a loss throughout its operating life[24].

The following year the Winchester-Simmons Company put Stainless Centerfire ammunition on the market[25]. This new type of ammunition used a mercuric, non-corrosive primer which drastically lessened barrel erosion. Its immediate success brought about the development of a new .22 caliber cartridge christened the Kopper-Klad (Color Plate 20) that employed a thin plating of a copper alloy on the bullet to reduce fouling[26]. Like its predecessor, this ammunition proved to be extremely popular.

To shore up the unstable Winchester-Simmons Company, attempts were

Plate 242

Winchester tool display illustrated on page 21 of the July/August 1924 issue of the **Winchester Herald**. Private Collection.

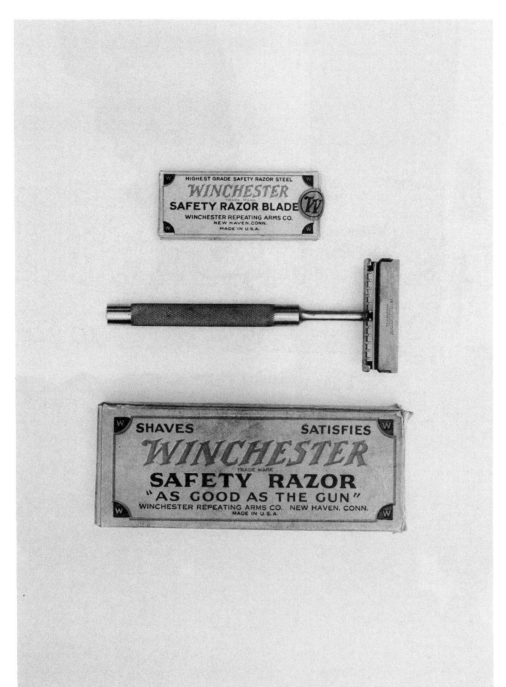

Plate 243
W*inchester razor and razor blades, circa 1925. Olin Corporation photograph.*

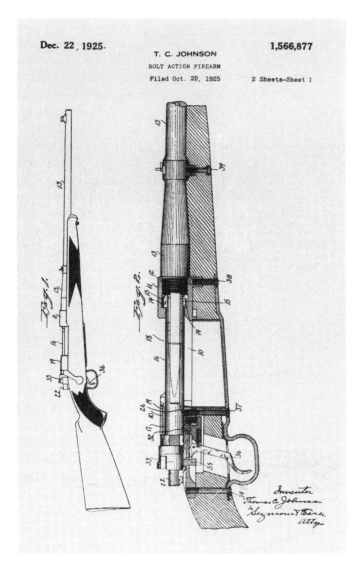

Plate 244

Sheet 1 of the specification drawings enrolled with Thomas C. Johnson's U.S. Patent Number 1566877 issued Dec. 22, 1925. Winchester Arms Collection Archives, Cody Firearms Museum.

Above: Plate 246

Frank Drew, president of the Winchester Repeating Arms Company from 1924-1928. Olin Corporation photograph.

Below: Plate 245

Winchester Model 54 sporting rifle introduced in 1925. Olin Corporation photograph.

Below: Plate 248

Frank F. Burton holding one of his most famous creations, a Winchester Model 21 shotgun, circa 1930. Olin Corporation photograph.

Above: Plate 247

William A. Tobler, president of the Winchester Repeating Arms Company from 1928-1931. Olin Corporation photograph.

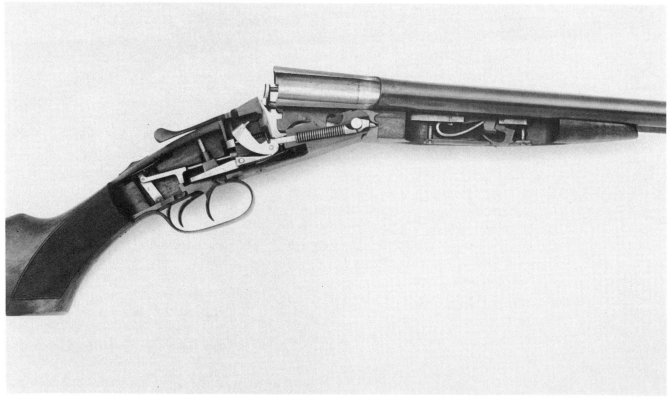

Top: Plate 249

*R*eceiver detail of the Model 21 shotgun engraved by Alden George Ulrich for Walter Chrysler. Kornbrath Papers. Buffalo Bill Historical Center, Cody, Wyoming.

Bottom: Plate 250

*S*keletonized Winchester Model 21 Shotgun, serial number 45.

made in early 1929 to reorganize its assets. On Feb. 5, the Winchester Repeating Arms Company of Delaware was established, and on May 23, the Winchester-Simmons Company changed its name to the Mercantile Securities Corporation[27]. The latter company essentially was a holding agency for the stock of the former. The collapse of the stock market in October 1929 finally sealed both firms' fate as there was no longer any money available from either Kidder, Peabody & Company or the public to offset the companies' losses. While the Winchester Repeating Arms Company of Delaware continued operations through 1930, and managed to introduce one new model, the 21 double barrel shotgun (Plates 248- 250) and stainless shot shells, the firm's debt load could not be serviced by its sales, consequently, bankruptcy was inevitable. To save whatever it could, the firm went into voluntary receivership effective Jan. 22, 1931[28]. Immediately thereafter, the receivers began searching for someone to purchase the company.

The Winchester Repeating Arms Company of Delaware's savior was to be one of its major competitors in the ammunition business, the Western Cartridge Company of Alton, Illinois. The principals of that firm, Franklin Olin and his sons John and Spencer, made a cash offer of $8,122,837.67 in early December 1931, which was accepted by the receivers[29]. The Olin family then established the Winchester Repeating

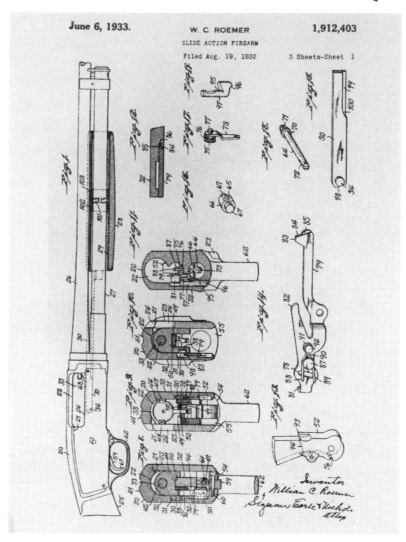

Above: Plate 251

Sheet 1 of the specification drawings enrolled with William C. Roemer's U.S. Patent Number 1912403 issued June 6, 1933. Winchester Arms Collection Archives, Cody Firearms Museum.

Below: Plate 252

Winchester Model 70 sporting rifle, serial number 30. Olin Corporation photograph.

Arms Company of Maryland on Dec. 14, and formal transfer of the old Winchester company's assets was completed by Dec. 22[30].

As with the company founded by Oliver F. Winchester, the new owners were to be actively involved in the firm's day-to-day operations, and all decisions regarding products and production quotas were approved by them. Their first order of business was to commission a thorough review of the firm's various operations. Completed on Feb. 29, 1932, this report by W.F. Siegmund summarized the Winchester product lines as follows[31]:

(a) **Shot Guns and Rifles**: It can be stated without fear of contradiction that the very best materials obtainable are used in the manufacture of Winchester shot guns and rifles. The treatment of the materials and the operations produce qualities in the finished product that have proven, beyond question, their superiority.

(b) **Shot Shells**: While it is believed that the WESTERN shot shell is superior to the Winchester shot shell, there is no doubt that under the management of the WESTERN CARTRIDGE COMPANY, Winchester shot shells will be made the equal of WESTERN shot shells.

The Winchester shot shell as compared with the WESTERN shell is inferior in that the battery cup assembly does not have a foil covering over the orifice in the front end of the battery cup to prevent powder getting into the battery cup.

The felt wad used in the Winchester shell is inferior to the WESTERN composition wad and I believe much more expensive to produce.

The Winchester shell head is not locked and reinforced by a steel flange firmly embedded in the base wad as is used in the WESTERN shell.

Very little time was spent by the undersigned in the Shot Shell Department.

(c) **Metallic Cartridges**: The same situation applies to metallic cartridges as in shot shells.

Winchester cartridges have to the best of my knowledge been satisfactory and compare favorably with any other manufacturer's product. It is my understanding that we are making Super-X 22's for them which undoubtedly is superior to any .22 the Winchester Company produced.

With the exception of walking through the Metallic Cartridges Department, no time was spent by the undersigned in the Department.

(d) **Bamboo Fishing Rods**: Winchester bamboo rods are manufactured from the best obtainable material for the various grades of rods and the process of heat treating coupled with the uniformity in cutting the strips and glueing insures a finished assembly of excellent quality. The use of serrated and water-

proof ferrules insures a minimum of trouble at the joints which is the sensitive point in a rod.

(e) Solid Steel Fishing Rods: The use of Chrome Vanadium steel and our experience in heat treating allows us to produce a rod which is not brittle and will stand a lot of abuse. The rods are tapered by grinding and are produced in both the round and octagonal forms and should be an outstanding product in its class.

(f) Tubular Steel Fishing Rods: The success or failure of the tubular steel rod lies in the material, design, and workmanship of the rod joint. In all Winchester rods, a very high grade of steel is used and that part of each section which receives the greatest strain just forward of the male ferrule is reinforced with an inner steel tube.

The various sections of the rod have an open seam and due to this seam, dampness can enter the section and in an ordinary rod corrosion of the inside surface soon weakens the rod. Winchester rods are not only protected externally against corrosion but the inside of each section is coated with a good corrosive preventative, which I believe is not done by any other manufacturer.

(g) Cutlery: Winchester experience in the selection and treatment of steel certainly qualifies the Company to produce cutlery of a very high grade and my impression is that it is as good, if not best, finished product that can be purchased. The question of whether a blade is forged or blank does not appeal to me to be of much importance if the product is satisfactory.

(h) Batteries: The merits of the Winchester battery deserves consideration as there is no doubt that the Fiber SuperSeal is superior to any other form used by our competitors.

The battery has a long shelf life and is marked with a code number so that it is easy to determine when the cell was made. A seamless can lends to the appearance of the battery although it is doubtful whether the added expense of making a seamless can instead of a soldered can is justifiable.

This battery has enjoyed a large volume of sales in the Orient where conditions are very severe for batteries.

(i) Ice Skates: No comments are necessary as the Barney & Barry line has established itself as a leader over a period of many years.

(j) Roller Skates: It is believed that the Winchester roller skate is superior both as to construction and longevity, which opinion is based on a roller skate comparison of the various manufacturers compiled at the Winchester factory.

(k) Whirl-dry Washing Machine: I have been assured that there has been practically no complaints on the Whirl-dry machine, and that it is a successful article with out serious competition. It is believed that a thorough investigation should be made as to its sales possibilities as it is my understanding that the distribution in the past has chiefly been through Sears, Roebuck & Company. The device appealed to me to be well designed and practical with an appeal to the house-wife.

(l) Radiators: Undoubtedly, the Winchester radiator has no peer and it is my opinion that only a prohibitive price would exclude this product in competition with any other make of radiator.

(m) Gun Oils, Grease and Solvents: The undersigned has used these materials for some time and has found them very satisfactory. Appears to be a profitable line and should be pushed.

(n) Tools: The quality and workmanship of the tools in my opinion are equal to any on the market, and under favorable market conditions should hold their own.

Despite Siegmund's positive comments concerning some of the non-firearms related lines, the Olins decided to end production of the majority of them. The Bar-

ney & Berry, Eagle Pocket Knife and New York Retail Store Companies, as well as The Whirldry Corporation, were all dissolved and their manufacturing or sales facilities shut down[32]. Likewise, unprofitable models, such as the 20, 41, 56, and 59, were withdrawn from production[33].

Realizing that the recovery of the company depended upon the development of new models, the Olin family actively promoted experimental work from the moment they purchased the firm. Unlike the previous management, they also allocated sufficient funds to pursue design projects and, more importantly, gave them their moral support. As a result, the Design Department became a productive part of the company's operations again. Over the next eight years it developed nineteen designs which were actually put into production and at least thirty others that were not taken up for various reasons[34]. The most important of the new were, without question, the Model 42 slide-action .410 bore shotgun and the Model 70 bolt-action rifle. The Model 42, introduced in 1933, was designed by William C. Roemer (Plate 251)[35]. Unlike previous .410 bore shotguns, the Model 42 was chambered for

a new three-inch shot shell that had been developed jointly by the Winchester and Western Cartridge Companies at the request of John Olin[36]. The light weight of the gun, combined with its effective cartridge, made the model an instant success[37]. The Model 70 bolt-action rifle (Plates 252 and 253), introduced in 1935, was designed by Albert F. Laudensack in 1932 (Plate 254)[38]. In many respects the Model 70 represented the final evolution of the centerfire bolt-action design work begun by Thomas C. Johnson with the Model A in 1913, and continued through the Model F just prior to the introduction of the Model 54.

Indeed, during its early development, the new rifle was known as the Model G (Plate 255)[39]. However, it differed from its predecessors in a number of ways. Chief among these was its lockwork, which was considerably advanced over that used by Johnson. When first introduced, the rifle was criticized as being a copy of the Mauser Model 1898 sporting rifle[40]. To counter this, the Winchester company circulated the following fact sheet to its salesmen and retailers to document the differences between the two arms[41].

"I wish I had Dad's Winchester"

■ Art and Firearms

Throughout the late 19th and early 20th centuries, the Winchester Repeating Arms Company regularly commissioned advertising art from the more famous artists of the times. Work by A.B. Frost, Phillip R. Goodwin, Lynn Bogue Hunt, Frederic Remington, and N.C. Wyeth appeared on the company's calendars and in their published advertisements. Yet, the most popular and endearing image ever to be used by the company was not by one of the above-mentioned artists, but by a relative unknown, Eugene Iverd. His painting "I Wish I Had Dad's Winchester" remains to this day one of the most sought after illustrations which Winchester published.

Comparison of Model '98 Mauser and Winchester Model 70

Model '98 Mauser	Model 70
1. Safety lug on right side of bolt.	1. No safety lug on bolt but bolt handle acts as safety lug in closed position.
2. Bolt release and ejector working together, made to swing horizontally at left rear of receiver. Left hand locking lug slit for ejector to work through.	2. Bolt release made to move vertically at rear left of receiver. The ejector is a separate piece working in the bottom of receiver.
3. Top of receiver cut for clip loading.	3. No cuts for clip loading.
4. No gas escape port in receiver ring, but locking lug channel in left side of receiver acts as gas escape.	4. Gas release port at right side of receiver ring and left locking lug channel also acts as supplementary gas release.
5. Safety swings in vertical plane.	5. Safety swings in horizontal plane.
6. Two stage trigger pull of military type.	6. Single stage trigger pull of sporting type.
7. Trigger directly connected to sear.	7. Sear will not work unless cocking piece is resting against it.
8. Firing pin and cocking piece are separate with cocking piece attached to firing pin by interlocking threads. Firing pin spring is retained by a permanent collar on the firing pin.	8. Firing pin and cocking piece permanently assembled together. Firing pin, spring retained by movable collar at front end of firing pin.

If the Model 42 shotgun and the Model 70 rifle are to be identified as the reborn Winchester company's best technological achievements prior to 1940, then the humble Model 37 shotgun must be recognized as that firm's chief money earner. Developed by Edwin Pugsley and William C. Roemer[42] to meet increasing consumer demands for a reliable and inexpensive single barrel shotgun, the Model 37 accounted for more than twenty-five percent of the company's firearms sales in 1936, the year it was introduced[43]. As the following chart graphically indicates, it was the Model 37 which finally pushed the Winchester Repeating Arms Company's arms sales above the level set in 1931[44].

	RIMFIRE RIFLES	CENTERFIRE RIFLES	SHOTGUNS	TOTAL
1932	50,410	8,568	12,523	71,501
1933	24,704	6,285	16,426	47,415
1934	114,333	8,446	18,393	141,172
1935	154,399	18,062	21,909	194,370
1936	194,175	31,966	145,674	371,815
1937	182,919	47,029	106,372	336,320
1938	104,844	42,716	53,823	201,383
1939	165,442	39,0438	8,016	292,501

■ Edwin Pugsley

Of all the Winchester company's employees during the 20th century, none is more widely remembered than Edwin Pugsley. A conscientious administrator and capable designer, Pugsley's bulldog appearance belied what one contemporary termed his "very gentle character."

Edwin Pugsley's immortality, however, will not come from anything he did for his employer, but rather from the work of his close friend and fellow arms collector, Charles Addams, the cartoonist. Addams, in his Addams Family cartoons, modeled the character Pugsley after his friend. Not only did he use Edwin's surname, he also made the character physically and apparently temperamentally (if accounts of Edwin Pugsley's mischief making are to be believe) resemble his arms collecting cohort.

Above: Plate 253

*R*eceiver detail of the Model 70 sporting rifle, serial number 30, illustrated in Plate 252.

Right: Plate 254

*S*heet 1 of the specification drawings enrolled with Albert F. Laudensack's U.S. Patent Number 1898670 issued Feb. 21, 1933. Winchester Arms Collection Archives, Cody Firearms Museum.

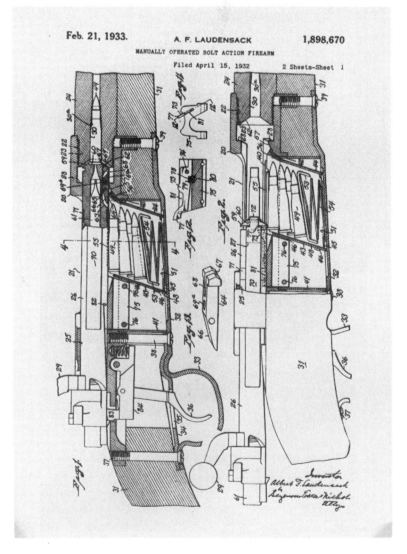

Within the company's rimfire product line, the Model 67 was its most successful seller in 1934, and the years following. In all, a total of 466,563 Model 67 rifles were shipped from 1934 to 1939[45]. Curiously, in the centerfire line, the Model 1894 Rifle proved to have the highest sales[46]. This can be attributed to the increased interest in deer hunting beginning in 1936[47].

As would be expected, considering the Olin family's previous interest, the development of ammunition was also not neglected. During the 1930s, the Winchester ammunition product lines were all modernized, and a number of technical improvements in cartridge design developed by the Western Cartridge Company were incorporated into

Winchester shells. In particular, the Super-X (Color Plate 23) was adapted for both rifle and shotgun cartridges[48]. In 1936, the company was the first to introduce a cartridge, the .220 Swift, having a standard muzzle velocity in excess of 4,000 feet per second[49]. In 1937, it began marketing rifled slugs for shot shells, and, in 1938[50], added another high velocity rifle cartridge to its line with the introduction of the .219 Zipper[51].

Under an active and truly interested management, the Winchester Repeating Arms Company, in the space of but a few years, had not only recovered from bankruptcy, but had become a thriving and profitable business again. This change in circumstances clearly validated the Olin family's 1931 assessment that the company would be a sound concern if it concentrated its resources on what it knew best, the manufacture of arms and ammunition.

Plate 255
Winchester Model G Musket, Olin Corporation photograph.

Endnotes

1. In 1919, it was estimated that the 1914 to 1917, building programs increased the New Haven plant facilities by thirty-nine percent (Memo from E. Pugsley to Henry Brewer dated Jan. 31, 1919. World War I miscellaneous Papers Concerning Production, Winchester Arms Collection Archives, Cody Firearms Museum.) The notes secured by the company to finance the building programs were due March 1, 1919 (Williamson, op. cid., 269).

2. Williamson, op. cit., page 269.

3. Ibid, page 286.

4. For a thorough discussion and financial review of the reorganization plan see, Williamson, op. cit., Chapter 22.

5. Ibid, pages 265-271.

6. Ibid, pages 263-264 and 272.

7. Summary of the Winchester Repeating Arms Company's Operations 1918-1931 prepared for John M. Olin, page 1. Documents Concerning The Purchase of the Winchester Repeating Arms Company, Winchester Arms Collection Archives, Cody Firearms Museum.

8. Ibid, page 1.

9. Ibid, page 2, Walden Knife Company report and William Read & Sons, Company report.

10. Ibid and Arthur Young Company Report dated April 27, 1925, page 3. Loc. cit.

11. Summary of Winchester Operations (1918-1931), op. cit., pages 3 and 4.

12. Arthur Young Company Report dated April 27, 1925, op. cit., pages 3 and 4.

13. Ibid.

14. Ibid.

15. While both models had been declared obsolete in 1919, final disposition of their tooling and parts inventories was delayed to 1924. For further information see: H.G. Houze "The End of a Marque: The Final Production of the Winchester Model 1873", **The Gun Report**, Volume 36, Number 12 (May 1991), pages 22 to 25); and H.G. Houze, **To The Dreams of Youth,** op. cit., pages 125,126,131, and 132.

16. This statement is based upon a statistical analysis of all the patents secured by the Winchester and Winchester-Simmons Companies from 1919 to 1930.

17. Watrous, op. cit.

18. The Model 54 Centerfire Rifle was introduced in 1925.

19. Based upon Watrous sales records (op. cit.) 12,865 Model 20s were sold from 1919-1932; 19,606 Model 36s were sold from 1920-1929, and; 20,197 Model 41s from 1920-1931.

20. Ibid. A total of 14,409 Model 53 rifles were sold from 1924-1931. During the same period ,18,198 Model 55 rifles were sold.

21. Ned Schwing, **Winchester's Finest,** op. cit., page 14.

22. Memoranda from M.A. Robinson to E. Pugsley dated Nov. 13, 1947, page 1 and Dec. 1, 1947, page 7.

23. Summary of Winchester Operations (1918-1931), op. cit., The Whirldry Corporation report.

24. Ibid. See also Winchester-Simmons and Winchester Repeating Arms Company of Delaware financial statements for 1927-1931.

25. Robinson-Pugsley memorandum of Nov. 13, 1947, op. cit., page 1.

26. Ibid.

27. Summary of Winchester Operations (1919-1931), op. cit., page 1, 3 and 4.

28. Ibid, pages 2 and 4.

29. Williamson, op. cit., page 378.

30. Summary of Winchester Operations (1918-1931), op. cit., pages 2 and 3. A statement of stock ownership prepared on Dec. 31, 1931, reveals the extent to which Kidder, Peabody & Company were financially involved in the bankrupt Winchester Company's operations.

Stock Ownership - December 31, 1831

W.R.A.Co.(Del.)-Common - 89 percent Mercantile Securities Corp.

4 percent Kidder, Peabody & Co.

7 percent Investors

Class A- 31 percent K.P.& Co.

Remainder by former Win.Co.Stockholder

Pfd. - 22 percent K.P.& Co.

Remainder former Win. Co. Stockholders

The Winchester Mfg.Co.- W.R.A.Co. (Del.)

(formerly WRA Co.Conn.)

The Mercantile Sec.Corp.- Common - 68 percent by K.P.& Co.

(formerly Win.-Sim.Co.) balance by public.

Pfd. - 50 percent by K.P.& Co.

balance by public.

31. Report of Trip to Winchester Repeating Arms Company by W.F. Siegmund to F.W. Olin dated Feb. 29, 1932, pages 6,7 and 8. Documents Concerning The Purchase of the Winchester Repeating Arms Company, loc. cit.

32. Summary of Winchester Operations (1918-1931), op. cit., page 2, Retail Store Company and The Whirldry Corporation reports.

33. Watrous, op. cit.

34. This statement is based upon the patents issued which were incorporated into production models and those issued that were never adopted for use during the period of 1932 to 1939.

35. United States, Patent Number 1912403 issued June 6, 1933, to W.C. Roemer.

36. Ned Schwing, **The Winchester Model 42** (Krause Publications, Inc.; Iola, WI: 1990), page 9.

37. Ibid. Also Watrous, op. cit., noted that 9,398 Model 42 Shotguns were sold in 1933, the year of its introduction.

38. United States Patent Number 1898670 issued Feb. 21, 1933 to A.F. Laudensack.

39. Design drawing dated October 1932. Winchester Arms Collection Archives, loc. cit.

40. Memorandum from E. Pugsley to J.M. Olin dated Dec. 2(?), 1935. Private Collection.

41. Comparison of Model '98 Mauser and Winchester Model 70. Undated information circular believed to have been prepared in late December 1935.

42. United States Patent Number 2125956 issued Aug. 9, 1938 and 2143923 issued Jan. 17, 1939 to W.C. Roemer; and United States Patent Number 2137808 issued Nov. 22, 1938 and 2158148 issued May 16, 1939 to E. Pugsley.

43. Watrous, op. cit.

44. Based upon Watrous, op. cit.

45. Ibid.

46. Ibid. A total of 97,599 Model 1894s were sold from 1936 to 1939.

47. Memorandum form G.R. Watrous to E. Pugsley dated Nov. 12, 1938. Pugsley Correspondence File Number 1. Winchester Arms Collection Archives, loc. cit.

48. Siegmund Report of Feb. 29, 1932. op. cit., page 5.

49. Robinson-Pugsley memorandum of Nov. 13, 1947, op. cit., page 1.

50. Robinson-Pugsley memorandum of Nov. 17, 1947, op. cit., page 1

51. Robinson-Pugsley memorandum of Dec. 1, 1947, op. cit., page 7.

CHAPTER 7

WORLD WAR II: 1939-1945

By Jan. 1, 1939, the modernization of the Winchester Repeating Arms Company's product line begun in 1932 by the Olin family was almost complete. Of the seventeen models in production when the company had been purchased in December 1931, eleven had been discontinued and fifteen new models introduced in their place[1]. As a result of these changes, the firm had gradually resumed its former prominence in the American arms industry and had, as the following sales table demonstrates[2], achieved a significant share of the sporting arms market despite the varying effects of the Great Depression.

> "I believe it is peace for our time."
>
> — Neville Chamberlain
> Sept. 30, 1938

Within the year, the addition of two new arms designed by Frank Burton (the Model 74 semiautomatic .22 caliber rifle[3] [Plate 256] and the Model 24 double barrel shotgun[4]) would further consolidate the Winchester company's position. Furthermore, it was anticipated that the introduction of a new

	YEARLY SALES			
	RIMFIRE RIFLES	CENTERFIRE RIFLES	SHOTGUNS	TOTAL SALES
1932	50,410	8568	12,523	71,501
1933	24,704	6285	47,415	78,404
1934	114,333	8446	18,393	141,172
1935	154,399	17,862	21,909	194,170
1936	194,175	31,966	145,674	371,815
1937	182,919	47,029	106,372	336,320
1938	104,844	42,716	53,823	201,383

semiautomatic shotgun, then in the final stages of development, would also increase the firm's market share.

Of equal potential importance to the company's future was a semiautomatic centerfire rifle then being worked on by the Design Department. Designated the G30R, this rifle was based on a design conceived by Jonathan E. Browning in 1930 (Plate 257), which could be adapted with equal ease to both civilian and military use[5]. Although it was generally believed that the Munich Agreement had forestalled the possibility of war in Europe, the management of the Winchester company wanted to have a design for a military rifle in hand should the need for it arise. Consequently, from June 7, 1938, through May 1939, an extensive series of tests were carried out using the original Browning

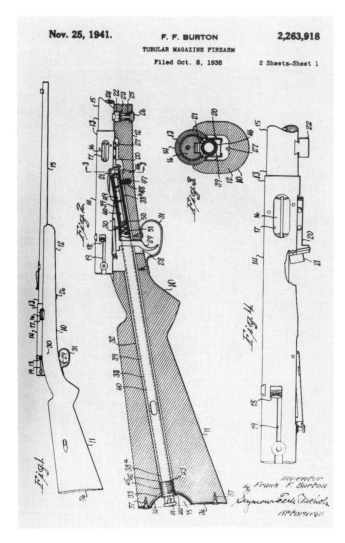

Plate 256

*S*heet 1 of the specification drawings enrolled with Frank F. Burtons's U.S. Patent Number 2263918 issued Nov. 25, 1941. Winchester Arms Collection Archives, Cody Firearms Museum.

Plate 257

*S*heet 1 of the specification drawings enrolled with Jonathon E. Browning's U.S. Patent Number 2247011 issued June 24, 1941 (application filed March 21, 1930). Winchester Arms Collection Archives, Cody Firearms Museum.

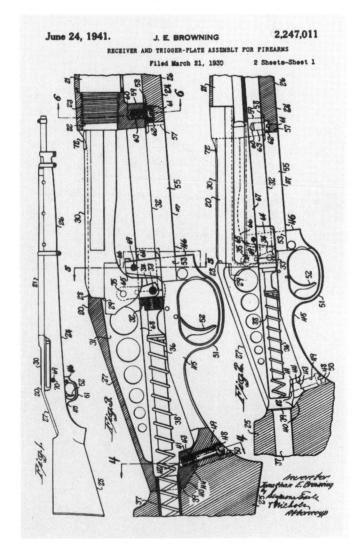

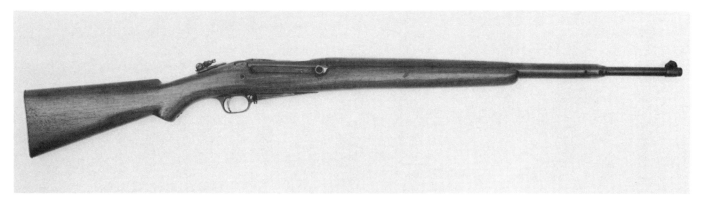

samples (Plates 258 and 259) and those subsequently made by the company[6]. During the testing of the first sample, a number of problems were encountered in the design. These were subsequently summarized in a report prepared by William C. Roemer, on April 10, 1940, as follows[7]:

Irregular Action – The gun would perform well for a time, then it would fail to feed or fail to eject or fail to make its automatic cycle. At other times it would fail on the first few shots. This difficulty was not eliminated until the annular gas piston was abandoned as later detailed in this report.

Poor Ejection – The ejection of the Winchester made gun was practically the same as Mr. Browning's sample, viz., toward and over the shooter. With Mr. Browning's cooperation we tried all manner of expedients to cause the empty shell to eject forwardly but were unable to effect this until we tried a deflecting member adjustably [sic] attached to the receiver. This was successful and was later incorporated as a part of the rear sight base.

Bolt Stop Failures – The member used to keep the action open automatically after the last shot was fired never functioned consistently in this gun. We felt this was due to a combination of effects involving irregular bolt trave, lack of consistent magazine follower position and close timing. This trouble was not completely removed in this model until February 1940.

Trouble with Firing Mechanism – In Mr. Browning's sample gun the firing pin was cocked by the link and held by a vertical sear in bolt which connected with a hook attached to the trigger mechanism. This mechanisms, especially the connection between sear and trigger mechanisms, was completely concealed and its action was uncertain due to the difficulty of making the proper fits. This mechanism gave so much trouble that it was replaced by a hammer mechanism of Winchester design.

Clip Loading – In Mr. Browning's military sample, no provision was made for loading the magazine with a clip. This was developed by Winchester, forming a part of the rear sight base.

Rear Sight – Mr. Browning's sample was not equipped with sights suitable for miliary purposes. The sights on the present guns were developed by Winchester but are not considered final.

Plate 258

Sample .30-06 semiautomatic sporting rifle with an annular piston designed by Jonathon E. Browning and tested by the Winchester company in 1938. Winchester Arms Collection (Inv. No. W1395), Cody Firearms Museum. Olin Corporation photograph.

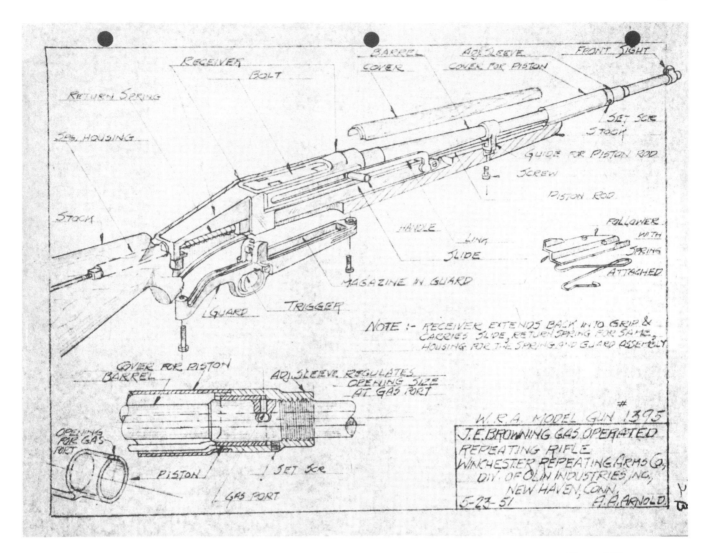

Plate 259

Schematic drawing by
A.A. Arnold of Jona-
thon E. Browning's
semiautomatic sporting
rifle illustrated in Plate
258 with an enlarged
detail of the annular piston. Winchester Arms
Collection Archives,
Cody Firearms Museum.

In July 1939, the annular piston designed by Browning was replaced by a more conventional version situated beneath the barrel (Plates 260 and 261), and most of the problems noted by Roemer were immediately corrected[8].

Interestingly, while the above work was being carried out, the Winchester company had already become involved in the production of another semiautomatic military rifle, the U.S. M1.

In 1938, the worsening political situation in Europe had prompted the United Sates Army General Staff to access the production capabilities of the Springfield Armory. Realizing that there would be a serious shortage of U.S. M1 rifles should a general mobilization occur, the Army decided to issue an educational contract to familiarize another manufacturer in the intricacies of the M1 production. In early April 1939, the Winchester company won this contract with a bid of $1,382,000[9].

Under the contract's provisions, the company then set about to make one tool, one fixture and one gauge for every component of the M1. Upon completion of this requirement, the company was then obliged to manufacture a total of 500 M1 rifles with the tooling they had made[10].

Concurrently with both of the above projects, the Design Department was finishing its work on the semiautomatic shotgun mentioned previously. Designed by William Roemer and Edwin Pugsley[11], this shotgun, to be known as the Model 40 (Color Plate 24), was the result of a development program that had begun in 1925, when the Model 1911 self-loading shotgun was discontinued. Originally conceived as a two-shot firearm intended solely for use in skeet or trap shooting[12], the design had evolved over the years into a multi-purpose shotgun for use by either game or competition shooters. In many ways

Top: Plate 260
Sample Jonathon E. Browning .30-06 semiautomatic military rifle with a modified operating piston. Winchester Arms Collection (Inv. No. W1393), Cody Firearms Museum. Olin Corporation photograph.

Bottom: Plate 261
Receiver detail of the modified Jonathon E. Browning sample military rifle illustrated in Plate 260.

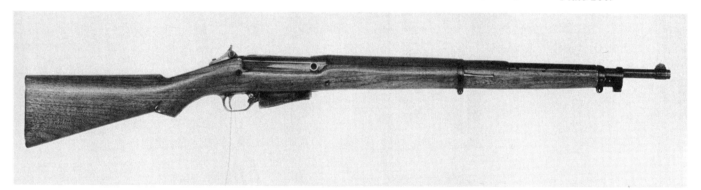

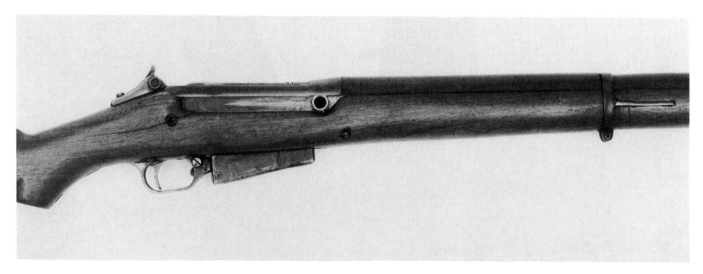

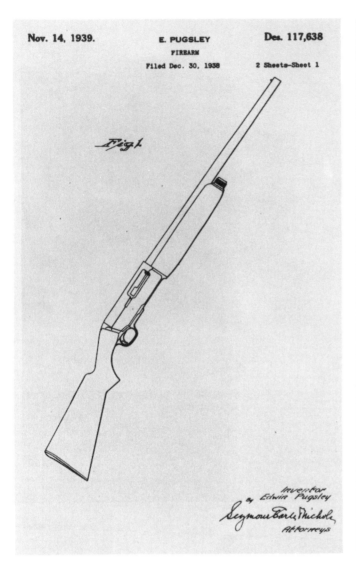

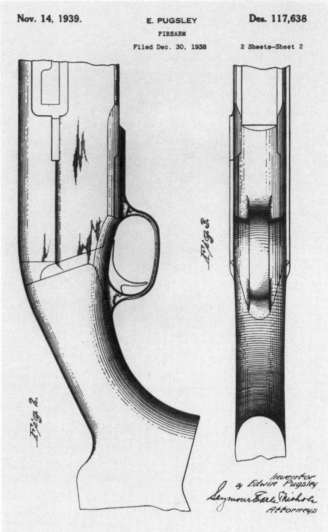

the Model 40 was a marked improvement over the autoloading shotguns manufactured by Winchester's competitors as its action was designed to minimize the effects of recoil. Indeed, this characteristic of the arm, as well as its other safety features, were stressed in the model's advertising[13]:

Upon firing either of these guns for the first time, the shooter is impressed by its unusually gentle action. This is provided for in the design of the gun. The action is the long-recoil type. The barrel and breech-block, locked together, recoil the full length of the receiver's interior. In doing so, they are retarded by the combined resistance of the action brake and coil spring – in the

magazine section within the fore end – and the breech-bolt spring at the rear. The braking increases toward the end of the recoil stroke, producing an easy stop at the recoil buffer.

The breech-bolt is released from the barrel at the end of the recoil stroke, and the barrel automatically returns to its forward position. In doing so, it ejects the empty shell. Meanwhile, the breech-bolt remains in its retracted position long enough for the empty shell to be ejected and for the carrier to raise another shell from the magazine to position for loading into the chamber. Then the breech-bolt automatically closes, loading the shell into the chamber and locks itself. The recoil spring

Left: Plate 262

*S*heet 1 of the specification drawings enrolled with Edwin Pugsley's U.S. Registered Design Number 117638 issued Nov. 14, 1939. Winchester Arms Collection Archives, Cody Firearms Museum.

Right: Plate 263

*S*heet 2 of the specification drawings enrolled with Edwin Pugsley's Registered Design illustrated in Plate 262.

encircles the magazine in the guns fore end, and the recoil brake is housed in the barrel lug, as in other automatic shotguns. The brake, however, is a new, exclusive Winchester design. It is made of self-lubricating metal, requiring no oil. Its design makes it also self-compensating, so that it correctly brakes recoil for all loads but exceptionally light ones. It is quickly and simply readjusted for the latter, and this can be done easily in the field, without tools.

The breech-locking mechanism is a Winchester design which has been thoroughly time proved. It positively locks the gun shut for firing and holds until unlocked automatically at the end of barrel recoil. The lock is an integral and sturdy pivoted member which, when locking, extends up against a substantial locking shoulder in the barrel extension.

This new gun has two important automatic safety features in its firing mechanism. One is the positive firing-pin retractor. It takes charge of the firing pin at the start of the recoil stroke and prevents it from going forward until the gun is completely locked. The firing pin is released from this control simultaneously with the final locking of the breech of the gun. The second safety feature mechanically discon-

nects the trigger and the sear, locking them apart for the full elngth [sic] of time that the action is open. Trigger and sear are reconnected only when the action is closed and locked. Thus the gun can be fired only after the action is closed and locked, and then only by pressing the trigger.

The streamlined configuration of the Model 40 was also stressed in the company's sales literature and was thought highly enough of to be protected by a Registered Design (Number 117638) issued by the U.S. Patent Office to Edwin Pugsley on Nov. 14, 1939 (Plates 262 and 263).

Unfortunately, the Model 40 semiautomatic shotgun was never to achieve the promise it appeared to have. Plagued by a variety of operating difficulties from the moment of its introduction, only 18,927 were eventually sold[14]. Of that number, 6,625 were taken back in exchange for Model 12 or 97 shotguns[15].

While the Model 40 was a disaster for the company, the losses incurred in its development and brief production life were more than compensated for by the company's success in other fields. In 1939, a total of 292,501 firearms were sold, and in 1940, a further 330,189[16]. The net sales of ammunition made by

Plate 264
U.S. M1 rifle manufactured by the Winchester Repeating Arms Company. Olin Corporation photograph.

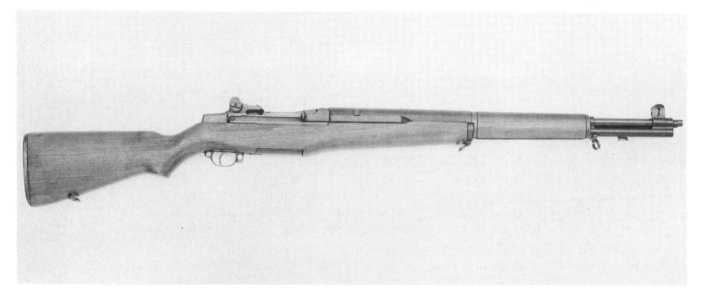

the company were also increasing at a rapid pace. In comparison with total sales of $2,466,225.36 in 1936, the company generated $3,616,189.09 in 1939 and an estimated $2,250,000 for the first six months 1940[17].

Unlike in August 1914, the declaration of war by France and Great Britain against Germany in September 1939 had little immediate effect upon the Winchester company's operations. This was solely due to the fact that the company could not accept any contracts for war material from any of the billigerents under the United States declaration of neutrality. The outbreak of war in Europe did increase the company's business in another way. In recognition that

its stocks of U.S. M1 rifles were insufficient to meet potential requirements, the United States Army asked for bids on a 65,000-unit contract in mid-September. The Winchester company, having gained valuable experience in the manufacture of that model due to the educational contract of earlier that year, was able to submit the lowest bid, and on Oct. 10, 1939 was awarded the contract[18] (Plates 264-279).

The company also stepped up work on the G30R, producing a second revised sample in December. When subjected to a sand test, however, the bolt stuck fast in the wedge-shaped stopping surface located in the rear of the receiver, totally disabling the rifle[19]. In

Plate 265

Billings & Spencer drop hammer forge used in the manufacture of the U.S. M1 rifle receiver. This photograph and the fourteen following are from a series of publicity shots commissioned by the Winchester company in 1941, to illustrate the various manufacturing procedures used in the production of the U.S. M1 rifle. Olin Corporation photograph.

Plate 266
*M*ichael Krantz inspecting a rough forging for the U.S. M1 rifle receiver. Olin Corporation photograph.

Plate 267

William J. Richardson broaching a U.S. M1 Rifle receiver. Olin Corporation photograph.

Plate 268

*P*rofiling machines used to machine various components of the U.S. M1 rifle. Olin Corporation photograph.

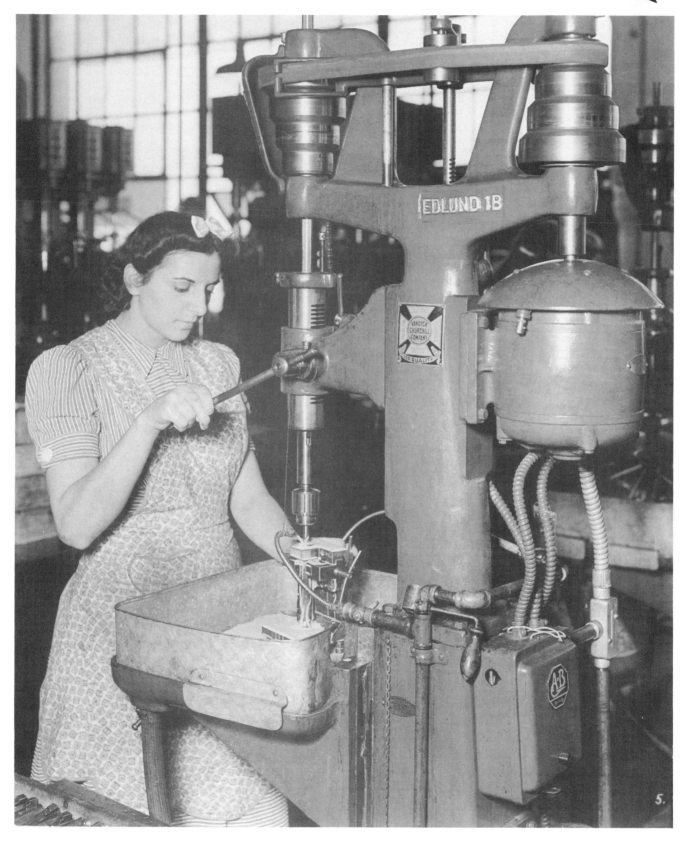

Plate 269

*J*osephine Bradanine operating a drill jig to partially finish a U.S. M1 rifle bolt. Olin Corporation photograph.

Plate 270

Helen Wilsznski and three unidentified women operating drill presses to make lock components for the U.S. M1 rifle. Olin Corporation photograph.

Oil Painting of Oliver F. Winchester by G.S. Hopkinson, circa 1875.
Winchester Arms Collection, Cody Firearms Museum, Buffalo Bill Historical Center, Cody, Wyoming.

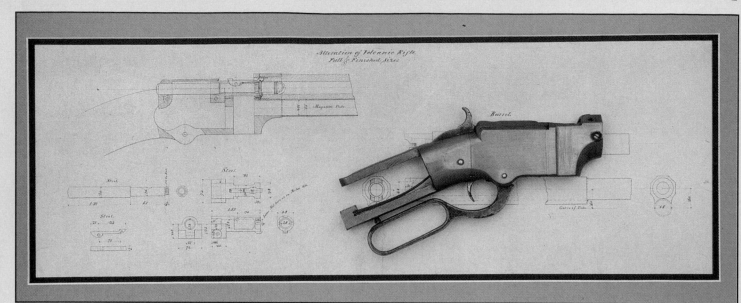

Design drawing and sample receiver prepared in mid-1859 to demonstrate the modification of New Haven Arms Company "Volcanic" Carbines for use with metallic cartridges.
Winchester Arms Collection (The receiver Inv. No. W2868), Cody Firearms Museum.

Winchester-Davies New Haven Shirt Manufactory advertising broadside, circa 1860.
Winchester Arms Collection Archives, Cody Firearms Museum. Olin Corporation photograph.

Sample James D. Smith .50 caliber musket made in August or September 1865.
Winchester Arms Collection (Inv. No. W253), Cody Firearms Museum. Olin Corporation photograph.

Sample Nelson King .45 caliber musket made in early 1866.
Winchester Arms Collection (Inv. No. W252), Cody Firearms Museum. Olin Corporation photograph.

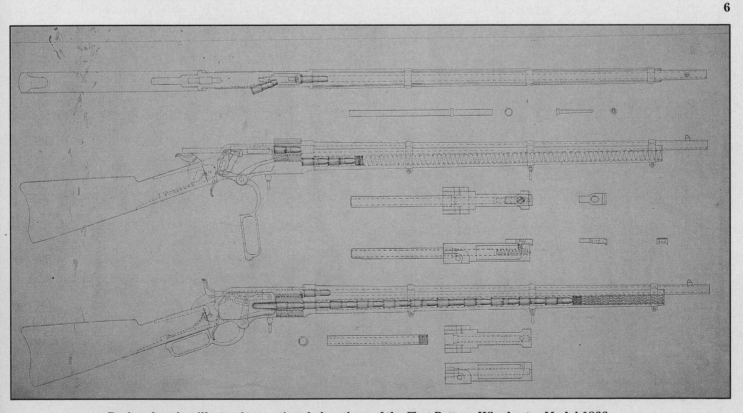

Design drawing illustrating sectional elevations of the First Pattern Winchester Model 1866 Swiss Sharpshooter's rifle, with a full-size delineation of the bolt and firing pin mechanism.
Private Collection.

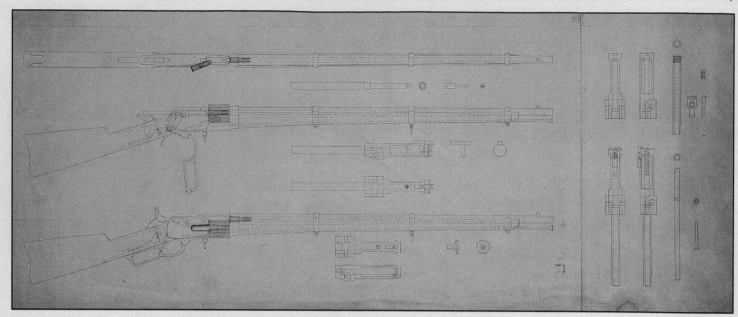

Design drawing illustrating sectional elevations of the Second Pattern Winchester Model 1866 Swiss Sharpshooter's rifle, with a full size delineation of the bolt and firing pin mechanism.
Private Collection.

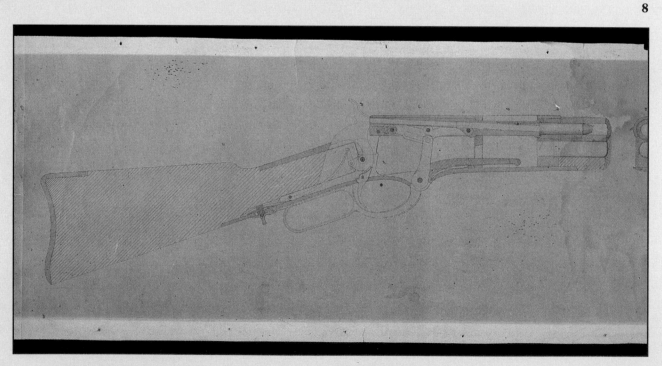

Design drawing illustrating the simplified lockwork developed by Luke Wheelock in 1872.
Winchester Arms Collection Archives, Cody Firearms Museum.

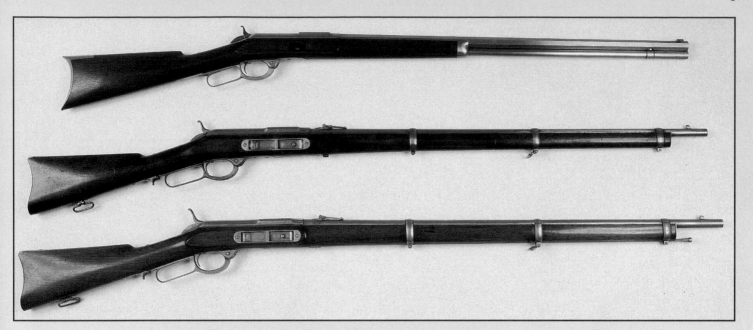

Sample Luke Wheelock .40 Dupee caliber sporting rifle, .45-70 caliber U.S. Army Trials Musket and .50 caliber musket made in 1872.
Winchester Arms Collection (Inv. Nos. [top to bottom] W249,W250 and W251), Cody Firearms Museum. Olin Corporation photographs.

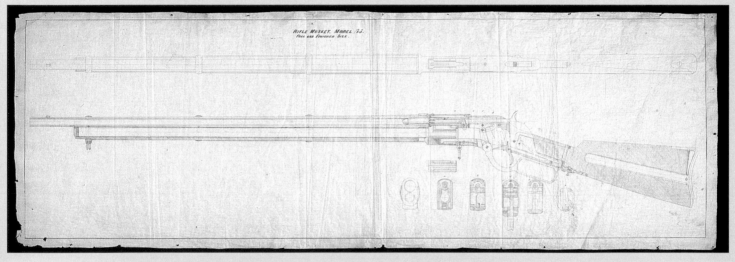

Design drawing illustrating sectional elevations of the Winchester Model /75 musket, prepared in mid-1875.
Cody Firearms Museum (Gift of Alexander Acevedo).

Colored lithograph illustrating the Winchester Repeating Arms Company's New Haven factory, circa 1875.
Private Collection.

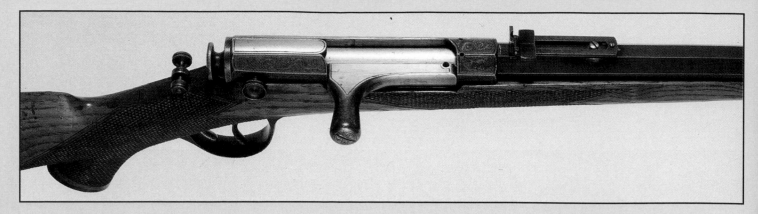

Detail of the Model 1880 Murata sporting rifle serial number 1, made by the Winchester Repeating Arms Company in 1879.
Cody Firearms Museum

Ammunition display board made by the Winchester Repeating Arms Company in 1884.
Winchester Arms Collection, Cody Firearms Museum. Olin Corporation photograph.

Ammunition display board made by the Winchester Repeating Arms Company in 1886. The vignettes based on paintings by Frederic Remington.
Winchester Arms Collection, Cody Firearms Museum. Olin Corporation photograph.

Winchester New Rival 12 gauge shot shell box label, circa 1900.
Private Collection.

17

18

Above: Sample Bennett-Mason .44 caliber self-loading carbine made in 1901.
Winchester Arms Collection (Inv. No. W325), Cody Firearms Museum.

Left: Cover of an advertising brochure for greaseless ammunition made by the Winchester Repeating Arms Company. Dated 1904.
Private Collection.

Below, Left: Rear cover of the July/August 1924 edition of *The Winchester Herald* with an advertisement for Winchester-manufactured baseball equipment.
Private Collection.

Below: Two brochures printed by the Winchester company to advertise Whirldry products. The larger with cover art by N.C. Wyeth. Circa 1928.
Private Collection.

19

20

Cover of an advertising brochure for Winchester "Kopper Klad" ammunition distributed in 1927.
Private Collection.

21　　　　　　　　　**22**

Above: Proof for a full-page advertisement announcing a new price for the Winchester Model 1897 shotgun, published in April 1933.
Private Collection.
Above Right: Proof for a full-page Winchester battery advertisement dated Aug. 2, 1937.
Private Collection.

23

Cover of an advertising brochure for Western Cartridge Company Super-X 12 gauge shot shells printed in 1940.
Private Collection.

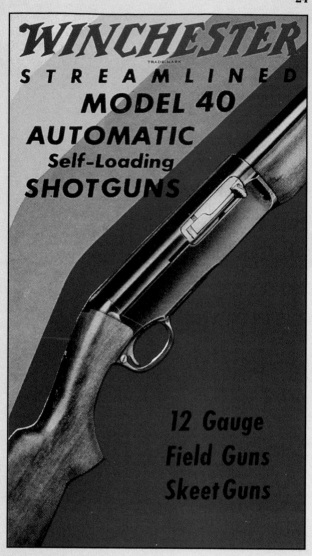

Cover of the advertising brochure announcing the Winchester Model 40 Semiautomatic Shotgun published in early 1940.
Private Collection.

Sample .22 caliber straight pull bolt action rifle and box magazine semiautomatic rifle designed by Carl G. Swebilius in 1940 and 1941.
Winchester Arms Collection (Inv. Nos. WRC 790 [top] and 787), Cody Firearms Museum.

Illustrations contained in *Winchester Goes To War*, a promotional booklet circulated by the Winchester company in December of 1943, to demonstrate its contributions to the war effort. *Private Collection.*

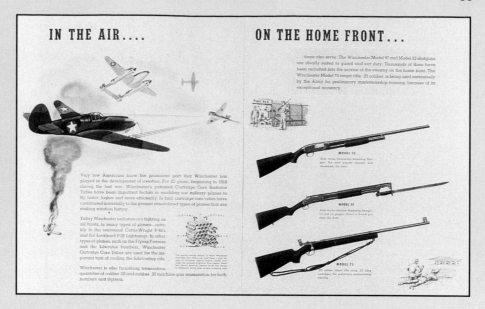

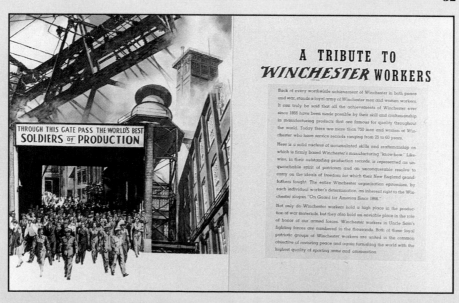

27

Illustrations contained in *Winchester Goes To War*, a promotional booklet circulated by the Winchester company in December of 1943, to demonstrate its contributions to the war effort.
Private Collection.

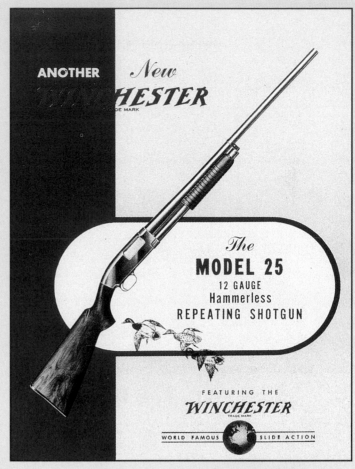

Left: Cover of the advertising brochure published in 1948, to announce the introduction of the Winchester Model 43 Rifle. *Private Collection.*

Right: Cover of the advertising brochure published in 1949, to announce the introduction of the Winchester Model 25 Shotgun. *Private Collection.*

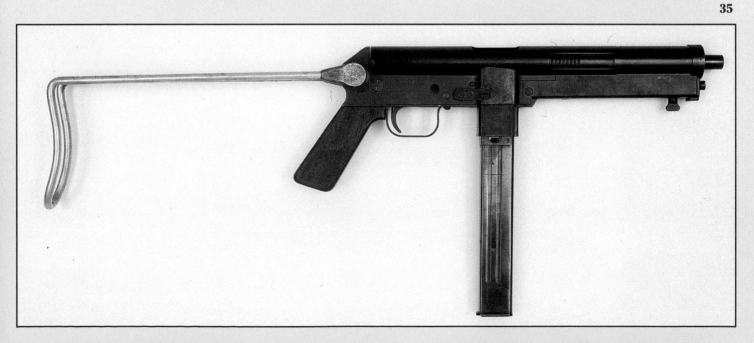

35

Sample Winchester Model N-l 9mm submachine gun designed by A.A. Arnold and M.M. Johnson in 1955, for possible adoption by the North Atlantic Treaty Organization.
Winchester Arms Collection (Inv. No. WRC 7), Cody Firearms Museum.

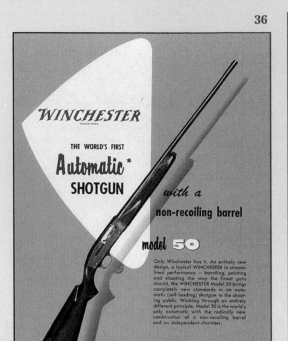

Left: Advertisement for the Winchester Model 50 semiautomatic shotgun introduced in 1954. *Private Collection.*

Right: Proof of a full-page advertisement for the Winchester Model 61, 67 and 74 rifles published in various magazines during late 1954. *Private Collection.*

38

Sample plastic-stocked and glass fiber reinforced barrel .22 caliber rifles made in 1961 and 1962, together with two conventionally made wood-stocked, identically designed samples. *Winchester Arms Collection (Inv. Nos. [top to bottom] WRC 1930, 1926, 1931, 1925, 1922 and 1929), Cody Firearms Museum.*

39. First, second and third samples made of the Winchester Special Purpose Infantry Rifle made in late 1962 and 1963.
Winchester Arms Collection (Inv. Nos. [top to bottom] WRC 1187,1185, and 1188), Cody Firearms Museum.

Winchester Mark II 16 gauge Liberator shotgun made in 1964.
Winchester Arms Collection (Inv. No. WRC 1177), Cody Firearms Museum.

Two sample .22 caliber semiautomatic rifles, designed in the early 1970s, as a possible replacement for the Winchester Model 63 semiautomatic rifle, which had been discontinued in 1958.
Winchester Arms Collection (Inv. Nos. WRC 2182 [top] and 1708), Cody Firearms Museum.

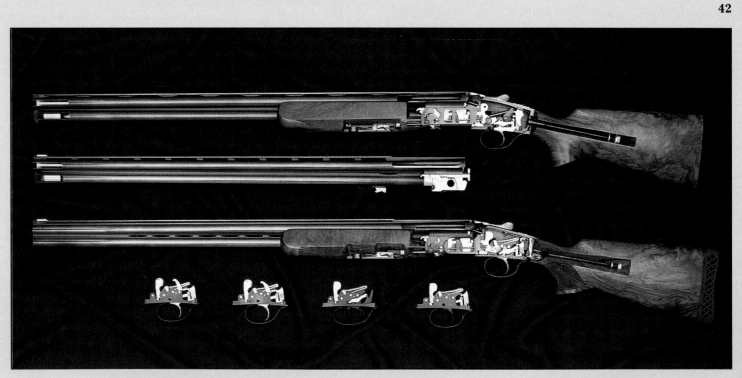

42

A skeletonized Perazzi Model MT6 (top) and MX8 (bottom) shotgun used by Olin Corporation for promotional purposes during the period it imported Perazzi arms. Also illustrated are a variety of interchangeable trigger and hammer units for the MX8.
Private Collection.

Plate 271

Ronald Payne rifling a U.S. M1 rifle barrel. Olin Corporation photograph.

Plate 272

H.S. Coy electro-welding two components of the U.S. M1 rifle. Olin Corporation photograph.

Plate 273
Sherwood Emerson profiling the stock blank for a U.S. M1 rifle. Olin Corporation photograph.

Plate 274
*E*dward Myscick inspecting the U.S. M1 rifle stocks prior to oiling and assembly. Olin Corporation photograph.

Plate 275
U.S. M1 rifles being assembled. Olin Corporation photograph.

Plate 276

Morris Bartlett installing the rear sight assembly to a U.S. M1 rifle. Olin Corporation photograph.

Plate 277

John Roche inspecting a completed U.S. M1 rifle. Olin Corporation photograph.

Plate 278

*T*est firing of the U.S. M1 rifle before final inspection. Olin Corporation photograph.

Plate 279
*E*arl Dormand and Leslie Friend packing U.S. M1 rifles for shipment. Olin Corporation photograph.

consequence of this, it was decided that it was necessary to redesign the rifle's lockwork.

The designer selected to perform this task was David Marsh Williams, who the company had hired under a one-year contract on July 1, 1939[20]. Williams immediately fitted a short stroke piston to the sample (Plates 280 and 281), which corrected some of the operating problems. The design of Browning's bolt, however, still made cycling erratic, so in late 1940, it was abandoned[21]. Williams then substituted a bolt of his own configuration. This bolt was of tubular form with two locking lugs located at its forward end and an angled slot cut in the bolt's body. The purpose of this slot was to receive a projection milled on the tip of the operating rod. When the rod moved rearward under pressure from the piston, the projection sliding in the bolt slot caused the bolt to rotate out of its locked position before any rearward movement of the bolt could begin. The delay which thereby occurred in the unlocking of the action allowed the pressure generated by the combustion of the cartridge powder to dissipate before the action began to cycle. This arrangement allowed the modified Browning-Williams rifle to be chambered for any high pressure cartridge

by the simple expedient of modifying the bolt slot length to adjust the bolt rotation to the point that the bolt could be safely opened. The versatility of the Williams' design was recognized by the company's management, and a series of samples (Plate 282) were authorized for field trials and endurance tests in January 1941.

Although the Winchester company relied primarily on its own designers, the personal friendship that existed between Edwin Pugsley and Carl G. Swebilius[22], founder of the High Standard Manufacturing Company, resulted in ten of Swebilius' designs being patented by Winchester[23]. While the majority of these designs, which were sold to the company for $1 each, were never selected for production, one did serve as the basis for the Winchester Model 77 semiautomatic rifle that was manufactured in limited quantities for the U.S. Marine Corps[24] (Color Plate 25 and Plates 283 and 284).

Though the Winchester company had been instrumental in the design and development of the .30 caliber light rifle cartridge for the U.S. Army Ordnance Department, it did not elect to submit a light rifle for the Army's trials[25]. In late May 1941, however, the company began seriously considering that option. In a letter to Col. Rene R. Studler, Edwin

Plate 280

Sample .30-06 caliber Jonathon E. Browning action semiautomatic rifle fitted with a short stroke piston designed by David M. Williams, submitted to the U.S. Marine Corps rifle trials held in San Diego in November 1940. Winchester Arms Collection (Inv. No. W1430), Cody Firearms Museum. Olin Corporation photograph.

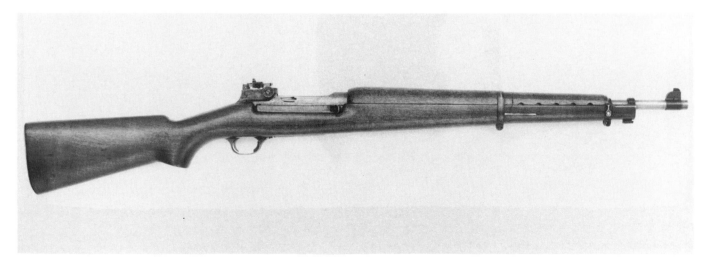

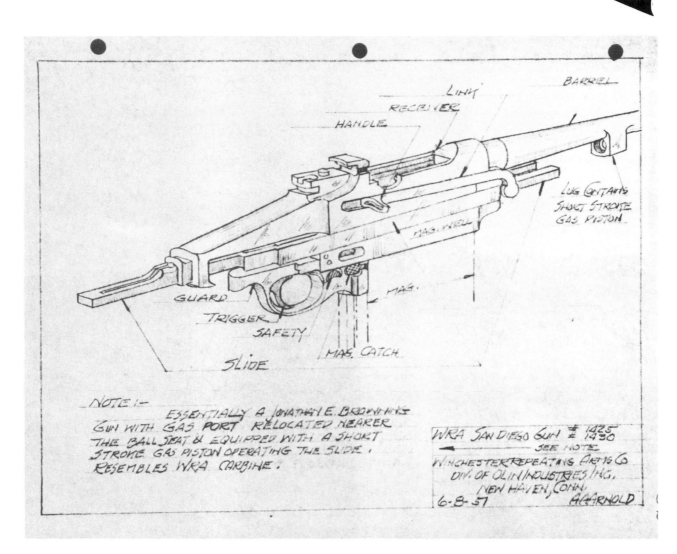

The labels visible in the drawing include: HANDLE, RECEIVER, LINK, BARREL, LUG CONTAINS SHORT STROKE GAS PISTON, MAG. WELL, MAG., GUARD, TRIGGER, SAFETY, MAG. CATCH, SLIDE.

NOTE:— ESSENTIALLY A JONATHAN E. BROWNING GUN WITH GAS PORT RELOCATED NEARER THE BALL SEAT & EQUIPPED WITH A SHORT STROKE GAS PISTON OPERATING THE SLIDE. RESEMBLES WRA CARBINE.

WRA SAN DIEGO GUN # 1425 # 1430
SEE NOTE
WINCHESTER REPEATING ARMS CO.
DIV. OF OLIN INDUSTRIES INC.
NEW HAVEN, CONN.
6-8-51   A.A. ARNOLD

Pugsley outlined the company's position[26]:

"While we have not as yet submitted a model for the light rifle, we thought it best to tell you of some experiments being carried on at the present time which, in their present state of development, are beginning to show considerable promise. It was felt, there fore, that you might be interested in hearing of this progress in connection with the current tests of light rifles as present indications are that these experiments may produce a light rifle along new lines which we believe will have great possibilities.

The experiments at the present time take the form of adopting some of the features which we have adopted in the Winchester semi-automatic .30-60 rifle to the M.1, notably the short stroke piston, the special chamber and simplification of the magazine and stock. We are pushing through a rifle embodying these features which we hope to be able to shoot this week that appears in its present state of completions to weight approximately 7- pounds. If a rifle that will handle the .30-60 cartridge can be produced with a weight of 7- pounds, it is then obvious that for a cartridge less than one-half the size the same mechanism should not weight more than 4- to 4-3/4 pounds. The advantage of our short stroke piston is that it is self- sealing, allowing the escape of practically no gas, so that our loss in ballistics with his type of mecha-

Plate 281

S*chematic drawing by A.A. Arnold of the sample Browning-Williams semiautomatic rifle illustrated in Plate 280. Winchester Arms Collection Archives, Cody Firearms Museum.*

267

nism should be negligible. It is not measurable on the .30-60 cartridges."

Upon seeing the Winchester sample, Studler asked the company to prepare a light rifle based upon the same design. The work on this project, which was to result in the U.S. M1 carbine, is best described in Edwin Pugsley's report written in June 1951[27].

"I thereupon agreed to build such a model, and the first model of the carbine [Plates 285-288] was the result. This was built in some thirteen days following Studler's visit, and was simply patched up, using a receiver and bolt which was a reduced size model of the receiver and bolt of the 7 lb. .30 M2 Winchester Military Rifle. Roemer and Humeston were the leading spirits in getting this gun going, Humeston making a sketch on a small drafting board he had at this bench of the essential sizes for the receiver and bolt. In looking for a trigger mechanism, Roemer found he could use the 1907 trigger guard and interrupting trigger mechanism complete, and sketched the way this could be adapted. He realized that we would not be able to get a double column magazine into this gun, but I decided it would be perfectly satisfactory to demonstrate to the Ordnance Department. Williams was extremely

Plate 282

Sample .30-06 military rifle fitted with a Williams' short-stroke piston and a U.S. M1 rifle style bolt made in early 1941. Winchester Arms Collection (Inv. No. W1457), Cody Firearms Museum.

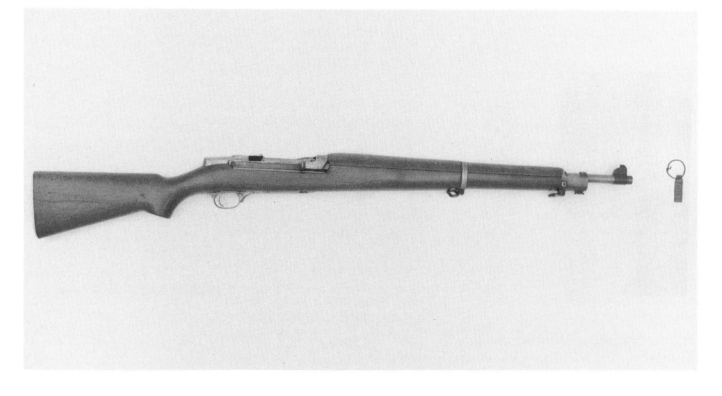

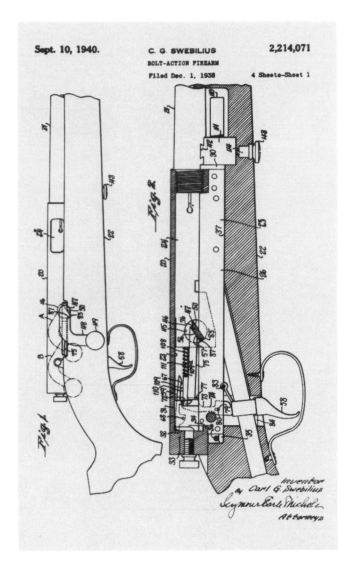

Sept. 10, 1940.   C. G. SWEBILIUS   2,214,071
                          BOLT-ACTION FIREARM
                          Filed Dec. 1, 1938   4 Sheets-Sheet 1

Above: Plate 283

*S*heet 1 of the specification drawings enrolled with Carl G.
Swebilius' U.S. Patent Number 2214071 issued Sept. 10, 1940.
Winchester Arms Collection Archives, Cody Firearms
Museum.

Below: Plate 284

*S*heet 1 of the specification drawings enrolled with Carl G.
Swebilius' U.S. Patent Number 2282903 issued May 12, 1942.
Winchester Arms Collection Archives, Cody Firearms
Museum.

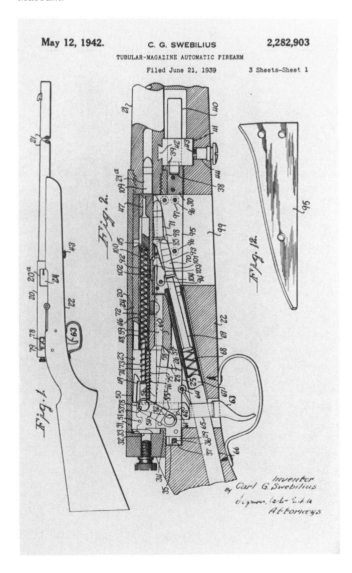

May 12, 1942.   C. G. SWEBILIUS   2,282,903
                  TUBULAR-MAGAZINE AUTOMATIC FIREARM
                  Filed June 21, 1939   3 Sheets-Sheet 1

Above: Plate 285

*R*eceiver detail of the sample .30 caliber carbine made in thirteen days during the summer of 1941. Winchester Arms Collection (Inv. No. W1348), Cody Firearms Museum.

Below: Plate 286

*D*isassembled view of the thirteen-day carbine illustrated in Plate 285.

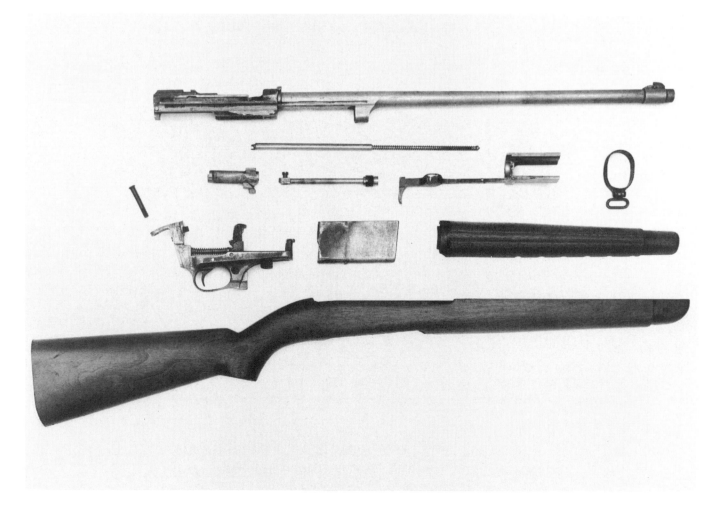

upset by the Winchester organization proceeding with this gun in spite of him, and he warned me several times that he would not be responsible for anything concerning it, that the did not wish his name associated with it in any way, and notified me that I was doing it entirely on my own responsibility. I accepted this situation and we proceeded to get the gun to operate without any help whatsoever from Williams. We did, however, practically copy the .30 M2 7 lb. Winchester Military Model which Williams had previously worked out, using the short stroke piston, general arrangement of the bolt, receiver, and slide as demonstrated in that gun.

When the gun was ready I called Studler and asked him to come up to see it and he agreed to be up the next morning. I then went up to have a talk with Williams, told him Studler was coming and that we were going to show this gun to him; that I would be glad to have Williams demonstrate the gun if he would cooperate and demonstrate the rifle to the best interest of Winchester, but that unless he would agree to this I would not have him present and would demonstrate the gun myself. Williams agreed to cooperate and accordingly Williams, Humeston and I took the gun to Pine Swamp and Williams demonstrated it in a very satisfactory manner.

Studler was captivated with its action, looks and general feel, and said he would take it with him to Washington. I refused to let him do this, telling him that I would bring it to Washington whenever he wanted me to but I had had very poor experience allowing untried models to be taken by Ordnance personnel. The next day Studler phoned me, asking that I be in Washington the day following, and at that time I showed the model to a conference headed by General Courtney Hodges who was then Chief of Infantry. General Hodges was also immediately capti-

vated by the gun and demanded to shoot it at Aberdeen the following Monday."

After Pugsley's return to New Haven, a revised sample was made in 30 days (Plate 289) and submitted to the Ordnance Department for testing on Sept. 15, 1941. As Pugsley later wrote, it "outdistanced all competitors and was so far ahead of the rest that it could only be the unanimous choice, which it was."[28] On Oct. 1, 1941, the Winchester light rifle was selected as the winner of the competition, and Pugsley immedi-

Plate 287

Sheet 1 of the specification drawings enrolled with David M. Williams' U.S. Patent Number 2308257 issued Jan. 12, 1943 (application filed Sept. 22, 1941). Winchester Arms Collection Archives, Cody Firearms Museum.

271

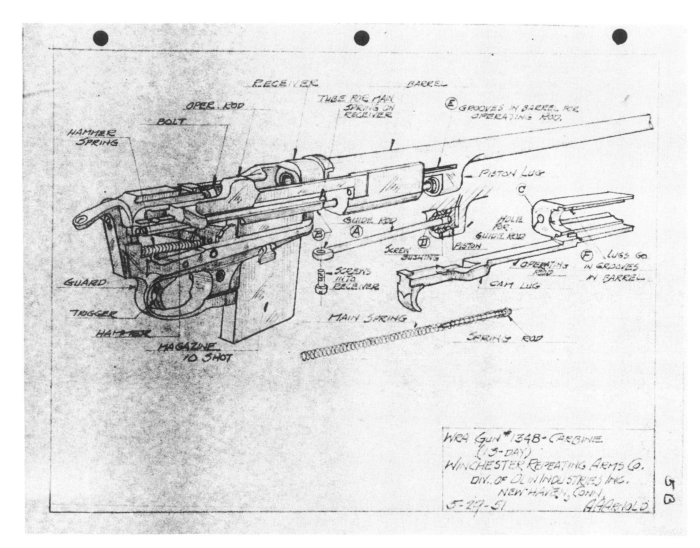

Plate 288

*S*chematic drawing by A.A. Arnold of the sample thirteen-day carbine illustrated in Plate 285. Winchester Arms Collection Archives, Cody Firearms Museum.

ately pressed the company to begin the production of the tools and fixtures needed to manufacture it. His proposal, however, was opposed by T.I.S. Boak[29], the company's Operating Manager and the members of the Operating Committee since it appeared that the government was going to award the production contract to the Inland Division of the General Motors Corporation. Ultimately, though, the Winchester company was to receive a production contract on Nov. 24, 1941 for 350,000 M1 carbines (Plate 290).

From the viewpoint of the speed with which the first and second carbine samples were made and the absence of any major changes in the basic design,

the Winchester light rifle marked a high water point in the company's ability to produce viable arms on short notice. The process, though, had demonstrated one of David M. Williams' shortcomings, namely, his inability to work under pressure[30].

While the Winchester Repeating Arms Company had been forbidden from accepting any contracts for Great Britain or France during the early stages of World War II, this situation changed after the passage of the Lend-Lease Act in March 1941. Almost immediately after that act was approved by the U.S. Congress, the company began to manufacture large quantities of ammunition for the British and Com-

Top: Plate 289

The sample Winchester carbine made in approximately thirty days during August and September 1941. Winchester Arms Collection (Inv. No. W1349), Cody Firearms Museum. Olin Corporation photograph.

Bottom: Plate 290

U.S. M1 carbine manufactured by the Winchester Repeating Arms Company. Olin Corporation photograph.

Plate 291

Charles Semper, Jr. and Charles Benson cupping brass planchets during the first stages of making .303 caliber cartridge cases. Olin Corporation photograph.

monwealth forces (Plates 291- 293) under contracts led by the U.S. Army Ordnance Department[31]. As the likelihood of the United States being drawn into the war increased during 1941, the volume of orders received from the U.S. government began to also incriminately rise[32].

"We must be the great arsenal of democracy."

— Franklin D. Roosevelt
Dec. 29, 1940

When the United States declared war on the Axis Powers on Dec. 8, 1941, the Winchester company put into effect a series of contingency plans developed over the previous year to change the plant's production facilities from civilian to military use[33]. The thoroughness of these plans, developed at the insistence of John M. Olin and Boak, allowed the company to change all its production lines, in both an orderly and speedy fashion, by the second week of February 1942[34]. Among the first orders to be processed on the new lines was a contract for 96,213 U.S. M1 rifles received in Jan. 28, 1942[35].

Although it was evident that the government was committed to the production and issuance of both the M1 rifle

Plate 292
Carolyn Perry operating a .303 caliber cartridge straightening machine. Olin Corporation photograph.

and M1 carbine, the Winchester company continued to work on the development of alternative designs. Chief among these were a series of arms based upon David M. Williams' design. While the carbine he had developed as an alternative to the M1 carbine was not completed until December 1941, it was viewed as "unquestionably an advance on the one that was accepted."[36]

One of the advantages of the Williams' design (Plates 294 and 295) was that it allowed the action to be stripped for cleaning or replacing broken parts simply by removing a bolt housing that was secured to the receiver by an interrupted thread locking ring. Williams also employed a superior lockwork

than that used in either the M1 carbine or M1 rifle. In acknowledgment of the design's advantages, samples were made in .30 carbine, .30-60 and .50 caliber.

Though Ordnance Department tests of the .30-60 rifle version demonstrated its marked superiority over the standard M1 rifle, it was to be the light machine gun (Plates 296-298) and anti-tank versions (Plate 299) that aroused the most interest. Both of the latter incorporated an ingenious device to dampen recoil. By placing two strong coil springs on either side of the barrel breech that were attached to a recoiling lug on the barrel, Williams was able to transfer a considerable amount of the recoil forces into the springs,

Plate 293

Marion Dance, Carmen Byrd, Lillian Brown and Hilda Johnson gauging and inspecting .303 caliber cartridges. Olin Corporation photograph.

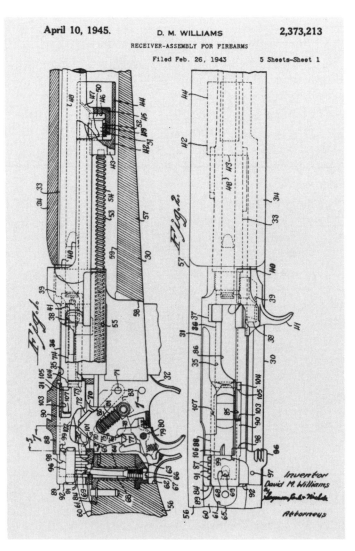

April 10, 1945.   D. M. WILLIAMS   2,373,213

RECEIVER-ASSEMBLY FOR FIREARMS

Filed Feb. 26, 1943   5 Sheets-Sheet 1

Above: Plate 294

Sample .30 caliber David M. Williams carbine completed in December 1941. Winchester Arms Collection (Inv. No. W1702), Cody Firearms Museum.

Left: Plate 295

Sheet 1 of the specification drawings enrolled with David M. Williams' U.S. Patent Number 2373213 issued April 10, 1945 (application filed Feb. 26, 1943). Winchester Arms Collection Archives, Cody Firearms Museum.

thereby absorbing its energy. The effect of this was to reduce the general recoil of both the light machine gun and the anti-tank rifle to the point that they were essentially recoilless. This meant that both arms could be used by infantrymen without undo stress being placed upon them during firing, a major benefit from the standpoint of accuracy as well as use. However, by the time these designs were selected for any serious testing, the war was almost over.

Curiously, it was during the testing of the .50 caliber Williams anti-tank rifle that the Winchester company seriously considered entering the automotive business for the second time in its history. On this occasion, however, unlike in 1909[37], the company toyed with the idea of manufacturing a light armored vehicle in which the anti-tank rifle could be mounted. Based upon a surviving photograph of the Winchester "Tank Killer,"[38] it had an overall length of approximately twelve feet and a height of four feet. The forward section of the vehicle had sloping armor, and the tracks were powered by a 1939 Chrysler Imperial engine. No record exists as to its width or crew capacity, though the size would probably have

only allowed two. Other than the one built in December 1944, it is doubtful whether any others were made.

One of the Winchester company's greatest contributions to later arms design took place in late 1944, when Edwin Pugsley fitted an electric motor to a Model 1883 Gatling gun (Plate 300). When it was found that the operating crank that was normally operated by hand could be automatically turned by electric power at various cyclic rates, the basic principle of the General Electric Corporation's Vulcan Automatic Cannon was born[39]. Why the Winchester Repeating Arms Company declined to pursue this design is unknown as are the events which eventually brought Pugsley's discovery to General Electric's attention.

By the close of World War II, the Winchester company had proved its worth to the Allied cause by producing an immense amount of war material. In all, the firm's "Soldiers of Production" (Color Plates 26-32) made the following[40]:

Unlike earlier wars, World War II was not to be ended by the force of arms, but by a simple equation: $E=mc^2$.

Above: Plate 297

Winchester Automatic Rifle made in 1944. Winchester Arms Collection (Inv. No. WRC69), Cody Firearms Museum.

Below: Plate 298

Disassembled view of the Winchester automatic rifle illustrated in Plate 297.

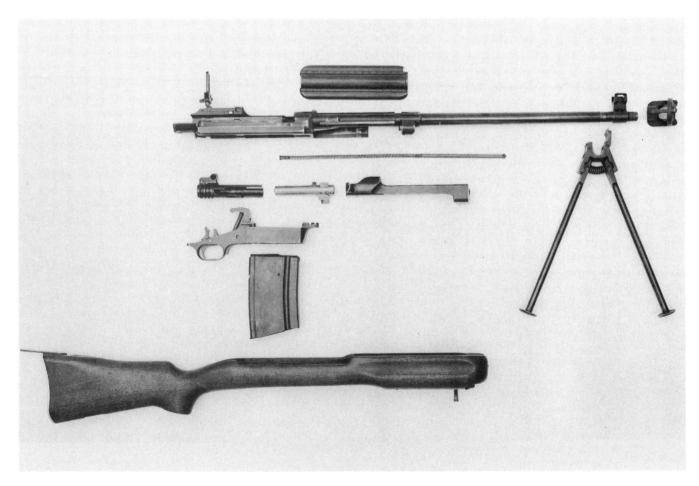

UNITED STATES GOVERNMENT

Description	Beginning	Conclusion	Quantity
U.S. Rifle Cal.,30 M1	12-27-40	6-28-45	507,880
Win. Rifle Cal. .30	6-15-45	7-5-45	10
Win. Rifle M/70-30-06	10-20-42	3-12-43	3,029
U.S. Carbine Cal..30 M1, M2 & T3	10-5-42	9-7-45	699,469
Win. M/12 Shotgun 12 ga.	4-1-42	3-21-44	61,014
Repairs to Win. M/12 Shotgun	11-10-44	9-12-45	19,207
Win. M/97 Trench Gun 12 ga.	1-31-42	9-29-43	24,829
Repairs to Win. M/97 Shotgun	11-10-44	9-12-45	8,889
Win. M/12 Shotgun 16 ga.	10-21-42	11-23-43	7,636
Win. M/75 Rifle	1940	1942	14,665
Repairs to Win. M/75 Rifle	12-28-44	9-12-45	4,584
Win. M/37 Shotgun	1941	1942	5,410
Ctge. Ball Cal. .38-200 gr.	12-13-44	4-9-45	863,450
Ctge. Ball Cal. .38 Spec. 158 gr.	3-21-45	8-7-45	87,000
Ctge. Blank Cal. .30 Army (30/40 Krag)	4-12-44	1-17-45	855,000
Ctge. Dummy Cal. .303	11-30-42	5-24-44	285,000
Ctge. Cal. .303	1-20-42	3-22-44	1,076,464,179
Ctge. Carbine Cal. .30 M1	1-19-42	9-13-45	278,139,976
Ctge. Carbine Cal. .30 M1 H.P.T.	5-27-42	9-6-45	13,105,665
Ctge. Dummy Carbine Cal. .30 M1	3-3-43	3-1-45	3,755,100
Ctge. Ball Cal. .30 M2	3-4-42	9-18-45	592,519,527
Ctge. Ball Cal. .45 M1911	3-2-42	8-23-45	281,998,170
Ctge. Cal. .50 Ball, AP, & Tracer	4-16-42	8-15-44	60,553,933
Ctge. 9 m/m Ball, Parabellum	6-23-42	2-7-44	414,351,260
Ctge. Cal. .22 Rim Fire	6-8-42	9-6-45	530,838,000
Paper Shot Shells 16 ga.	2-2-43	3-16-43	500,000
Paper Shot Shells 12 ga.	12-17-42	7-18-45	140,463,000
All Brass Shot Shells 12 ga.	12-29-42	9-11-45	6,086,700
Paper Shot Shells .410 ga.	7-4-42	4-30-43	169,500
Paper Shot Shells .410 ga. Slugs	10-7-43	12-2-43	150,000
Ignition Ctge. M5	9-19-41	8-24-45	72,979,889
Ignition Ctge. M4	3-27-42	8-24-45	9,923,965

Ignition Ctge. M3	3-17-42	5-26-45	8,839,140
Ignition Ctge. T2	2-22-45	9-11-45	80,420
Ignition Ctge. T26	8-31-44	1-8-45	70,000
Ignition Ctge. T17	1-12-44	1-12-45	150,000
Ignition Ctge. M6	12-22-41	3-9-42	2,000,000
Ignition Ctge. T1	8-18-42	12-16-42	4,000
*Primers #110	4-23-42	9-14-42	11,000,000
*Primers #2 Navy	5-8-42	6-20-45	26,765,009
Primers #1 U.S. Navy	6-4-42	8-3-44	1,412,000
*Primers M39	8-3-44	8-30-45	42,775,000
Primers #209B	12-31-41	1-30-45	88,635,657
Primers #3	11-8-43	1-12-44	700,000
*Primers Mark V	4-14-41	8-13-45	209,272,436
*Primers New No.4	4-27-42	8-31-45	147,123,381
*Primers M29	5-7-41	8-30-45	93,668,500
*Plunger Housing for Fuzes	10-10-44	8-21-45	5,014,190
Case Cups Cal. .50	4-24-44	6-29-45	22,310,365 lbs
Case Cups Cal. .30	2-29-44	7-14-44	2,379,362 lbs
Case Cups Carbine Cal. .30	2-29-44	7-14-4	25,191 lbs
Carbine Bullet Jackets Cal. .30	2-29-44	7-14-4	14,790 lbs
*6" 10 ga. Primed Shells for Flares	4-13-42	8-13-4	1,536,900
*Includes sub-contracts			
Steel Air Rifle Shot	7-14-42	5-29-44	074,000 lbs
Ctge. Clips U.S. Rifle .30 M1	8-15-41	3-30-43	11,310,000
Ctge. Clips 7.92 m/m Packed in Cans for Govt. of China	11-23-44	3-28-4	1,458,240

• Plus an unknown number of batteries, flashlights and airplane engine radiator tubes (Plate 301).

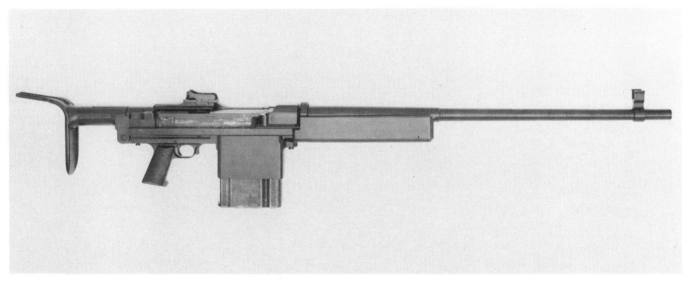

Plate 299

Winchester .50 caliber semiautomatic antitank rifle designed by David M. Williams in 1944. Olin Corporation photograph.

Plate 300

Colt .45-70 caliber Model 1883 Gatling Gun, serial number 449, dated 1886, fitted with an electric drive mechanism by Edwin Pugsley in 1945, to demonstrate the feasibility of operating the normally hand-cranked firing mechanism automatically. Olin Corporation photograph.

Plate 301

*K*arl Hummel inspecting Winchester manufactured airplane radiators in
1942. Olin Corporation photograph.

Endnotes

1. The following models were discontinued between late December of 1931 and 1939: 1903 (1932); 1906 (1932); 57 (1936); 60 (1934); 1886 (1935); 1892 (1932); 1910 (1932); 53 (1932); 55 (1932); 54 (1936), and; 41 (1934). The following models were introduced during the same period: 61 (1932); 62 (1932); 63 (1933); 67 (1934); 68 (1934); 69 (1934); 677 (1937); 697 (1937); 72 (1938); 75 (1938); 74 (1939); 64 (1933); 65 (1933); 71 (1935); 70 (1935); 42 (1933), and; 24 (1939).

2. Watrous, op. cit.

3. Frank Burton's United States Patent Number 2263918 issued Nov. 25, 1941.

4. The Model 24 was based primarily on Burton's patents for the Model 21 issued in 1930 and 1931.

5. William C. Roemer, "Development of the Model 30, Auto Rifle" (April 10, 1940), page 1. M1 Carbine File 1. Winchester Arms Collection Archives, Cody Firearms Museum.

6. Ibid.

7. Ibid, pages 1 and 2.

8. Ibid, page 2.

9. U.S. M1 Rifle Educational Contract (Order Number W-ORD-343) File. Winchester Arms Collection Archives, Cody Firearms Museum.

10. Ibid.

11. William Roemer's United States Patents Number 2229390 issued Jan. 21, 1941, and Number 2333677 issued Nov. 9, 1943; and Edwin Pugsley's United States Registered Design Number 117638 issued Nov. 14, 1939.

12. For mention of the Grant Hammond two-shot shotgun, see Chapter 5, page 186.

13. "Data on the New Winchester Automatic Shotguns," pages 3 and 4. Model 40 Production File. Winchester Arms Collection Archives, Cody Firearms Museum.

14. Watrous, op, cit.

15. Ibid. The exchange program continued at least through 1956.

16. Watrous, op. cit.

17. Report dated July 13, 1944, detailing Net Sales of Ammunition for 1936 to June 1, 1940. World War II Contracts–Miscellaneous. Winchester Arms Collection Archives, Cody Firearms Museum.

18. Contract Number W852 ORD-4622.

19. Roemer, Model 30, op. cit., pages 2 and 3.

20. Edwin Pugsley, Confidential Report on the Development of the U.S. M1 Carbine dated June 20, 1951, page 3. M1 Carbine File 1. Winchester Arms Collection Archives, Cody Firearms Museum. The full text of this report is reproduced in **ARMAX**, Volume II, Number 1 (1988), pages 79-89.

21. Ibid.

22. A brief biography of Swebilius is to be found in Lt. Col. William S. Brophy, **Marlin Firearms: A History of the Guns and the Company That Made Them** (Stackpole Books; Harrisburg, PA: 1989), pages 42-45.

23. Swebilius' United States Patents assigned to the Winchester Repeating Arms Company are as follows: Number 1852440 (issued April 5, 1932); 1928871 (issued Oct. 3, 1933); 2155512 (issued April 25, 1939); 2203035 (issued June 4, 1940); 2214071 (issued Sept. 10, 1940); 2279931 (issued April 14,

1942); 2282903 (issued May 12, 1942); 2290778 (issued July 21, 1942); 2328108 (issued Aug. 31, 1943); and 2334798 (issued Nov. 23, 1943).

24. C.G. Swebilius' United States Patent Number 2282903 was used as the basis for the Model 77 design. However, a box magazine was substituted for Swebilius' butt magazine.

25. For a complete and detailed history of the U.S. M1 carbine's development, as well as for the .30 caliber carbine cartridge, see Larry L. Ruth, **War Baby! The U.S. Caliber .30 Carbine** (Collector Grade Publications, Inc.; Toronto, Canada: 1992).

26. Pugsley, Confidential Report, op. cit., pages 3 and 4.

27. Ibid, pages 4 and 5.

28. Ibid, page 10.

29. Although T.I.S. Boak was disliked by many members of the Winchester company, including Pugsley, he had an uncanny ability to arrange production schedules, as well as insure timely deliveries. In many respects he must be credited with the success the Winchester company achieved in meeting and often exceeding contract fulfillment dates.

30. Pugsley, Confidential Report, op. cit., pages 7 and 12.

31. For example, Contract Number DAW-478-ORD-40 dated Sept. 20, 1941, for 750 million rounds of .303 British ammunition.

32. For example, Contract Number W478-ORD-3 dated Nov. 27, 1941, for twenty million rounds of .50 Armor Piercing M2 ammunition.

33. T.I.S. Boak, War Transition Plan (undated, pre-December 1941). World War II Contracts-Miscellaneous. Winchester Arms Collection Archives, Cody Firearms Museum.

34. Edwin Pugsley, Report on the Operations of the Winchester Repeating Arms Company 1941-46, page 1. World War II Contracts– Miscellaneous. Winchester Arms Collection Archives, Cody Firearms Museum.

35. Contract Number 852-ORD-4622.

36. Pugsley, Confidential Report, op, cit., page 13.

37. In early 1909, the Winchester company briefly considered making automobiles for Hotchkiss & Cie of Paris, France. After royalty arrangements could not be mutually agreed on, the matter was dropped. Cf. Beverly R. Kines and Henry A. Clark, Jr., **Standard Catalog of American Cars 1805-1942** (Krause Publications; Iola, WI: 1992), page 1504.

38. An 8x10-inch black-and-white print of this photograph with manuscript notations of the vehicle's specifications was in the collection of the late Lt. Col. William S. Brophy of North Haven, Connecticut.

39. For a description of the Vulcan Cannon, see Lt. Col. George M. Chinn, **The Machine Gun, History, Evolution, and Development of Mannual, Automatic and Airborne Repeating Weapons** (U.S. Navy; Washington, D.C.: 1953), pages 87-103.

40. Report on contracts fulfilled for the U.S. government dated Sept. 19, 1945. World War II Contracts–Miscellaneous. Winchester Arms Collection Archives, Cody Firearms Museum.

CHAPTER 8

RESURGENCE AND CHANGE: 1946-1960

When World War II ended on Sept. 2, 1945, the Winchester Repeating Arms Company, like much of North America, began the readjustment back to civilian life. This transition, however, was made much easier and less traumatic upon the company's work force due to the fact that detailed preparations had been made well beforehand.

Consequently, military production lines were gradually dismantled as contracts were cancelled or completed, and then, over a period of several months, refitted with the tooling necessary to manufacture civilian arms. When this was completed, the Winchester factory closely resembled how it had appeared in 1941, but there were some differences. Three of the production lines that had been disassembled in December 1941 and January 1942 were absent, as were a large number of machines devoted to the manufacture of specific variations previously offered for particular models. These changes in the company's product line were all the result of decisions made during World War II concerning postwar marketing strategies.

The origins of the leaner Winchester company that emerged from the war can be directly traced to the events which occurred immediately after Dec. 7, 1941. When the company decided to close down all of its civilian production lines, it realized that it had a unique opportunity to review each component of its product line without the normal hinderance of maintaining manufacturing schedules or reacting to market pressures. As a result, in the spring of 1942, George R. Watrous was commissioned by John M. Olin and T.I.S. Boak to prepare a complete and dispassionate analysis of all the models which had been in production the previous year[1]. In particular, Watrous was to assess the specific weaknesses or strengths of individual models and to provide an estimate of their market position relative to the competition. This report[2], completed in early June 1942, was circulated to company representatives nationwide for comment on June 8[3]. Eventually, it was to be the synthesis of Watrous' comments with those he received that was to form the basis for the company's postwar production and marketing program.

Distributed on Jan. 15, 1943 to the senior management of the Winchester company, the final combined report made the following recommendations concerning the firm's 1941 product line[4]:

Shotguns:

Model 12 – improve the smoothness of the action as it is criticized for being rough
  – consider the production of a lightweight version
  – introduce a 28 gauge version
Model 21 – no changes
Model 24 – improve its extractors
  – cosmetically change its appearance so that it does not look awkward or clumsy
  – use a better quality wood for its stocks
Model 37 – no changes
Model 40 – abandon this model totally as "It worked bad, looked bad and it shot bad – in fact, it was a lemon."
Model 42 – no changes

Rimfire Rifles:

Model 52 – no changes
Model 61 – no changes
Model 62 – no changes
Model 63 – no changes
Model 67/68 – discontinue one or both
Model 69A – no changes
Model 72 – improve the design (specifically the safety) so that it can compete with the Remington Model 512
Model 74 – improve the action and redesign it so that .22 caliber short, long and long rifle cartridges can be used interchangeably
Model 75 – no changes

Centerfire Rifles

Model 07 – discontinue when parts supply is exhausted
Model 64 – discontinue
Model 65 – discontinue
Model 70 – no changes
Model 71 – no changes
Model 94 – discontinue .25-35 caliber and market as "Deer Rifle"

The general recommendations for postwar changes made in this report can be summarized as follows[5]:

1. Improve all packaging and literature.

2. Reduce the number of variations manufactured for each   model so that ordering and the sales literature can be simplified.

3. Change the appearance of those arms being purchased by the   United States Government in quantity so that if they are dumped on the market after the war, they will have little to no effect upon the company's sales of similar arms.

4. *Introduce a new bolt action sporting rifle chambered for cartridges such as the .22 Hornet, .25-20 or .32-20.*

5. *Introduce a low to medium cost bolt action sporting rifle chambered for high velocity cartridges up to .30-06 caliber.*

6. *Introduce a self-loading centerfire rifle.*

7. *Consider the manufacture of a combination rifle/shotgun in .22rf/.410 or .22Hornet/.410 calibers.*

8. *Develop a single barrel trap shotgun to compete with Ithaca.*

9. *Consider the introduction of full-length military style stocks for arms such as the Model 52, 75 and 70, to take advantage of returning servicemen's possible preference for that style of stock.*

10. *Seriously consider the substitution of plastic stocks (grained to resemble walnut or bird's-eye maple) for wood stocks.*

After the relative merits of all the recommendations had been debated by the company's Operating Committee, it was decided in mid-1943 to implement some of the changes that had been suggested[6]. The Models 65, 68 and .25-35 caliber 94 were to be discontinued, and all the special order variations offered for models to be kept in production were to be unilaterally reduced in number[7]. Though there had been a strong call for the Model 64 to be discontinued, the Operating Committee decided to retain it in the company's product line as they believed that there would be a continued demand for a higher grade version of the Model 94 carbine[8]. The accuracy of this assessment was later proven by the strong sales generated by the Model 64 from 1946 to 1957[9].

Action on the remainder of the report's proposals was to be tabled until early 1944, when the volume of war-related work being done by the Design Department had decreased to the point where other discretionary projects could be assigned to it.

Among the first commercial projects to be worked on by the Design Department in 1944 were cosmetic changes to the Models 67 and 69 so that they resembled military arms[10]. Later in the year, though, a much broader development program was undertaken. An enclosed striker .22 caliber single-shot rifle was completed, and samples were made of the .25-20 caliber bolt-action rifle that had been suggested in 1942[11]. Attempts also were made to develop a combination rifle/shotgun, but these were abandoned in favor of pursuing the simple expedient of producing interchangeable rifle barrels for the Model 37 shotgun[12]. Preliminary work was also begun on the design of a self-loading centerfire rifle[13].

Although this work only resulted in two new production models after the war (the Model 43 and 47), it did allow the Winchester company to explore a variety of new product options before reentering the civilian arms market in late 1945. This, coupled with the decisions reached concerning the models previously manufactured, gave the

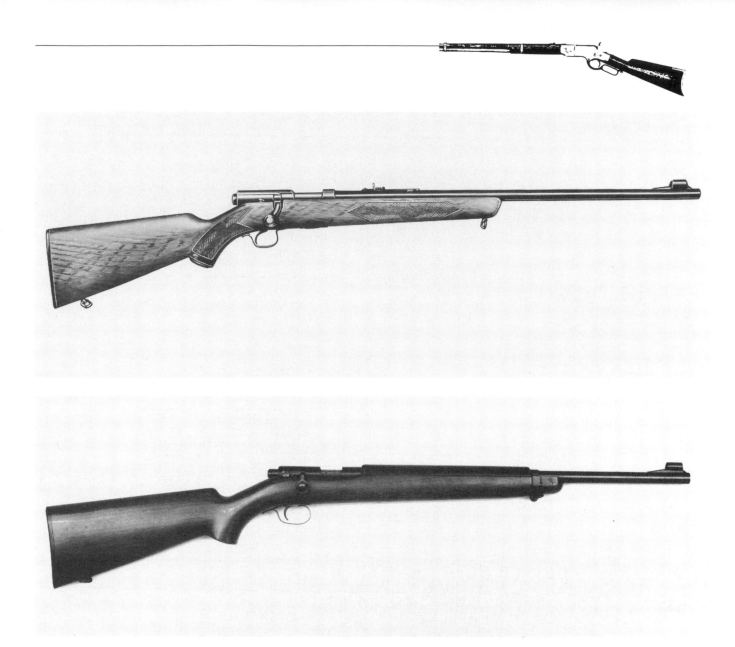

company a considerable competitive edge. Moreover, as the Design Department had already switched gears and had begun the planning of civilian arms, it was able to aggressively work on new designs as soon as it was free of the constraints placed upon it by war-related work. As a result, it was able to turn out, in a rather short period, a number of design proposals which would later result in production models.

During the immediate postwar period, the Winchester company introduced the Model 43 bolt-action rifle (Color Plate 33 and Plate 302) in .22 Hornet, .25-20 and .32-20 caliber and the Model 47 single-shot .22 caliber rifle (Plates 303-305)[14]. It also briefly flirted with the idea of manufacturing a sporting version of the U.S. M1 carbine (Plate 306) until difficulties concerning the regaining of exclusive production rights from the government caused that plan to be set aside[15].

By 1948, work was well advanced on another of the 1942 suggestions, the self-loading shotgun (Plate 307). Spearheaded by John L. Lochhead (Plate 308), this project involved a number of the company's designers, including Harry H. Sefried II and David M. Williams (Plate 309)[16]. Lochhead and H.L. Crockett also were independently working on sample centerfire semiautomatic rifle designs during the same period[17].

While the greater part of the Design Department's attention was directed

Plate 302

C*onceptual drawing of the Model 43 sporting rifle. Olin Corporation photograph.*

Plate 303

S*ample Model 47 single-shot rifle fitted with a M1 carbine style stock made in June or July of 1948. Winchester Arms Collection (Inv. No. WRC661), Cody Firearms Museum.*

289

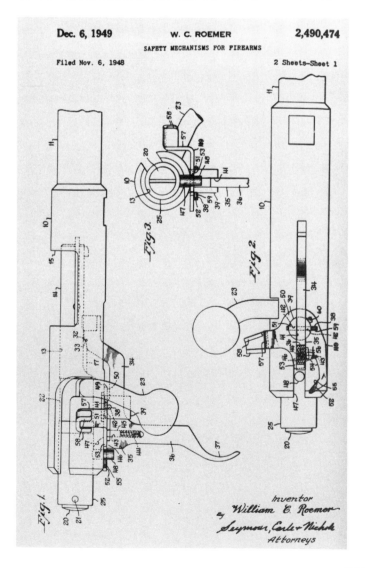

Dec. 6, 1949

W. C. ROEMER

2,490,474

SAFETY MECHANISMS FOR FIREARMS

Filed Nov. 6, 1948

2 Sheets—Sheet 1

Above: Plate 304

Detail of the sample Model 47 rifle illustrated in Plate 303.

Left: Plate 305

Sheet 1 of the specification drawings enrolled with William C. Roermer's U.S. Patent Number 2490475 issued Dec. 6, 1949, for an improved Model 47 rifle safety. Winchester Arms Collection Archives, Cody Firearms Museum.

Plate 306

*C*ommercial version of the U.S. M1 carbine designed by H.L. Crockett. Olin Corporation photograph.

Plate 307

*W*inchester Design Department photograph of sample Model 50 shotguns numbers 3-6, circa 1948/49. Olin Corporation photograph.

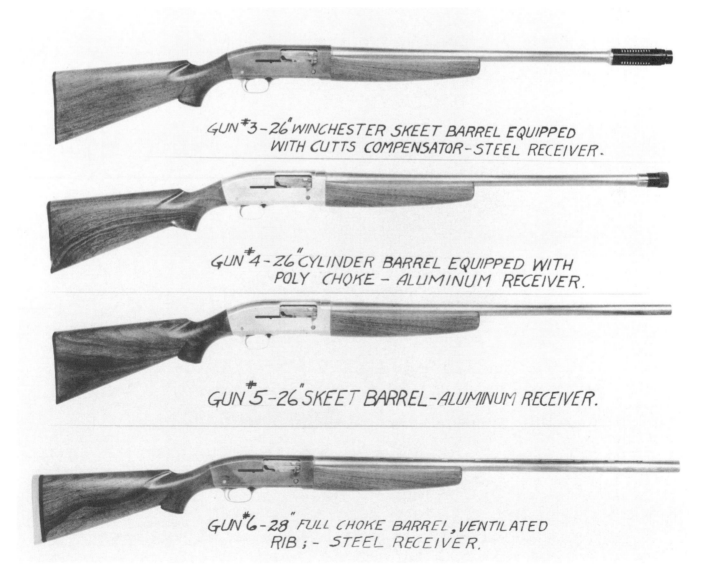

GUN #3-26" WINCHESTER SKEET BARREL EQUIPPED WITH CUTTS COMPENSATOR-STEEL RECEIVER.

GUN #4-26" CYLINDER BARREL EQUIPPED WITH POLY CHOKE - ALUMINUM RECEIVER.

GUN #5-26" SKEET BARREL-ALUMINUM RECEIVER.

GUN #6-28" FULL CHOKE BARREL, VENTILATED RIB ;- STEEL RECEIVER.

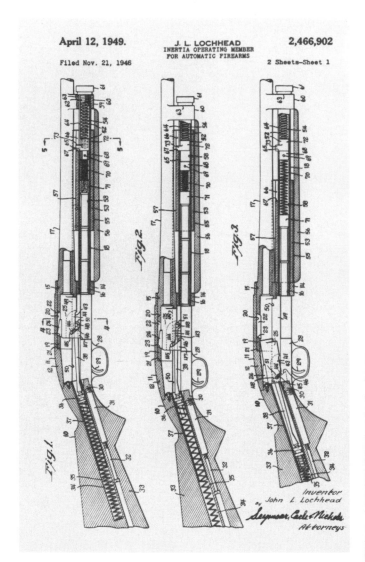

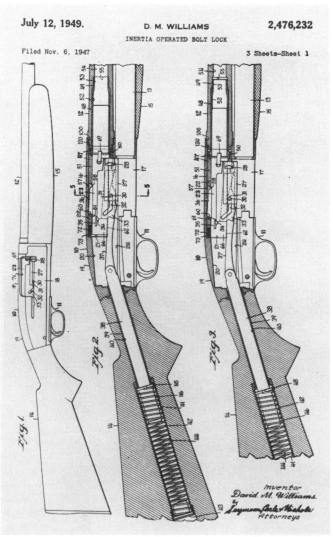

Above: Plate 308

*S*heet 1 of the specification drawings enrolled with J.L. Loch-head's U.S. Patent Number 2466902 issued April 12, 1949. Winchester Arms Collection Archives, Cody Firearms Museum.

Below: Plate 309

*S*heet 1 of the specification drawings enrolled with David M. Williams' U.S. Patent Number 2476232 issued July 12, 1949. Winchester Arms Collection Archives, Cody Firearms Museum.

toward the development of commercial arms, it did not neglect pursuing work on arms which had military application. In particular, the Winchester automatic rifle project, which had begun during World War II, was continued, though the principle was modified by Harry H. Sefried II. In place of the Williams' designed rifle originally proposed, the revised model was based on a U.S. M1 rifle (Plates 310 and 311)[18].

> "We are in the midst of a cold war which is getting warmer."
>
> — Bernard Baruch
> 1948

Throughout the 1950s, the expertise of the Design Department was demonstrated again and again as a whole new generation of Winchester rifles and shotguns were introduced. Within a space of seven years, between 1954 and 1960, the Winchester Repeating Arms Company's product line was thoroughly modernized by the introduction of the following models:

- Model 50 Semiautomatic Shotgun – 1954 (Plates 312-314)
- Model 77 Lever Action Hammerless Rimfire Rifle – 1955 (Plate 315)
- Model 88 Lever Action Hammerless Centerfire Rifle – 1955 (Plate 316)
- Model 55 Single Shot Semiautomatic .22 caliber Rifle - - 1957
- Model 59 Semiautomatic Shotgun – 1959 (Plate 317)
- Model 100 Semiautomatic Centerfire Rifle – 1960 (Plate 318)

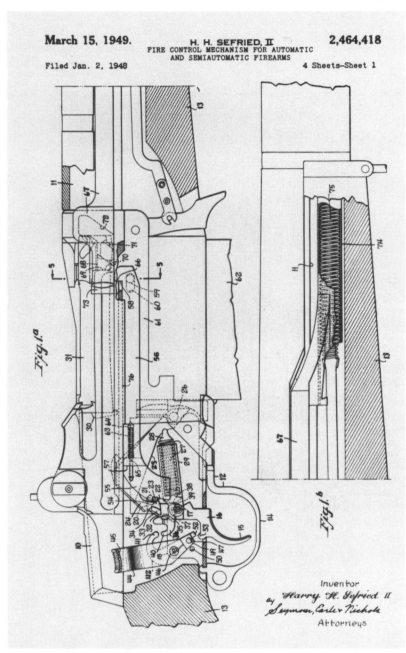

Characterized by exceptionally clean lines and well engineered actions, the new Winchester rifles and shotguns demonstrated that the company was committed to the production of quality arms that met the public's needs.

The Model 50 semiautomatic shotgun (Color Plate 36) typified the company's dedication to engineering excellence. Although development of this model was authorized on July 1, 1947[19], it was to take just under seven years before

Plate 310

Sheet 1 of the specification drawings enrolled with Harry H. Sefried, II's U.S. Patent Number 2464418 issued March 15, 1949. Winchester Arms Collection Archives, Cody Firearms Museum.

the first production example was delivered to the company's warehouse on April 15, 1954[20]. The reason for this delay was due to the fact that the company had to be absolutely certain that the shotgun's design was perfect as it did not want a repetition of the Model 40 "black eye."[21] Throughout the development program, sample Model 50s were exhaustively tested to ensure that the action would function properly under all conditions. Excessive wear was simulated on critical components of the action which were then installed in samples that served as test fixtures for the firing of proof loads. If the component failed, it was then redesigned to the point that it could sustain its role under such conditions[22]. As a result, when the Model 50 was introduced to the public, the company could justifiably claim that it was the safest semiautomatic shotgun then made[23]. The Model 50 had the additional distinction of being the first shotgun made with a floating chamber and inertia rod action (Plate 312).

If the Model 50 was a technical triumph, the Model 59 (Plate 317) marked the Winchester company's embrace of modern science. In place of a standard steel barrel, the Model 59 had a barrel composed of a thin steel tube encased within a fused web of glass fiber[24]. Structurally as strong as a solid steel barrel, the combination glass-steel barrel never met with commercial success as many shooters considered the model too light. The experience gained from its development, however, was later to be put to good use by the Design Department in other arms projects.

In many respects the Model 88 rifle (Plate 316) represented a marked departure from previous design practices for the company. In place of the standard sliding bolt used in lever-action rifles made to that point, the Model 88 was fitted with a tubular bolt which rotated on its axis when the finger lever was initially lowered and then was drawn rearward by the continuation of the finger lever's downward travel. The advantage of this style of bolt design was that the bolt could be fitted with locking lugs at its forward end that engaged cuts in the barrel breech so that a positive lock up of the bolt and barrel could be effected when the bolt rotated into its closed position. This design feature allowed high pressure cartridges to be used in a lever-action rifle without fear that the bolt

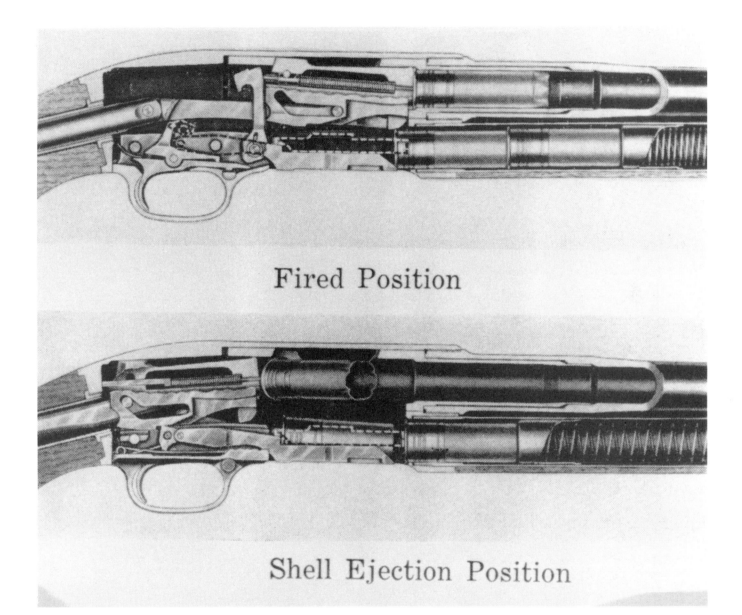

Fired Position

Shell Ejection Position

Plate 312

Illustrations of the Model 50 shotgun's action during the various stages of operation published in the maintenance brochure accompanying each shotgun sold. Private Collection.

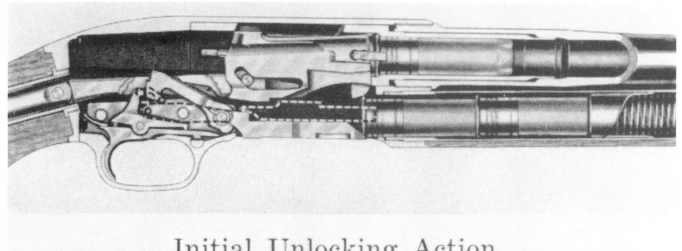

Initial Unlocking Action

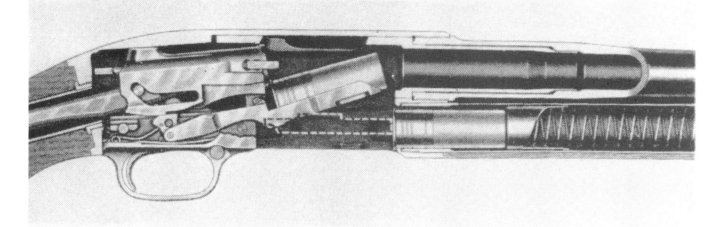

Shell Reloading Position

Plate 312

Illustrations of the Model 50 shotgun's action during the various stages of operation published in the maintenance brochure accompanying each shotgun sold. Private Collection.

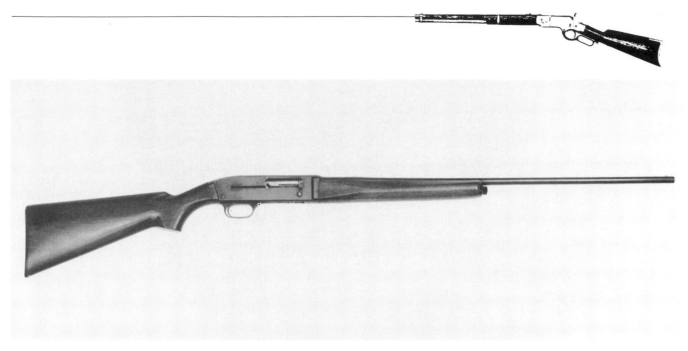

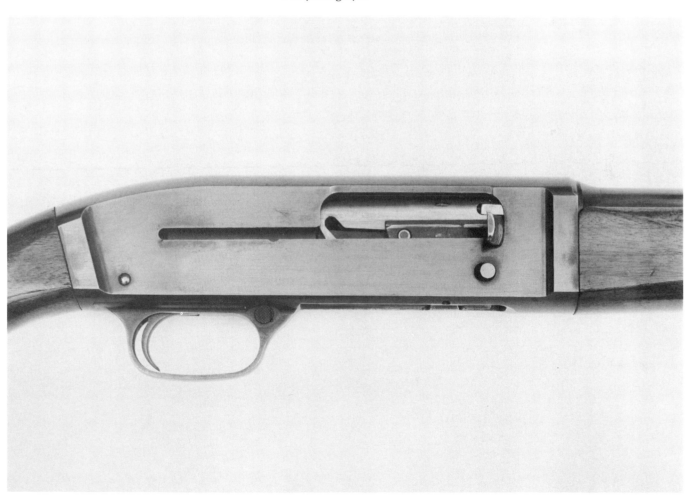

Plate 313

*S*ample Model 50 shotgun in .410 bore, made in 1953 or 1954. Olin Corporation photograph.

Plate 314

*R*eceiver detail of the sample Model 50 shotgun illustrated in Plate 313.

Above: Plate 315

Illustration of the box and tubular magazine variations of the Model 77 sporting rifle published in the introductory sales brochure issued in 1955. Private Collection.

Below: Plate 316

Winchester Model 88 lever-Action sporting rifle in .308 caliber. Olin Corporation photograph.

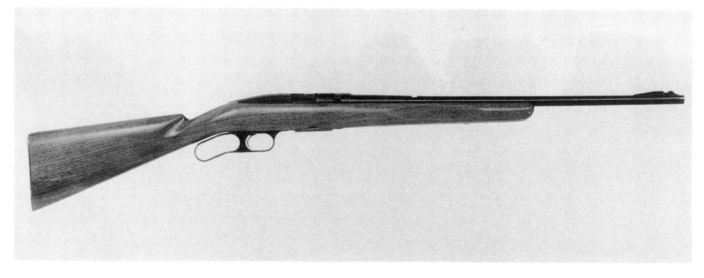

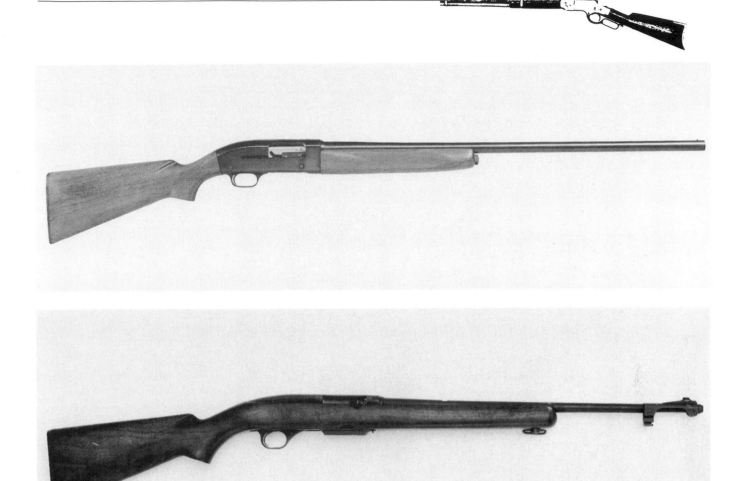

would blow open if there was a cartridge failure. Thus, the company finally solved the dilemma William Mason and John M. Browning had struggled with some seventy years earlier.

To many, the finest rifle to be developed by the Winchester Repeating Arms Company during the 1950s was one which never went into production. In 1957, the company decided to enter a lightweight military rifle into a competition sponsored by the United States Army Continental Army Command[25]. Ignoring more recent action designs such as those employed in the Model 50 and 100 (which was then under development), the Winchester company chose instead to build a rifle on

the Model G30R Williams' pattern which had been perfected in 1944. Though this may have appeared as a regressive step to some, it was in fact a recognition of the Williams design as being the most suitable for the purpose.

This testament to Williams' genius resulted in the creation of an aesthetically attractive and very versatile little rifle (Plates 319 and 320), which incorporated a number of modern improvements, such as an automatic firing pin retractor and a reworked selective fire mechanism. Chambered for the Winchester .224 caliber cartridge, the samples furnished to the Army performed well in all the tests they were subjected to during the trials that took place

Top: Plate 317

Winchester Model 59 shotgun. Olin Corporation photograph.

Bottom: Plate 318

Sample Model 100 semiautomatic rifle with a military style stock and integral bayonet lug made in 1961. Olin Corporation photograph.

between March and August 1958[26]. Ultimately, though, the politics of the test were to deny the Winchester light military rifle the contract it should have received by virtue of its performance.

After it became clear, in September 1958, that the Army had decided to recommend the Armalite AR-15 for adoption into service[27], the Winchester company considered the commercial production of a semiautomatic version of the Light Rifle. However, this plan was set aside when the firm's management decided that there was no real market for a high-velocity semiautomatic sporting rifle. Likewise, brief consideration was also given to the production of a 7.62 x 54mm or .308 caliber version of the rifle, but that, too, was abandoned due to the advanced stage of development which the later Model 100 (also a semiautomatic .308 caliber rifle) had reached by that time[28]. The final footnote to this project occurred in March 1959 when the U.S. Army Continental Army Command requested that the Winchester company turn over all samples made of the light rifle for destruction[29]. Though some were transferred, three made at varying stages of the projects development at the expense of the company were retained. Thus, the model was preserved for posterity, and its relative merits can still be judged.

With respect to the Winchester company's ammunition division, a fundamental change in it occurred during the postwar period. Beginning in the mid-1950s, the energies of its Research and Development section were increasingly directed toward the design of new military ammunition. This is not to say that civilian ammunition was neglected, for a number of new sporting cartridges were developed and introduced into the market between 1950 and 1960[30], but the primary goals of the company gradually became centered on the improvement of military ammunition. In many ways, this turn of events was to be expected as the United States government was the largest purchaser of ammunition from Winchester in the late 1950s. In 1959, it bought $9,900,000 worth of cartridges, and in 1960, $8,700,000[31].

The increasing alliance between the Winchester company and the government became even more entrenched when the company was awarded a contract to manufacture 35,000 U.S. M14 rifles at $69.75 apiece on Feb. 17, 1959[32]. Beset with manufacturing problems from the very beginning, excessive production costs and unanticipated design changes, the M14 rifle contracts resulted in a net loss to the company even though it managed to produce 356,501 of them[33].

The absorption of these operating losses by the company was to result in a number of changes over the following years that would alter the firm's destiny.

300

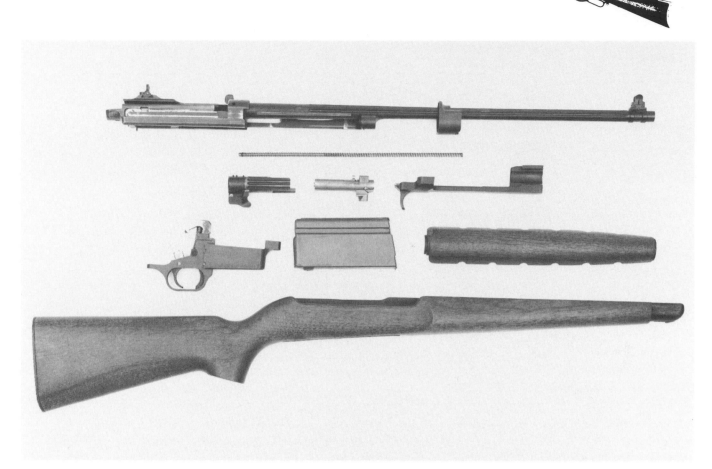

Plate 320

*D*isassembled view of the sample lightweight military rifle illustrated in Plate 319.

Plate 321

Winchester manufactured U.S. M14 rifle made in 1959. Olin Corporation photograph.

301

Endnotes

1. Manuscript note attached to typescript copy of George R. Watrous's Survey of Winchester Firearms-1941, dated June 1, 1942. World War II–Miscellaneous Production Records. Winchester Arms Collection Archives, Cody Firearms Museum.

2. Watrous, 1941 Survey, op. cit.

3. George R. Watrous, Recommendation For Arms-Post War Line, page 1. World War II–Miscellaneous Production Records. Winchester Arms Collection Archives, Cody Firearms Museum.

4. Ibid.

5. Ibid.

6. Minutes of Operating Committee Meeting, July 12-14, 1943, pages 1 and 2. World War II–Miscellaneous Production Records. Winchester Arms Collection Archives, Cody Firearms Museum.

7. Ibid.

8. Ibid, page 3.

9. Based upon Watrous' sales records (1904-1945), op. cit., a total of 28,571 Model 64 rifles were sold from 1933 to 1945. Total sales of the model by the time of its discontinuance is January 1957 amounted to 66,783 rifles, indicating postwar sales of 38,212.

10. Houze, Dreams of Youth, op. cit., page 154.

11. Ibid, page 165. Work on the Model 43 was authorized on May 31, 1944.

12. Winchester Firearms Reference Collection, op. cit., Inv. No. W2486, page 359.

13. The exact date when work began on this project is unknown. It was in progress, however, in December 1944.

14. The Model 43 and 47 Rifles were both introduced in January 1949.

15. The commercial version of the U.S. M1 carbine was developed by H.L. Crockett in late 1945.

16. The major patents for this model were granted to: John L. Lochhead, United States Patent Number 2466902 issued April 12, 1949; Harry H. Sefried, II, United States Patent Numbers 2482880 and 2491218 issued Sept. 27 and Dec.r 13, 1949; and David M. Williams, United States Patent Number 2476232 issued July 12, 1949.

17. For example, see Inv. Nos. W1817-W1819, Winchester Firearms Collection Reference Collection, op. cit., page 270.

18. Harry H. Sefried, II, United States Patent Number 2464418 issued March 15, 1949.

19. Model 50 Shotgun Production File. Winchester Arms Collection Archives, Cody Firearms Museum.

20. Ibid.

21. Watrous, Recommendation for Post-War Line, op. cit. (the statement was made by G.L. Nichols).

22. Model 50 Production File, op. cit.

23. Model 50 Introduction Notice dated May 1954, page 1. Model 50 Production File. Winchester Arms Collection, Cody Firearms Museum.

24. The Winchester company's engineers estimated that approximately 500 miles of glass fiber was used in the production of a standard thirty-inch Model 59 barrel.

25. For a detailed account of this competition see R. Blake Stevens and Edward C. Ezell, **The Black Rifle - M16 Retrospective** (Collector Grade Publications; Toronto, Ontario: 1987).

26. Ibid.

27. Ibid.

28. The Model 100 was introduced in 1960.

29. Manuscript notes to D.F. Butler dated March 8 (?), 1959, reading "**Do Not Turn Over** to Gov't for Destruction" were found in the magazine housings of two of the Winchester .224 caliber light military rifles in the Winchester Arms Collection. The author of the notes is unknown as the signatures have been obscured by oil.

30. The most notable additions to the sporting cartridge line during this period were the .243, .358 and .458.

31. Arms & Ammunition Operations, Government Ammunition Sales 1959-1970. M14 Production File. Winchester Arms Collection Archives, Cody Firearms Museum.

32. M14 Production File. Winchester Arms Collection Archives, Cody Firearms Museum.

33. Ibid.

CHAPTER 9

THE FINAL DECADES: 1961-1981

Although concerns had been voiced about high production costs as early as 1946[1], they were to become more and more acute as the 1950s progressed. By 1960, these costs, coupled with the operating losses associated with the U.S. M14 rifle contract, caused the management of Olin-Mathieson Chemical Corporation to seriously consider what means could be taken to decrease or at least stabilize this expense being incurred by its subsidiary, the Winchester company.

One avenue explored was the transfer of production to a foreign country where labor and, hopefully, raw material costs were cheaper. Though impractical for arms then in production, as intolerable manufacturing delays would have resulted from the dismantling and shipping of assembly lines abroad or the cost of duplicating them elsewhere, this solution was quite practical for new models yet to be made. Consequently, when the Forward Planning Committee of the Winchester company recommended the development of a superimposed double barrel shotgun (which would require considerable hand finishing)[2], the use of offshore production site was not only entertained but actively pursued.

After reviewing all possible locations (Austria, Belgium, Germany, Great Brit-

Plate 322

Stan Musial, member of the Baseball Hall of Fame, holding a Model 101 shotgun during the 1969 Winchester Claybird Tournament. Olin Corporation photograph.

ain, Japan, the Philippines and Spain), it was decided that Japan offered the best possible venue[3]. Olin-Mathieson then commissioned a survey of all the arms manufacturers operating there to determine which one would be most compatible with the Winchester company. Furthermore, as many of those firms were already producing superimposed shotguns, Olin-Mathieson authorized a second study to ascertain which one might be best suited to the American market[4].

Ultimately, this research was to result in the selection of Miroku Limited in the Tochigi Prefecture as the best possible candidate[5]. Shortly thereafter, Miroku and Olin-Mathieson agreed on a working relationship, and a new company called Olin-Kodensha Limited was established in 1961 to manufacture shotguns bearing the Winchester name[6]. Although subsequent sales literature regarding the Model 101 shotgun made by Olin-Kodensha stated that it was the result of a process in which "Winchester designers, quality control

and production engineers" oversaw the "development and continued production of the new Winchester over-and-under shotgun,"[7] the Model 101 (Plate 322) was in reality almost a pure Miroku product of which some 2,000 had already been made before the partnership with Olin began[8].

While the Olin-Kodensha arrangement solved one aspect of the Winchester company's problem, it did not address the continued rise in production costs in the United States. Therefore, a number of other alternatives were examined in New Haven.

One rather attractive solution to the problem was the development of a series of plastic-stocked rifles and shotguns having glass fiber reinforced barrels. This marriage of the Winchester company's arms technology with the chemical expertise of Olin-Mathieson did hold considerable promise as it used the strengths of both firms to advantage. During 1961 and 1962, the Winchester Design Department built a variety of single-shot and repeating .22

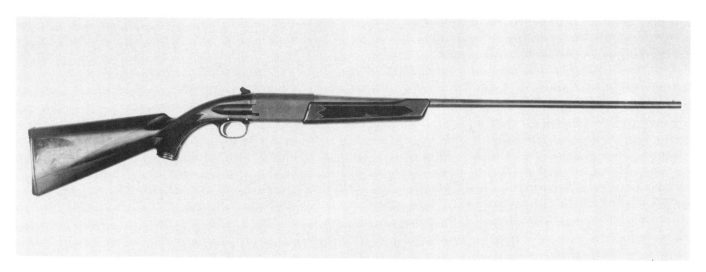

caliber rifles (Color Plate 38 and Plate 323), as well as several single-shot shotguns (Plate 324) on this principal for evaluation[9]. Though all these arms performed well in tests and displayed substantial structural integrity, their development beyond the sample stage was not pursued due to apprehension about market resistance to "plastic rifles,"[10] even though manufacturing costs would have been approximately half that of identical conventionally made arms[11].

The company then turned its attention to two other manufacturing processes which were known to be cost effective. The first of these was the use of aluminum extrusions for labor intensive parts such as receivers. While the use of this material had been successfully employed in the production of the Model 59 shotgun, tests demonstrated that it was unsuitable for centerfire rifles[12], a major portion of the Winchester company's output. As a result, its use was authorized only for new shotguns and rimfire rifles then under development[13].

The second process to be considered was one that had been perfected by William B. Ruger and Alexander M. Sturm of Sturm, Ruger & Company, Inc. in Southport, Connecticut, namely, the use of precision investment castings[14]. By casting chrome molybdenum steel into forms closely approximating that of the final components rather than hammer forging and machining them to

Above: Plate 323
Sample plastic single-shot .22 caliber rifle, weighing two pounds and 9/10ths of an ounce, made in 1962. Winchester Arms Collection (Inv. No. WRC1929), Cody Firearms Museum.

Below: Plate 324
Sample plastic shot 28 gauge shotgun built in 1961 or 1962. Winchester Arms Collection (Inv. No. WRC251), Cody Firearms Museum.

that stage, not only could savings be realized by the reduction of waste, but also, a large number of machining operations needed to produce any given part could be eliminated. Recognizing that considerable savings could be quickly brought about by modifying their production techniques to use the investment casting process, the management of the Winchester company authorized the change in 1962[15].

At the same time the Design Department was directed to make the necessary changes in each of the models then in production to accommodate the manufacturing requirements of the new process. By the late summer of 1963, these changes had been made, and on Oct. 7, the first Winchester rifles

and shotguns made with investment castings began to come off the production lines[16].

To take advantage of the publicity campaign that the company was planning for the introduction of its improved product line, four new models (two variations of the Model 200 series [Plate 325], the Model 1200 and Model 1400 [Plate 326]) made with aluminum extrusion receivers) were also to be brought into production[17].

When announced on Jan. 1, 1964, the new Winchester models were heralded by the company as a major advancement in arms design and an improvement over all the arms that had been made before[18]. Consumer reaction, however, did not mirror the company's

Above: Plate 325

Model 255 lever-action .22 caliber sporting rifle introduced in 1964. Olin Corporation photograph.

Below: Plate 326

Model 1400 shotgun introduced in 1964. Olin Corporation photograph.

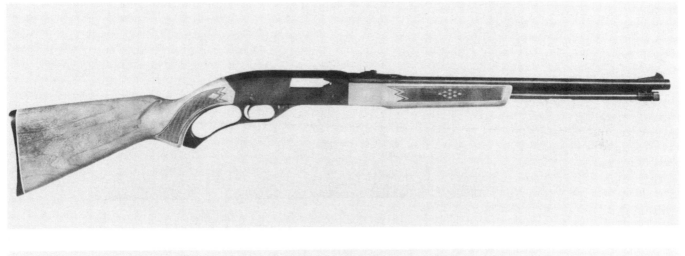

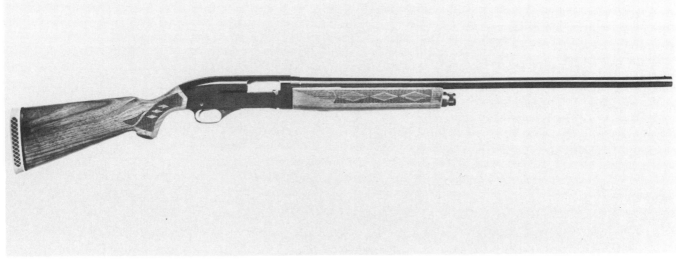

Left: Plate 327

Receiver detail of the second sample made for the Special Purpose Infantry Rifle competition by the Winchester company in 1963. Winchester Arms Collection (Inv. No. WRC1185), Cody Firearms Museum.

Below: Plate 328

Receiver detail of the third sample made for the Special Purpose Infantry Rifle competition by the Winchester company in late 1963. Winchester Arms Collection (Inv. No. WRC1188), Cody Firearms Museum.

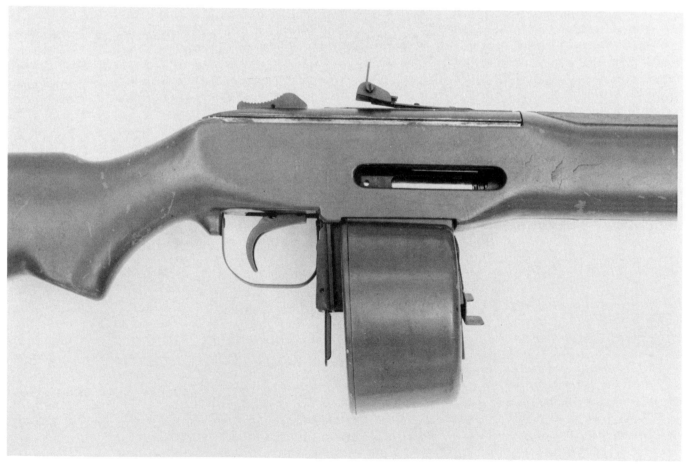

publicity. Instead of embracing the revised product line as improvements, the reworked old models were derided as being reduced cost imitations. This sentiment grew during 1964, as design and production problems became more evident in the "improved" versions of the Model 70 and 94 rifles. To the embarrassment of the company, it was found that the blued receivers of these rifles had a tendency to change color to a vibrant purple hue[19] after a period of time. Though this was to be corrected in the Model 70[20], its persistence in the Model 94 receivers eventually resulted in the Winchester company using black chrome plating as the finishing process for that model[21]. Though this setback and others were weathered by the company, they were never really overcome, and to this day the firm's products are described as being either pre- or post-1964, with a premium being placed on those made before the manufacturing change.

While the company had seriously underestimated the conservatism of its customers, there was a certain laissez-faire attitude about the civilian market among some members of the management. They had little regard and even less interest in the commercial production of arms as they saw the future of the company as being based upon government contracts rather than the more traditional area of civilian sales[22]. To a large degree these sentiments rose from the ever-increasing ammunition orders the United States government placed during the 1950s, and became even more pronounced as the Cold War deepened in the 1960s.

Plate 329

*P*ainted wooden model of the Mark I Liberator shotgun made in 1964. Winchester Arms Collection (Inv. No. WRC408), Cody Firearms Museum.

The importance of the government market was undeniable, though, as it accounted for $8,700,000 worth of ammunition sales in 1960, $21,400,000 in 1964 and over $45,400,000 in 1966[23].

The increasing reliance upon the government as the company's prime customer manifested itself in other ways. Beginning in the early 1960s, the firearms Design Department found itself being assigned research and development programs aimed solely toward the creation of military weapons. While some of these projects were funded directly by the government (such as the Special Purpose Infantry Weapon), others were independently undertaken by Winchester in the hope of government purchases (for example, the Model 1400 selective fire, box magazine

shotgun, and the 12, 16 and 20 gauge Liberator shotguns).

Likewise, the company's ammunition Design Department had increased its involvement in development work for the government, particularly in the area of caseless ammunition ranging in size from 5.56mm to 25mm. While there were some benefits to be gained by the application of the technologies experimented with under these programs, vis-a-vis the future production of commercial arms and ammunition, the diversion of resources to the military sector did have a detrimental effect upon the continued development of commercial products during the 1960s and early 1970s.

Perhaps the most interesting of the government-sponsored projects undertaken by the Winchester company was

Plate 330
*L*eft side view of the Liberator shotgun model illustrated in Plate 329.

the Special Purpose Infantry Rifle. Winchester was offered the opportunity to participate in this program shortly after its contract for the U.S. M14 rifle had been canceled, and it is probable that the project was taken up as a means to recoup some of the losses that had been brought about by the abrupt termination of the M14[24]. The Winchester company's involvement with the SPIW program began in October 1962, and by December of that year[25] it had submitted a detailed proposal to the Army Weapons Command for a rifle that embodied the following characteristics set forth by the government[26]:

- Maximum Length – Forty inches
- Maximum Weight – Ten pounds
- Have a Semiautomatic, Controlled Burst and Automatic Fire Capability
- A Magazine capacity of no less than sixty rounds
- A Semiautomatic Grenade Launcher with at least a three-round magazine
- An Integral Safety
- A Tamper-Proof Firing System
- Integral Sights
- The Simplest Possible Design
- A Minimum Number of Operating Controls
- Provision for Sling, Bipod and Bayonet

Plate 331
S*ample Mark II Liberator 16 gauge shotgun made in 1964, with the wire shoulder stock stored and the winter trigger folded up. Winchester Arms Collection (Inv. No. WRC1177), Cody Firearms Museum.*

The SPIW was, as the above specifications demonstrate, to be the perfect, multi-purpose infantry weapon of the future, and whoever fulfilled the design requirements potentially stood to be rewarded.

Winchester's proposal was accepted in February 1963[27], and immediately thereafter the Design Department began an intensive development program to transform the ideas it had proposed on paper into an actual working sample.

After a number of attempts (Color Plate 39 and Plates 327 and 328), a design was finally settled on in late 1963[28]. Using a conventional rotating bolt and Williams' short piston operating mechanism, the Winchester SPIW had an innovative recoil control mechanism. To reduce the effects of recoil during controlled burst (three-round) firing, the barrel and breech mechanism were designed to move rearward

with each successive shot until they butted up against the rear receiver wall at the conclusion of the burst. This necessitated the use of a long receiver that could accommodate the ever rearward travel of the bolt during firing and the use of high pressure springs in the entire operating mechanism. The grenade launcher also was of unique design with a forward recoiling barrel, fixed breech and side-mounted magazines. Unfortunately, the rifle weighed 12 pounds fully loaded and never worked satisfactorily (mainly due to its recoil system and the complexity of its design)[29].

Even though the Winchester company had failed to develop a reliable design for the SPIW, the engineering work on the recoil system was to be of use in another project undertaken in 1964. At the request of the government, the company was asked to develop a shotgun which could be easily used by

Plate 332

The Mark II Liberator shotgun illustrated in Plate 331 with the wire shoulder stock in place and the winter trigger guard folder down.

a ninety-pound individual for defense[30]. The resulting arm, to be known as the Liberator shotgun (Plates 329 and 330), was a wonderful amalgamation of old and new technology.

By adapting the rotating firing pin mechanism designed by Christian Sharps in the 1850s[31] for use in a four-barreled shotgun, the company's designers found that a very effective short range weapon could be made. Further, by installing a recoil absorbing buffer mechanism to the rear of the hammer, they could control the adverse effect of recoil upon the user. To minimize recoil even more, the first samples were made in 20 and then 16 gauge with simple squeeze bar triggers (Color Plate 40 and Plates 331-334). Though this design worked perfectly, the government later requested that 12 gauge samples (Plates 335-337) be made with a conventional double-action trigger mechanism[32]. The result-

ing increase in recoil and the arrangement of the trigger mechanism made the resulting arm less than user-friendly. This notwithstanding, the company went ahead with plans to introduce the new weapon in early 1965 (Plate 338), and a small number were actually sold before the model was discontinued[33].

While many aspects of the Winchester company's involvement in arms development for the government between 1963 and 1974 are well documented; others are not. For example, it is not known when or for whom the company built selective fire and silenced versions of the Model 290 semiautomatic .22 caliber rifle, or what the circumstances were which brought about the development of a selective fire box magazine Model 1400 shotgun, yet examples of both exist with full government acceptance markings[34].

Plate 333

*L*eft side view of the *Mark II Liberator shotgun illustrated in Plate 331.*

Apart from the work being done on military projects, the firearms Design Department produced only two notable new commercial designs (the Model 9422 rifle [Plates 339-345] and Super-X Model 1 shotgun [Plates 346-351]) between 1963 and 1974[35]. The balance of its civilian output was devoted to the production of new variations on old themes (Plates 352-356)[36]. It was as if after the great creative burst of the 1950s and 1960s, the company's design engineers were spent.

In contrast, great strides forward were being made in ammunition design at the Winchester works in Alton, Illinois. Not only had a variety of caseless cartridges been developed, but also their potential application to commercial use had been fully explored. Eventually, this process was to lead to the

more challenging problem of designing a caseless shotgun cartridge. After determining its feasibility and solving some of the technical problems associated solely with the use of caseless ammunition in a shotgun, the development of a working sample was begun in 1966[37].

Interestingly, it was the production of this sample which demonstrates the degree to which the arms and ammunition design sections had become insulated from each other by that time. Instead of having the sample designed and built in New Haven, the design work was contracted to the Van Dyke Corporation,[38] and the actual construction of the sample was only partially done in-house with a number of critical components sub-contracted to other manufacturers[39].

Plate 334

Detail of the Mark II Liberator shotgun illustrated in Plate 331 opened for loading. The recoil absorbing buffer mechanism is contained in the housing directly above the pistol grip.

■ John Clymer

Continuing a tradition established almost a century earlier, the Winchester-Western Division of Olin Corporation commissioned the Bridgewater, Connecticut artist John Clymer to paint three oil paintings depicting his vision of the American frontier. Completed in 1970, the paintings illustrated a gold train (pictured above in the process of being completed), a wagon train and Indians on horseback. After a brief period on exhibition in Connecticut, the paintings were presented by Olin Corporation to the Whitney Gallery of Western Art at the Buffalo Bill Historical Center in Cody, Wyoming.

Plate 335

Sample Mark III Liberator 12 gauge shotgun made in January or February 1965. Winchester Arms Collection (Inv. No. WRC388), Cody Firearms Museum.

Though the testing of the resulting sample in the summer and autumn of 1967 revealed that a caseless cartridge shotgun could be made and that its operating characteristics would approximate those of a conventional shotgun[40], the commercial production of neither the ammunition nor shotgun was ·to follow. As with the "plastic rifles," the concern was market acceptance of new technology.

Following the United States' withdrawal from Vietnam, the reduction in government orders renewed Winchester's reliance on the commercial market. Unfortunately, this was not to be as easily accomplished by the arms division as by the ammunition division. Though some models were selling quite well, others were not, and there was a growing tiredness in the market to Winchester's product line. To revive the lackluster firearms sales, Winchester again looked to the introduction of new models (Color Plate 41). However, this time, the company looked increasingly abroad for ideas. A semiautomatic shotgun made by Benelli of Italy (Plate 357) was considered for adoption as was a double barrel shotgun made by Manufrance[41]. An Australian-designed .22 caliber bolt-action rifle design (Plates 358 and 359) was actually purchased and marketed as the Winchester Model 310[42]. In addition, the company became the importer of Perazzi shotguns (Color Plate 42 and Plate 360) in an attempt to establish itself in the first quality shotgun market[43]. None of these efforts, however, were to achieve the results the company desired.

Moreover, the company's sales techniques of using regional distributors and individual retailers was obsolete. Competitors selling to national distributors and mass merchandisers were able to consistently outsell Winchester. In addition, Winchester's concentration on the shotgun market, which was controlled by its competitors, had not resulted in any inroads being made[44]. This consumer resistance to

Top: Plate 336

*L*eft side view of the sample Mark III Liberator shotgun illustrated in Plate 335.

Bottom: Plate 337

*T*he sample Mark III Liberator shotgun illustrated in Plate 335 opened for loading.

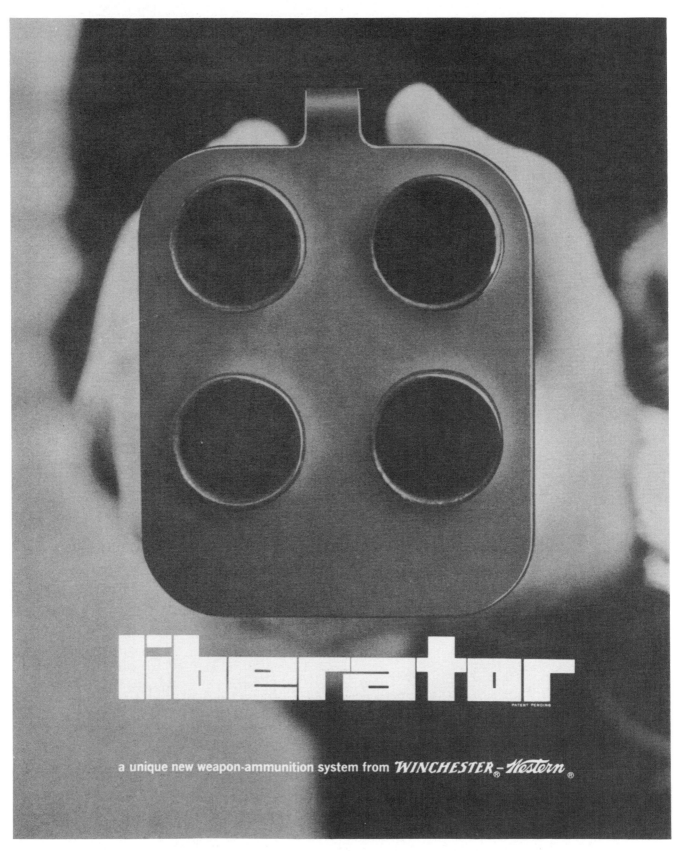

Plate 338
*A*dvertising brochure for the Mark III Liberator shotgun published in March 1965. Private Collection.

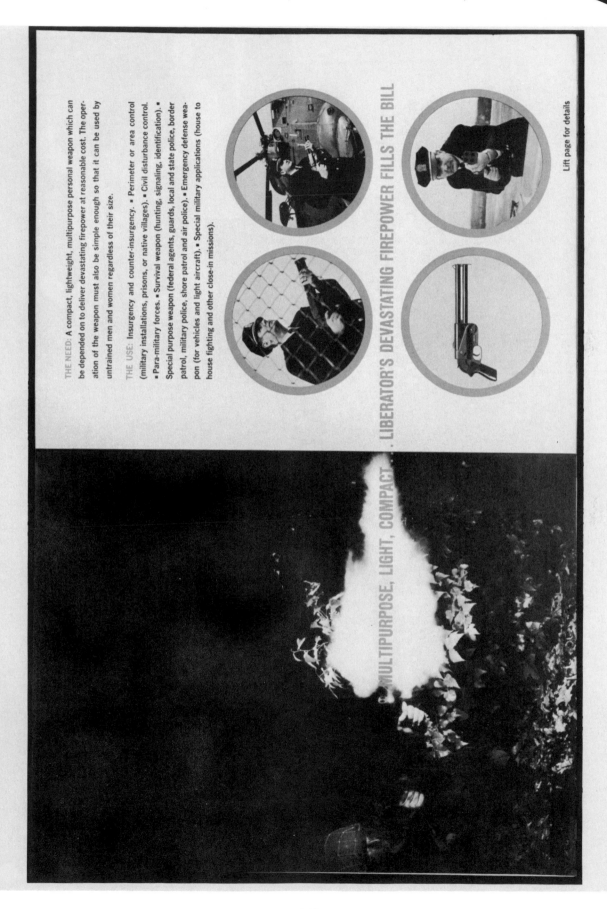

THE NEED: A compact, lightweight, multipurpose personal weapon which can be depended on to deliver devastating firepower at reasonable cost. The operation of the weapon must also be simple enough so that it can be used by untrained men and women regardless of their size.

THE USE: Insurgency and counter-insurgency. ▪ Perimeter or area control (military installations, prisons, or native villages). ▪ Civil disturbance control. ▪ Para-military forces. ▪ Survival weapon (hunting, signaling, identification). ▪ Special purpose weapon (federal agents, guards, local and state police, border patrol, military police, shore patrol and air police). ▪ Emergency defense weapon (for vehicles and light aircraft). ▪ Special military applications (house to house fighting and other close-in missions).

MULTIPURPOSE, LIGHT, COMPACT . . . LIBERATOR'S DEVASTATING FIREPOWER FILLS THE BILL

Lift page for details

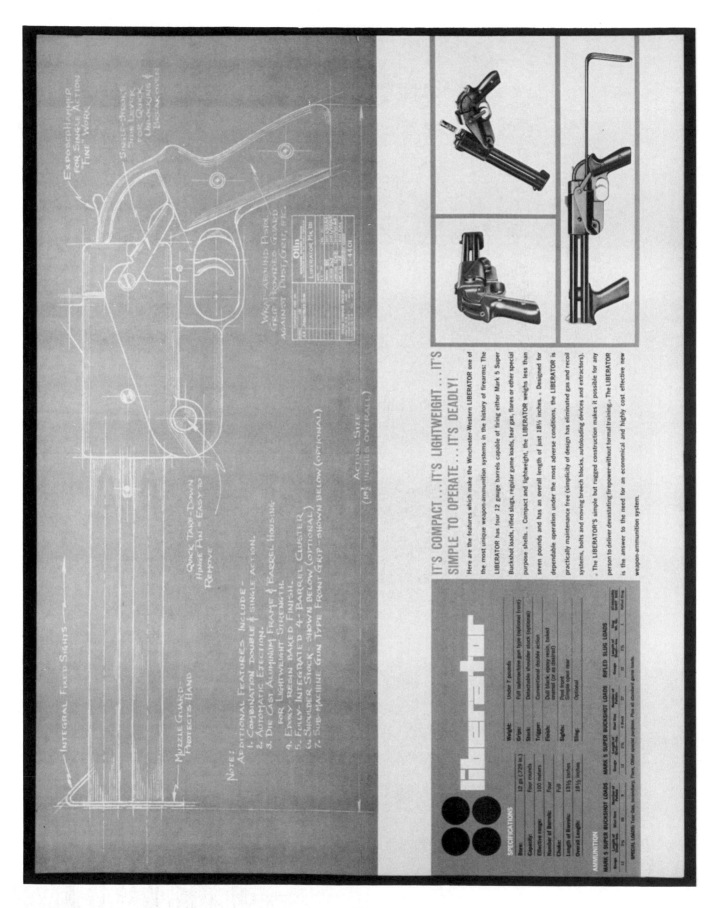

A PERFECT COMBINATION:
The LIBERATOR and MARK 5 SUPER BUCKSHOT LOADS

20% MORE EFFECTIVE RANGE UP TO 20% MORE PUNCH!

Winchester-Western Mark 5 Super Buckshot loads shoot farther, hit harder and pattern better than any other shot shells ever made.

The special polyethylene collar wrapped around the shot protects the pellets from deformation during the vital pattern forming split-second it leaves the muzzle. Then, its job done, it falls away. In addition, the Mark 5 collar virtually eliminates barrel leading and tube wash.

The appearance of the LIBERATOR alone is enough to deter some aggressions. When looks aren't enough . . . all you have to do is pull its trigger . . . one, two, three or four times.

PERFORMANCE:
In less than three seconds, the LIBERATOR can deliver thirty-six .33 caliber projectiles with devastating effectiveness, or using Mark 5 loads with No. 4 Buck, the LIBERATOR can deliver one hundred eight .25 cal. projectiles. Firing Mark 5 Super Buckshot loads, the LIBERATOR puts over 80 percent of each shell's 9 pellets in a 30-inch circle at 30 meters.

PENETRATION:
Two ¾-inch pine boards, spaced one inch apart, don't stop Mark 5 Super Buckshot pellets fired from the LIBERATOR . . . not even at 60 meters.

THESE SHELLS GIVE THE LIBERATOR ITS VERSATILITY!

RIFLED SLUG LOAD
Bullet-shaped slug with hollow base and scientifically rifled sides for greater accuracy and power.

FLARE LOAD

SPECIAL PURPOSE LOAD

INCENDIARY LOAD

TEAR GAS LOAD

9 PELLETS
(.33 caliber)
MARK 5 SUPER BUCKSHOT LOAD
Regular Mark 5 collar and exclusively cushioned pellets eliminate pattern-destroying shot deformation.

FOR ADDITIONAL INFORMATION CONTACT:

WINCHESTER-WESTERN DIVISION
NEW HAVEN, CONNECTICUT
MANAGER, GOVERNMENT SALES · PHONE: 777 7911, AREA CODE 203

WM122

3-65

PRINTED IN U.S.A.

321

Plate 339
Sample Model 9422 sporting rifle made in 1971. Olin Corporation photograph.

Winchester firearms and a general recession in the arms market beginning in late 1976 had a disastrous effect upon the company. The firearms division managed to turn a net profit of $988,000 on sales of $43,502,000 in 1976, but over the next three years it showed losses of $6,027,000, $7,227,000 and $4,166,000[45].

The deteriorating financial situation together with the effects of a six-month strike, which idled the New Haven factory in 1979[46], finally caused Olin Corporation to examine its future in the arms business. After deciding that the ammunition division would be retained, Olin Corporation formally announced on Dec. 12, 1980, that it would divest itself of the Winchester firearms business[47]. In 1981, the arms division was purchased by a consortium of former members of the Winchester management and a new company, the U.S. Repeating Arms Company, was established. Thus ended a 115-year tradition of firearms being made in Connecticut by a company bearing the Winchester name[48].

■ The End

One anonymous Olin Corporation executive identified the problems plaguing the Winchester-Western firearms division during the late 1970s as follows:

Lack of adequate new investment in the factory, manufacturing processes and product development.
Lack of management continuity.
Lack of marketing continuity.
Declining sales due to existing sales techniques.
Inappropriate and excessively large investments in unsuccessful product lines.
The discontinuing of several popular and cost-effective models.
Costly labor contracts.
"Several could be dealt with, but together they created an insurmountable obstacle to the company's continued operation."

Plate 340
*D*rilling machine used to drill and ream the Model 9422's bolt. Olin Corporation photograph.

Plate 341

*B*arrel-swagging machine used in the production of the Model 9422. Olin Corporation photograph.

Plate 342
Model 9422 finger lever profiling machine. Olin Corporation photograph.

Plate 343

*M*odel 9422 bolts being inspected. Olin Corporation photograph.

Plate 344

A Model 9422 being assembled. Olin Corporation photograph.

Plate 345

The final step in the Model 9422's manufacture, test firing. Olin Corporation photograph.

Plate 346
Cincinnati Grinder used to shape the Super-X Model 1 shotgun's barrel extension. Olin Corporation photograph.

Plate 347

*T*en station drilling machine used in the manufacture of the Super-X Model 1 shotgun's receiver. Olin Corporation photograph.

Plate 348

Numerically controlled stock checkering machine used in the Super-X Model 1 shotgun's manufacture. Olin Corporation photograph.

Plate 349

Inspection of Super-X Model 1 barrel extensions. Olin Corporation photograph.

Plate 350
*F*unction testing of the Super-X Model 1 shotgun using weighted action test cartridge simulators. Olin Corporation photograph.

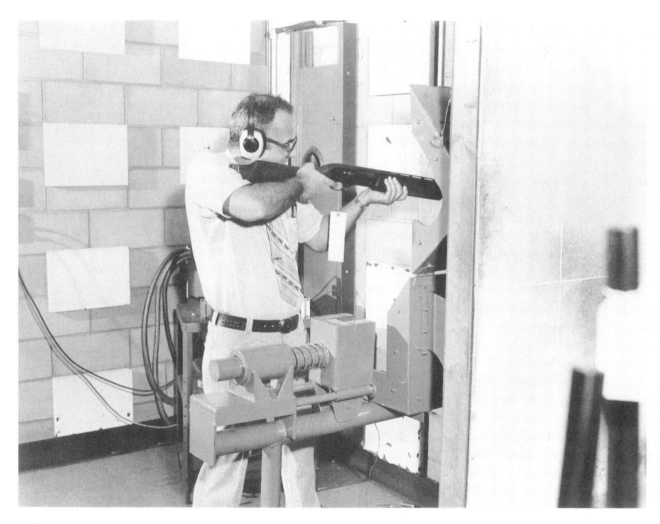

Plate 351

Test firing of the Super-X Model 1 shotgun prior to boxing and shipping. Olin Corporation photograph.

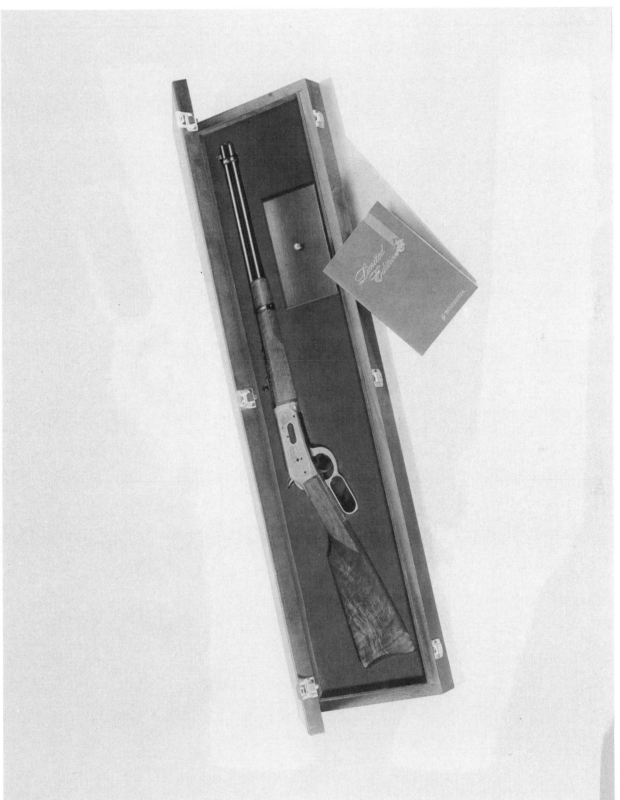

Plate 352

Boxed Model 94 Limited Edition rifle made in 1977. Olin Corporation photograph.

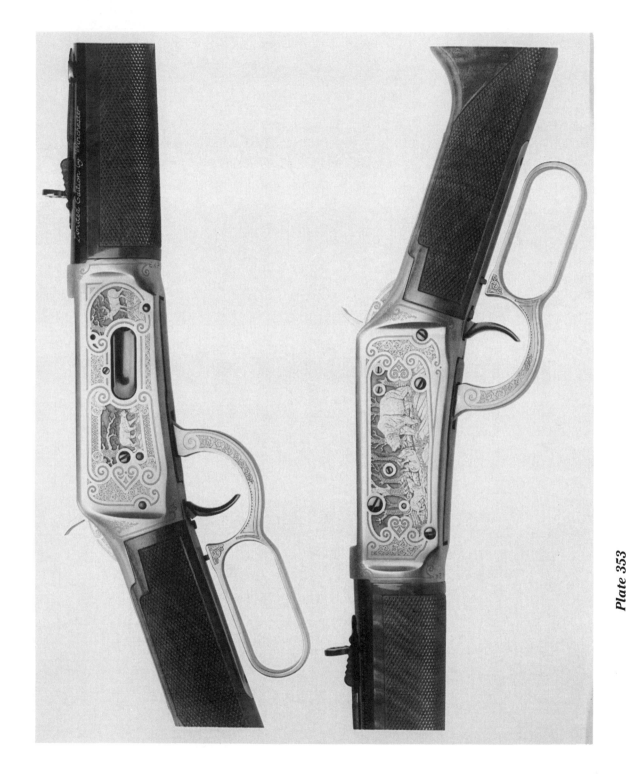

Plate 353
Receiver details of the Model 94 Limited Edition rifle. Olin Corporation photograph.

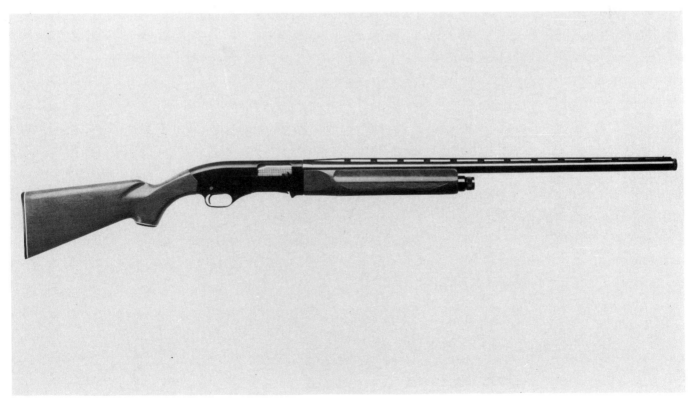

Above: Plate 354

Model 70 A XTR introduced in 1978. Olin Corporation photograph.

Below: Plate 355

Model 1500 XTR introduced in 1978. Olin Corporation photograph.

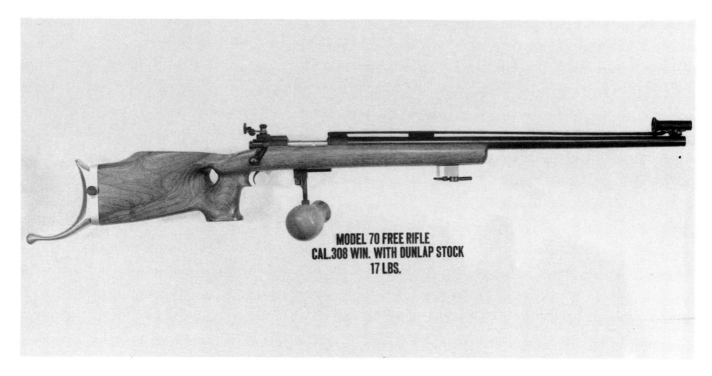

MODEL 70 FREE RIFLE
CAL.308 WIN. WITH DUNLAP STOCK
17 LBS.

Above: Plate 356

*M*odel 70 target rifle fitted with a Dunlap stock. Olin Corporation photograph.

Below: Plate 357

*P*rototype Benelli Model 201 semiautomatic 20 gauge shotgun made for Olin Corporation in the late 1970s. Winchester Arms Collection, Cody Firearms Museum.

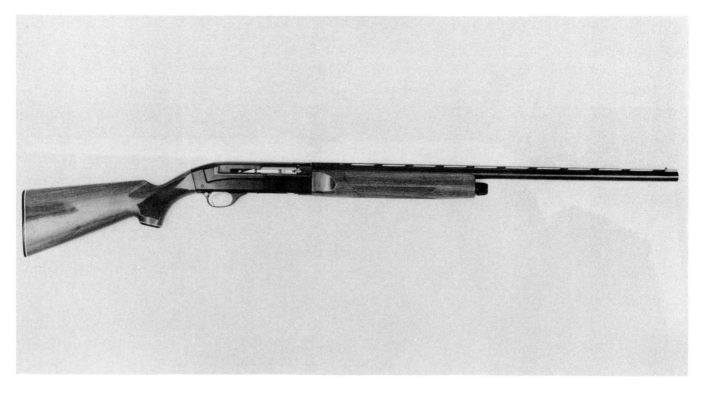

Above: Plate 358

*P*rototype .22 caliber single-shot rifle made by Sportco of Australia for Olin Corporation. Winchester Arms Collection (Inv. No. WRC440), Cody Firearms Museum.

Below: Plate 359

*R*eceiver detail of the Sportco prototype illustrated in Plate 358.

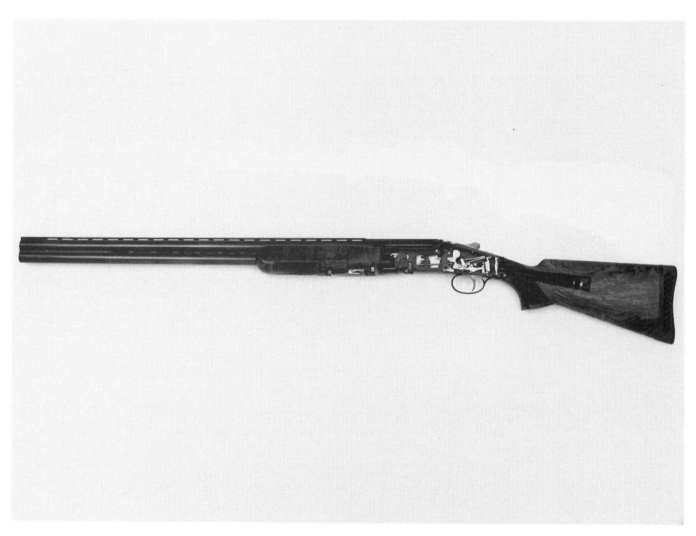

Plate 360

*S*keletonized Perazzi Model MX8 shotgun used by the Winchester company for promotional purposes during the period the firm imported Perazzi shotguns. Olin Corporation photograph.

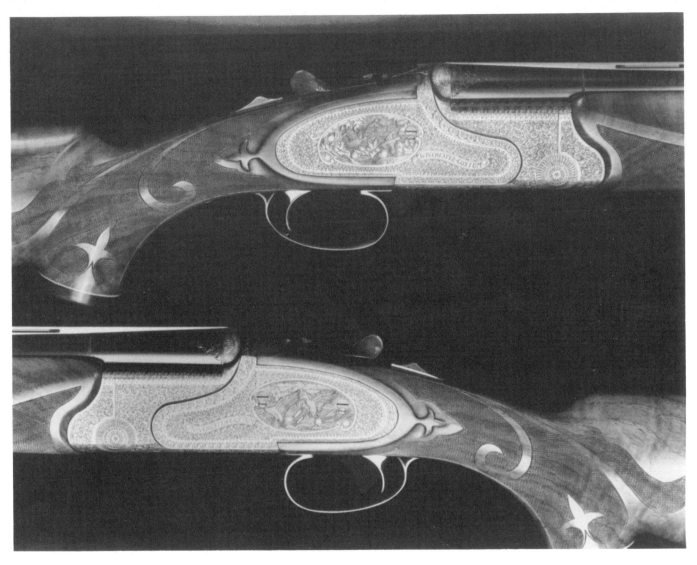

Plate 361

Receiver details of two Japanese-made sample Winchester Custom over and under sidelock trap shotguns made in late 1979, for possible introduction by the Winchester division of Olin Corporation in 1980. Olin Corporation photograph.

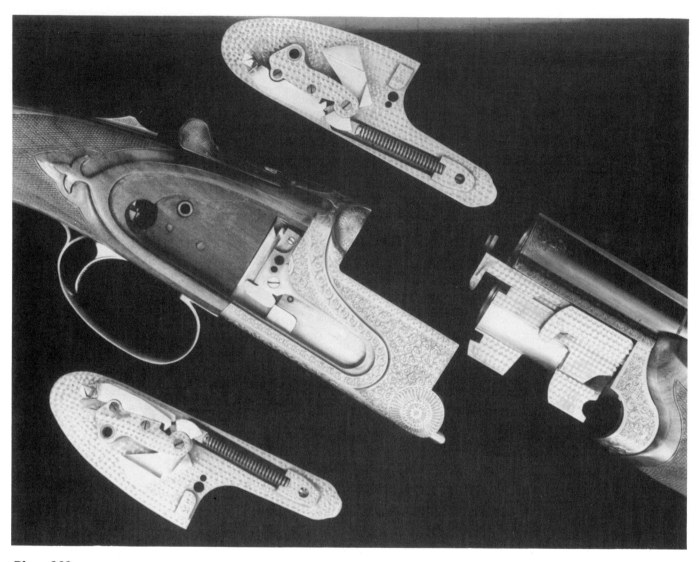

Plate 362

One of the sample Winchester Custom over and under sidelock trap shotguns, illustrated in Plate 361, with the locks and barrels dismounted. Olin Corporation photograph.

Endnotes

1. Memorandum from Edwin Pugsley to John M. Olin dated Jan. 10, 1946. World War II General Production File. Winchester Arms Collection Archives, Cody Firearms Museum.

2. Development of a superimposed shotgun was authorized sometime in 1959.

3. Survey of Arms Manufactures 1960. Winchester Repeating Arms Company Archives, Olin Corporation.

4. Arms Companies in Japan 1960 (with Summary). Winchester Repeating Arms Company Archives, Olin Corporation.

5. Ibid, page 1.

6. Olin-Mathieson Chemical Corporation Public Relations Press Release for the Model 101 Production File. Winchester Arms Collection Archives, Cody Firearms Museum.

7. Ibid.

8. Olin-Kodensha memorandum from R.E. Roby to J.F. Walsh dated May 20, 1971, regarding serial numbers of the Model 101. Manufacture of the 101 commenced in October 1959 at serial number 50,000 and was at 52,000 when Olin-Kodensha was established. Model 101 Production File. Winchester Arms Collection Archives, Cody Firearms Museum.

9. Virtually all the samples (including the conventionally made equivalents) made during this design exercise are preserved in the Winchester Arms Collection of the Cody Firearms Museum.

10. Memorandum from W.R. Kelly, Jr. to D.R. Butler dated December 1962. Miscellaneous Arms File. Winchester Arms Collection Archives, Cody Firearms Museum.

11. Ibid. Cf., Note 9 above.

12. Notes on Aluminum Extrusion Receivers, undated. Miscellaneous Arms File. Winchester Arms Collection Archives, Cody Firearms Museum.

13. The Model 255 and 275 rifles and the Model 1200 and 1400 shotguns.

14. For a brief biography of William Ruger, see James M. Triggs, "William B. Ruger," **Arms Gazette**, Vol. 4, No. 12, pages 12-15 and 42. An account of the Sturm, Ruger & Company, Inc. by the same author appears on page 43 of the same journal.

15. Personal communication from William E. Talley, June 11, 1993.

16. Model 70 Production File. Winchester Arms Collection Archives, Cody Firearms Museum.

17. While the Model 255 and 275 rifles were introduced shortly after Jan. 1, 1964, production of the Model 1200 and 1400 shotguns was delayed. The Model 1200 was finally introduced in March and the Model 1400 in late June.

18. Olin-Mathieson Chemical Corporation Public Relations Press Release dated Jan. 1, 1964, pages 1 and 2. Model 70 Production File. Winchester Arms Collection Archives, Cody Firearms Museum.

19. The problem was first reported in February of 1964 Personal communications from J.F. Walsh and W.E. Talley.

20. Ibid.

21. Ibid and an unsigned manuscript note regarding Model 94 receiver finish modifications from 1964 to 1967. Model 94 Production File. Winchester Arms Collection Archives, Cody Firearms Museum.

22. A statement variously quoted as "The commercial gun department can go to Hell" or "Who cares about commercial gun sales" has been attributed both to David R. Butler and T.W. van Wilgen. Given the political climate within the company at the time, it is possible that anyone associated with either the military development or sales departments could have made these remarks.

23. Government Ammunition Sales, 1962-1966. Miscellaneous Arms File. Winchester Arms Collection Archives, Cody Firearms Museum.

24. The M14 rifle contract was terminated in the early autumn of 1962.

25. R.Blake Stevens and Edward C. Ezell, **The SPIW The Deadliest Weapon That Never Was** (Collector Grade Publications; Toronto, Ontario: 1985), page 47.

26. Ibid, page 53.

27. Ibid, page 47.

28. Notes on the Winchester SPIW. Miscellaneous Arms File. Winchester Arms Collection Archives, Cody Firearms Museum.

29. Steven and Ezell, SPIW, op. cit., page 58.

30. Personal communication from T.E. Henshaw.

31. Sellers, Sharps Firearms, op. cit., pages 125-127.

32. Personal communication from T.E. Henshaw.

33. A three-color brochure titled "Liberator a unique new weapon ammunition system from Winchester-Western" was published and distributed in March 1965. This brochure illustrated the Mark III 12 gauge Liberator developed in January 1965.

34. Examples of all these arms are preserved in the Winchester Arms Collection of the Cody Firearms Museum.

35. The Model 94 was introduced in 1972, and the Super-X Shotgun in 1974.

36. For example, a plethora of Model 94 commemorative rifles and carbines, as well as numerous variations of the Model 70.

37. David F. Butler, Preliminary Report On: Caseless Shotguns and Tests Fixtures, dated October 1, 1967, page 12.

38. Ibid.

39. Ibid.

40. Ibid, pages 13-14.

41. Negotiations with Benelli evidently reached an advanced state as both Model 121 and 201 shotguns by that manufacturer bearing full Winchester markings are preserved in the Winchester Arms Collection of the Cody Firearms Museum. Inventory card notes for those arms indicated that the Benelli-Winchester association continued into 1980. Cf. [Public Auction] **Antique and Modern Firearms at the Buffalo Bill Historical Center, Cody, Wyoming**- Christie's East, July 5, 1984, Lot 79. An example of the Manufrance prototype for the Winchester Model 23 shotgun was sold at the same auction as Lot 132. Eventually, Olin Corporation contracted with Laurona of Spain to manufacture two shotguns for the firm in 1975. These were the Model 22 double barrel and Model 91 superimposed shotguns, which were marketed outside of the United States under the Winchester name.

42. Houze, Dreams of Youth, op. cit., pages 187-188.

43. Perazzi Shotguns, regarded by many shooters as being among the best made, were initially imported into the United States by Ithaca.

44. Even as late as 1980, the company was still pursuing this market, and plans had been made to market a detachable sidelock double barrel shotgun made or patterned after one by Nikko of Japan (Plates 361 and 362). L.L. Larson, Winchester's 1980 O/U & S/S Shotgun Line. Olin Corporation 1980 Product File. Winchester Arms Museum Archives, Cody Firearms Museum.

45. Summation of Arms Sales 1976-1979. Miscellaneous Financial Documents Relating to Winchester Sale. Winchester Arms Collection Archives, Cody Firearms Museum.

46. The anticipated loss for the firearms division in 1980 was $2,076,000 per an addendum to the document cited in Note 44. The strike by members of the International Association of Machinists and Aerospace Workers (AFL-CIO) against the Winchester company lasted from January to July 1979, and was the result of a dispute concerning the firm's wish to establish job standards to increase productivity.

47. The announcement was made immediately after a meeting of Olin Corporation's Board of Directors held on Dec. 12, 1980.

48. Although the products of the U.S. Repeating Arms Company were the same as those previously made by the Winchester-Western Division of Olin Corporation, they only bore the Winchester name under a licensing agreement with Olin Corporation, the owner of that tradename.

PREFACE
THE DECORATION OF WINCHESTER
FIREARMS 1865-1981

One facet of the Winchester company's operations between 1865 and 1981, which has yet to be addressed, is the manner in which the arms the company manufactured were sometimes decorated. The primary reason for omitting any substantive reference to this subject in Part One is that the development of the company's engraving styles does not mirror either the technological or economic chronologies used to outline the firms' history. Therefore, any discussion presented in the preceding pages would have been necessarily disjointed. As a result, it was thought best to present a separate account of the Winchester company's engraving practices following a chronological progression based solely upon the working careers of the engravers involved.

In order that the following account not be considered an

endorsement of any living engraver's work, primary attention has been given to the period from 1865 to 1949 and only passing mention to that period which followed. With respect to the earlier era, the major sources of information were drawn from Winchester corporate records and the papers of Louis D. Nimschke, Rudolph J. Kornbrath, as well as, the Ulrich family. In addition to supplying documentary evidence, two members of the Ulrich family (Dorothy Ulrich and her cousin David Mercer Ulrich) also provided personal reminiscences that were of inestimable value.

Finally, it should be mentioned that unlike Part One, which is an objective analysis of the Winchester company's history,

some of the conclusions presented in Part Two, especially those concerning the authorship of particular engraved arms, are subjective in nature. Every attempt, however, has been made to base such conclusions upon verifiable grounds.

INTRODUCTION

As the industrialization of the American firearms industry increased during the 1850s, a new class of artisans associated with the production of arms began to emerge. Engravers, specializing in the decoration of pistols, rifles and shotguns, were actively recruited by nearly all of the major, as well as minor, manufacturers. Their task was to impart some measure of individuality to the machine-made products of their employers. In some respects, it was the work of these engravers which perpetuated the crafts of local gunsmiths, who had previously dominated the trade. Even the most modest amount of engraving, such as a few cut scrolls, changed an impersonal mass-produced arm into one which bore evidence of hand labor and, therefore, some originality.

Oliver F. Winchester was well aware of the contributions these craftsmen could make to a company's success. Beginning with the founding of the New Haven Arms Company in 1856, he instituted a policy of offering engraving and special finishes (eq., gold and silver plating) as an extra cost option to prospective purchasers[1]. Winchester also appreciated the potential of decorated arms as advertising vehicles. Consequently, a number of the early Henry Rifles were engraved for presentation to individuals who could further the fortunes of his company, such as Secretary of War Edward Stanton and President Abraham Lincoln[2].

Even though the vast majority of the Henry rifles produced during the Civil War were plain arms destined for defense or military use, the Letter Book of the New Haven Arms Company contains ample evidence that engraved and plated Henrys were sold on a regular basis. The availability of these arms was also advertised from the very introduction of the model (Plate 363).

However, during the brief business life of the Winchester Arms Company from 1865 to early 1867, the practice of offering engraving or special finishes was not continued. Similarly, after the founding of the Winchester Repeating Arms Company on April 1, 1867, it was discouraged by the adoption of a cost schedule which made the option prohibitively expensive. In contrast to the Henry rifle price schedule for engraving and plating, which ranged from $5 to $13 above the cost of the rifle, that published in 1867 (Plate 364)[3], quoted prices of $60 to $100 above the base cost for similar extras. To a large extent, the company's policy deterring orders for engraving and special finishes was no doubt due to the fact that the arms then being manufactured

Office of New Haven Arms Company,

NEW HAVEN, Conn., Oct. 15th, 1862.

The price of "HENRY'S REPEATING RIFLE" was fixed some twelve months ago as low as possible, and leave a fair profit to us as manufacturers. Since then the cost of materials and the labor of competent Gunsmiths (in consequence of the great demand to execute Government orders,) with the addition of the National Tax, has so enhanced the cost as to make a slight advance of Two Dollars in the price necessary to protect us from loss.

Lead and Copper, used in the manufacture of the ammunition, have recently advanced 50 per cent., making the cost of Cartridges more than the price at which we are now selling them. If this advance is maintained any considerable length of time, or increased, we shall have to advance the price of Cartridges.

We shall endeavor to avoid, if possible, any further increase of price either in the items of ammunition; but in the present of said tendency of every thing entering into the cost of our Goods, we cannot guarantee the prices for a week.

Below please find List of

RETAIL PRICES:

Rifle, plain, - - - - -	$42.00
Engraving, and Fancy Stock, - extra, $5	47.00
Silver Plating and Engraving, and Fancy Stock, " 10	52.00
Gold " " " " " 13	55.00
Cartridges, per 1000 - - - -	17.50
Leather Cases, - - - - -	5.00
Extra for Strap and Fixtures for Slinging, - -	2.00

O. F. WINCHESTER, President.

J. H. CONKLIN, Secretary.

Plate 363

Obverse of a printed letter dated Oct. 15, 1862, which was sent by the New Haven Arms Company to potential clients who had requested information regarding the price schedule adopted by the firm for the Henry rifle. Private Collection.

thout the letter H̄ or W raised in the end of the copper cartridge.
e following price list the cost of packing will be added in all cases.   Box for single guns seventy-five cents.   Case
ning boxes with tin for shipment holding ten guns, $3.50 each extra.

Rifles with varnished Stocks and Slings,	$50.00
Carbines with oiled Stocks without Slings,	40.00
Cartridges, per 1000,	20 00
Slings for Carbines,	2.50
Leather Cases,	6.00 to 7.50
Extra finish with plating and engraving will cost from	60 00 to 100.00

CAUTION.

uch of the accuracy and power of any good Rifle depends upon the *care* and accuracy with which the amunition is 1

were primarily destined for military, rather than civilian, consumption.

Consequently, those individuals who purchased Winchester rifles and carbines for private use either could order engraving, etc., from the company or arrange for it at a much lower cost from retailers and independent contractors. Given price differentials, it is likely that most selected the second source.

Chief among the independent engravers active at this time was Louis D. Nimschke (1832-1904) of New York City. His Work Book, preserved in the collection of Richard C. Marohn, M.D., contains numerous pulls (inked impressions of engraved decoration) of both Henry and Winchester rifles engraved for clients during the late 1860s[4].

Typical of the standard patterns executed by Nimschke are the designs shown in the pulls mounted on pages 54 through 56 of the Work Book (Plates 365-367). In general, his work is characterized by the use of well-formed foliate scrollwork either alone or in conjunction with shaped blank panels and ribbands. At times, Nimschke accentuated his scrollwork by incorporating animal figures into the composition. In particular, he was fond of using portrait heads of setters as shown by one set of

pulls on page 47 of the Work Book (Plate 368).

Though even the simplest of Nimschke's engraving exhibits a balanced and elegance that demonstrates devotion to his craft, it is the specially commissioned pieces which reveal his true virtuosity. Drawing upon a variety of published sources, as well as his own imagination, Nimschke created a number of beautifully engraved arms decorated with panel scenes such as the Winchester Model 1866 rifle illustrated in Plates 369 to 372. While the content of some of the tableaus, like the abduction scene on the rifle just mentioned, may seem to be naive by today's standards, they were, when first engraved, equal to the best work being done in Europe. More importantly, it is work of this type which demonstrates Nimschke's ability to create an illusion of three dimensionality through the use of perspective. He further enhanced that illusion by using deeper and, therefore, darker, cuts for those elements of the design in the foreground and finer, lighter cuts for those objects or individuals to the rear. Nimschke also provided a sense of movement to his work by positioning moving elements, animals and people at angles to the surface, thereby also heightening dimen-

Plate 364

Detail of advertising broadside issued by the Winchester Repeating Arms Company after April 1, 1867, which is illustrated in Plate 65. The $60 to $100 additional charge for plating and engraving remained in effect until 1870. Olin Corporation Photograph.

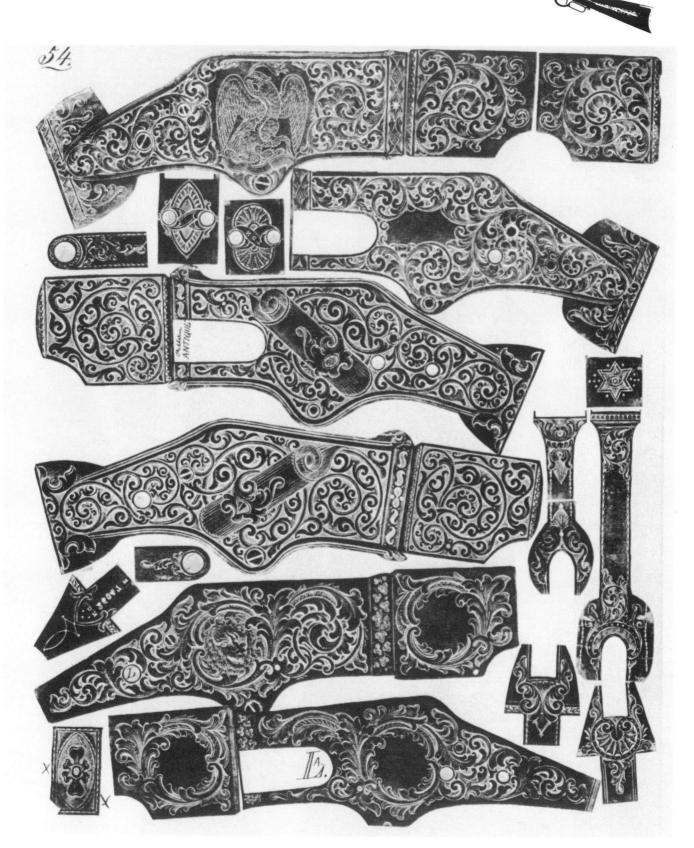

Plate 365

*P*age 54 of Louis D. Nimschke's Work Book containing various pulls (inked impressions) of Winchester Model 1866 rifles, which Nimschke engraved during the late 1860s. Reproduced with permission of the copyright holder from **L.D. Nimschke Firearms Engraver.**

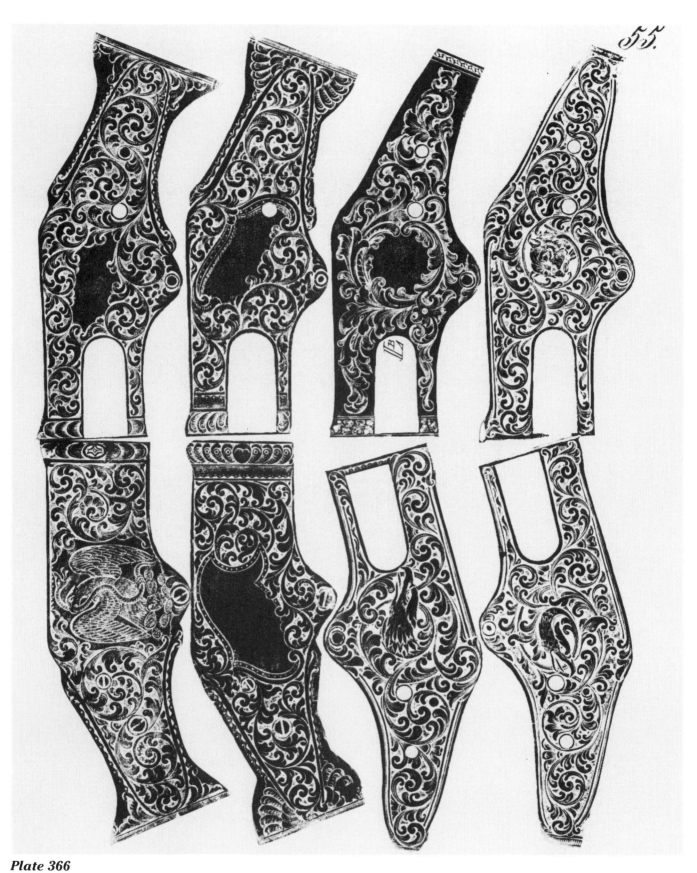

Plate 366

Page 55 of Louis D. Nimschke's Work Book. Reproduced with permission of the copyright holder from **L.D. Nimschke Firearms Engraver.**

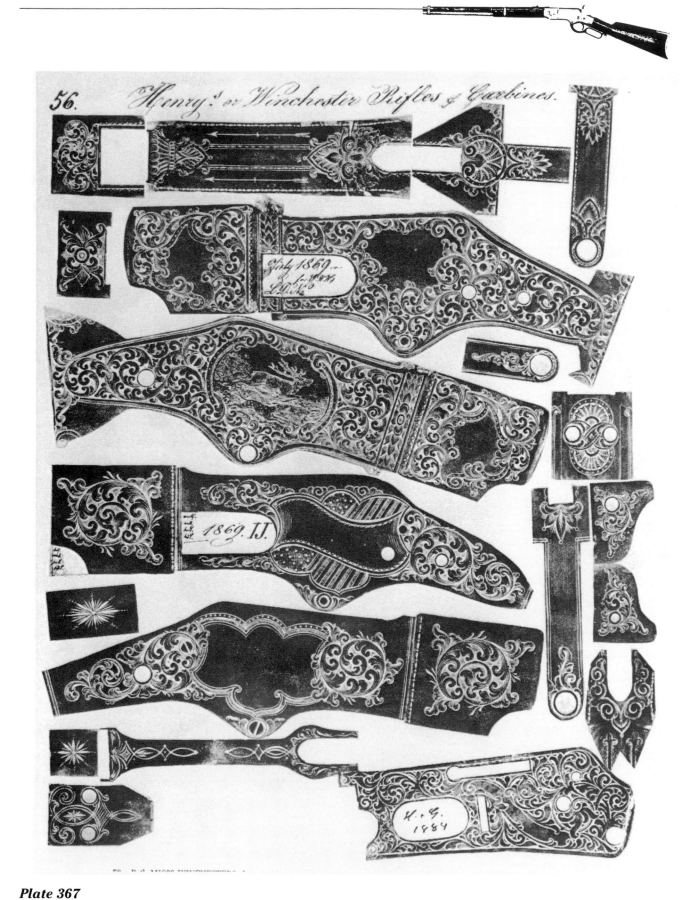

Plate 367

*P*age 56 of Louis D. Nimschke's Work Book. Reproduced with permission of the copyright holder from **L.D. Nimschke Firearms Engraver.**

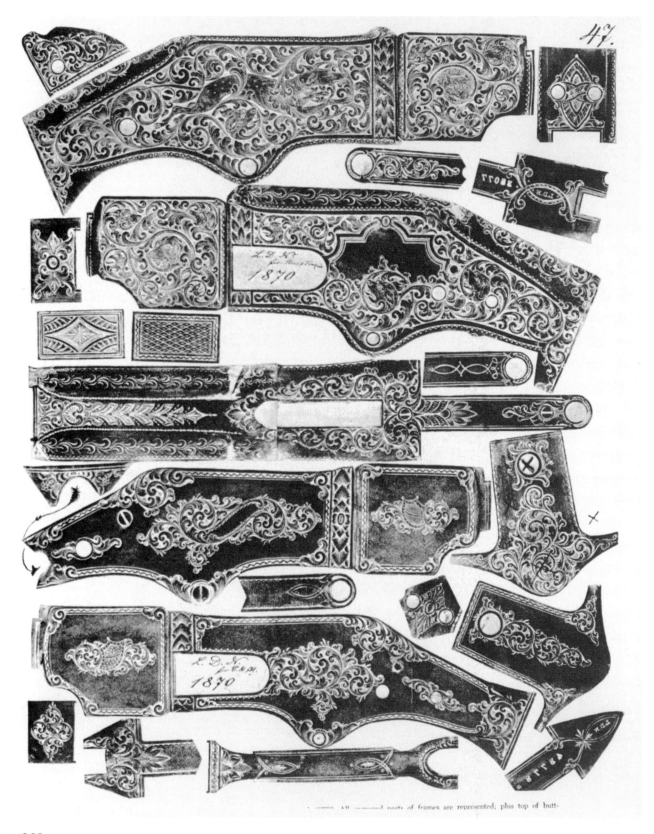

47.

... parts of frames are represented; plus top of butt-

Plate 368

*P*age 47 from Louis D. Nimschke's Work Book illustrating Nimschke's use of setters' heads in the upper two pulls. Reproduced with permission of the copyright holder from **L.D. Nimschke Firearms Engraver.**

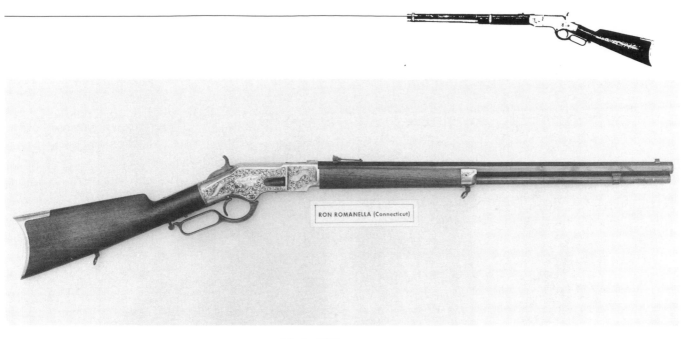

Plate 369

Winchester Model 1866 rifle, serial number engraved by Louis D. Nimschke in September of 1869. R.C. Romanella Collection, Olin Corporation Photograph.

Plate 370

Right receiver detail of the Model 1866 rifle illustrated in Plate 369. Olin Corporation Photograph.

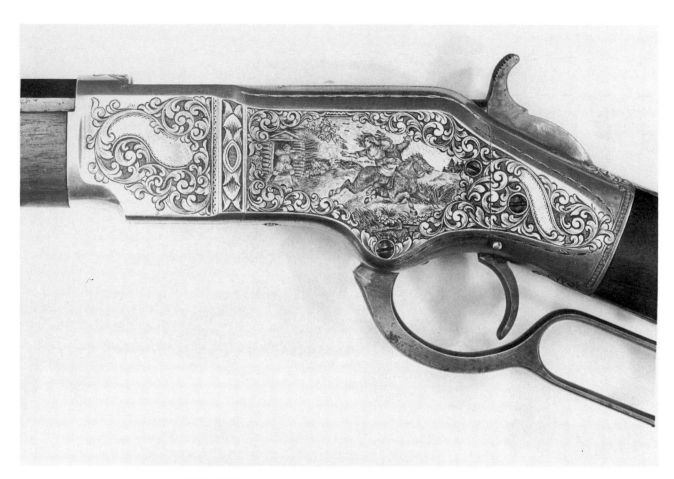

Plate 373

*E*nlarged detail from page 45 of Louis D. Nimschke's Work Book illustrating a pull taken from a Spencer sporting rifle engraved in August 1868. Reproduced with permission of the copyright holder from **L.D. Nimschke Firearms Engraver.**

Plate 374

*E*nlarged detail from page 45 of Louis D. Nimschke's Work Book illustrating a pull of a stage coach hold-up scene engraved on the left sideplate of a Winchester Model 1866 rifle. Reproduced with permission of the copyright holder from **L.D. Nimschke Firearms Engraver.**

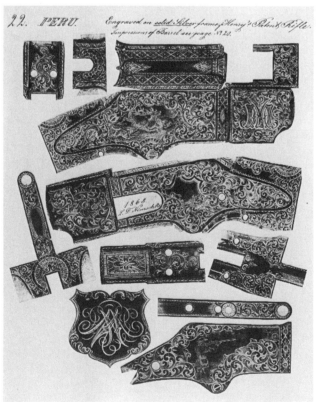

Above: Plate 375

Detail of a relief cut monogram engraved by L.D. Nimschke on the left receiver of a solid silver Winchester Model 1866 rifle in 1868. Olin Corporation Photograph.

Left: Plate 376

Page 22 of Louis D. Nimschke's Work Book containing pulls of his engraving on the silver Model 1866 rifle illustrated in Plate 375. Reproduced with permission of the copyright holder from **L.D. Nimschke Firearms Engraver.**

sionality. Thus, in the abduction scene (Plate 371), not only does the galloping horse appear to be moving toward the viewer, but the imminent fall of the victim and abductor from the horse is implied by their contorted position. Even when the main figures are depicted in a static pose, as with the Union cavalryman shooting at guerrillas which Nimschke engraved on a Spencer rifle (Plate 373) or the seated figures in the stagecoach robbery scene used as part of a Winchester rifle's decoration (Plate 374), the angle of these elements with respect to the surface of the arm implied imminent action.

Another aspect of decoration which Nimschke excelled at was relief work. By cutting away surrounding metal, he created true three-dimensional monograms and scrolls. Though difficult to illustrate in two-dimensional pulls and photographs due to the rather shallow nature of the relief work, some idea of this class of engraving can be seen in the crowned monogram shown at mid-right on page 57 of the Work Book (Plate 372) and the monogram cut in

the left receiver of the silver Winchester Model 1866 decorated by Nimschke in 1868 (Plates 375-376).

Whether Nimschke ever executed work for the Winchester company directly is not presently known. However, given the volume of Winchester rifle pulls, preserved in his Work Book which dates from 1868 to 1870, together with the unique character of some of those arms, it is probable that some of the work might have been done under contract. Due to an absence of absolute evidence, though, this question must remain in the realm of conjecture.

While Nimschke was inarguably one of the best engravers active during the late 1860s, he was not the only one. In Hartford, Connecticut, Gustave Young was producing superlative work for the Colt's Patent Fire Arms Manufacturing Company, and more importantly, teaching a new generation of engravers who would ultimately influence the decoration of Winchester arms for over seventy years[5].

Endnotes

1. For the price schedule adopted at that time, see the New Haven Arms Company advertising broadside reproduced in R. Bruce McDowell, **Evolution of the Winchester**, op. cit., page 113.

2. Illustrations of these particular presentation rifles are to be found in R.L. Wilson, **Winchester Engraving** (Beinfeld Books; Palm Springs, CA: 1989), pages 11 and 13.

3. Undated Winchester Repeating Arms Company advertising broadside published between March 4, 1867 and Feb. 16, 1869 (the dates Oliver P. Davis served as secretary of the company). Winchester Arms Collection Archives, Cody Firearms Museum.

4. Louis D. Nimschke's Work Book was published in full in R.L. Wilson, **L.D. Nimschke Firearms Engraver** (John J. Malloy; Teaneck, NJ: 1965 – reprinted by R & R Books; Livonia, NY: 1992).

5. R.L. Wilson, Nimschke, op. cit., page 50.

6. A biography of Gustave Young together with a summary and illustrations of his work is to be found in R.L. Wilson, **Colt Engraving** (Beinfeld Publishing, Inc.; North Hollywood, CA: 1982), pages 51-145.

CHAPTER 10

THE BEGINNING OF THE ULRICH ERA

In many respects, the founding of the Winchester Arms Company and later the Winchester Repeating Arms Company could not have occurred at a worse time. The United States had settled into a postwar recession and the American arms industry into a depression which it would not recover from until the supplies of cheap surplus arms from the Civil War had been dissipated some four to five years later.

Recognizing that the sales of any new arm, even one with such promise as King's Improvement of the Henry rifle, would be questionable in the volatile American market, Oliver F. Winchester decided in 1866 to concentrate his firms' marketing efforts on the procurement of foreign military orders. Not only would the receipt of such orders, if they proved to be forthcoming, provide a stability to production, but also they would generate substantial revenues which would ensure the economic survival of his endeavors. Though there was an element of risk involved, Winchester hoped to capitalize upon the changes then taking place in military strategy throughout the world. Throughout Western Europe, as well as elsewhere, military theoreticians had come to recognize that single-shot service rifles had become obsolete due to the rapid advancements which had

taken place in the development of repeating firearms. The manufacturers of such arms, therefore, had a competitive edge if they could prove the efficiency and reliability of their products. Since the new Winchester rifle was battle-proven by virtue of its lineage to the Henry rifle, O.F. Winchester began an aggressive campaign to promote its tactical value[1].

The wisdom of Winchester's decision to pursue this marketing strategy was to be proven correct almost immediately, and throughout 1866, 1867 and 1868, the bulk of the company's production was exported abroad for use by a variety of nations as either a primary or auxiliary service weapon[2]. While the success of this sales policy did ensure the financial success of his fledgling company during the first critical years of its existence, Winchester knew that the continued well-being of the firm depended upon the creation of a broader based market. Thus, when military sales began to fall off in late 1868[3], he decided that it was time to reenter the civilian arms market. Consequently, in December of that year, he instructed the Bridgeport factory's superintendent, Nelson King, to begin a gradual retooling of the production lines there to accommodate an increase in the manufacture of Model 1866 sporting

PRICE LIST OF ARMS
MANUFACTURED BY THE
Winchester Repeating Arms Company.

Rifle, with varnished Stock and Sling,	$50.00
Rifle, with oiled Stock,	48.50
Infantry Rifled Musket, with Angular Bayonet and Sling,	45.00
Infantry Rifled Musket, with Sabre Bayonet and Sling,	47.00
Carbine with oiled Stock, without Sling,	40.00
Cartridges, per 1,000,	20.00
Slings for Carbine,	1.50
Leather Case for Rifle,	7.50
" " " Carbine,	7.00
Globe and Peck Sights, extra,	7.50
Fancy Stock, additional,	5.00
Extra Finish, with plating and engraving, will cost, additional, from	10 to 50.00

Office, 193 CHAPEL STREET.

NEW HAVEN, CONN.

W. W. WINCHESTER, Sec'y.   O. F. WINCHESTER, Pres't.

rifles[4]. At the same time, he also began a subtle shift in the company's advertising so that it addressed civilian uses of Winchester rifles rather than solely their military applications, which it had previously stressed[5].

Just as his decision to pursue military contracts three years earlier had proved successful, the timing of Winchester's reentry into the general market also proved to be propitious. Faced with little or no competition due to the collapse of their chief rival, the Spencer Rifle Company[6], the Winchester company rapidly achieved a dominant position within the repeating rifle field. The firm was also able to capitalize upon a demand for their products, which had been brought about not only by the reputation their arms had won abroad over the previous years but, more importantly, their relative scarcity in the United States. Thus, when the company began advertising the availability of Model 1866 sporting rifles and carbines in January 1869, the response was immediate. According to George Walker and H.B. Dow's records concerning the production of the Model 1866, orders far outpaced the company's ability to fulfill them during all of 1869 and the first quarter of 1870[7].

While it is probable that O.F. Winchester planned to offer engraving as a standard option for the Model 1866 during the first year of its real commercial availability, the retention of the prohibitively expensive 1867 price schedule ($60 to $100 above the cost of a carbine or rifle) through 1869 and into 1870 suggests that he did not consider it a priority. Instead, it appears that his primary concern was the production of plain arms for which a ready and eager market existed. However, when production began to keep pace with orders received, the policy concerning engraving and special finishes was reexamined. Whether the subsequent change was brought about by an increased volume in requests for decorated arms or by the realization that significant profits could be made by the company if it offered reasonably priced engraving

Plate 377
Price list issued by the Winchester Repeating Arms Company in 1870, noting the reduced cost for plating and engraving. Private Collection.

Plate 378

*T*intype photograph of Herman Leslie Ulrich taken about 1868. Ulrich Family Collection.

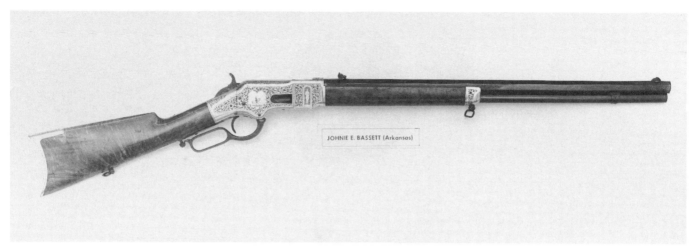

JOHNIE E. BASSETT (Arkansas)

cannot now be determined. It is known that in mid-1870, the Winchester Repeating Arms Company radically altered the cost of engraved arms to a level set at from $10 to $50 above the base cost of the arm to be decorated (Plate 377). The firm also hired its first in-house engraver at this time.

Interestingly, the individual employed by the firm was a relative unknown in the field. Yet, given O.F. Winchester's insistence upon excellence, Herman Leslie Ulrich's reputation must have belied his age of not quite twenty-four years.

Born in Mansbach, Germany, on Sept. 24, 1846, Herman Ulrich (Plate 378) was the third son of Conrad and Marguerite Viel Ulrich[8]. The family had emigrated from Germany in mid-1849 and settled briefly in New York City before relocating to Hartford, Connecticut, where the father entered the employ of the Colt's Patent Fire Arms Company. Although absolute proof is now lacking, it is believed that Herman Ulrich was apprenticed to either Herman Bodenstein or Gustave Young at the Colt company in 1859 or 1860. By 1867, he had completed his apprenticeship and established himself as an independent engraver in Hartford. His employment at the Winchester works began in July 29, 1870, at a salary of 32.5 cents per hour. It should be noted here that Herman was not the first Ulrich to be employed by the Winchester company. His younger brother John (Aug. 13, 1850-Aug. 9, 1924) had been hired in November 1868 by Leander Russell as an assembler in the Gun Shop[9].

Herman Ulrich was to remain the company's sole engraver only for eight months. Due to a sharp rise in demand for decorated arms, he had to call upon the aid of his elder brother Conrad Friedrich (March 24, 1844-April 22, 1925) in March 1871[10]. Conrad's arrival at the Winchester factory resulted in a number of changes which his younger brother probably did not foresee. First, his position as chief engraver was taken over by Conrad and the younger brother John was transferred from the Gun Shop to Conrad. Conrad's exercise of the rights of an elder brother must have been especially galling when he gave John a salary of 33.2 cents per hour while maintaining Herman's at the previous level of 32.5 cents[11].

The most curious aspect of Conrad Ulrich's tenure as chief engraver or chief engraving contractor for the Winchester company is the little amount of work he did. While he billed the company for 129 hours in April 1871, in May he billed only eight, in June he billed seventeen, and in July just six. In comparison, Herman billed the firm for 250, 258, 184, and 112 hours for the same period, and John billed the firm for 257, 263, 258, and 215 hours from April

Plate 379

Winchester Model 1866 rifle, serial number 26283, engraved by Herman L. Ulrich in 1870, for exhibition by the Winchester company at the Exposition of the American Institute in New York City. Formerly in the collection of the late Johnie E. Bassett. Olin Corporation Photograph.

362

Above: Plate 380

*R*ight receiver detail of the Model 1866 rifle illustrated in Plate 379. Herman Ulrich's use of animal and bird head terminals for his scrollwork is also to be found on his personal revolver (Plates 432-436). Olin Corporation Photograph.

Below: Plate 381

*L*eft receiver detail of the Model 1866 rifle illustrated in Plate 379. While the circular panel scene exhibits some naivete, the portrait of Liberty is extremely well modelled (a characteristic of all of Herman Ulrich's figural work). Olin Corporation Photograph.

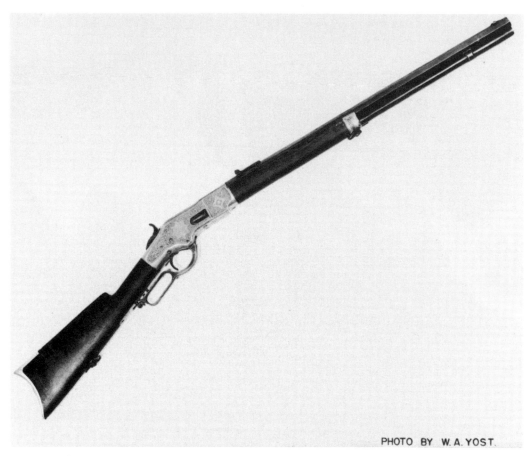

PHOTO BY W.A. YOST.

Left: Plate 382

Winchester Model 1866 rifle, serial number 28549, engraved by Herman Ulrich in the simplest pattern offered by the Winchester company. W.A. Yost Photograph.

Below: Plate 383

Right receiver detail of the Model 1866 rifle illustrated in Plate 382. The general form of Herman Ulrich's scrollwork is quite evident in this piece. W.A. Yost Photograph.

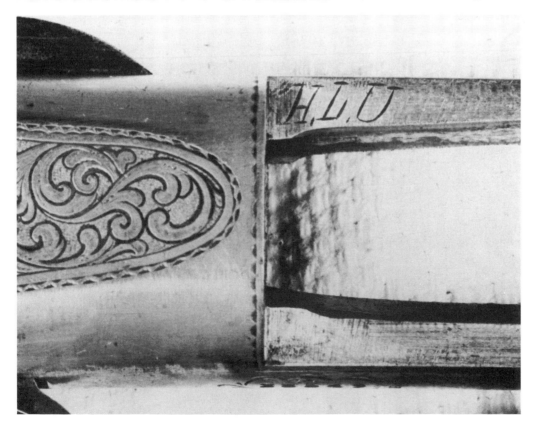

Above: Plate 384
*L*eft receiver detail of the Model 1866 rifle illustrated in Plate 382. W.A. Yost Photograph.

Left: Plate 385
*D*etail of Herman L. Ulrich's signature cut in the upper tang of the Model 1866 rifle illustrated in Plate 382. The presence of this signature may indicate that this arm was engraved prior to H.L. Ulrich's employment by the Winchester company as it was against the firm's general policy for engravers to sign their works. W.A. Yost Photograph.

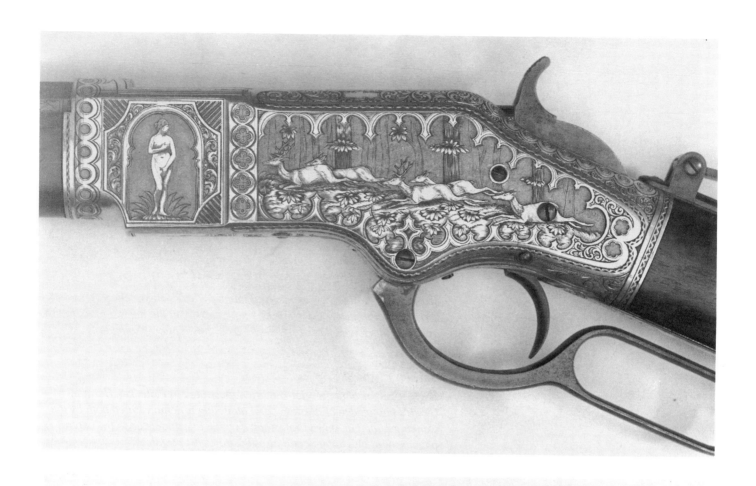

Top: Plate 394

*L*eft receiver of the Model 1866 rifle illustrated in Plate 392. The positioning of the running deer (patterned after drawings by Claesen) within a formal architectural frame is quite dramatic. Interestingly, Herman Ulrich did another Model 1866 for the Vienna Exhibition, which was almost identically decorated as this piece. However, in place of the running deer, that rifle (now only known from pulls) has a hunting scene set within the frame. In keeping with where the rifle was to be first exhibited, the hunters are shown in typical German dress and are armed with hunting swords. Olin Corporation Photograph.

Bottom: Plate 395

*D*etail of the engraving found on the Model 1866 rifle illustrated in Plate 392. Olin Corporation Photograph.

H. L. Ulrich & Company
Stock Brokers
No. 4 Myrtle Avenue
Brooklyn, New York

Monday May 5, 1884

Samuel T. Baker
Oraville [sic], California

Dear Sir

Yours of the 21st has been received. The news you relate concerning the marking of your rifles
is most disturbing. I have however been informed reliably that Mr. John Ulrich has adopted the
fashion of stamping Winchester Repeating Arms Company rifle &c with his touch mark when
they are sent to that company's works for any reason.

Should you wish redress, I am positive that Gov. Winchester's successor Mr. William Converse
will be able to assist you.

Your obt servant
H.L.Ulrich

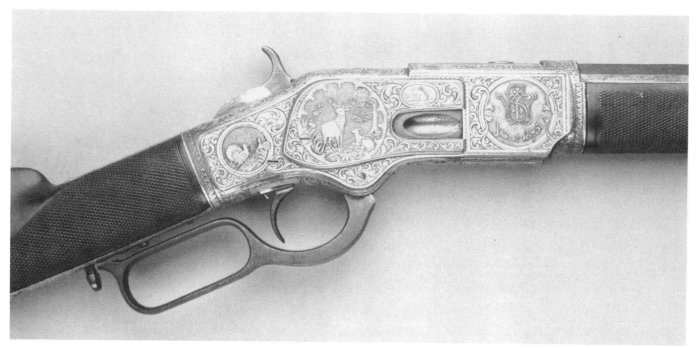

Plate 396

*R*ight receiver of Winchester Model 1873 rifle, serial number 2681, engraved by Herman Ulrich during the period he was sole engraver for the Winchester company. Christie, Manson & Woods International, Inc. Photograph.

Plate 397

*D*etail of the relief cut monogram chiselled in the forward right receiver of the Model 1873 rifle illustrated in Plates 396. Given the difference in quality between all the engraving and that of the squirrel, it has been suggested that the latter was added later (perhaps at the time when the rifle was stamped with John Ulrich's signature die). For examples of Herman Ulrich's squirrels, see Plates 390, 432 and 436. Christie, Manson & Woods International, Inc. Photograph.

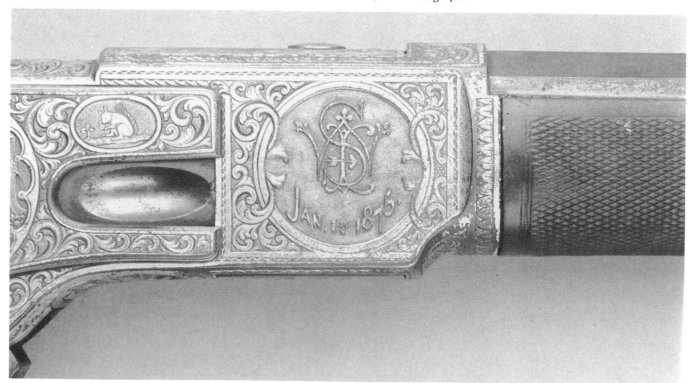

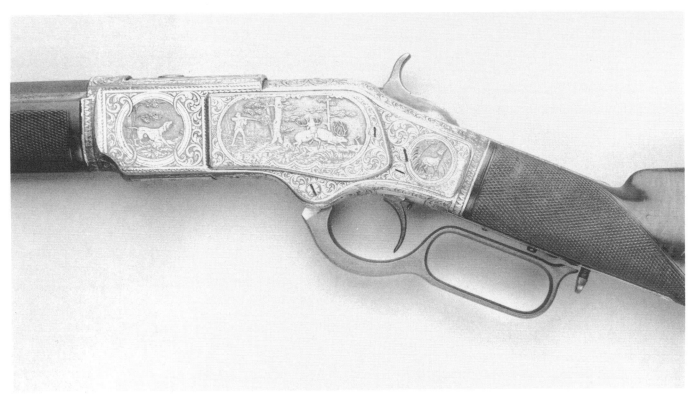

through July[12]. Due to a change in accounting procedures after Dec. 2, 1871, it is unfortunately not possible to track the hours of work for each of the brothers. However, the gross amounts paid to Conrad Ulrich strongly suggest that the work schedule did not change appreciably during 1872[13]. In 1873, though, the amounts paid to Conrad diminished to the extent that they would not support one brother, let alone three[14]. Therefore, it is likely that Conrad worked alone that year and until March 14, 1874, when he left the company[15]. The fate of Herman and John during this period is unknown, although they may have worked in the Gun Shop.

While it has been suggested that Conrad Ulrich continued to do contract work for the Winchester company during the last quarter of the 19th century, evidence suggests that he did not. Rather, he engraved Winchester arms as private commissions. A manuscript order form dated May 4, 1885[16] demonstrates that he purchased rifles for cli-

ents, engraved them and then had them finished by the company before being returned to him for delivery to his clients.

When Conrad Ulrich left the company, Herman Ulrich again assumed the position of chief engraving contractor as of April 1, 1874. He remained in that position until May 22, 1875, when the volume of orders again fell to the level that continuing there was economically unfeasible[17].

The Winchester company then did without an engraver for almost a year. On March 1, 1875, orders had risen sufficiently for the firm to engage the services of John Ulrich, then still working in the Gun Shop, as a full-time engraver[18].

While there is a similarity between the three brothers' work, which is due not only to a familiar relationship, but also, the circumstances of their training (Conrad and Herman at the Colt works and John's apprenticeship to Conrad), there are also marked differences that

Plate 398

*L*eft receiver of the Model 1873 rifle illustrated in Plate 397. The format of the relief cut hunting scene was to remain a standard offering of the Winchester company for over forty years. Christie, Manson & Woods International, Inc. Photograph.

allow each brother's products to be differentiated from each other's.

The character of Herman Ulrich's engraving (Plates 379-398, 423-425, 430-436 and 440-444) is perhaps best defined by the exquisitely cut and balanced scrollwork it contains. Not only does it have a plastic fluidity, his addition of lines on the curving planes gives it an illusion of depth that was never quite matched by either Conrad or John. On occasion, Herman also included portrait heads of animals and birds, as well as masques into his scrollwork (Plates 380-381 and 432-433) in the manner of Gustave Young (his probable teacher). It was his work in special order pieces, however, which best demonstrates his abilities. On pieces of this quality (Plates 379-381 and 389-398), he incorporated panel scenes frequently enclosed with architectural elements that are distinguished by his knowledge of anatomy

and the use of shading combined with modelling to create an illusion of depth. A further characteristic of his work, especially on higher grade arms, was Herman Ulrich's consistent use of finely lined or crosshatched backgrounds against which his scrollwork was set (Plates 432-436). This feature served to accentuate the scrolls in a manner which a punchdot or pointelle ground could never achieve no matter what its fineness. One other field in which Herman Ulrich excelled was relief work. Whether done with scrollwork or in panel scenes, his technique revealed a complete mastery of the nuances needed to create a balanced effect.

In contrast to Herman Ulrich, who terminated his scrolls with well defined curling knobs (see Plate 385), Conrad Ulrich consistently used terminals that rolled into the scroll itself so that the end is not a separate element (see Plates 399). In those instances where

Plate 399
Right receiver of a Winchester Model 1866 rifle, serial number 79580, engraved by Conrad Friedrich Ulrich, illustrating the manner in which he ended his scrolls with rolled knobs. Olin Corporation Photograph.

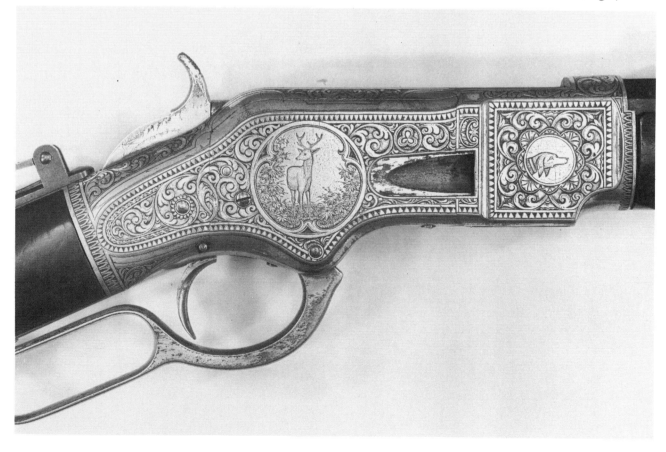

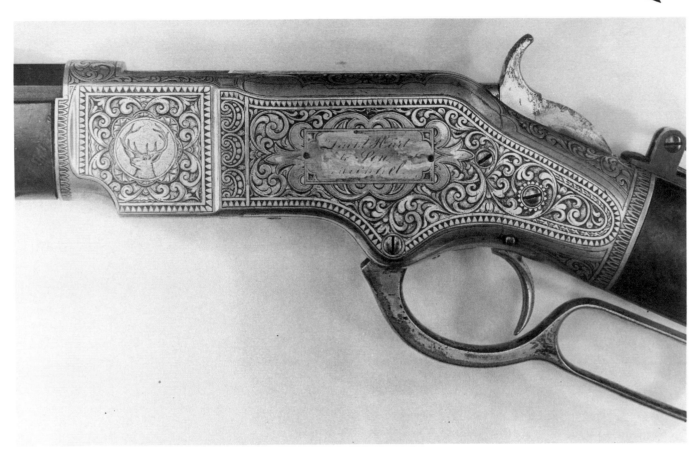

Above: Plate 400

*L*eft receiver of the Model 1866 rifle illustrated in Plate 399. Olin Corporation Photograph.

Below: Plate 401

*W*inchester Model 1866 rifle, serial number 79924, engraved by Conrad F. Ulrich. Formerly James S. Fowler Collection, Olin Corporation Photograph.

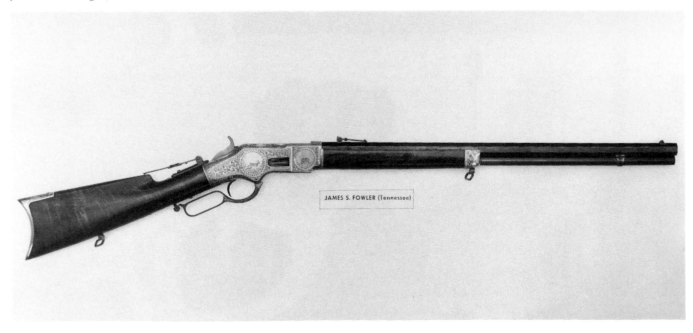

JAMES S. FOWLER (Tennessee)

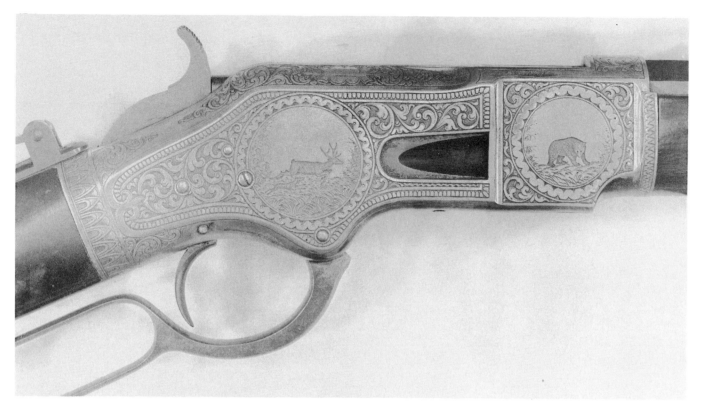

Above: Plate 402

*R*ight receiver of the Model 1866 rifle illustrated in Plate 401. Olin Corporation Photograph.

Below: Plate 403

*L*eft receiver of the Model 1866 rifle illustrated in Plate 401. C.F. Ulrich's incomplete appreciation of foreshortening is illustrated in his figure of the doe. The head of that animal is grossly out of proportion to the remainder of the body. Olin Corporation Photograph.

Above: Plate 404

*W*inchester Model 1866 rifle, serial number 96020, engraved by Conrad Ulrich for presentation by the Winchester company to H. Reynolds on Feb. 1, 1872. Harry H. Sefried Collection, Olin Corporation Photograph.

Below: Plate 405

*R*ight receiver of the Model 1866 rifle illustrated in Plate 404.

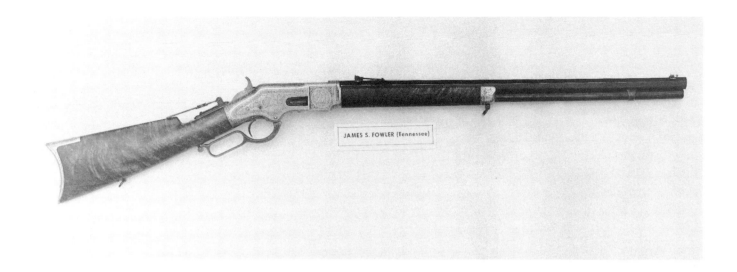

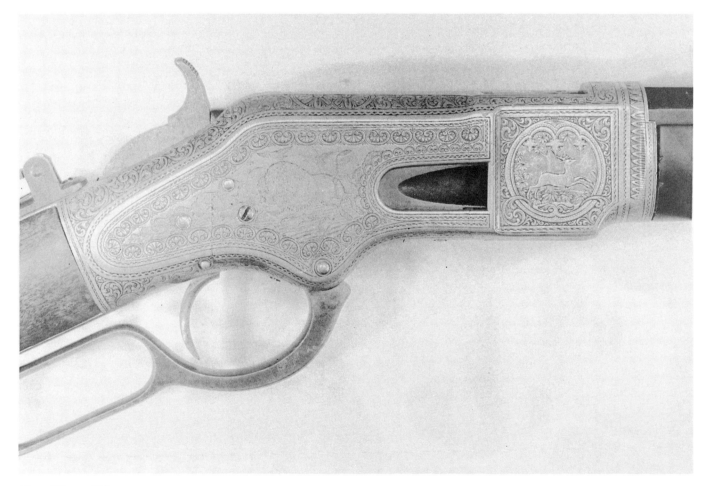

Top: Plate 406

*W*inchester Model 1866 rifle, serial number 96749, engraved by Conrad Ulrich. Formerly James S. Fowler Collection, Olin Corporation Photograph.

Bottom: Plate 407

*R*ight receiver of the Model 1866 rifle illustrated in Plate 406. The buffalo stampede with the fleeing rabbits represents one of C.F. Ulrich's finest works. Olin Corporation Photograph.

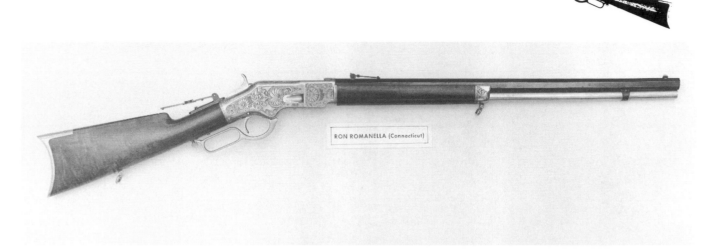

RON ROMANELLA (Connecticut)

Above: Plate 408

*W*inchester Model 1866 rifle, serial number 109544, engraved by Conrad Ulrich in a style somewhat similar to Louis D. Nimschke. R.C. Romanella Collection, Olin Corporation Photograph.

Middle: Plate 409

*R*ight receiver of the Model 1866 rifle illustrated in Plate 408. Olin Corporation Photograph.

Bottom: Plate 410

*L*eft receiver of the Model 1866 rifle illustrated in Plate 408. Olin Corporation Photograph.

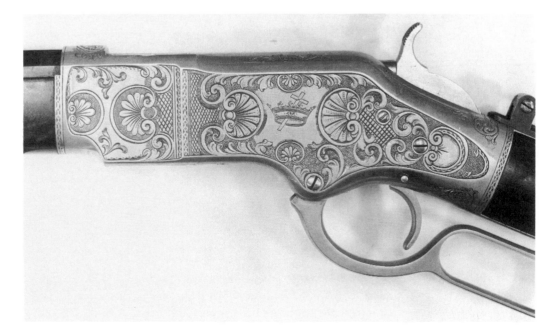

terminals are not rolled into themselves, Conrad Ulrich favored rounding them off without forming a ball ending (Plate 405). In addition, Conrad Ulrich's scrolls are fuller (i.e., thicker) than his brother Herman's. While Conrad Ulrich used lined and cross latched grounds for some elements of his work, for the most part he preferred to use a punch-dot or pointelle background, even on his best work (Plates 399 and 402). The most striking difference between Conrad and Herman Ulrich's work is to be found in their figural studies. Whereas Herman's have a vitality and three dimensional character even in static poses, those executed by Conrad never achieve the same sense of animation. Even in his portrait of the goddess of the hunt, Diana, with her accompanying stag (Plate 411), which was copied from a print by Rennasson[19], there is a flatness not found in Herman's work. To a great extent the lack of dimensionality is due to the absence of subtle shad-

ing, however, another cause is poor modelling. If the stag rondel found on the Model 1866 rifle engraved by Conrad Ulrich, illustrated in Plate 399, is compared with an almost identical rondel done by Herman (Plate 390), the difference between the two brother's appreciation of foreshortening as a means to create the illusion of depth is easily understood. Conrad placed the stag so that its hooves are virtually on the same horizontal plane, with the hoof of the partially obscured right rear leg almost touching that of the right foreleg. In contrast Herman, slightly staggered the three visible legs so that the image has a sense of depth. Herman also used more pronounced modelling of muscles and curves together with careful shading to achieve depth perception.

The easiest of the brothers' work to identify is that of John (Plate 411). Not only does it differ considerably in the style of scrollwork but also in his exe-

Plate 411

Right receiver of a Winchester Model 1866 rifle, serial number 112270, engraved by Conrad Ulrich for exhibition by the Winchester company at the Centennial Exhibition of the United States held in Philadelphia, Pennsylvania, in 1876. Winchester Arms Collection (Inv. No. W3283), Cody Firearms Museum.

Plate 412

*P*hotograph of John Ulrich taken between 1870 and 1875. Ulrich Family Collection.

Top: Plate 413

*W*inchester Model 1866 rifle, serial number 104463, engraved by John Ulrich. Hy Vogel Collection, Olin Corporation Photograph.

Bottom: Plate 414

*R*ight receiver of the Model 1866 rifle illustrated in Plate 413. Olin Corporation Photograph.

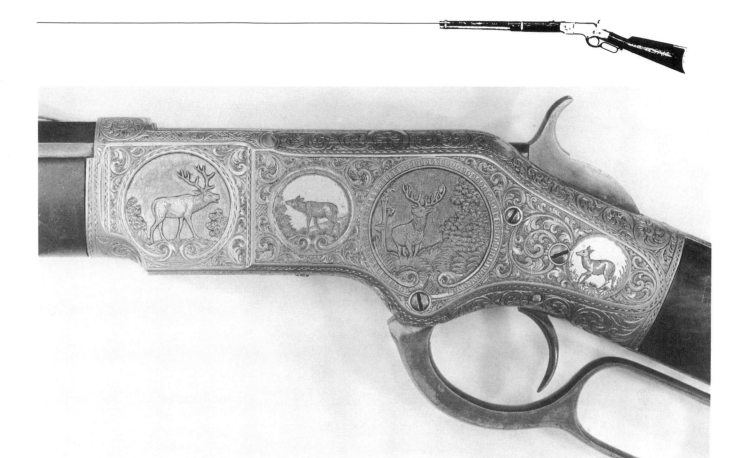

Above: Plate 415

*L*eft receiver of the Model 1866 rifle illustrated in Plate 413. Olin Corporation Photograph.

Below: Plate 416

*W*inchester Model 1866 rifle, serial number 107209, engraved by John Ulrich. Formerly James S. Fowler Collection, Olin Corporation Photograph.

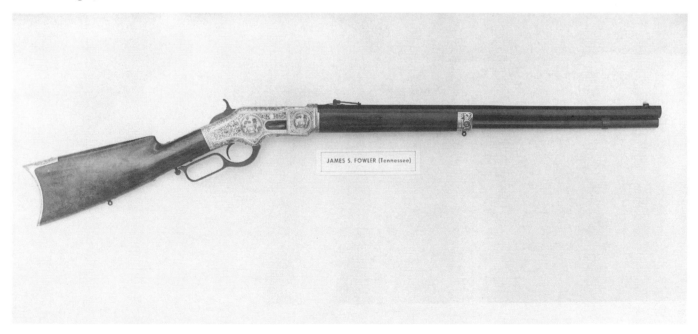

Above: Plate 417

*R*ight receiver of the Model 1866 rifle illustrated in Plate 416. Olin Corporation Photograph.

Below: Plate 418

*L*eft receiver of the Model 1866 rifle illustrated in Plate 416. Olin Corporation Photograph.

Above: Plate 419

*R*ight receiver of a Winchester Model 1876 rifle, serial number 38647, with panel scenes engraved by John Ulrich and originally owned by Theodore Roosevelt. The scrollwork represents one of the earliest known examples of William E. Stokes work for the Winchester company. While the buffalo scene is well executed, that of the antelope resembles nothing more closely than a llama. Olin Corporation Photograph.

Below: Plate 420

*L*eft receiver of the Model 1876 rifle illustrated in Plate 419. The deer in the center panel is patterned after a drawing by George Catlin. Olin Corporation Photograph.

Above: Plate 421

*D*etail of the fore end cap engraved by William E. Stokes fitted to the Model 1876 rifle illustrated in Plate 419. Olin Corporation Photograph.

Right: Plate 422

*D*etail of the escutcheon engraved by John Ulrich, which is inlaid in the stock of the Model 1876 rifle illustrated in Plate 419. Olin Corporation Photograph.

cution of panel scenes. He used rolled scroll terminals with strongly cut inner turns often accompanied by a subsidiary 'c' shaped cut in the turn (Plates 414 and 417). In comparison to both Conrad and Herman's work, John's scrollwork lacks imagination and often appears forced into the space covered rather than flowing free within it. If there is one singular feature about John Ulrich's work, it is his lack of technical expertise. This is clearly evident in his panel scenes. They contain lifeless and poorly drawn figures that are totally devoid of dimensionality (Plates 414-415, 417-418 and 419-420). Even with the addition of shading, the basic anatomical correctness of the figural elements stands out (see especially Plate 419). While there was some improvement in his work over the years, it never did equal the quality of either of his brothers. Yet today, he is lauded as one of the company's best engravers due to the assumption that he was responsible for a large volume of particularly fine work done from 1886 to 1914.

As Chapter 11 will demonstrate, this assumption is fallacious.

The major problem encountered in the study of engraving produced by the Ulrich brothers is the disquieting habit of both Conrad and John to sign work which may or may not be the result of their labor.

Although it was the policy of the Winchester company not to allow engravers working under their control to sign work produced for sale, the injunction was relaxed in the case of pieces made solely for exhibition[20]. Consequently, Winchester rifles made after July 1870, bearing the signatures of an engraver, should, if made under company auspices, be of exhibition quality and be recorded in the company's serial number registers in a manner consistent with that purpose[21]. The signature policy also could not, however, be enforced on those arms engraved under private contract, even by engravers who also were under contract to the company.

JAMES S. FOWLER (Tennessee)

Top: Plate 423

Winchester Model 1866 rifle, serial number 107209 with panel scenes engraved by Conrad F. Ulrich and scrollwork by Herman L. Ulrich. Formerly James S. Fowler Collection, Olin Corporation Photograph.

Bottom: Plate 424

Right receiver of the Model 1866 rifle illustrated in Plate 423. Olin Corporation Photograph.

Plate 425

Left receiver of the Model 1866 rifle illustrated in Plate 423. Olin Corporation Photograph.

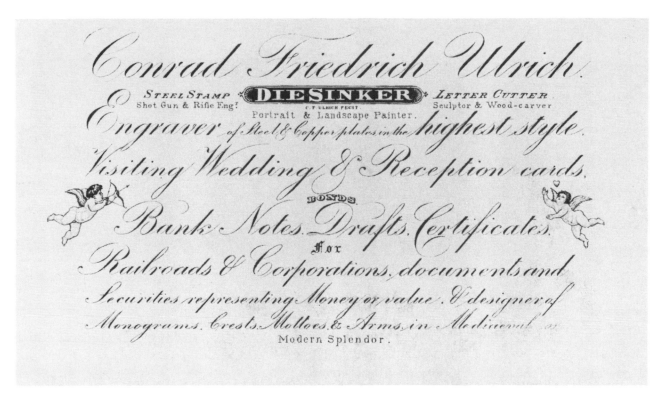

Plate 426

*C*onrad F. Ulrich's trade card distributed by him after he left the Winchester company. Private Collection.

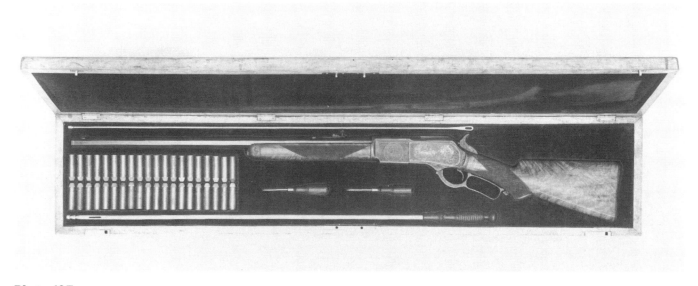

Plate 427

*C*ased Winchester Model 1876 rifle, serial number 53072, engraved by Conrad F. Ulrich in 1886, as a private commission. Typical of those arms engraved by C.F. Ulrich privately, the Winchester company's record for this rifle makes no mention of engraving. Instead, it describes only the factory-made features ("June 22/86 rifle Ex Oct Pl 26 CHCSPG   mag SB Rub B Plate Matted Bbl &c June 23/86"). Olin Corporation Photograph.

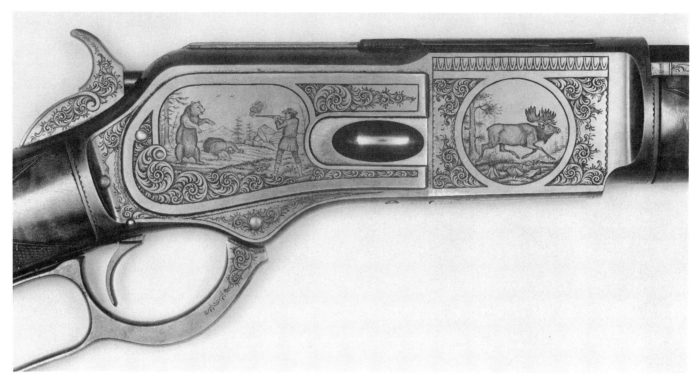

Plate 428

*R*ight receiver of the Model 1876 rifle illustrated in Plate 427. Olin Corporation Photograph.

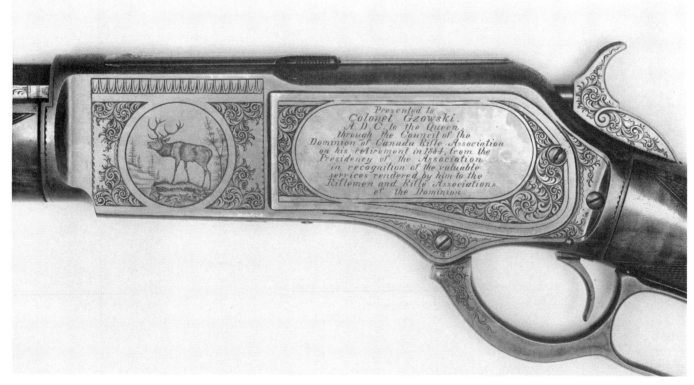

Plate 429

*L*eft receiver of the Model 1876 rifle illustrated in Plate 427. Olin Corporation Photograph.

Plate 430
Winchester Model 1873 One of One Thousand rifle, serial number 23385, believed to have been engraved by Herman Ulrich in 1876, based upon the form of the scrollwork. The quality of the work is also more indicative of Herman Ulrich's hand than that of his younger brother, John, who was then the only engraver at the Winchester company. Olin Corporation Photograph.

Above: Plate 431

*L*eft receiver of the Model 1873 rifle illustrated in Plate 430. Olin Corporation Photograph.

Below: Plate 432

*C*olt New Line revolver, serial number 5018, engraved and gold inlaid by Herman L. Ulrich for his own use. Ulrich Family Collection.

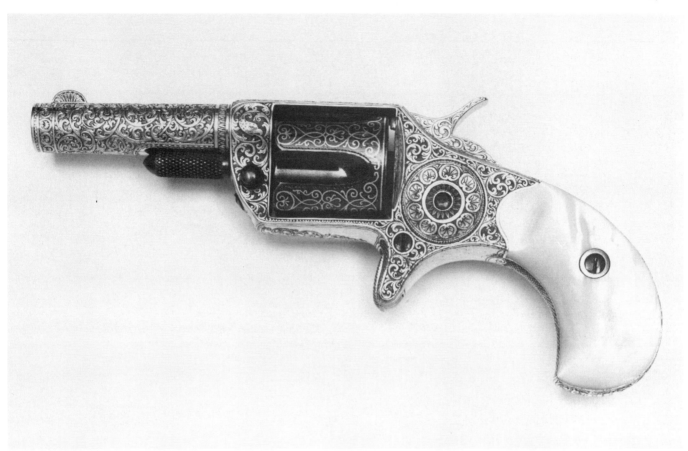

Plate 433

*L*eft-hand view of Herman L. Ulrich's personal Colt New Line revolver illustrated in Plate 432. With the exception of the lower frame strap below the cylinder, all of the scrollwork on this revolver is cut in relief with the background either finely shaded with crosshatched lines or minutely punched with a circular die. Ulrich Family Collection.

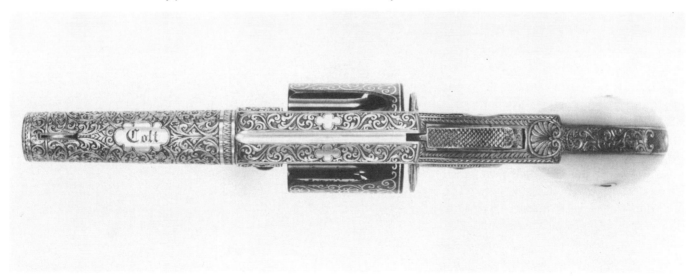

Plate 434

*T*op view of Herman L. Ulrich's personal Colt New Line revolver illustrated in Plate 432. The scrollwork and geometric motifs used on the topstrap above the cylinder are virtually identical to the work to be seen on the Winchester Model 1866 rifles illustrated in Plates 389-394. Ulrich Family Collection.

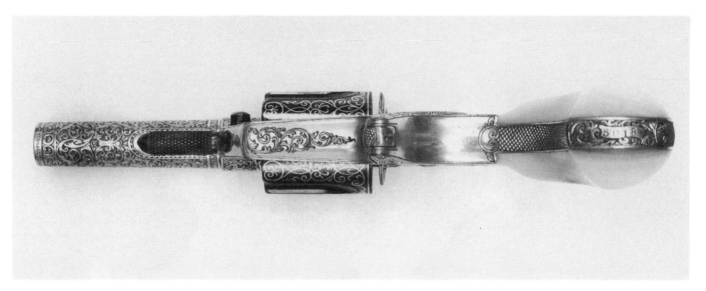

Plate 435

Bottom view of Herman L. Ulrich's personal Colt New Line revolver illustrated in Plate 432. Ulrich Family Collection.

Therein lies the seeds of a problem which still perplexes arms enthusiasts. Further complicating the situation is the fact that it was standard practice for a contractor to sign pieces made in his shop by assistants or journeymen. Thus, a rifle signed by Conrad Ulrich during the period he was chief engraving contractor to the Winchester company (April 1, 1871 to March 14, 1874) can be the work of his hand or one of his brothers. Identification is clouded even more by the fact that on occasion the brothers shared engraving work, with one cutting panel scenes and another completing the surrounding scrollwork (Plates 423-425).

With respect to arms signed by John Ulrich, the problems associated with attribution and whether they are the results of private contracts or intended for exhibition purposes is much more problematical. The source of this confusion is based on the fact that John Ulrich both signed arms which were returned to the Winchester factory for work (see sidebar and Plates 396-398) and pieces decorated under factory orders. Thus, arms predating his tenure as chief engraving contractor are to be found with his signature stamp as well as non-exhibition pieces made during the period he was the engraving contractor. Further compounding the prob-

Plate 436

Enlarged detail of the right frame decoration on Herman L. Ulrich's personal Colt New Line Revolver illustrated in Plate 432. Ulrich Family Collection.

BROOKLYN STOCK EXCHANGE.

H. L. ULRICH & CO.

STOCK BROKERS,

No. 4 Myrtle Avenue,

COR. FULTON STREET.   BROOKLYN, N. Y.

Plate 437
*T*rade card for the H.L. Ulrich & Company, Brooklyn, New York, circa 1881-1889. Ulrich Family Collection.

Plate 438
*V*ignette of an elk engraved by Herman L. Ulrich for the American Bank Note Company of New York City, in 1883 or 1884. American Bank Note Company Archives.

Plate 439

*P*hotograph of Herman L. Ulrich taken shortly after his retirement from the securities trading business in 1889. Ulrich Family Collection.

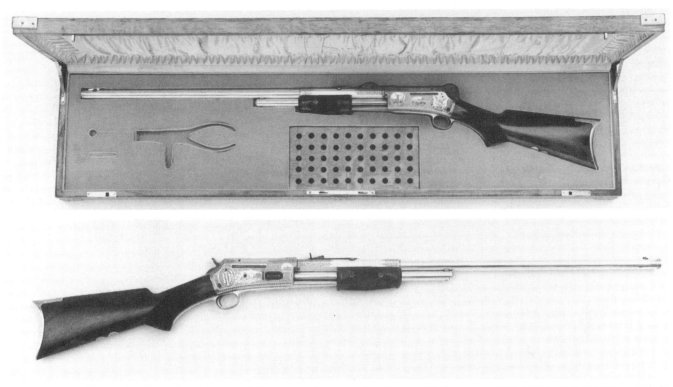

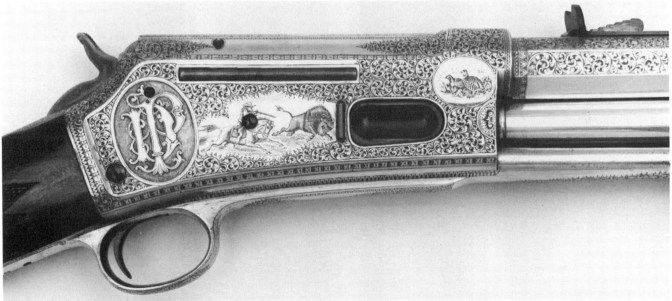

Top: Plate 440

*C*ased Colt Lightning magazine rifle, serial number 5164, engraved by Herman L. Ulrich either for the Colt's Patent Fire Arms Manufacturing Company or for the New York arms distributor Hartley & Graham, who presented the rifle in 1891 to His Excellency, General Don Porfirio Diaz, President of Mexico. Douglas Arms Collection (Inv. No. D63), Royal Military College of Canada, Kingston, Ontario.

Middle: Plate 441

*R*ight-hand view of the Colt Lightning Magazine rifle illustrated in Plate 440.

Bottom: Plate 442

*R*ight receiver of the Colt Lightning magazine rifle illustrated in Plate 440. Herman L. Ulrich's initials are finely engraved into the background of the PD monogram panel.

lem was his practice after 1885 of signing arms engraved by his assistant, William E. Stokes. The latter, however, can be properly attributed due to the differences in style between the two men.

Despite his relative anonymity, Herman Leslie Ulrich would, some two decades later, play an important role in the development of Winchester engraving. Consequently, some mention should be made of his activities after he left the company in 1875. Although his brother, Conrad, continued to engrave Winchester carbines and rifles on a regular basis after his departure from the firm (Plates 427- 429), Herman Ulrich, in contrast, is believed to have done only one between 1875 and 1896 (Plates 430 and 431). Instead, he chose to work primarily for the Colt's Patent Fire Arms Manufacturing Company in Hartford (Plates 432-436)[22]. While he was a superb craftsman, Herman Ulrich's true interests lay in another direction, and by the close of the decade he had, by following the engraving trade, made enough money to pursue his real ambition, a career in finance.

Plate 443

*L*eft receiver of the Colt Lightning magazine rifle illustrated in Plate 440. The standing elk is identical to that done by Herman L. Ulrich for the American Bank Note Company (Plate 438).

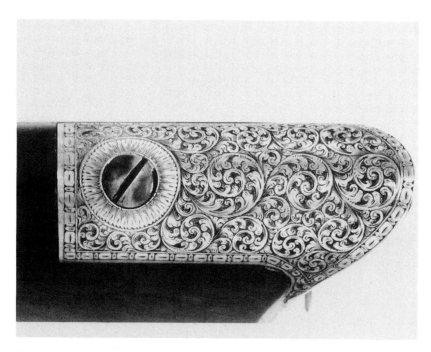

Plate 444

*D*etail of the scroll engraving on the butt plate tang of the Colt Lightning magazine rifle illustrated in Plate 440.

With E.P. Atkinson as a minority partner, Herman L. Ulrich purchased the New Haven Stock Exchange seat of N.S. Roberts & Company in late January or early February 1880[23]. The partners then formed a new corporation named the H.L. Ulrich & Company. The purchase of the Roberts company was, however, merely one move in a larger scheme. In October 1880, Ulrich moved to Brooklyn where he purchased a seat on that city's stock exchange, continuing to operate under the name of H.L. Ulrich & Company (Plate 437). Over the next eight years, he amassed a considerable fortune not only from the trading of securities, but also from the underwriting of new stock issues. During this period, he occasionally did some engraving work as a diversion for it is known that he designed stock certificates and decorative motifs for several security printing houses, including the American Bank Note Company (Plate 438).

In 1889, after a protracted bout with what was described as "pulmonary disease,"[24] he retired and sold his seat on the Brooklyn Stock Exchange. At that time, one contemporary stated that Ulrich had "accumulated a sufficient fortune to meet his every need for the next fifty years, should in the unlikely event he survive that length of time."[25] Shortly thereafter, he returned to Hartford, where he began working on a contractual basis with the Colt company again (Plates 440-444)[26].

Endnotes

1. O.F. Winchester's promotion of the King's Improvement rifle as a military arm and the results of those efforts are reviewed in detail in Chapter 1.

2. Ibid.

3. The decline in military contracts for the standard Model 1866 after August 1868 is documented in George Walker's Production Notes for the Model 1866, op. cit.

4. Ibid.

5. Though press notices were published as early as September 1866, the Winchester company did not begin any widespread advertising campaign for the Model 1866 until early 1869. Likewise, the firm's catalogs from 1867 to 1870 stressed the military applications of Winchester rifles and especially the results of the Swiss Rifle Trials, which involved the Models 1866 and 1867 Iron Frame rifles. By 1868, though, the firm's broadsides (for example, that illustrated in Plate 65) had begun to more prominently mention the standard Model 1866.

6. Marcot, Spencer, op. cit., pages 153-156.

7. Walker, Model 1866 Notes, op. cit. and H.B. Dow, Notes on Winchester Arms, op. cit., page 6.

8. The information presented here and following is extracted from Herbert G. Houze, "The Appearance of Evidence: A Brief Examination of the Life and Work of Herman Leslie Ulrich," **ARMAX, The Journal of the Cody Firearms Museum**, Volume IV, Number 2, pages 35-71.

9. George Walker, Notes on the Ulrich Family. Engraving File, Winchester Arms Collection Archives, Cody Firearms Museum.

10. Houze, Herman Ulrich, op. cit., page 37.

11. Ibid.

12. Winchester Repeating Arms Company, Payroll Ledger (April 1871-May 1873), period April to July 1871. Winchester Arms Collection Archives, Cody Firearms Museum.

13. Ibid. The total payments to Conrad F. Ulrich for the year 1872 were $4,076.66.

14. Ibid. The total paid to Conrad F. Ulrich in 1873 was $1,016.44.

15. Houze, Herman Ulrich, op. cit., page 69.

16. This order is preserved in the collection of Paul Heinz. The rifle referred to is a Model 1876 sporting rifle recorded in the Serial Number Ledgers for that model as follows: "May 12/85 Rifle 40/60 Oct Set CH & CSPG May 12/85." For another example of a privately commissioned Model 1876 rifle engraved by C.F. Ulrich, see Plates 427-429. In common with the rifle recorded in the order cited here, the record for the rifle illustrated makes no mention of engraving.

17. Houze, Herman Ulrich, op. cit., pages 37 and 69.

18. Ibid, page 69, and; Winchester Repeating Arms Company, Gun Contractors Ledger I, page 75.

19. Stephen V. Granscay, **Master French Gunsmiths' Design of the XVII-XIX Centuries** (Winchester Press; New York, NY: 1970), pages 111-113.

20. Weber Ruesch, op. cit., page 12.

21. Exhibition arms are normally recorded in the serial number ledgers with a sequence of shipment and return dates (sometimes numbering over twenty instances), reflecting when a piece was sent out of the factory for promotional purposes. In contrast, it is rare for a commercially sold rifle to be recorded in the ledgers with more than two "Return" and "Repair" dates. Indeed, most arms never were returned to the factory for alteration.

22. There is evidence which suggests that Herman Ulrich did some engraving work for Parker Brothers of Meriden, Connecticut at this time. H.L. Ulrich also worked for this firm during the 1920s (personal communication from David Mercer Ulrich, April 1994).

23. Records of R.G. Dun Company, Connecticut, Volume 41, page 402.

24. Confidential report prepared by "E.D." dated February 1889, Brooklyn City Bank Confidential Notes, 1889, page 62. Private Collection.

25. Ibid.

26. Houze, Herman Ulrich, op. cit., pages 52-64.

CHAPTER 11

A PERIOD OF CHANGE

As noted in the preceding chapter, the reputation of John Ulrich as an engraver has in large part been due to the survival of a number of exquisitely decorated Winchester arms postdating 1885 which bear his signature. However, a close examination of these pieces with arms engraved by him immediately before reveals that they are the product of a different hand.

The identity of this artist might have remained unknown had it not been for the fortunate survival of a series of factory photographs showing identically engraved Winchester arms with the notations that they had been done by someone with the surname Stokes[1]. The discovery several years ago of a

partial print illustrating one of the same rifles (a Model 1894 rifle made in 1912) fortunately clarified the matter as it is inscribed with a notation that the engraving was done "by W.E. Stokes."[2]

Based upon surviving evidence, William Stokes entered the employ of the Winchester company in 1885, or at the very latest 1886, since he is first listed in New Haven city directories as a Winchester employee in the 1887 edition (compiled in 1886)[3].

What is known is that Stokes was an accomplished engraver when he started work for the company. This is amply proved by one of his first works, a Model 1873 rifle, serial number 206057, shipped on March 7, 1886, that

Plate 445

Winchester Model 1873 Short rifle, serial number 206057, engraved by William E. Stokes in 1886, originally owned by His Excellency, General Don Porfirio Diaz, President of Mexico. Douglas Arms Collection (Inv. No. D 362), Royal Military College of Canada, Kingston, Ontario.

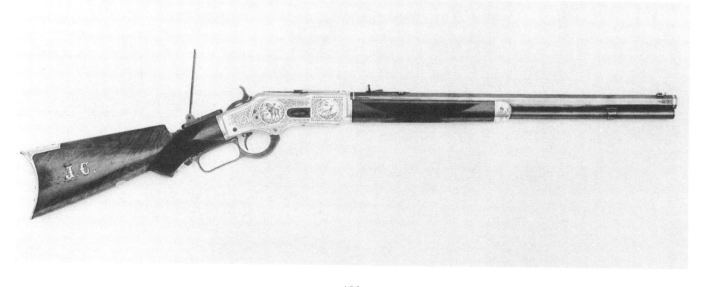

Above: Plate 446

*R*ight receiver of the Model 1873 rifle illustrated in Plate 445. The distinctive form of Stokes' scrollwork is visible here in its earliest form. Within a few years it would evolve into the segmented or scale pattern to be seen in Plates 454 to 461. Stokes' ability as a draftsman is also evident in the composition and execution of the panel scenes.

Below: Plate 447

*L*eft receiver of the Model 1873 rifle illustrated in Plate 445.

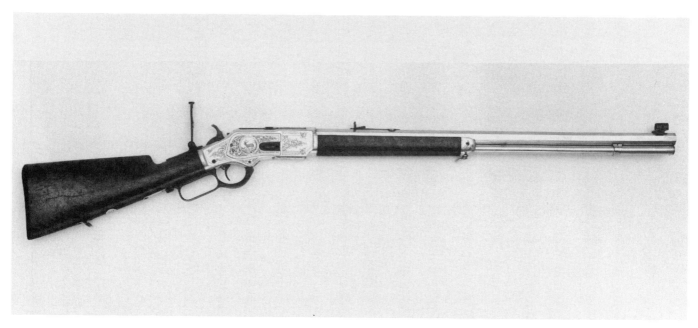

Above: Plate 448

*W*inchester Model 1873 rifle, serial number 222286, engraved by William E. Stokes in 1887, originally owned by His Excellency, General Don Porfirio Diaz, President of Mexico. Douglas Arms Collection (Inv. No. D252), Royal Military College of Canada, Kingston, Ontario.

Below: Plate 449

*R*ight receiver of the Model 1873 rifle illustrated in Plate 448.

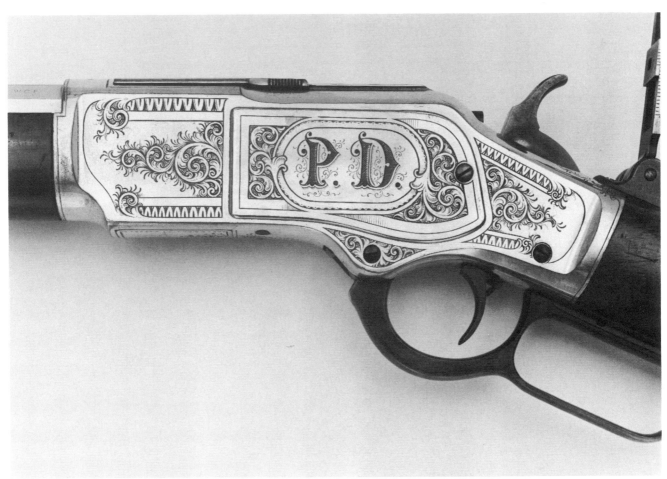

Plate 450

*L*eft receiver of the Model 1873 rifle illustrated in Plate 448.

Plate 451

*I*ncomplete proof of the line engraving prepared to illustrate a Winchester Model 1886 rifle engraved and gold inlaid by William E. Stokes. The complete version of this print was published in the 1897 edition of the Winchester company's **Highly Embellished Arms** catalog. Private Collection.

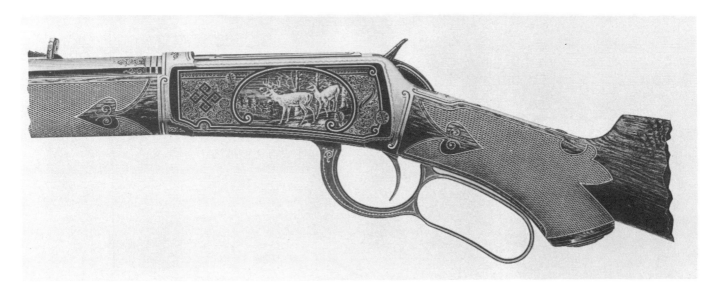

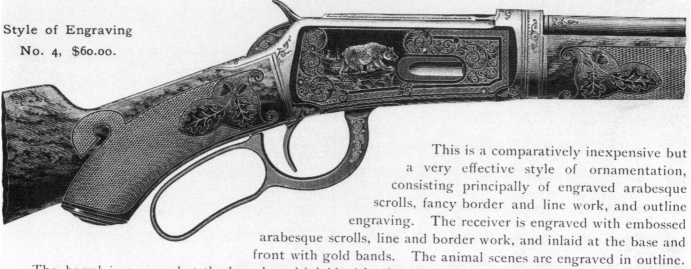

HIGHLY FINISHED WINCHESTER RIFLES.

AN ENGRAVED MODEL 1894 WINCHESTER RIFLE.

Style of Engraving
No. 4, $60.00.

This is a comparatively inexpensive but a very effective style of ornamentation, consisting principally of engraved arabesque scrolls, fancy border and line work, and outline engraving. The receiver is engraved with embossed arabesque scrolls, line and border work, and inlaid at the base and front with gold bands. The animal scenes are engraved in outline. The barrel is engraved at the breech and inlaid with a band of gold. The finger lever, hammer, and all screw heads are engraved.

Plate 452

*P*age 7 of the Winchester Repeating Arms Company's 1897 **Highly Embellished Arms** catalog illustrating a Model 1886 rifle engraved and gold inlaid by Herman L. Ulrich. Private Collection.

Plate 453

*P*age 18 of the Winchester Repeating Arms Company's 1897 **Highly Embellished Arms** catalog illustrating a Model 1890 rifle engraved jointly by William E. Stokes (the scrollwork) and Herman L. Ulrich (the panel scene). Private Collection.

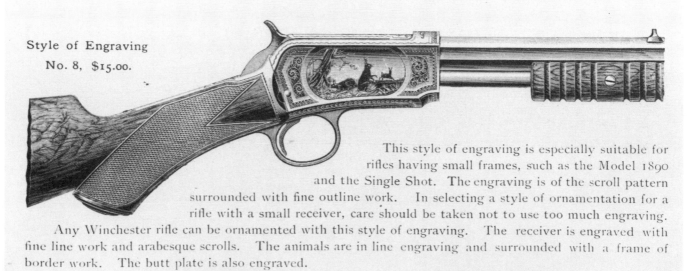

HIGHLY FINISHED WINCHESTER RIFLES.

A STYLE OF ENGRAVING SUITABLE FOR THE MODEL 1890 WINCHESTER RIFLE.

Style of Engraving
No. 8, $15.00.

This style of engraving is especially suitable for rifles having small frames, such as the Model 1890 and the Single Shot. The engraving is of the scroll pattern surrounded with fine outline work. In selecting a style of ornamentation for a rifle with a small receiver, care should be taken not to use too much engraving. Any Winchester rifle can be ornamented with this style of engraving. The receiver is engraved with fine line work and arabesque scrolls. The animals are in line engraving and surrounded with a frame of border work. The butt plate is also engraved.

Price of this style of Engraving, $15.00.

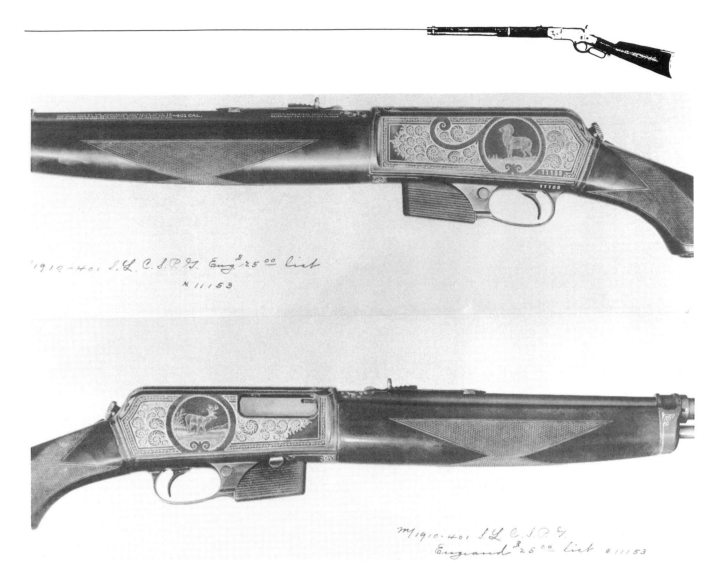

1919-401 S.L.C.S.P.G. Eng'd 25.00 list
× 11153

m 1910-401 S.L.C.S.P.G.
Engraved 3 25.00 list × 11153

was later presented to His Excellency, General Don Porfirio Diaz, President of Mexico (Plates 445-447)[4]. Though long credited to John Ulrich, the form of the scrollwork differs markedly from his work as do the panel scenes. It does, however, closely resemble that of Conrad Ulrich, and it is entirely possible, if not probable, that Stokes studied under Conrad Ulrich[5].

Typical of Stokes' work are the tightly coiled scrolls almost completely filled with curving tendril extensions. Where scrolls border or extend into plain fields, they are edged with separate single line curved tendrils reminiscent of the attached tendril extensions used by Conrad Ulrich. In sharp contrast to John Ulrich, the panel scenes engraved by Stokes are well drawn and show a keen appreciation for modelling, as well as the use of shading together with

positioning to create an illusion of depth. Some elements of his early work display a lack of technical expertise in his cutting of animal figures (eq., the pig-like snout on the bear engraved on the Model 1873 illustrated in Plate 447), but this deficiency was overcome as he matured.

During the course of his work at the Winchester company, William Stokes' scroll engraving gradually evolved into a more stylized form, but the coiled form was retained. It did, however, assume almost a segmented appearance. This is particularly evident in work he created after 1890.

Beginning with Stokes' arrival at the Winchester company, the problems associated with identifying the authorship of engraving produced by the firm become more problematical. This is due to the fact that labor was divided

Plate 454

***W**inchester company photograph of a Model 1910 rifle, serial number 11153, engraved by William E. Stokes. Winchester Arms Collection Archives, Cody Firearms Museum.*

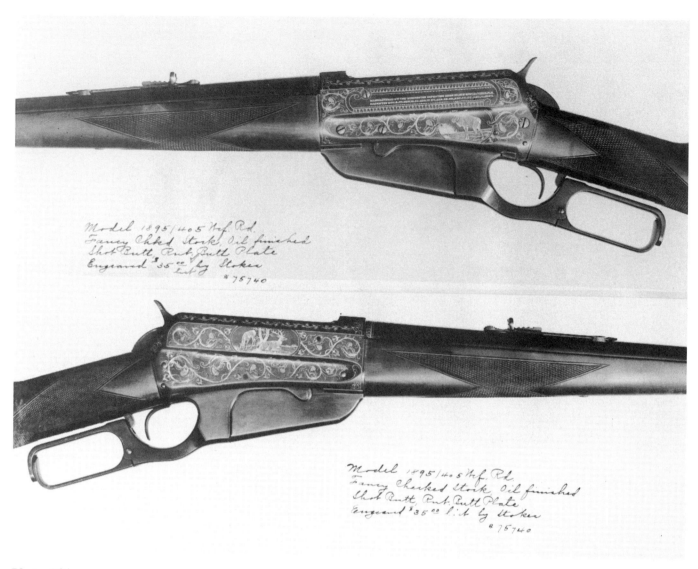

Plate 455

Winchester company photograph of a Model 1895 rifle, serial number 75740, engraved by William E. Stokes. Winchester Arms Collection Archives, Cody Firearms Museum.

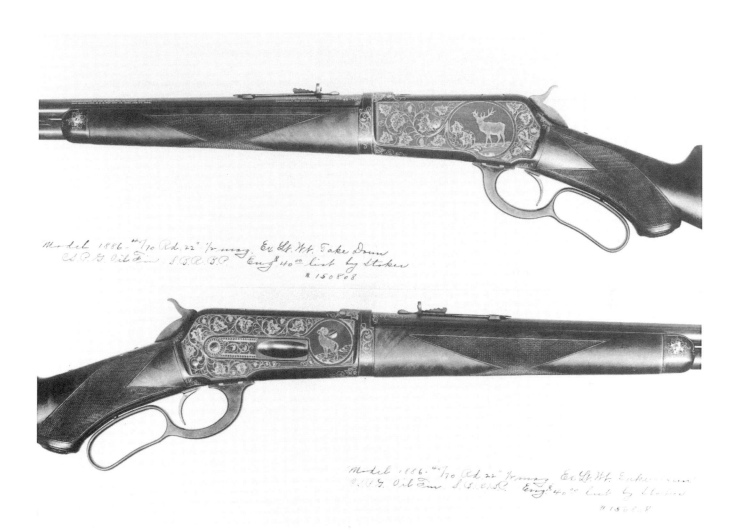

Plate 456

Winchester company photograph of a Model 1886 rifle, serial number 150808, engraved by William E. Stokes. Winchester Arms Collection Archives, Cody Firearms Museum.

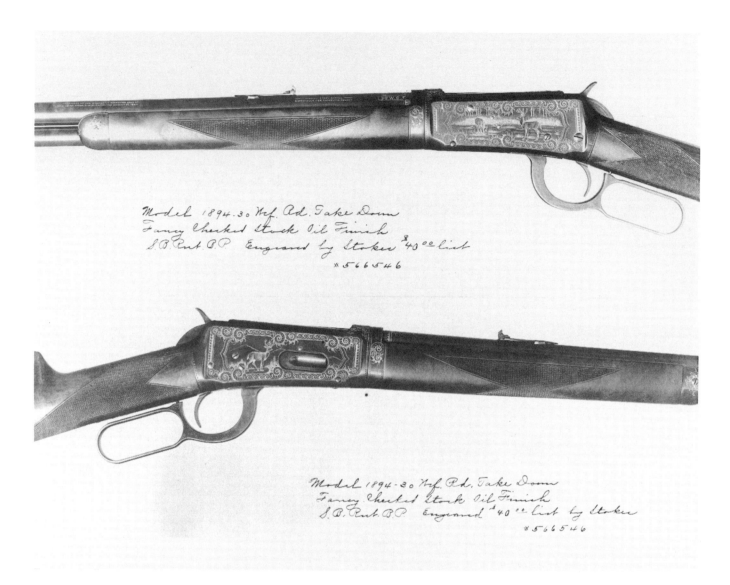

Plate 457

Winchester company photograph of a Model 1894 rifle, serial number 566546, engraved by William E. Stokes. Winchester Arms Collection Archives, Cody Firearms Museum.

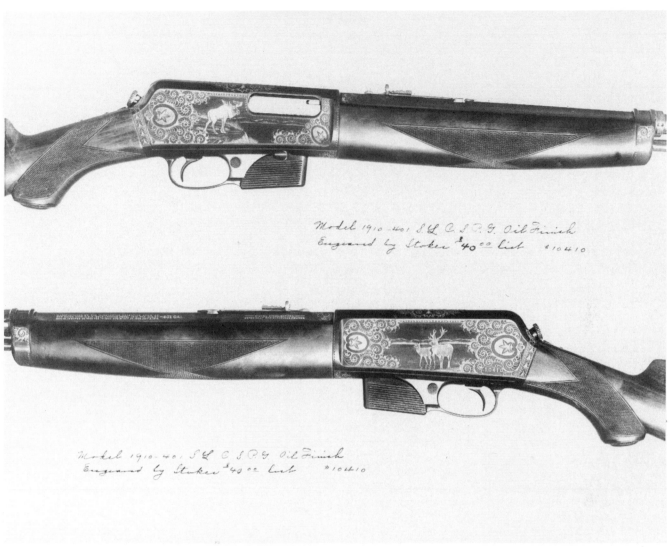

Plate 458

W̶inchester company photograph of a Model 1910 rifle, serial number 10410, engraved by William E. Stokes. Winchester Arms Collection Archives, Cody Firearms Museum.

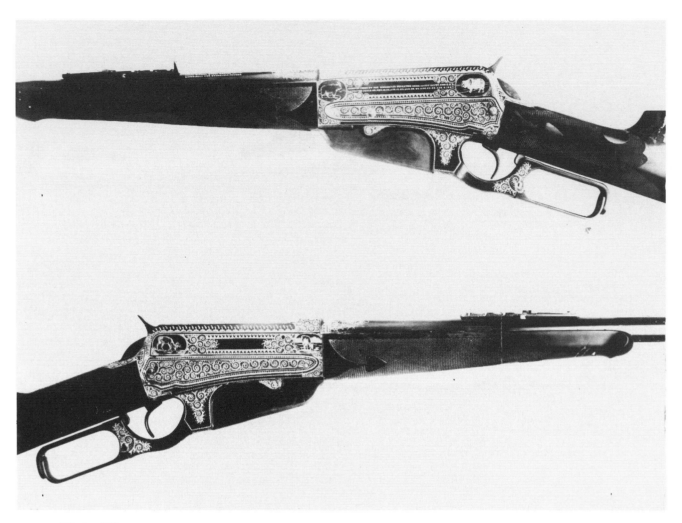

Plate 459
*W*inchester company photograph of a Model 1895 rifle engraved by William E. Stokes. Winchester Arms Collection Archives, Cody Firearms Museum.

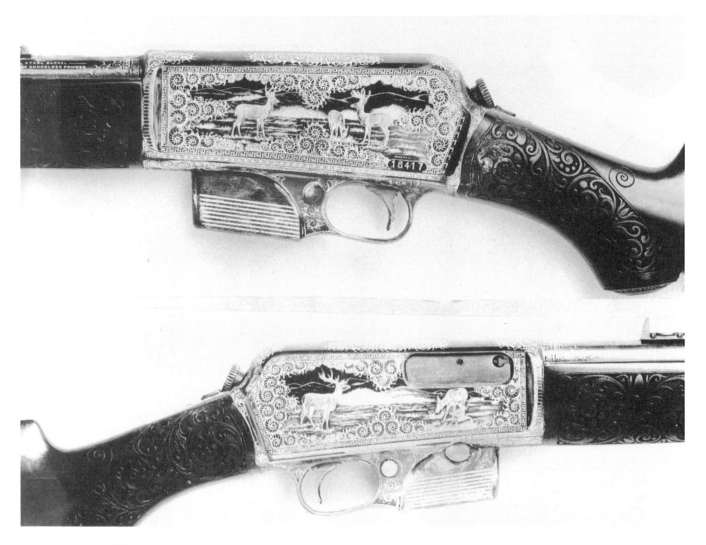

Plate 460

*W*inchester company photograph of a Model 1907 rifle, serial number 16417, engraved by William E. Stokes. Winchester Arms Collection Archives, Cody Firearms Museum.

between John Ulrich and Stokes. While some pieces were engraved totally by Stokes or Ulrich (Plates 448-450), in other instances Ulrich only cut the panel scenes while Stokes was assigned the task of completing the panel surrounds (i.e., scrollwork)[6]. This accounts for a number of arms cut with scrollwork typical of Stokes, having game scenes clearly identifiable as being the work of John Ulrich. The problem of identification becomes even more blurred in those pieces made after 1897, when Herman Ulrich again joined the firm. There are sufficient differences in the Ulrich brothers' style, as well as Stokes', to allow identification of each artist's work to be differentiated with a high degree of certainty. In 1896, the company became aware of or was forced to acknowledge that John Ulrich's work was not always of the best quality when two Model 1893 shotguns engraved by him were returned to the factory due to what Thomas C. Johnson described as "Bad engraving."[7] Whether this was the catalyst that caused Thomas G. Bennett to seek Herman Ulrich's assistance the following year is not known, but it probably was a significant cause.

Whatever the case, the Winchester Repeating Arms Company reassessed the role of engraving during the first half of 1897, and decided to make some organizational changes in that department. Herman Ulrich was engaged to oversee the artistic content of the engraving produced in the factory on a part-time basis since he continued to live in Hartford[8].

One of his first assignments on behalf of the company was the codification of

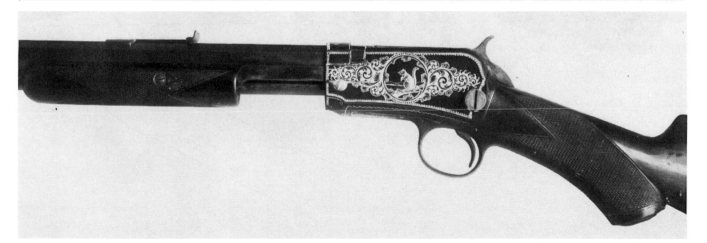

Top: Plate 463

*W*inchester company photograph of a Model 1903 rifle engraved by Herman L. Ulrich in 1904. Winchester Arms Collection Archives, Cody Firearms Museum.

Middle: Plate 464

*W*inchester company photograph of a Model 1890 rifle engraved by Herman L. Ulrich. Winchester Arms Collection Archives, Cody Firearms Museum.

Bottom: Plate 465

*L*eft side of the Model 1890 rifle illustrated in Plate 464. Winchester Arms Collection Archives, Cody Firearms Museum.

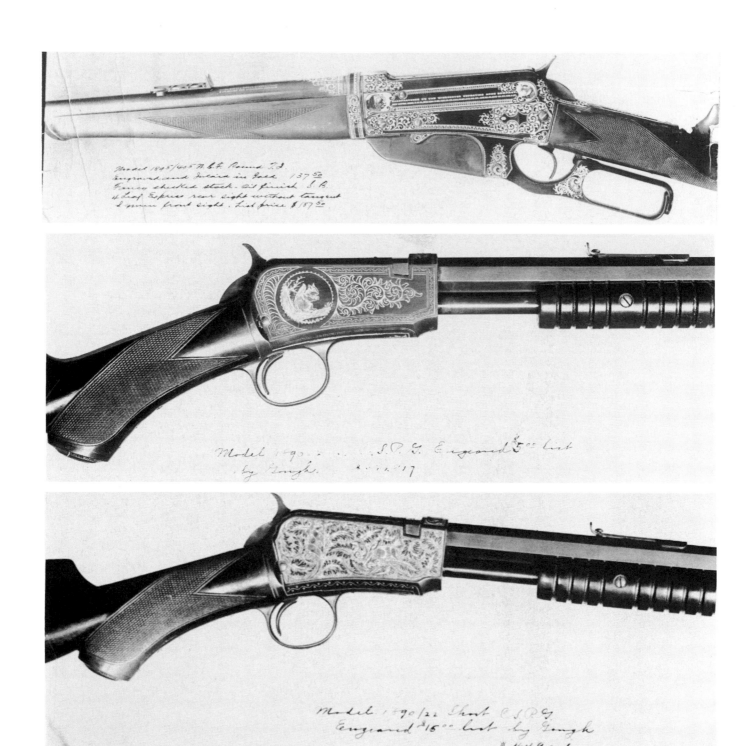

Top: Plate 466

Winchester company photograph of a Model 1895 rifle engraved and gold inlaid by Herman L. Ulrich. Winchester Arms Collection Archives, Cody Firearms Museum.

Middle: Plate 467

Winchester company photograph of a Model 1890 rifle, serial number 582817, engraved by John A. Gough. Winchester Arms Collection Archives, Cody Firearms Museum.

Bottom: Plate 468

Winchester company photograph of a Model 1890 rifle, serial number 449006, engraved by John A. Gough with stylized northern oak leaf foliage instead of conventional scrollwork. Winchester Arms Collection Archives, Cody Firearms Museum.

the engraving styles to be offered by the firm and the setting of their retail prices. In this project, he was primarily assisted by William E. Stokes. The result of this collaboration was the Winchester Repeating Arms Company's 1897 *Highly Embellished Arms* catalog (Plates 451-453),[9] which must be regarded as Stokes' greatest contribution to the development of Winchester engraving. Throughout the work, Stokes' coiled scrollwork is to be found as are a variety of game and hunting scenes that reflect patterns developed from those designed by Conrad and Herman Ulrich.

While the publication of this catalog should have brought about a public recognition of William Stokes' abilities (for examples of his work see Plates 454-461), it did not. Instead, John Ulrich was to be the beneficiary as it was incorrectly assumed by clients and later arms enthusiasts that Ulrich was, due to his position as chief engraver, chiefly responsible for the work. Further reinforcing this misconception was John Ulrich's renewal of the practice of applying his personal signature stamp to arms engraved under his supervision. This activity eventually was brought to the attention of the company's management, and in reaction, T.G. Bennett reorganized the Engraving Shop for a second time.

On Sept. 1, 1904, Bennett merged the independent engraving design office (which consisted only of Herman Ulrich) with the Engraving Shop. The amalgamated department was then named the Design and Engraving Laboratory (commonly called the Design Lab), and Herman Ulrich was named as its superintendent (for examples of Herman Ulrich's work during this period, see Plates 463-466). The same day Bennett wrote the following two memoranda to Herman Ulrich and Oscar Thiel[10]:

Sept. 1, 1904

Mr. Herman Ulrich
Engr. Design Lab.

The marking of guns with unauthorized inspection signature stamps is expressly forbidden. All dies used for that purpose used by members of your department are to be turned over to Mr. Hodson.

Thomas G. Bennett

Sept. 1 1904

Mr. Thiel
Gun Department

Please collect all engraved rifles now in stock for review tomorrow by Mr. Hodson or myself.

T.G.B.

The latter memorandum has a manuscript postscript in Bennett's hand, stating, "Those in the display cases excepted."

Interestingly, the die stamps turned over to Hodson, then vice president of the Winchester company, were still held by the firm's management as late as 1937, when Edwin Pugsley allowed one of John Ulrich's to be used to mark several engraved rifles, which had been sent to the factory for refinishing by Charles Foster[11]. Whether the stamps were used in other occasions is unknown, but there is a strong likelihood.

Sometime after 1906, John A. Gough joined the Design Lab staff[12]. Based upon the quality of his earliest work (Plates 469- 471), it appears that his initial employment was as a journeyman engraver. By 1911, however, he had

Plate 469

Winchester company photograph of a Model 1905 rifle, serial number 18871, engraved by John A. Gough. Winchester Arms Collection Archives, Cody Firearms Museum.

Plate 470

Winchester company photograph of a Model 1903 rifle, serial number 78359, engraved by John A. Gough with designs composed of formal panel game scenes surrounded by stylized California white oak leaves. Winchester Arms Collection Archives, Cody Firearms Museum.

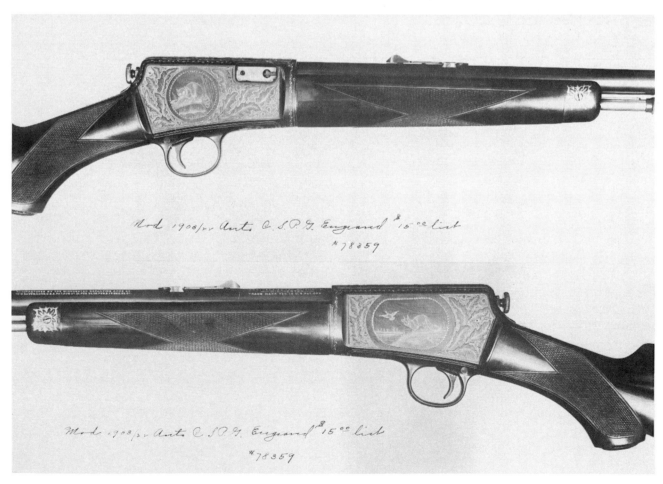

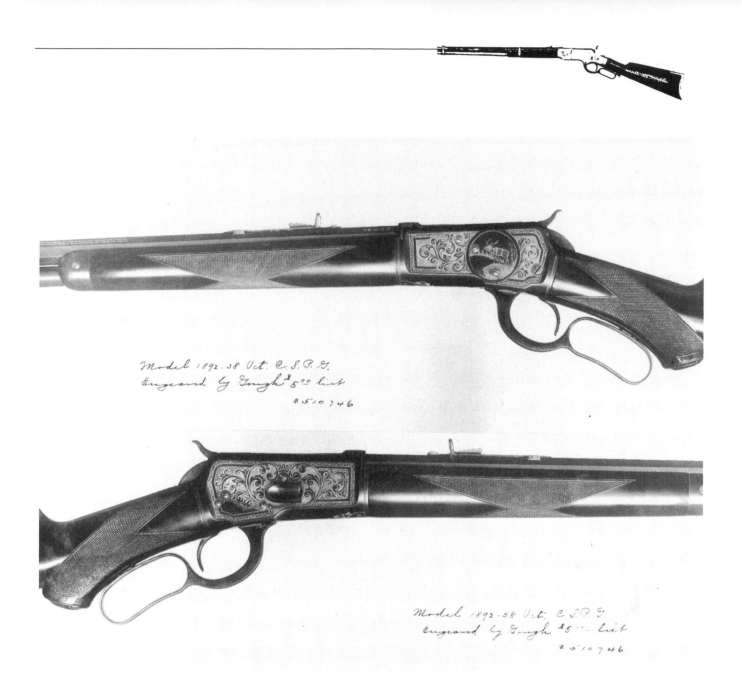

Plate 471

*W*inchester company photograph of a Model 1892 rifle, serial number 510746, engraved by John A. Gough. Winchester Arms Collection Archives, Cody Firearms Museum.

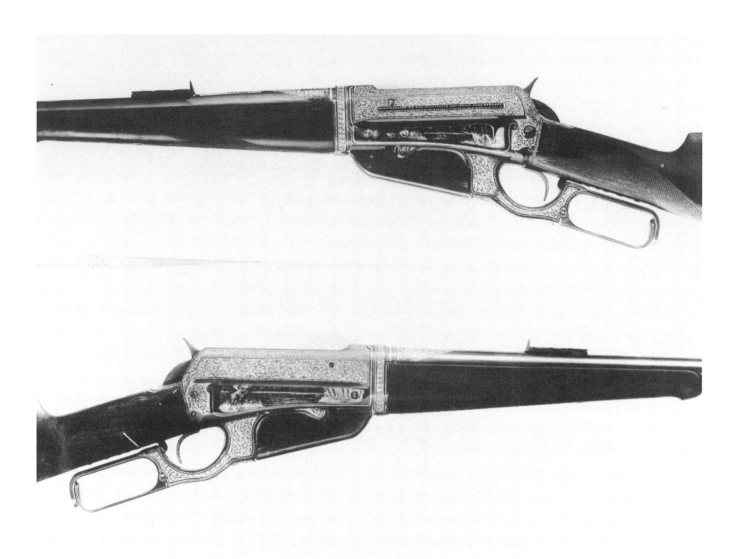

Plate 472

*W*inchester company photograph of a Model 1895 rifle engraved and gold inlaid by John A. Gough. Winchester Arms Collection Archives, Cody Firearms Museum.

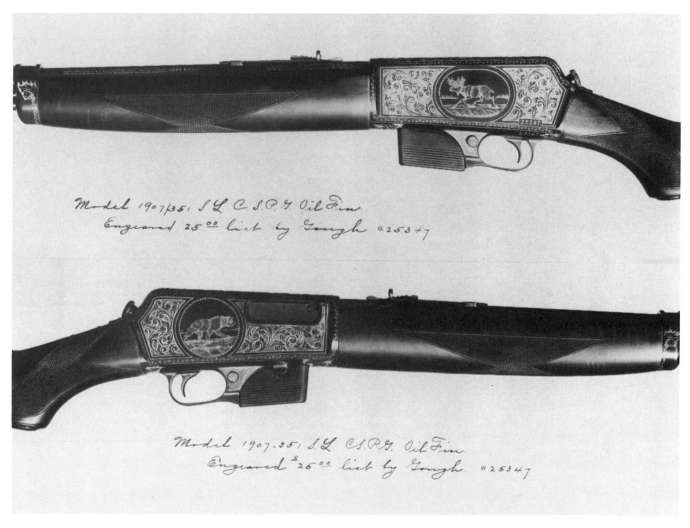

Model 1907/351 S.L. C.S.P.G. Oil Fin.
Engraved 25⁰⁰ list by Gough #25347

Model 1907-351 S.L. C.S.P.G. Oil Fin.
Engraved ª 25⁰⁰ list by Gough. #25347

Plate 473

Winchester company photograph of a Model 1907 rifle, serial number 25347, engraved by John A. Gough. Winchester Arms Collection Archives, Cody Firearms Museum.

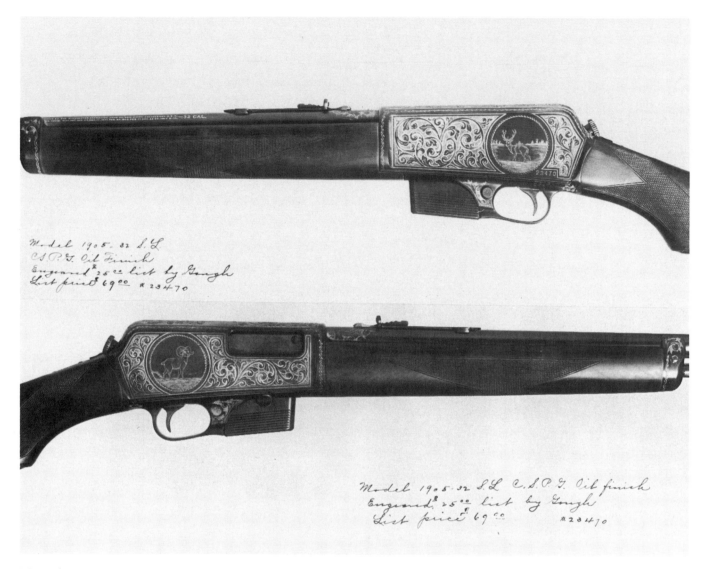

Plate 474

*W*inchester company photograph of a Model 1905 rifle, serial number 23470, engraved by John A. Gough. Winchester Arms Collection Archives, Cody Firearms Museum.

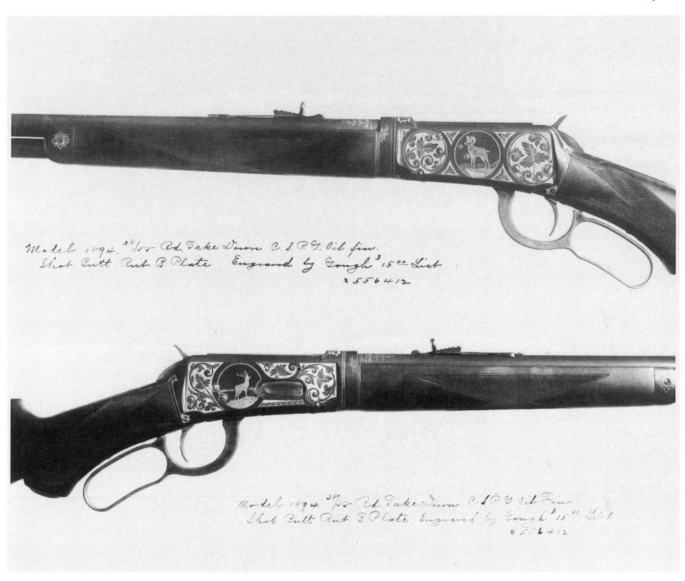

Model 1894. ³⁵/₁₀₀ Ad. Take Down C.S.P.G. Oil fin.
Shot Butt Put. B. Plate   Engraved by Gough'₅ 15⁰⁰ List
                                        ₂556412

Model 1894 ³⁵/₁₀₀ Ad. Take Down C.S P G Oil Fin
Shot Butt Put B. Plate Engrav'd by Gough'₅ 15⁰⁰ List
                                        ₂556412

Plate 475

Winchester company photograph of a Model 1894 rifle, serial number 556412, engraved by John A. Gough with panel game scenes and scrolls containing ashleaf maple leaves. Winchester Arms Collection Archives, Cody Firearms Museum.

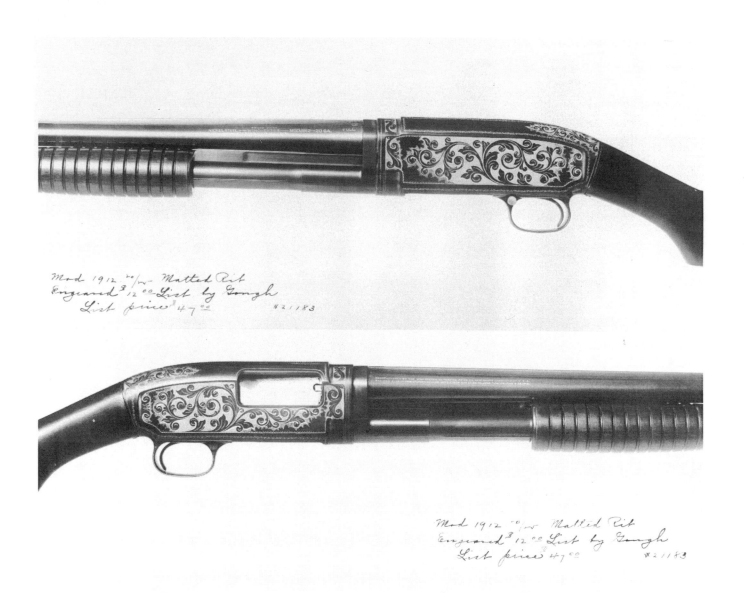

Plate 476

Winchester company photograph of a Model 1912 shotgun, serial number 21183, engraved by John A. Gough with relief cut foliate scrollwork. Winchester Arms Collection Archives, Cody Firearms Museum.

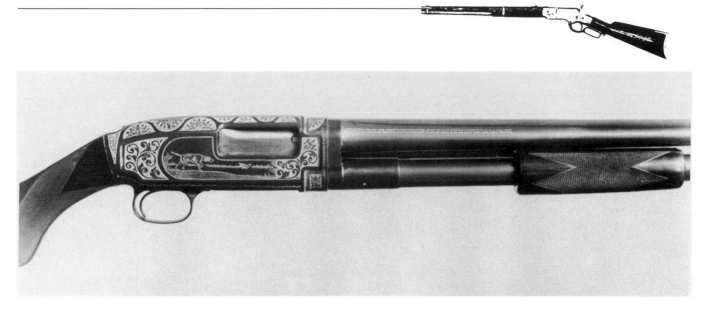

Plate 477

Winchester company photograph of a Model 1912 shotgun, serial number 42951, engraved by John A. Gough with relief cut scrollwork, palmetto leaf fans and game scenes. Winchester Arms Collection Archives, Cody Firearms Museum.

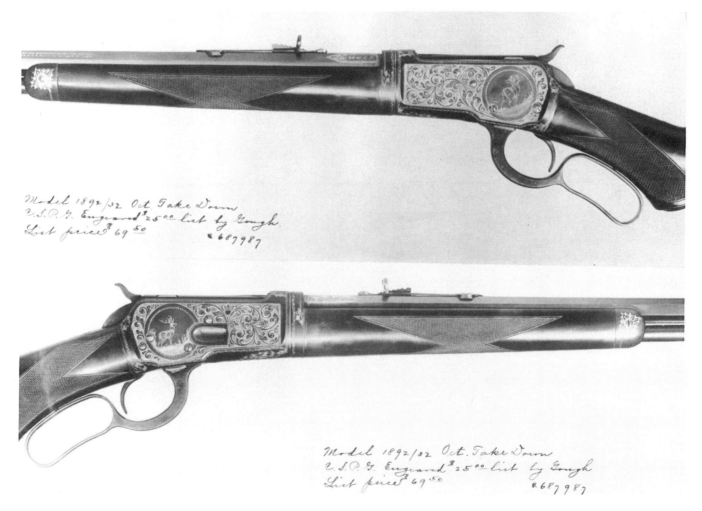

Plate 478

Winchester company photograph of a Model 1892 rifle, serial number 687987, engraved by John A. Gough. Winchester Arms Collection Archives, Cody Firearms Museum.

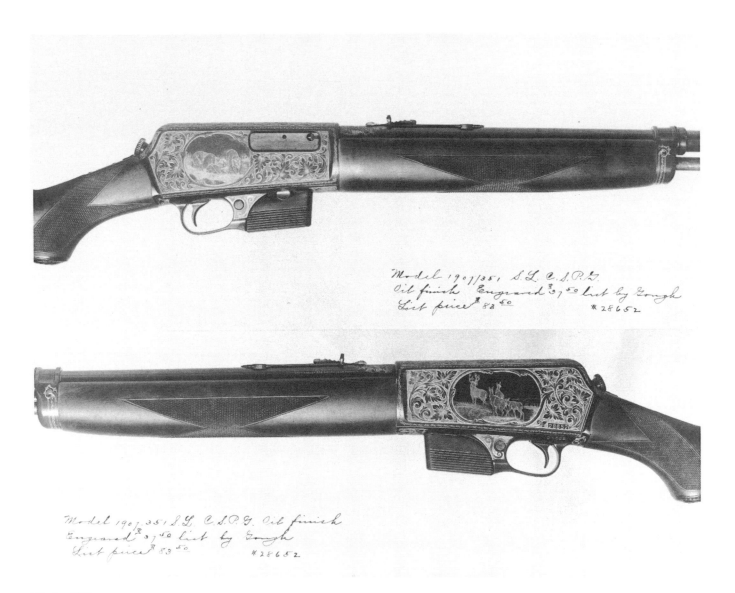

Model 1907/351, S.L. C.S.P.G.
Oil finish   Engraved $37.50 list by Gough
List price $83.50
        #28652

Model 1907, 351 S.L. C.S.P.G. Oil finish
Engraved $37.50 list by Gough
List price $83.50
        #28652

Plate 479

*W*inchester company photograph of a Model 1907 rifle, serial number 28652, engraved by John A. Gough with game scenes and scrolling ashleaf maple leaves. Winchester Arms Collection Archives, Cody Firearms Museum.

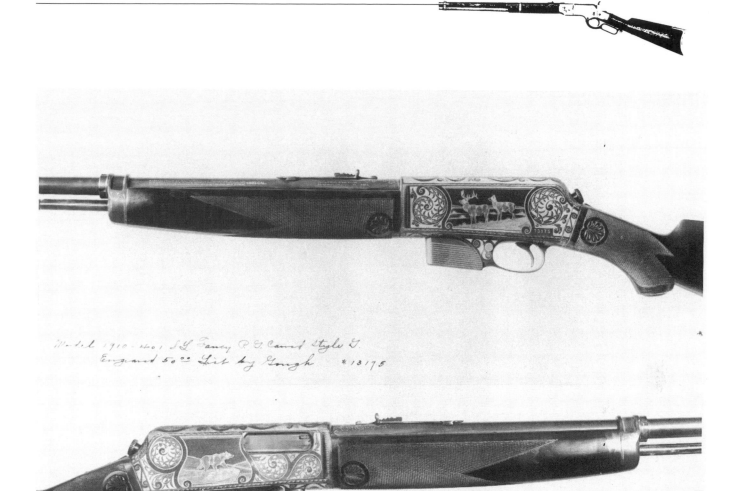

Model 1910 - 401 S.L. Fancy P.G. Carved Style G.
Engraved 50⁰⁰ List by Gough #13175

2nd Sept 1910 - 401 S.L. Fancy P.G. Carved Style G.
Engraved 50⁰⁰ List by Gough #13175

Plate 480

Winchester company photograph of one of John A. Gough's finest works, a Model 1910 rifle, serial number 13175, which is engraved with finely detailed game scenes surrounded by scrolling willow leaf foliage cut in relief. Winchester Arms Collection Archives, Cody Firearms Museum.

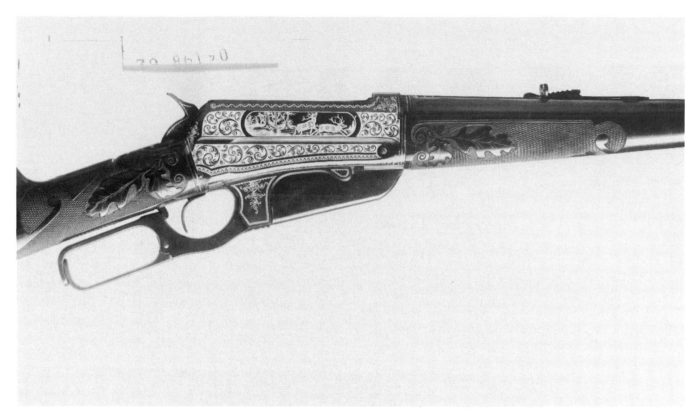

Plate 481

*W*inchester company photograph of a Model 1895 rifle engraved and gold inlaid by John Ulrich. Winchester Arms Collection Archives, Cody Firearms Museum.

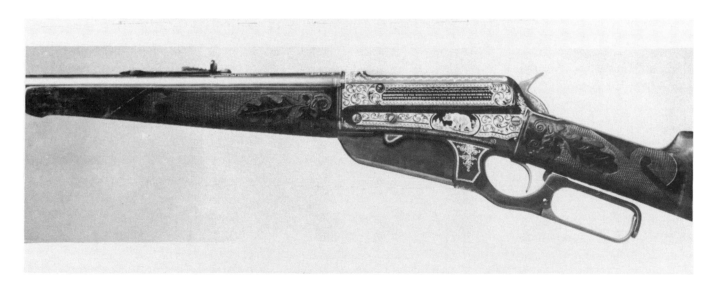

Plate 482

*W*inchester company photograph of the left side of the Model 1895 rifle illustrated in Plate 481. Winchester Arms Collection Archives, Cody Firearms Museum.

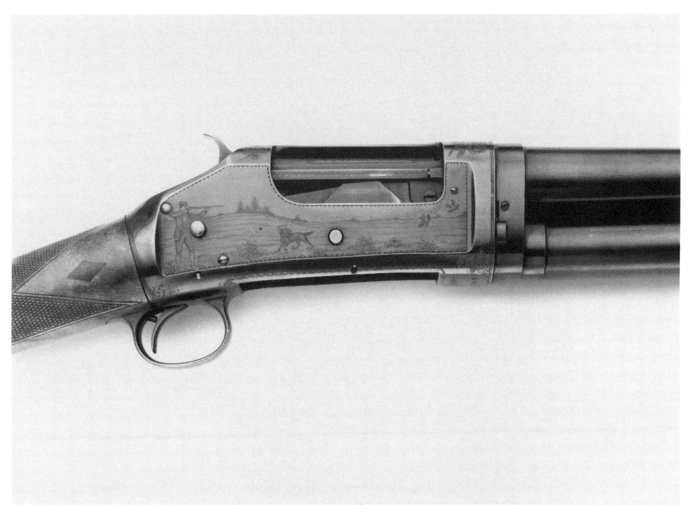

Plate 483
*R*ight receiver of a Winchester Model 1897 shotgun engraved with an upland game shooting scene by John Ulrich. Private Collection.

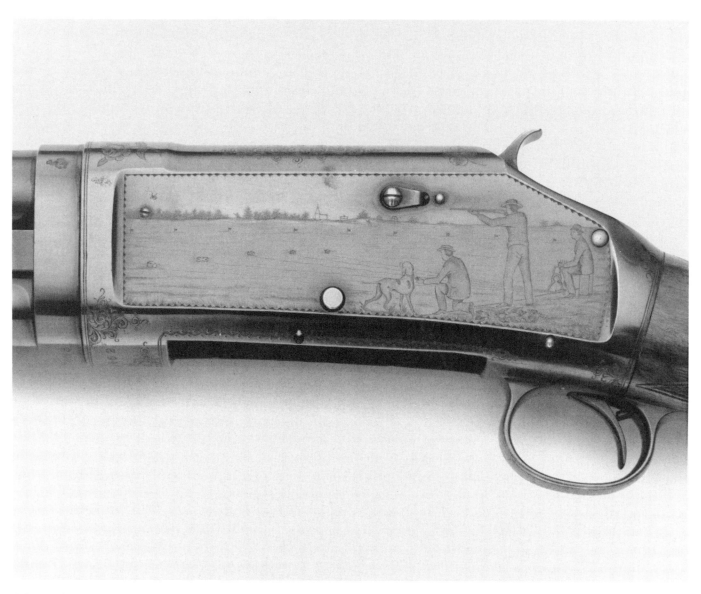

Plate 484

Left receiver of the Model 1897 shotgun illustrated in Plate 483, engraved with a live bird competition shooting scene by John Ulrich. Private Collection.

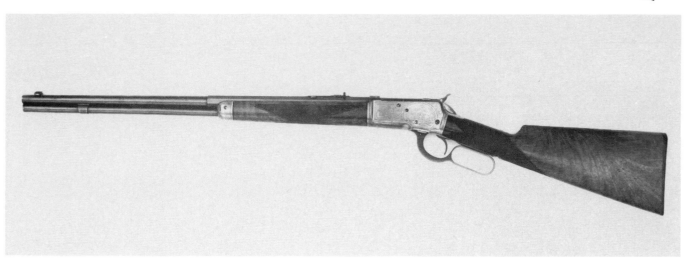

Plate 485

*W*inchester Model 1892 rifle, Serial number 41023, engraved by John Ulrich and William E. Stokes and originally owned by Annie Oakley. Buffalo Bill Museum (Inv. No. 1-69-1866). Gift of Mr. and Mrs. Spencer T. Olin, Buffalo Bill Historical Center, Cody, Wyoming.

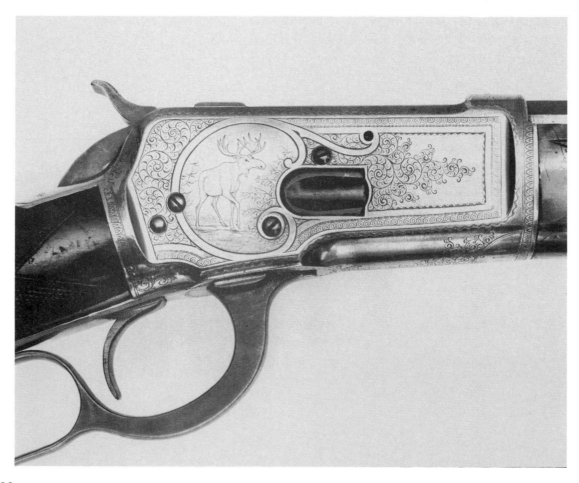

Plate 486

*R*ight receiver of the Model 1892 rifle illustrated in Plate 485.

Plate 487

Enlarged detail of OAKLEY ownership stamp struck in both sides of the wrist on the rifle illustrated in Plates 485 and 486. It is believed that this inscription was applied at the Winchester factory.

Plate 488

D.F. Barry portrait photograph of Annie Oakley holding the Winchester Model 1892 rifle, serial number 41023, engraved by John Ulrich, which is illustrated in Plates 485-487. Buffalo Bill Historical Center, Cody, Wyoming.

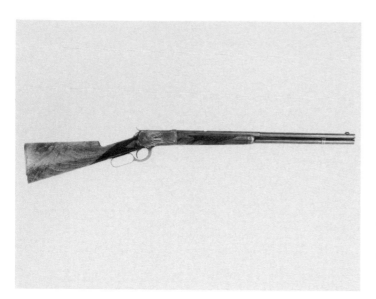

Plate 489

Winchester Model 1892 smoothbored rifle, serial number 301670, engraved by Leslie Bordon Ulrich and originally owned by Annie Oakley. Buffalo Bill Museum (Inv. No. 1.69.25). Gift of Fred Stone, Buffalo Bill Historical Center, Cody, Wyoming.

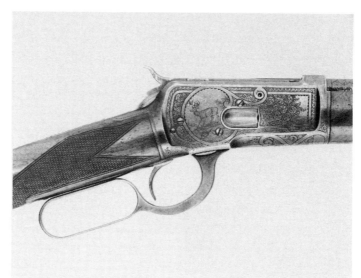

Plate 490

Right receiver of the Model 1892 smoothbored rifle illustrated in Plate 489.

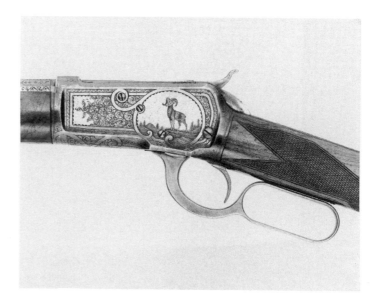

Plate 491

Left receiver of the Model 1892 smoothbored rifle illustrated in Plate 489.

mastered his craft, and from that date forward he worked alongside William Stokes and Herman Ulrich. Though his work (Plates 467-480) reveals a strong influence from Herman Ulrich, particularly in the composition of panel scenes and conventional scrollwork, it was his development of a theme created by Stokes that was to establish his reputation. Gough transformed the use of leaves and foliage, introduced into the company's repertoire by Stokes in the late 1890s[13], into an art form. Intertwined as well as free-standing maple, oak and sycamore tree leaves or broad and spear point leafed plants were used by Gough in place of scrolls with an effectiveness that had no equal (Plates 468, 470 and 476). Often offset by plain scrolling ribbands (Plates 475, 479 and 480), the net result of these designs was both novel and extremely attractive.

A new generation of Ulrichs was to become part of the Design Lab when Leslie Bordon Ulrich (188?-1966), John's second son, joined the company in 1907[14], the same year his father retired[15] (for examples of John Ulrich's later work, see Plates 481-487). Unfortunately, few examples of Leslie Bordon Ulrich's work can now be identified due to the fact that he primarily followed the patterns published in the 1897 and 1905 editions of the Winchester company's *Highly Embellished Arms* catalogs. One rifle does exist, however, about which there is no question as to his authorship. This piece is a Model 1892 short rifle (Plates 489- 491) with a half-octagonal smoothbored barrel, serial number 301670, which was made for the world-famous exhibition shooter Annie Oakley (Plate 488)[16]. Though L.B. Ulrich's engraving closely parallels that of his father, John Ulrich, the influence of William E. Stokes is to be found in his scrollwork. Leslie B. Ulrich remained at the company until late 1915 or early 1916.[17]

Another son who briefly worked for the firm at about the same time was Angelo Stokes. Unfortunately, little is known about him either personally or professionally. Based upon extant records, his career with Winchester only lasted from 1904 to 1907[18].

The new era heralded by Gough's work was, unfortunately, to be shortlived. With the United States' entry into World War I in April 1917, the Winchester Repeating Arms Company closed the Design Lab and transferred its employees to other departments needing experienced personnel to ensure the production of war contracts[19].

Plate 492

Colored advertising ink blotter given to Herman Ulrich by John A. Gough after Gough had left the Winchester company to work on his own as an independent artist and engraver, circa 1920. Harold McCracken Research Library, Gift of Dorothy Ulrich, Buffalo Bill Historical Center, Cody, Wyoming.

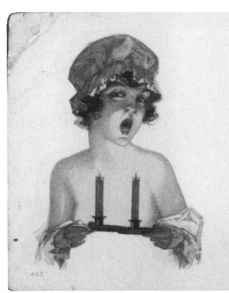

JOHN A. GOUGH

ENGRAVER

PICTURES   ANTIQUES

56 COLLEGE STREET

NEAR TAFT HOTEL

NEW HAVEN, - - - CONNECTICUT

THE BEST MFG. CO. NEW HAVEN. CT.

After the war ended, the lab was reopened, but its staff was significantly smaller than before. Indeed, it would appear that in 1919, only William Stokes and Herman Ulrich were employed full time as John Gough, who had shown so much promise, had left the company sometime before April of that year to pursue a career in engraving, painting and selling antiques (Plate 492)[20].

Fortunately, in 1920, Alden George Ulrich (Sept. 15, 1888-Oct. 18, 1949), Conrad's third son, joined the Winchester company[21]. A highly accomplished engraver who had produced a number of superb pieces for his former employer, the Marlin Fire Arms Company[22], Alden George was to head the Winchester company's Design Lab for the next three decades.

His arrival could not have occurred at a better time as William E. Stokes was badly injured in an automobile accident on May 14, 1920[23]. According to a pencilled notation on a factory roster dated Sept. 1, 1920, he suffered compound fractures of the right arm and wrist, which limited their movement. In consequence, he was transferred to the Gun Shop at his former salary as "a general employee."[24]

Attribution of the Design Lab's staff continued when Herman L. Ulrich finally retired on Dec. 31, 1923[25]. Fittingly, just prior to his retirement, Herman was presented with the company's long service gold medal, the die for which he had cut in 1912[26].

Thus, for the greater part of the 1920s, the company's only engraver was Alden George Ulrich.

Endnotes

1. Over twenty photographs dating from approximately 1910 to 1917, which illustrate Winchester rifles and shotguns engraved by William E. Stokes, are preserved in the Winchester Arms Collection Archives at the Buffalo Bill Historical Center.

2. This photograph (preserved in the Winchester Arms Collection Archives) is vertically cracked in half just to the left of the middle point. The rifle shown in the print is a Model 1894 serial number 566546 and the visible inscription reads as follows:

...30 WCF. Rd. Take Down

...d Stock Oil Finish

...Engraved $40.00 list by W.E. Stokes

566546

3. New Haven City Directory for 1887.

4. Identification of this rifle as being from the hand of William E. Stokes is amply demonstrated by the style of the scrollwork and the well-drawn game scenes. This rifle is preserved in the Douglas Arms Collection (Inv. No. D362), Royal Military College of Canada, Kingston, Ontario.

5. For similar scrollwork by Conrad F. Ulrich, see Plates 428 and 429.

6. Personal communication from David Mercer Ulrich, April 29, 1994.

7. Thomas C. Johnson maintained a notebook log of all Model 1893 shotguns that were returned to the factory for any reason. The two arms mentioned here appear under the dates March and April 1896, with identical entries that read as follows:

One - <u>Bad</u> engraving JU

T.C. Johnson Model 1893 Notebook No. 2, Winchester Arms Collection Archives, Cody Firearms Museum.

8. Herman L. Ulrich maintained his residence in Hartford until 1904.

9. This catalog was issued in October 1897.

10. Both memoranda are preserved among the Edwin Pugsley papers that were formerly in the collection of the late Alan S. Kelley. Photostatic copies are also in the Edwin Pugsley Miscellaneous Documents file, Winchester Arms Collection Archives, Cody Firearms Museum.

11. Letter from Albert Foster to Edwin Pugsley dated Saturday, Nov. 27, 1937. The relevant section is as follows: "Thank you for correcting the late Mr. Ulrich's oversight by stamping both rifles with his little J ULRICH stamp." Unfortunately, the serial numbers of the Winchester rifles are not known. Edwin Pugsley Correspondence, Winchester Arms Collection Archives, Cody Firearms Museum.

12. Nothing is known about John A. Gough's origins or early training.

13. See the 1897 edition of the **Highly Embellished Arms** catalog, pages 12 and 13.

14. R.L. Wilson, **Winchester Engraving** (Beinfeld Books; Palm Springs, CA: 1989), pages 346 and 347.

15. Some confusion surrounds John Ulrich's retirement as company records list two dates (Nov. 29, 1907 and May 26, 1917). The first of these is believed to be the date of his retirement from full-time employment and the second his retirement from part-time employment. This assumption is based upon the fact that he carved stocks for the company between 1908 and 1917, yet New Haven City Directories no longer list him as an employee of the Winchester company from 1908 forward.

16. This rifle was engraved in April 1908.

17. R.L. Wilson, Winchester Engraving, op. cit., page 347.

18. The only record of Angelo Stokes having been employed as an engraver at the Winchester factory is to be found in the New Haven City Directories for the years 1905 to 1907, where he is listed as an "engraver W.R.A. Co." living at 687 Dixwell Avenue.

19. The Design and Engraving Laboratory was formally closed in November 1917, when Herman Ulrich was transferred to the Gun Shop. It is likely that most of the employees in the lab were assigned other positions within the company beginning in the late spring or early summer of that year.

20. John A. Gough established his business at 56 College Street in New Haven.

21. Ulrich Family Notes, Winchester Arms Collection Archives, Cody Firearms Museum.

22. For examples of Alden George Ulrich's work dating from this period, especially a Model 31 Marlin shotgun made for Czar Nicholas II or Russia, see Brophy, Marlin Firearms, op. cit., pages 382-383 and 533-539; and Wilson, Winchester Engraving, op. cit., pages 347 and 349.

23. Undated note written by H.B. Dow (?). Miscellaneous File (Employees). Winchester Arms Collection Archives, Cody Firearms Museum.

24. Gun Shop Employee Roster dated Sept. 1, 1920. Next to W.E. Stokes name is a marginal note reading "formerly Des. Lab - salary as before." Miscellaneous File (Employees), Winchester Arms Collection Archives, Cody Firearms Museum.

25. Ulrich Family Notes, op. cit.

26. Houze, Herman Ulrich, op. cit., page 68.

CHAPTER 12

DECLINE AND RENAISSANCE: 1924-1936

Less than a year after Herman L. Ulrich's retirement, the Design and Engraving Laboratory at the Winchester plant was closed. Except for sixteen months during World War I and immediately thereafter, the lab had been in operation for just over two decades. At the height of its activity, at least six, and possibly more, engravers had been employed there, but when it was closed, only one, Alden George Ulrich, remained[1]. The fortunes of the Design Lab had not fallen on hard times because of the quality of work produced, but rather due to a radical change in consumer tastes.

Almost immediately after World War I ended, a new style of art began to influence the production of all kinds of consumer products. Derived from work first done in Vienna, the new style was rapidly embraced initially in Europe, then England and finally North America. Characterized by austere simplicity both in material and form, its influence came to dominate architecture, clothing, the design of household goods and even luxuries such as jewelry. In many ways the public's enthusiastic adoption of the new style represented a total rejection of the old order, which had dominated prewar society as well as the ostentation of that era. As the American public became ever more enamored of simple, "modern" products, orders for highly decorated firearms began to decrease apace.

The decline accelerated to the degree that George R. Watrous recorded at the close of 1927, that only twenty-six arms had been engraved at the Winchester factory that year[2]. More poignantly, of that number, twenty-one had only monograms cut or inlaid in them. Curiously, in a decade now remembered for both its moral and financial excess, the rigidity of consumer tastes severely limited the work of classically trained artists who were employed as industrial designers or decorators of commercial wares.

Given the almost universal acceptance of the modern style, it was inevitable that someone would eventually request a gun decorated according to its dictates. Ironically, the order was received at the very end of the decade shortly before the "modern" was to be cast aside by the effects of the Great Depression. On Nov. 20, 1929, just four weeks after the collapse of the New York stock market, a Parisian publisher placed an order with the Winchester company for a Model 12 trap shotgun to be stocked in the English fashion (i.e., a straight wrist) and inlaid in four colors of gold[3]. The nature of the inlay work was not to be decided upon at the

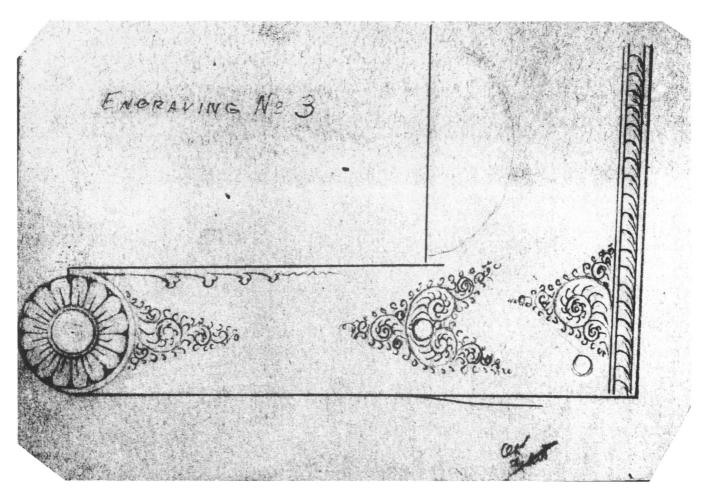

ENGRAVING № 3

company's discretion, but instead was to consist of concentrically formed whorls to be alternately inlaid in green, yellow, red and white gold after a design drawn by the book binder, Paul Bonet[4]. Subsequently, perhaps at the request of the company, the order was modified to include only "trois couleurs" (three colors) of gold: yellow, red and white. The deletion of the green appears to have been due to an apprehension that it would not stand out sufficiently from the blued ground of the shotgun receiver.

Apart from the gold whorls, the receiver was to be inlaid with three thin platinum lines running the length of the upper surface (one straight one along the sight line and a slightly angled fretted line on either side that partially converged at the forward end of the receiver), and the bow of the trigger-

guard was to be inlaid in platinum with the monogram H M de V. As befits the unusual nature of the commission, this shotgun was fitted with a plain, highly polished ebony buttstock and an unribbed ebony fore end. When completed in January 1930, the customer was billed $372 for this shotgun plus $48 for shipping.

Sadly, this was to be the last major work Alden George Ulrich was to do for almost two years. The deepening Depression steadily eroded sales and especially orders for decorated arms. Paradoxically, however, it was at this time that the seeds of Alden George Ulrich's later fame were sown.

Despite being crippled by a lack of operating funds, the staff of the Winchester company continued to put into motion plans made the year before to bring a new model into production.

Plate 493

Pencil sketch drawn by Alden George Ulrich illustrating the proposed form for the Number 3 style of engraving to be used on the Winchester Model 21 shotgun. The inscription at the lower right reads "OK GRW" (i.e., approved by George R. Watrous). Kornbrath Papers, Harold McCracken Research Library, Buffalo Bill Historical Center.

440

ENGRAVING № 4

Plate 494

*P*encil sketch drawn by Alden George Ulrich illustrating the proposed form for the Number 4 style of engraving to be used on the Winchester Model 21 shotgun. Kornbrath Papers, Harold McCracken Research Library, Buffalo Bill Historical Center.

Plate 495

*P*encil sketch drawn by Alden George Ulrich illustrating his proposal for the Number 5 style of engraving to be used on the Winchester Model 21 shotgun. Kornbrath Papers, Harold McCracken Research Library, Buffalo Bill Historical Center.

Plate 496

*P*encil sketch drawn by Alden George Ulrich illustrating his proposal for the Number 6 style of engraving to be used on the Winchester Model 21 shotgun. Kornbrath Papers, Harold McCracken Research Library, Buffalo Bill Historical Center.

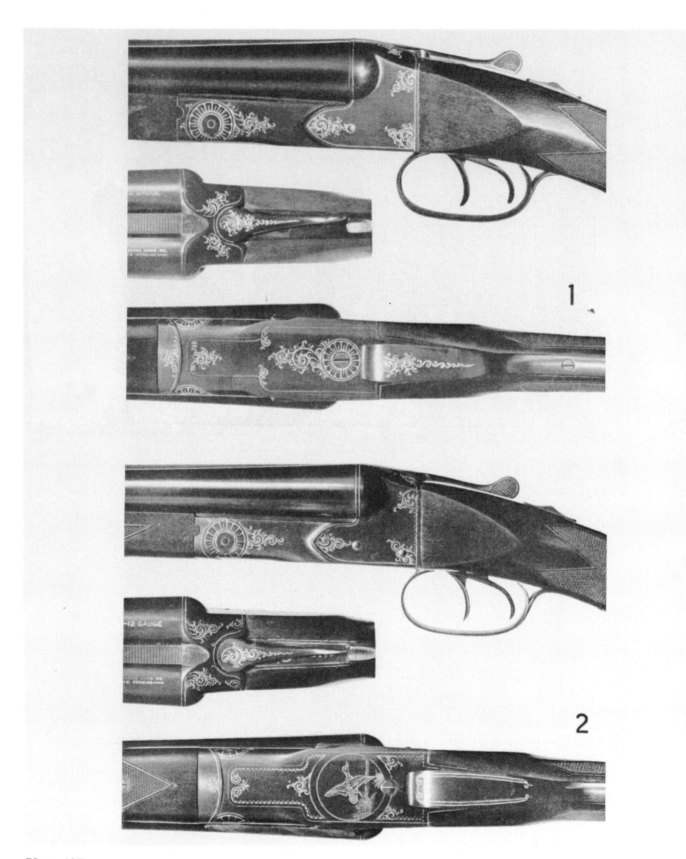

Plate 497

*I*llustrations of the Number 1 and 2 styles of Model 21 shotgun engraving published in 1933. Olin Corporation Photograph.

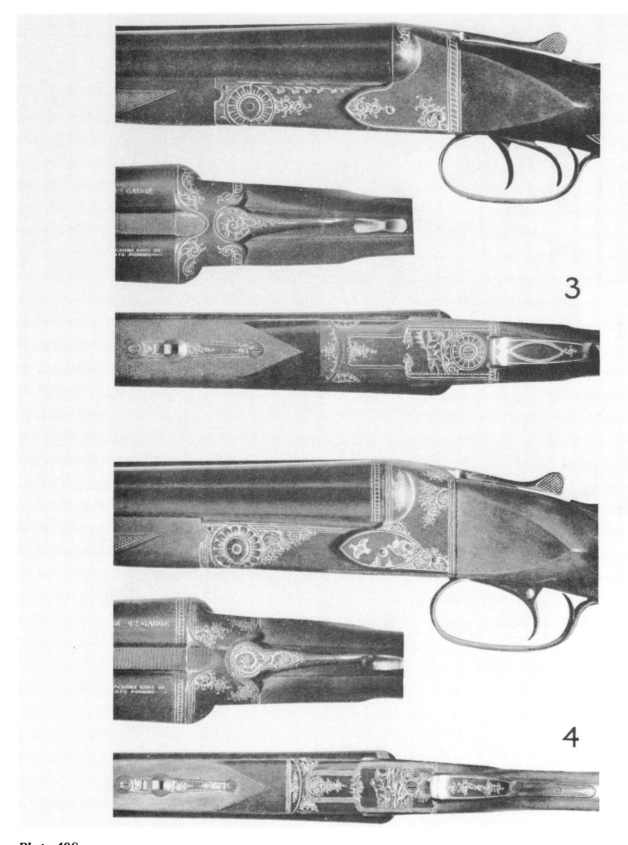

Plate 498

Illustrations of the Number 3 and 4 styles of Model 21 shotgun engraving published in 1933. Olin Corporation Photograph.

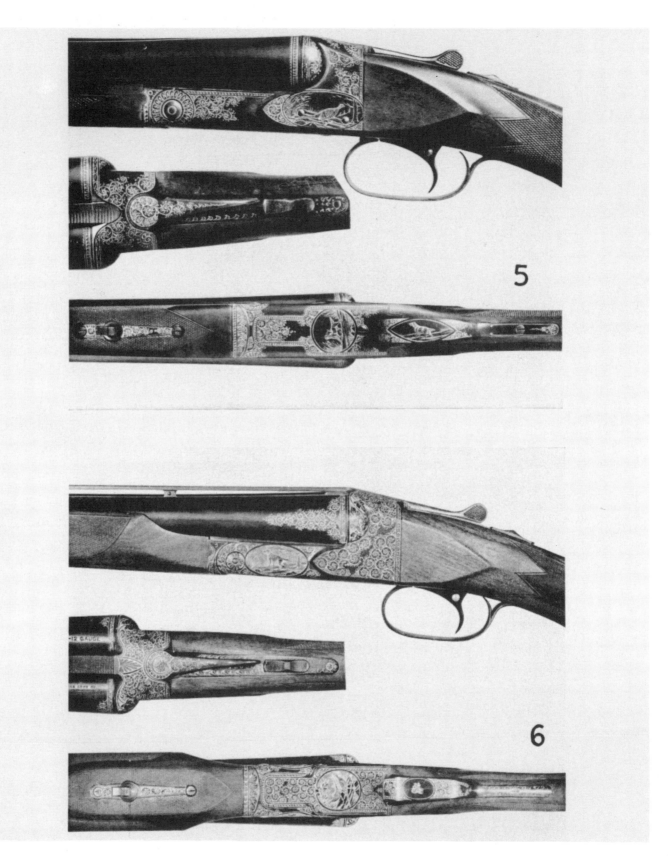

Plate 499

*I*llustrations of the Number 5 and 6 styles of Model 21 shotgun engraving published in 1933. Olin Corporation Photograph.

The Winchester Model 21 Shotgun In Hollywood

While the Model 21 Shotgun was purchased by a cross section of American society ranging from farmers to heads of industry, perhaps its most enthusiastic supporters were the members of the Hollywood film community. Between 1931 and 1940, a significant number of Model 21's were purchased by a variety of actors, actresses, and movie producers. Among the more well known of these were:

Ward Bond
Clara Bow
Charlie Chaplin
Gary Cooper
Cecil B. DeMille
Douglas Fairbanks
Errol Flynn
Myrna Loy
Mary Pickford
Dick Powell
Gilbert Roland
Barbara Stanwyck
Erich von Stroheim
Jack Warner

Interestingly, the prop departments of several major studios also acquired Model 21 Shotguns during this period. Consequently, the distinctive raised side panels of this model are to be occasionally seen in films produced by RKO, 20th Century Fox, and Warner Brothers.

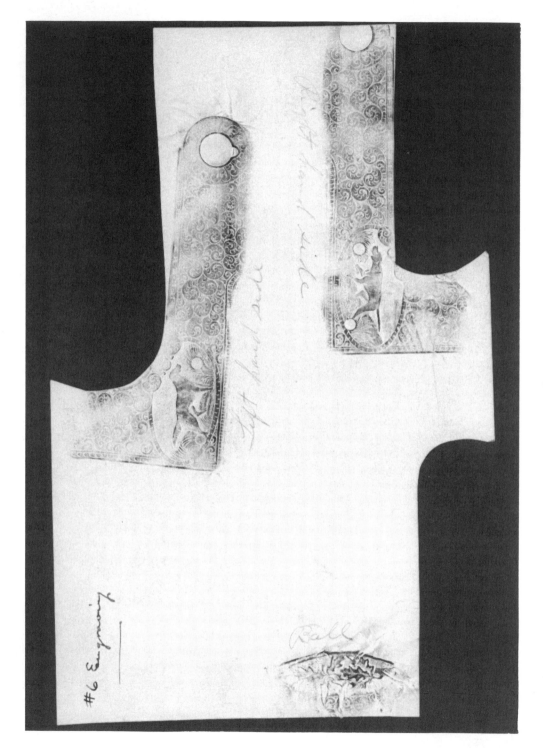

Plates 500-504 (On this page and the following pages).
A complete set of pulls taken from the engraved decoration cut by Alden George Ulrich on the Winchester Model 21 shotgun, serial number 6868, built in November 1933 for Robert W. Woodruff, president of the Coca-Cola Company. The finished appearance of this shotgun resembled that of the Ulrich-engraved Model 21 shotgun illustrated in Plate 552. The pencilled notations were added by Ulrich to identify each element shown. Kornbrath Papers, Harold McCracken Research Library, Buffalo Bill Historical Center.

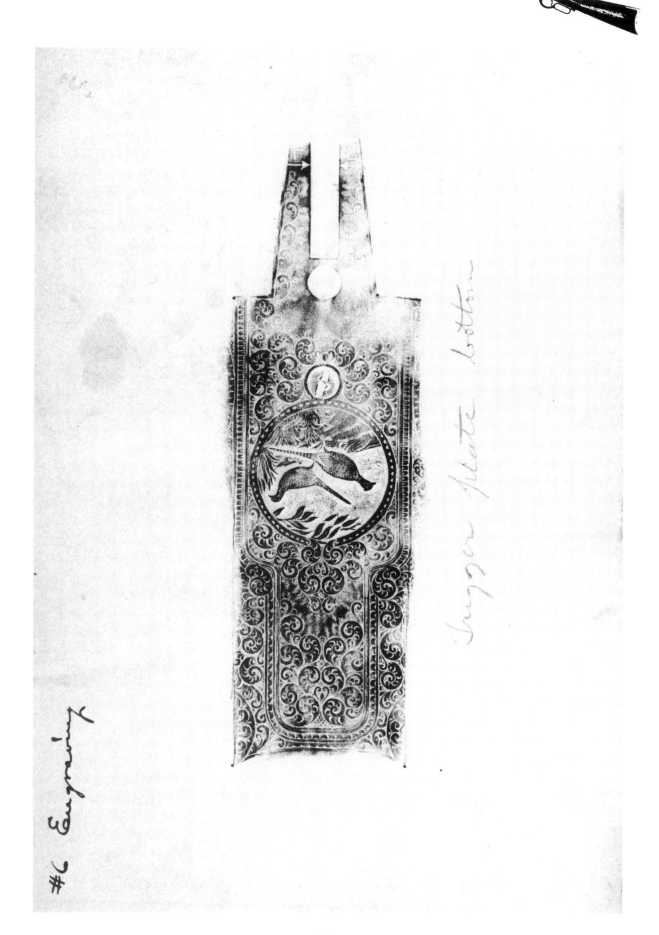

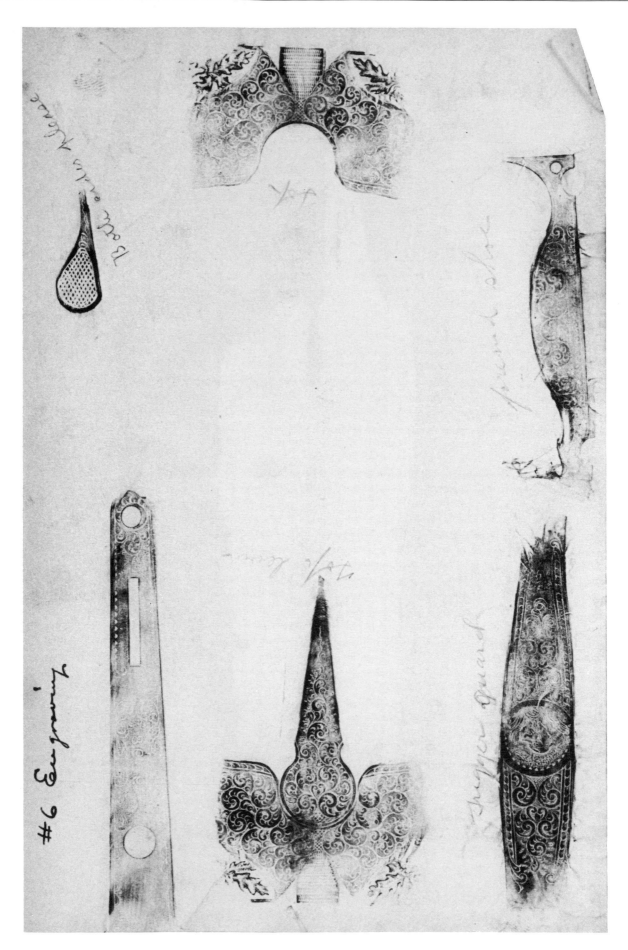

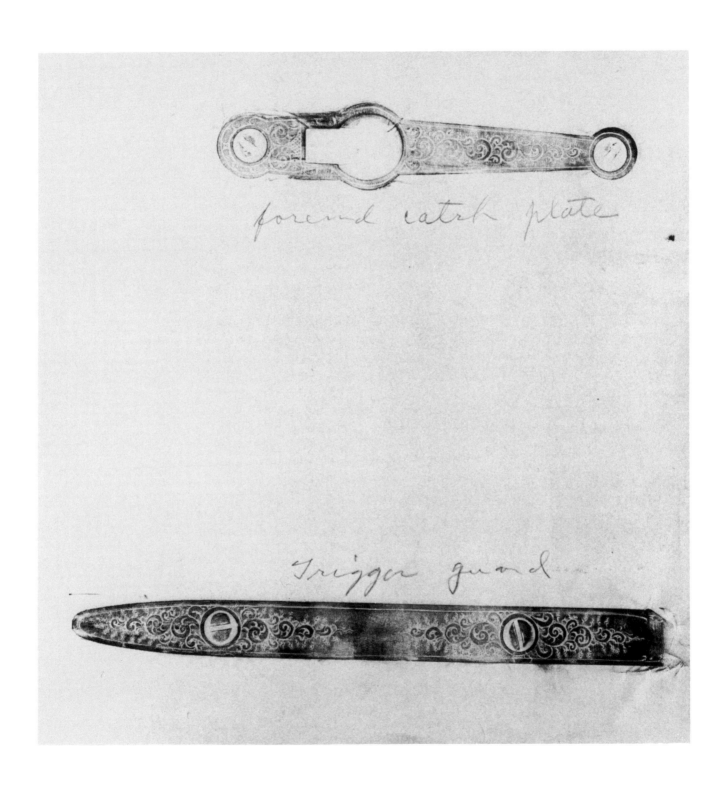

Through considerable ingenuity, a modest manufacturing line was set up in the late winter of 1929, and the first Model 21 shotguns were delivered to the company's warehouse the following March[5].

Although the Model 21 had been brought into existence in spite of tremendous odds and the conventional wisdom of the time, Winchester's management realized that its success depended upon a number of different factors. Chief among these was the expansion of the gauges, chokes, and barrel lengths that the model could be offered with. Secondly, to compete with other first quality shotguns made by firms such as Parker, L.C. Smith and Fox, it was decided to introduce various grades. To accomplish this, George R. Watrous, manager of the Gun Sales and Line Department, instructed Alden Ulrich to prepare a series of engraving designs ranging from inexpensive scrollwork to relatively expensive coverage involving detailed panel scenes. The four surviving sketches from this series (Plates 493-496) reveal a carefully graduated progression of coverage as well as complexity.

While these patterns were approved for use by Watrous[6], some question exists as to the amount of their use since only 615 Model 21s were shipped in 1930 and 1931, most of which were plain. By the late autumn of 1931, the financial position of the Winchester Repeating Arms Company started to show signs of improvement. Reductions in staff along with drastic cuts in pay for those who remained had resulted in the paring of operating costs to a point where the firm's income from orders equalled expenses. Shortly thereafter, the company was to be purchased by the Olin family, an event which was to drastically affect the firm's fortunes. In marked contrast to the previous period when development, production and advertising funds had been severely restricted, the Olins provided the company with all the money it needed to become a viable and thriving business again.

One of the unexpected benefits of the Olin purchase was that John M. Olin was an enthusiastic devotée of the Model 21. He believed that it was far superior to any other double barrel shotgun then on the market, due to both its construction and handling characteristics[7]. As a result, he personally began a campaign to publicize its worth. At his orders, production of the Model 21 was increased and a greater selection of styles introduced. Believing that the model could become the firm's showpiece, he also authorized Alden George Ulrich to refine his previ-

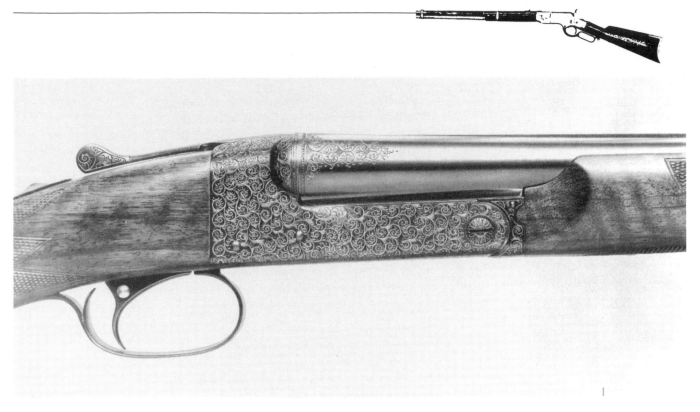

Plate 505

*R*ight receiver detail of Walter Chrysler's Model 21 shotgun, serial number 5437, engraved by Alden George Ulrich in 1934. Olin Corporation Photograph.

Plate 506

*P*ull from an unfinished Custom Grade Model 21 shotgun receiver illustrating the position of the scrollwork and inlays yet to be completed by Alden George Ulrich. Kornbrath Papers, Harold McCracken Research Library, Buffalo Bill Historical Center.

ous engraving patterns so that they contained a greater amount of decoration than the price to be charged would normally have justified (especially in the higher grades). These revised patterns (Plates 497-499) were to remain in use with only minor changes for the next fifty years.

The timing of these changes coincided with an unexpected increase in orders for decorated arms. In a curious contradiction to the health of the United States, sales of engraved arms increased substantially in 1932. The reasons for this turn of events have never been explored, but it may have reflected either a reaction to the modernist ideals of the 1920s or a realization that engraved arms represented objects of true value. Whatever the case, Alden George Ulrich suddenly was a very busy man. It is also interesting to note that the majority of the orders received, whether for Model 21 shotguns or other Winchester firearms, were for the higher grades of work[8]. In the midst of the worst economic catastrophe the United States has ever known, the Winchester company was able to exploit what little remained of its former markets and to create a new market with its Model 21. From farmers in the South and North purchasing utilitarian firearms for hunting, to captains of industry and movie stars buying highly decorated rifles and shotguns for sport shooting, the reborn Winchester company catered to all with equal success.

For Ulrich, this was to be a halcyon age, since the production of higher grade arms allowed him the opportunity to fully express his artistic abilities. Among his many accomplishments of this period were a Model 21 engraved in the Number 6 style for Robert W. Woodruff, president of the Coca-Cola Company (Plates 500-504) and the Custom Grade Model 21 built for Walter Chrysler (Plate 505). Though these pieces amply demonstrate his command of the engraving craft, Ulrich's talents are perhaps best illustrated in a pull he made from a partially engraved Model 21 Custom Grade (Plate 506). The bare form of the layout reveals Alden George Ulrich's compositional

Plate 507
Photograph of the receiver from John M. Olin's Model 12 Winchester shotgun engraved by Rudolph J. Kornbrath in 1930. Kornbrath Papers, Harold McCracken Research Library, Buffalo Bill Historical Center.

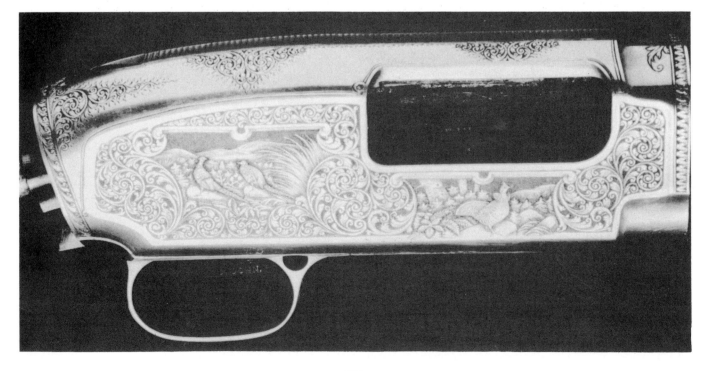

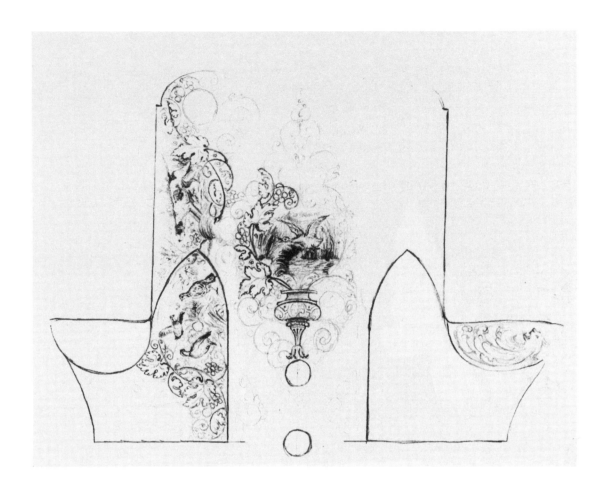

Plate 508

*P*encil sketch drawn by Rudolph J. Kornbrath illustrating a possible decorative composition for the decoration to be engraved on the exhibition Model 21 shotgun commissioned by John M. Olin for the Winchester company in 1932. Kornbrath Papers, Harold McCracken Research Library, Buffalo Bill Historical Center.

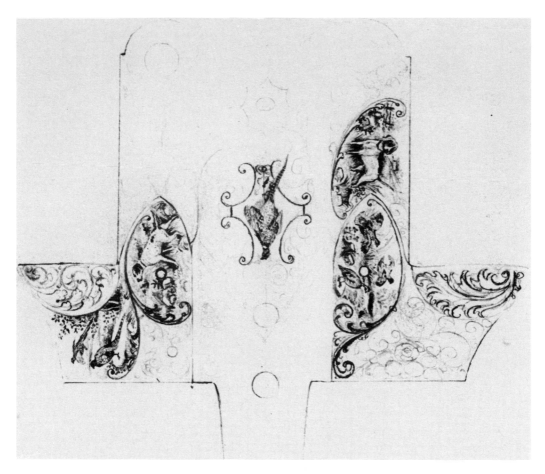

Plate 509

Pencil sketch drawn by Rudolph J. Kornbrath illustrating another possible design for the decoration to be engraved on the exhibition Model 21 shotgun commissioned by John M. Olin for the Winchester company in 1932. Kornbrath Papers, Harold McCracken Research Library, Buffalo Bill Historical Center.

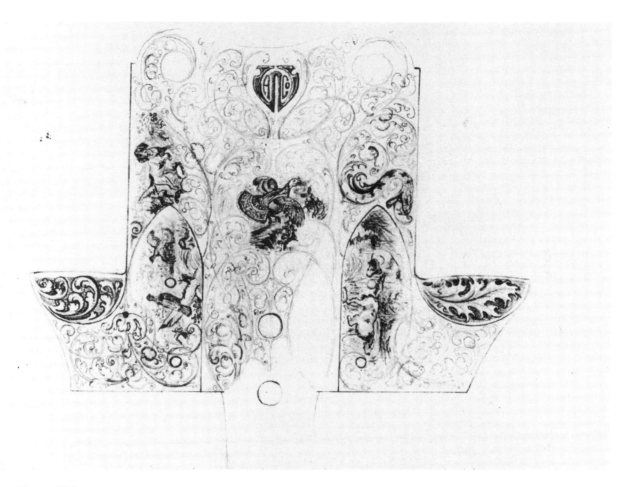

Plate 510

Pencil sketch drawn by Rudolph J. Kornbrath illustrating a third possible design for the decoration to be engraved on the exhibition Model 21 shotgun commissioned by John M. Olin for the Winchester company in 1932. Kornbrath Papers, Harold McCracken Research Library, Buffalo Bill Historical Center.

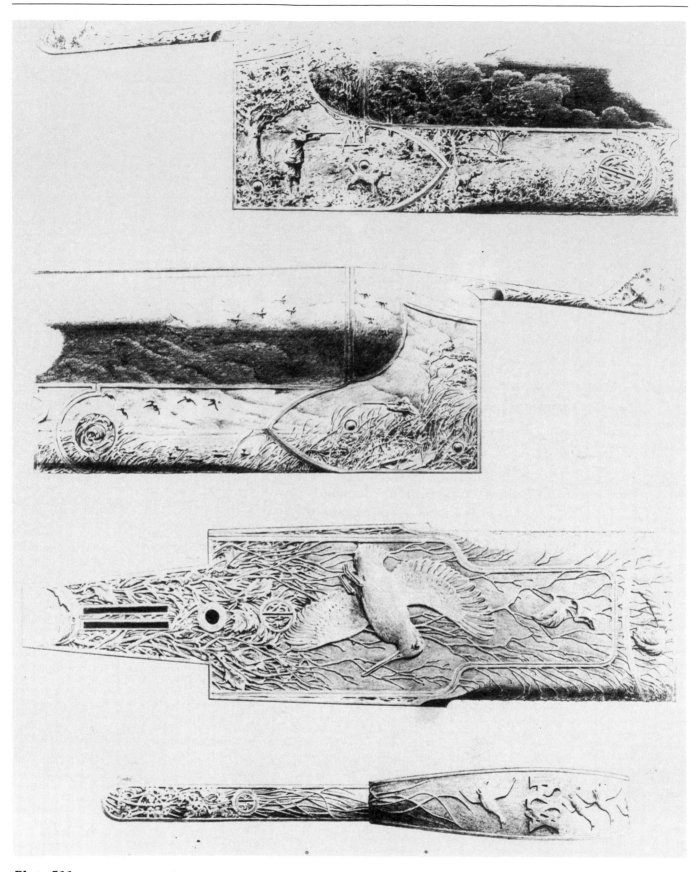

Plate 511

*P*hotograph of the pencil design drawings done by Fred Foster, art director of **The National Sportsman**, used by Rudolph J. Kornbrath as patterns for John M. Olin's Model 21 shotgun (Plates 512-515). Kornbrath Papers, Harold McCracken Research Library, Buffalo Bill Historical Center.

skills that would make the finished product aesthetically pleasing.

Shortly after the Olin family purchased the Winchester company, another engraver was to become integrally linked with the firm. Even though he was never a full-time employee, the volume and character of Rudolph J. Kornbrath's contract work would eventually immortalize him as perhaps the finest engraver to have ever decorated Winchester firearms.

While Kornbrath had had only a passing relationship with the company prior to 1931[9], his work was well known to John M. Olin. In 1929, Kornbrath had engraved a L.C. Smith shotgun for him and in 1930, a Model 12 shotgun (Plate 507)[10]. In 1932, Olin, for reasons that are not now fully known, commissioned Kornbrath to engrave an exhibition grade Model 21. In keeping with his normal practice, Kornbrath drew up a series of design sketches (three of which are illustrated in Plates 508-510) for Olin's review[11]. Olin approved a variation of the design shown in Plate 510, which did not include the scrolling snake and had chiselled oak leaves on the fence in place of the scrollwork suggested by Kornbrath. Completed prior to Oct. 1, 1932, this Model 21's engraving was to cost Mr. Olin $96[12].

The following year, Kornbrath received another commission from John M. Olin, which was to result in what is justifiably regarded as the finest engraved Winchester ever made. Ordered sometime shortly after April 13, 1933, the decoration of this shotgun was not designed by Kornbrath, but rather, was to be based upon a series of pencil sketches drawn for Olin by Fred Foster, art director of **The National Sportsman** (Plate 511)[13]. Totally devoid of scrollwork, the decoration was to be uniquely composed of chiselled game scenes. While Kornbrath's final work (Plates 512-515) faithfully translated Foster's drawings onto the steel canvas

of the Model 21's receiver, it contained several compositional improvements. To give the upland game hunting scene on the right side a greater vitality, Kornbrath changed the stance of the rearmost dog so that it is more realistically positioned and portrayed the foremost dog starting to move toward the quarry. The only other change from Foster's design was Kornbrath's substitution of a blank escutcheon on the triggerguard bow in place of the Winchester Arms Company monogram originally suggested.

Perhaps the most striking feature of the right and left hunting scenes are the clouds chiselled in relief on the barrel breeches. Not only do they seem to convey a sense of movement with careful shading, but Kornbrath managed to imbue the clouds with a depth simulating reality.

Given the complexity of the decoration and the amount of time needed to complete it, Kornbrath's bill of $350 was relatively modest[14].

Over the next three years, Kornbrath engraved a number of Winchester rifles and shotguns both under contract from the company and for private clients. The quality of this work ranged from rather pedestrian game scenes (Plates 516-519) and simple inlay work (Plate 520) to exquisitely conceived scrollwork (Plate 521). Among the more famous of Kornbrath's special commissions dating from this period are the Model 21 shotguns made for J.E. Vincent of Fairmont, West Virginia (Plate 522) and the one presented to Wiley Post by the Pratt & Whitney Aircraft Company in 1934 (Plates 523 and 554). Equally important, but less well known, are two Model 42 shotguns and Model 52 rifle engraved and gold inlaid by Kornbrath in 1934. The first of these, serial number 18179 (Plates 524-527), decorated with chiselled oak leaf foliage surrounding gold game inlays, was made for Ben Hayes[15]. The second,

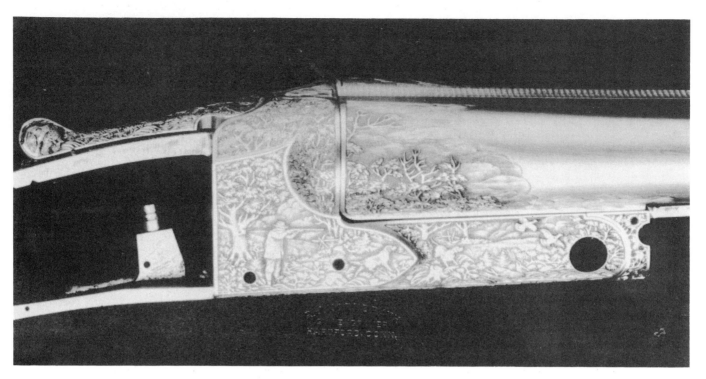

Plate 512

Detail of John M. Olin's Model 21 shotgun, serial number 8186, engraved by Rudolph J. Kornbrath in April 1933 after designs drawn by Fred Foster (Plate 511). Kornbrath Papers, Harold McCracken Research Library, Buffalo Bill Historical Center.

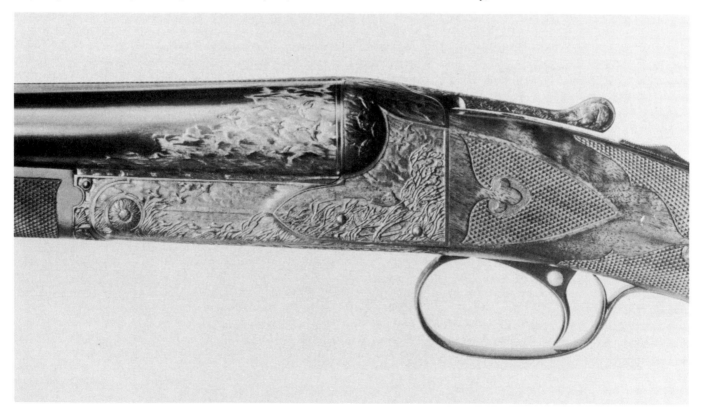

Plate 513

Left receiver detail of John M. Olin's Model 21 shotgun illustrated in Plate 512. Olin Corporation Photograph.

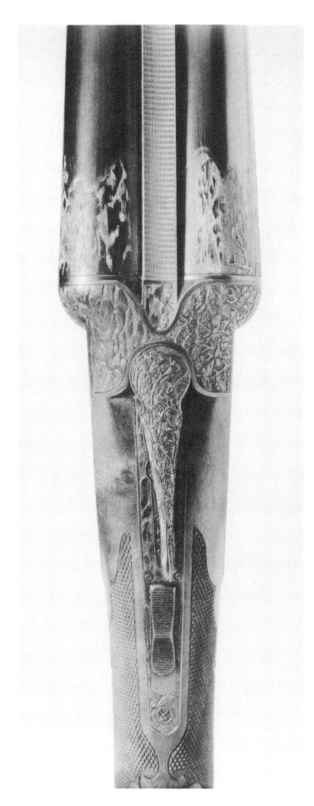

Plate 514
*D*etail top view of John M. Olin's Model 21 shotgun illustrated in Plate 512. Olin Corporation Photograph.

Plate 515
*L*ower water table and triggerguard detail of John M. Olin's Model 21 shotgun illustrated in Plate 512. Olin Corporation Photograph.

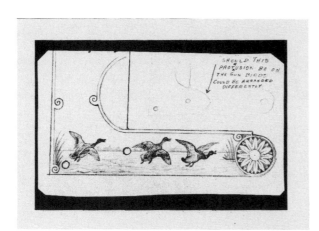

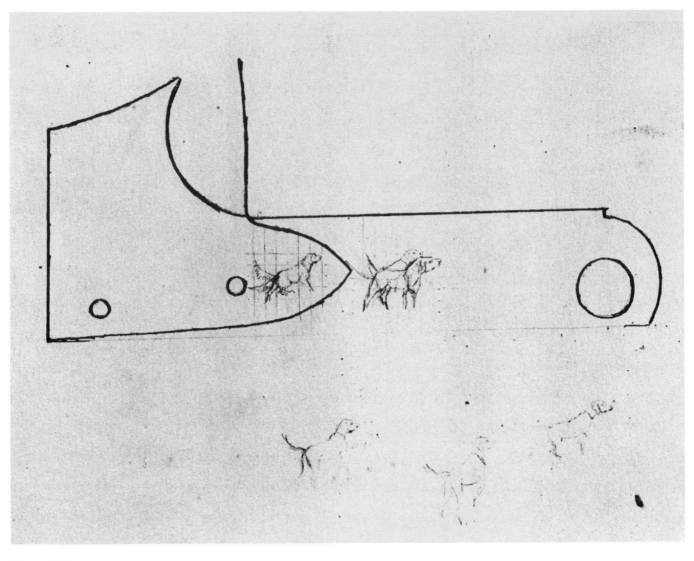

Plate 520

Preparatory sketch by Rudolph J. Kornbrath illustrating the possible position for two dogs to be engraved on a Model 21 shotgun receiver. The location of the dogs suggests that this drawing might have been made during the design phase for John M. Olin's Model 21 shotgun illustrated in Plate 512. Kornbrath Papers, Harold McCracken Research Library, Buffalo Bill Historical Center.

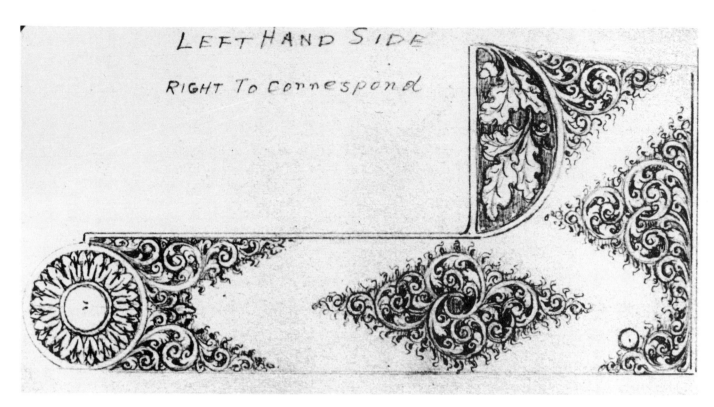

Plate 521

*P*encil sketch illustrating custom grade scrollwork to be cut in a Model 21 shotgun. Kornbrath Papers, Harold McCracken Research Library, Buffalo Bill Historical Center.

Plate 522

*P*encil design sketch illustrating the proposed decoration to be engraved on J.E. Vincent's Winchester Model 21 shotgun, serial number 6290, built in 1935. Kornbrath Papers, Harold McCracken Research Library, Buffalo Bill Historical Center.

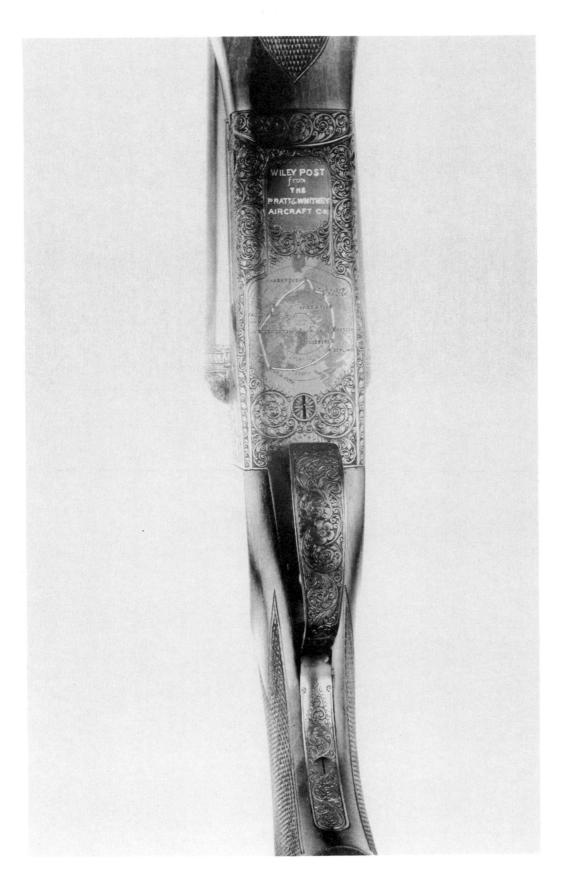

WILEY POST
from
THE
PRATT&WHITNEY
AIRCRAFT Cº

Plate 523
*L*ower water table
detail of Wiley Post's
Model 21 shotgun illus-
trating the engraved
world map with Post's
route inlaid in gold.
Olin Corporation Photo-
graph.

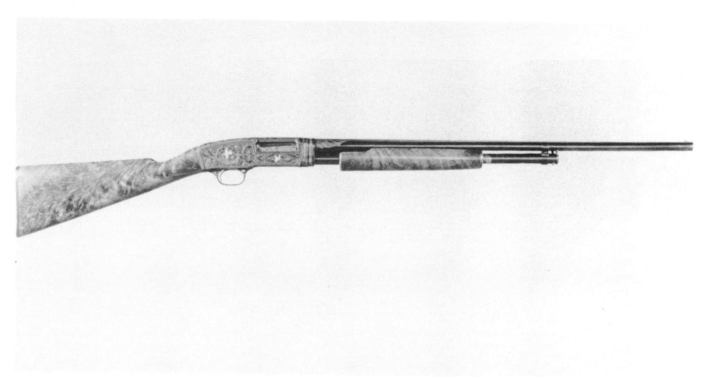

Plate 524

*R*ight overall view of the Winchester Model 42 shotgun, serial number 18179, engraved by R.J. Kornbrath for Ben Hayes. Olin Corporation Photograph.

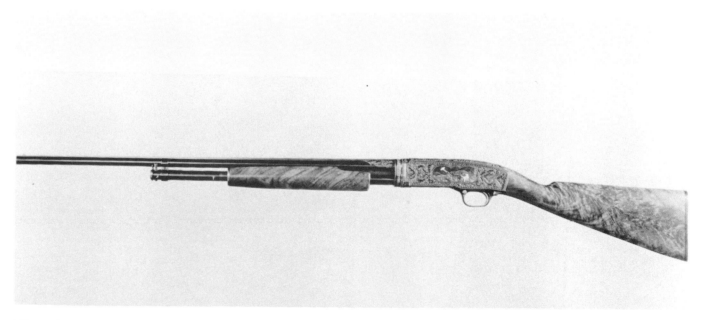

Plate 525

*L*eft overall view of the Model 42 shotgun illustrated in Plate 524.

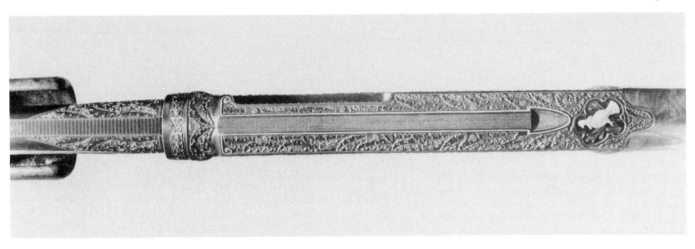

Plate 526
*U*pper receiver detail of the Model 42 shotgun illustrated in Plate 524.

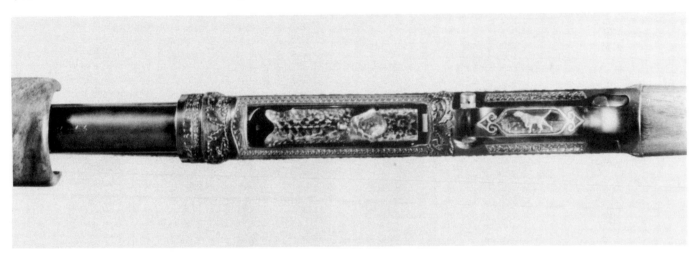

Plate 527
*L*ower receiver detail of the Model 42 shotgun illustrated in Plate 524.

Plate 528
*R*ight overall view of the Winchester Model 42 shotgun, serial number 23456, engraved by Rudolph J. Kornbrath for C.A. Tilt. *Olin Corporation Photograph.*

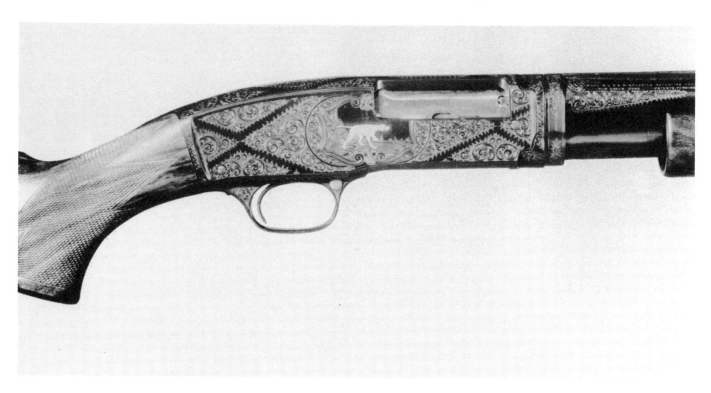

Plate 529

*R*ight receiver detail of the Model 42 shotgun illustrated in Plate 528.

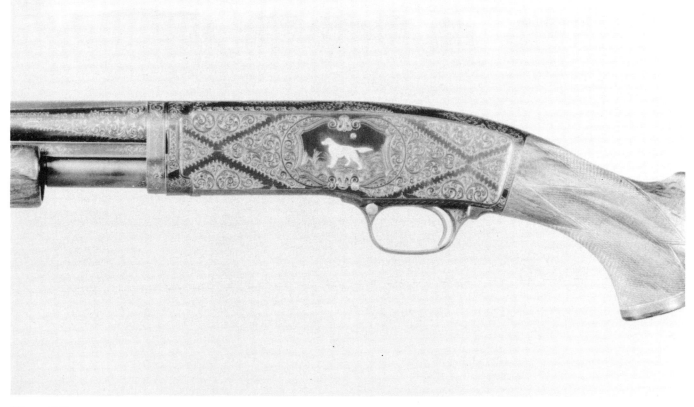

Plate 530

Left receiver detail of the Model 42 shotgun illustrated in Plate 528.

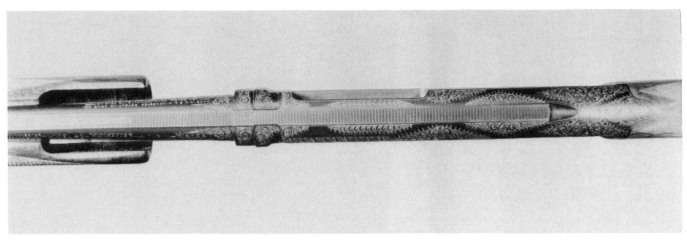

Plate 531
*U*pper receiver detail of the Model 42 shotgun illustrated in Plate 528.

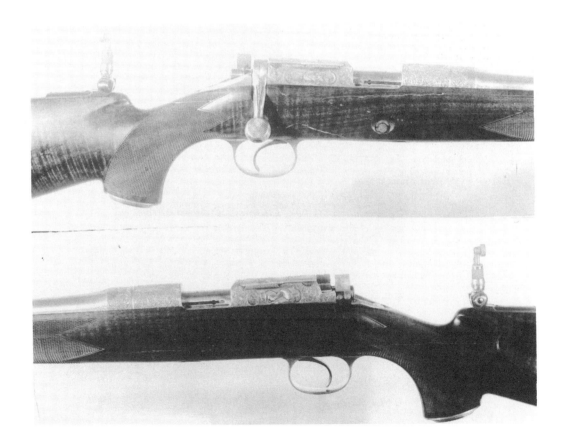

Plate 532
*P*eriod photographs of a Winchester Model 52 sporting rifle engraved by Rudolph J. Kornbrath. The groundhog and squirrel panels (right and left receiver sides, respectively) are also to be seen in Plate 535. Kornbrath Papers, Harold McCracken Research Library, Buffalo Bill Historical Center.

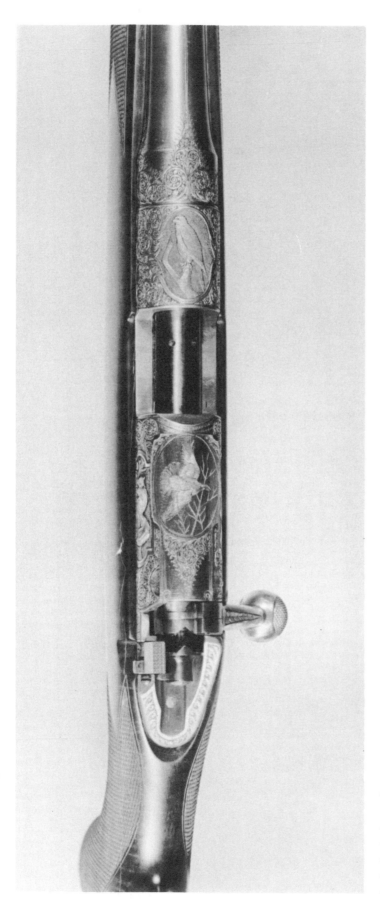

Plate 533

*U*pper receiver detail of the
Model 52 sporting rifle illus-
trated in Plate 532. Kornbrath
Papers, Harold McCracken
Research Library, Buffalo Bill
Historical Center.

number 23456 (Plates 528-531), was engraved with conventional scrollwork in geometrical panels enclosing at their center shaped cartouches containing game scenes with gold inlaid hunting dogs. Its original owner is noted as having been C.A. Tait[16]. The Model 52 was engraved with deeply cut scrollwork and small game scenes (Plates 532-535) for an unknown client.

Perhaps the most aesthetically attractive and technically innovative work to be produced by Rudolph J. Kornbrath was his use of colored enamel for inlaying portraits of animals and gamebirds into the steel receivers of firearms. First developed about 1930, Kornbrath perfected the technique sometime in 1932. Kornbrath's reasons for first experimenting with enamel are explained in the following statement written by him as part of a patent application[17].

"Since the first sporting firearm came into existence, it has been the practice to beautify these firearms by decorating or engraving them. Up to the present time the art of engraving has been much the same, except that in some cases, precious metal inlay work has been used in imparting color and richness and added beauty to the decoration.

Gun engraving consists mainly of Scroll work cut or engraved into the surface of a Shotgun, Rifle, Pistol or revolver etc. Hunting scenes, animals and birds are also used, being executed in the same manner on any suitable surface of a gun.

The finished artists, gun engraver, in this way is unable to produce some highly decorative work which adds much to the beauty of the firearms and the fancy of its owner.

The finish on such engraved firearms consists of blueing or Browning, or case hardening which adds to the protection against rust, but at the same time, it gives the firearms a monoto-

Plate 534

Pencil sketch for the engraving cut on the muzzle of the Model 52 sporting rifle illustrated in Plate 532. Kornbrath Papers, Harold McCracken Research Library, Buffalo Bill Historical Center.

nous appearance no mater how well executed the engraving on the firearm may be.

As a gun engraver of note I have executed many such decorations on firearms, and I have long been impressed with the idea that there is something lacking in this present art of gun engraving and this, <u>something</u>, is the lack of <u>color</u>, natural color of the object engraved. The most beautiful conception of any is, without question, nature with its multiple coloring in every aspect, and I now have produced an entirely new conception of the art of gun engraving whereby the monotonous appearance of an engraved sporting firearm is given a touch of natural coloring of the object.

I have executed hunting scenes, animals, birds and landscape in their natural colors and have worked out a process whereby these natural colored

471

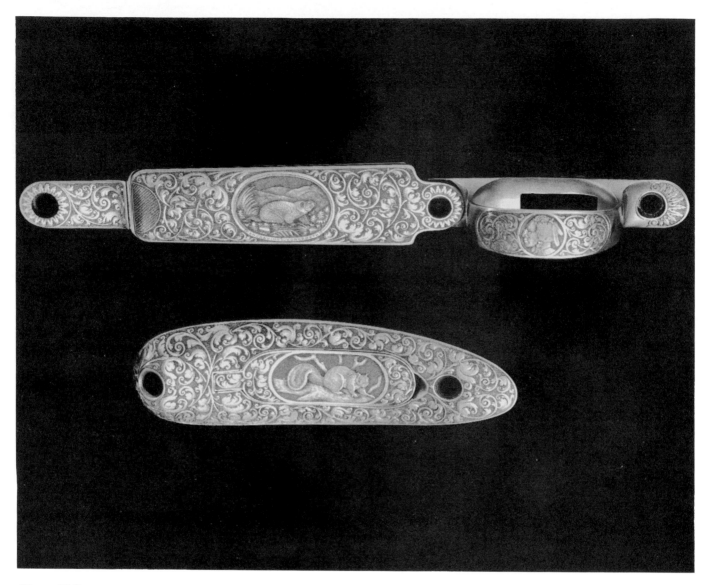

Plate 535

A magazine floorplate and triggerguard together with a butt plate from an unidentified sporting rifle. The floor and butt plates engraved with panel scenes are identical to those found on the Winchester Model 52 sporting rifle illustrated in Plate 532.

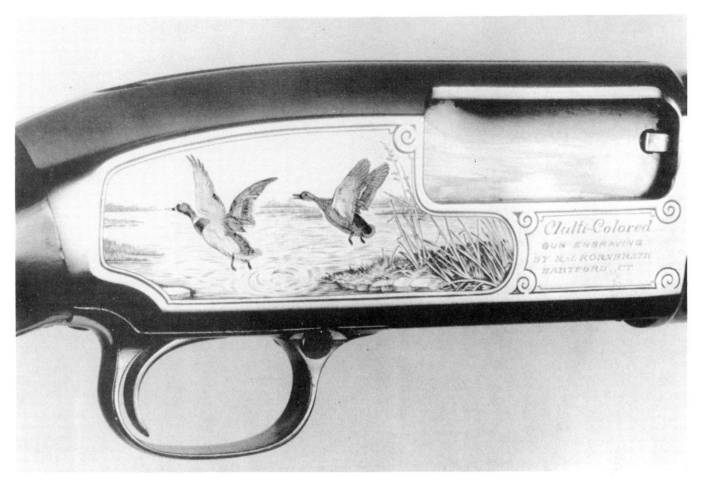

Plate 536

*D*etail of a Winchester Model 12 shotgun receiver inlaid in colored enamel by Rudolph J. Kornbrath. Kornbrath Papers, Harold McCracken Research Library, Buffalo Bill Historical Center.

Plate 537

Left receiver detail of the enamel inlaid Model 12 shotgun illustrated in Plate 536. Kornbrath Papers, Harold McCracken Research Library, Buffalo Bill Historical Center.

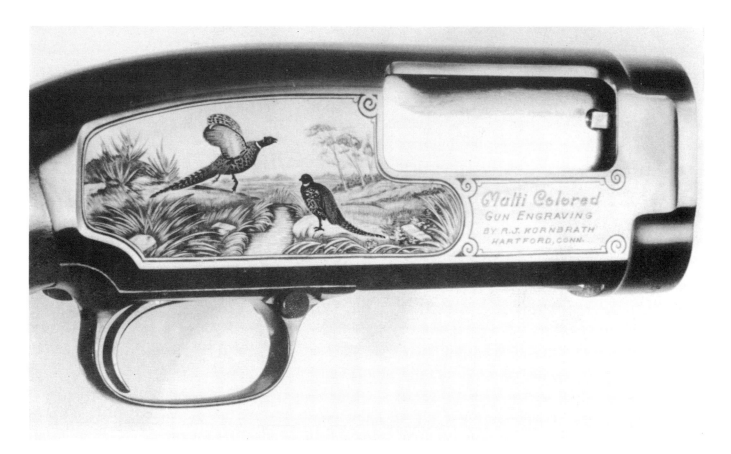

Plate 538

Detail of the Winchester Model 12 shotgun receiver inlaid in colored enamel by Rudolph J. Kornbrath for E. Field White of Hartford, Connecticut. Kornbrath Papers, Harold McCracken Research Library, Buffalo Bill Historical Center.

Plate 539
Left receiver detail of the enamel inlaid Model 12 shotgun illustrated in Plate 538. Kornbrath Papers, Harold McCracken Research Library, Buffalo Bill Historical Center.

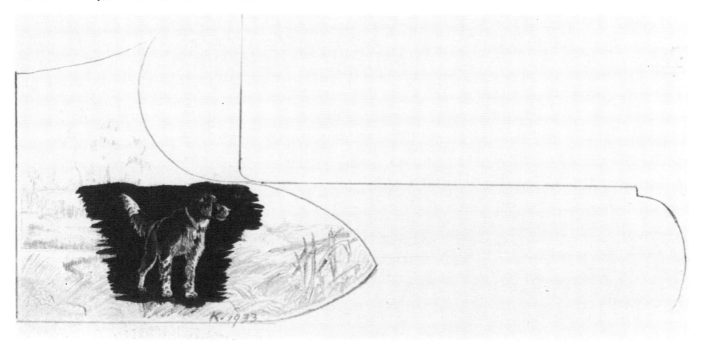

Plate 540
Pencil and watercolor sketch by Rudolph J. Kornbrath illustrating the portrait of a spaniel to be inlaid in colored enamel on Major John R. Hessian's Winchester Model 21 shotgun. Kornbrath Papers, Harold McCracken Research Library, Buffalo Bill Historical Center.

Plate 541
Pencil and watercolor sketch by Rudolph J. Kornbrath illustrating the portrait of a spaniel to be inlaid in colored enamel on Major John R. Hessian's Winchester Model 21 shotgun. Kornbrath Papers, Harold McCracken Research Library, Buffalo Bill Historical Center.

objects may be properly protected against ordinary wear."

Though primarily used in the decoration of slide-action shotguns, especially the Winchester Model 12 (Plates 536-539), Kornbrath did do at least one Model 21 in this manner. In a letter dated June 13, 1933, Kornbrath wrote Captain Paul A. Curtis, editor of *Field & Stream* magazine, that he had "Major John W. Hessians' little 20 gauge skeet gun in the works and he is to have his two bird dogs reproduced in colors on that gun."[18] While the whereabouts of this Model 21 are presently unknown, the form of the decoration can be seen in two color sketches (Plates 540-541) drawn by Kornbrath probably for Major Hessians' approval before the work was begun.

Although Rudolph J. Kornbrath received a number of engraving contracts from the Winchester company which could have as easily been done by Alden George Ulrich, there does not appear to have been any rivalry between the two engravers. Actually, evidence suggests quite the opposite as both men freely exchanged pencil design drawings, pulls and photographs of their work. More importantly, this exchange was not limited just to engraving done on Winchester firearms, but extended to other makes and subjects (such as calling cards and stationery)[19]. Thus, it appears that Kornbrath and Ulrich recognized each other's particular talents and that work was apportioned between them on that basis.

The chief benefactor of this spirit of cooperation was the Winchester Repeating Arms Company since it was able to offer consumers an unlimited variety of decoration from standard engraving and chiselled decoration to colored inlay work. Realizing the potential sales value of the Kornbrath-Ulrich partnership, the company began work on a new embellished arms catalog in late 1934. Issued in April 1935[20], this booklet, titled *Winchester Custom-Built Shotguns...Rifles* (Plates 542-559), illustrates the degree to which the two engravers cooperated. It also demonstrates how much their work complemented the other's. Of the thirteen pages (including the recto and verso of the front cover) containing reproductions of engraved arms, a total of nine illustrated works are by Ulrich and the remaining four are by Kornbrath. Specifically, the authorship of the engraving is as follows:

Alden George Ulrich

Front Cover – the Chrysler Model 21 shotgun, serial number 5437 and the background scrollwork

Plate 542-559 (On this page and the following 15 pages)

*W*inchester Custom Built shotguns...rifles catalog issued in April 1935 containing illustrations of work by both Rudolph J. Kornbrath and Alden George Ulrich. Private Collection.

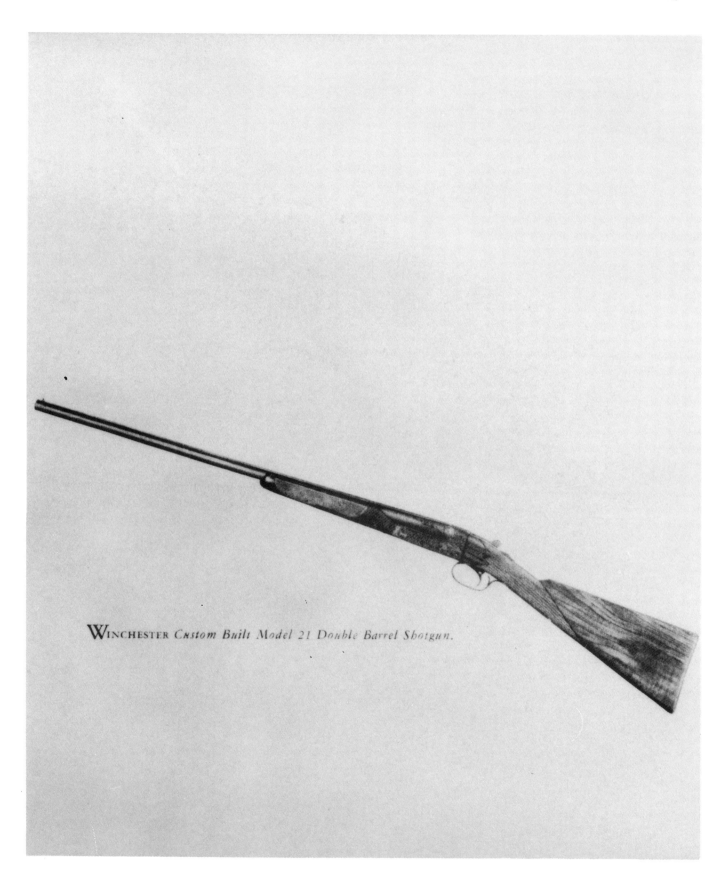

Winchester *Custom Built Model 21 Double Barrel Shotgun.*

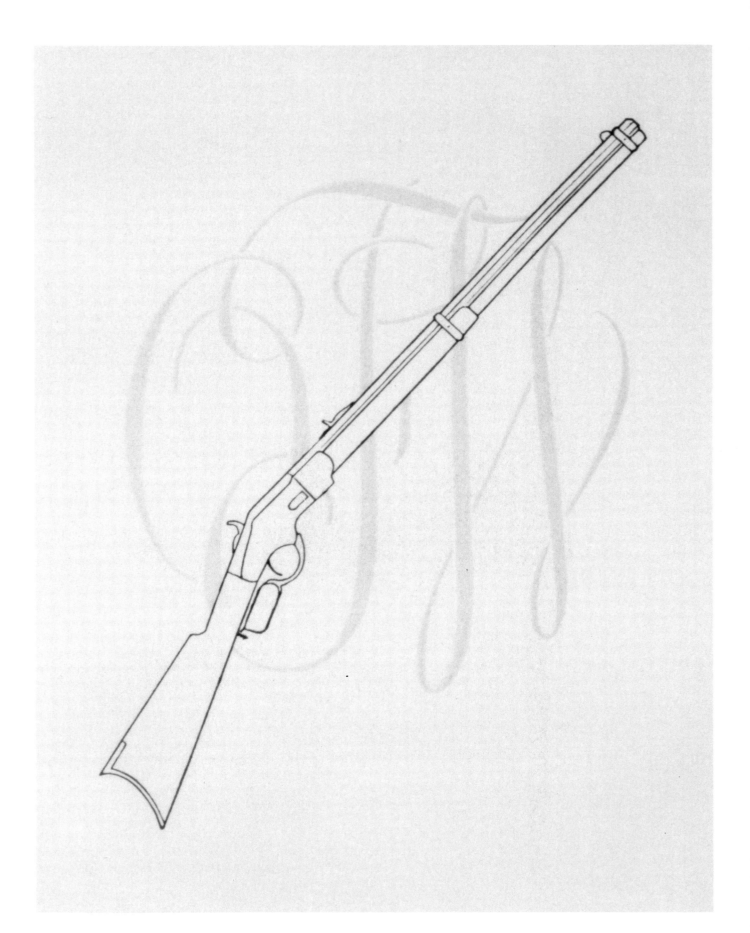

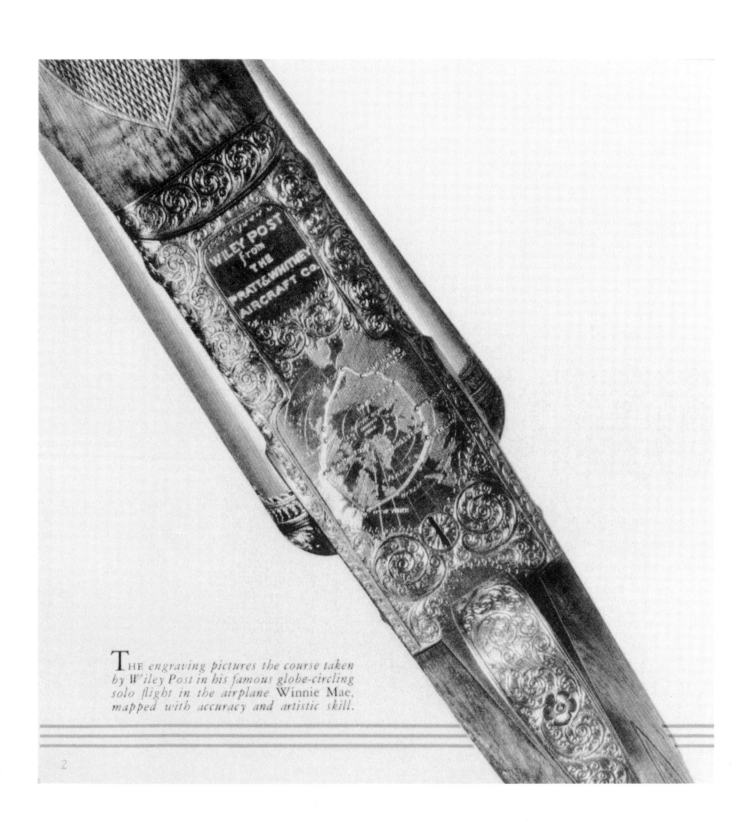

THE *engraving pictures the course taken by Wiley Post in his famous globe-circling solo flight in the airplane* Winnie Mae, *mapped with accuracy and artistic skill.*

2

HUNTING dogs in action, engraved far better today than in former years, are very popular panel subjects for the sides of shotgun receivers. Customers' own favorite dogs can be faithfully pictured. On rifles, these spaces usually are decorated with game subjects. True-to-life subjects only are reproduced, and the work is strictly authentic, with truly artistic rendering.

THE pistol-grip cap on shotgun or rifle offers an excellent base for ornamentation, with a wide range of decorative possibilities.

MEDALLION game scene from under side of frame of a Winchester Custom Built Model 21 Shotgun, in shallow relief engraving. Choice of such scenes may be made from a variety of stock designs. Customers' own designs are executed with the same high degree of artistic skill. We also combine engraving with gold or platinum inlays of game, of monogram initials or of presentation legends.

THE variety of monogram designs used on firearms is infinite. We execute customers' own designs, or any of a number of popular styles which offer interesting combinations of lettering and design. The choice ranges from simple plain engraving on steel, nickel silver or gold, to the most beautiful combination of engraving and inlay work in gold or platinum.

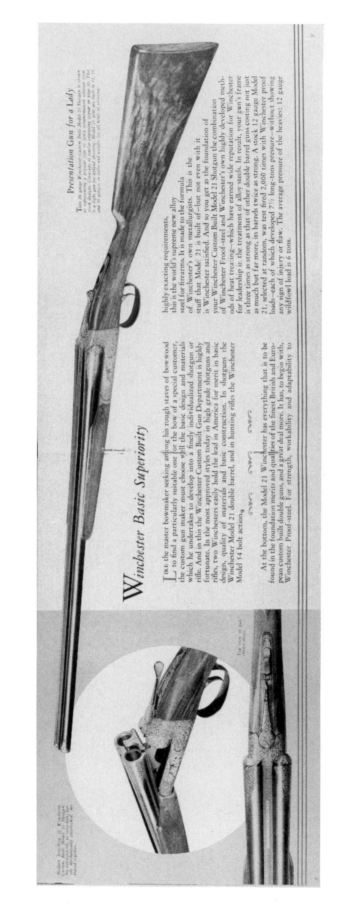

Winchester Basic Superiority

Like the master bowmaker seeking among his rough staves of bow-wood to find a particularly suitable one for the bow of a special customer, the custom gun maker must choose well the basic design and materials which he undertakes to develop into a finely individualized shotgun or rifle. And in this the Winchester Custom Built Gun Department is highly fortunate. In the most approved styles today in high grade shotguns and rifles, two Winchesters easily hold the lead in America for merit in basic design, quality of materials and basic construction. In shotguns the Winchester Model 21 double barrel, and in hunting rifles the Winchester Model 54 bolt action.

At the bottom, the Model 21 Winchester has everything that is to be found in the foundation merits and qualifies of the finest British and European custom built double guns, and a great deal more. It has, to begin with, Winchester Proof-steel. For strength, workability and adaptability to

highly exacting requirements, this is the world's supreme new alloy steel for firearms. It is made to the formula of Winchester's own metallurgists. This is the stuff that Model 21 is built of—but not even with it is Winchester satisfied. And so you get as the foundation of your Winchester Custom Built Model 21 Shotgun the combination of Winchester Proof-steel and Winchester's own highly developed methods of heat treating—which have earned wide reputation for Winchester for leadership in the treatment of alloy steels. In result, your gun's frame is three times as strong as that of other double barrel guns costing not just as much but far more, its barrels twice as strong. A stock 12 gauge Model 21, selected at random, was test fired 2,000 times with Winchester proof loads—each of which developed 7½ long-tons pressure—without showing any sign of injury or flaw. The average pressure of the heaviest 12 gauge wildfowl load is 6 tons.

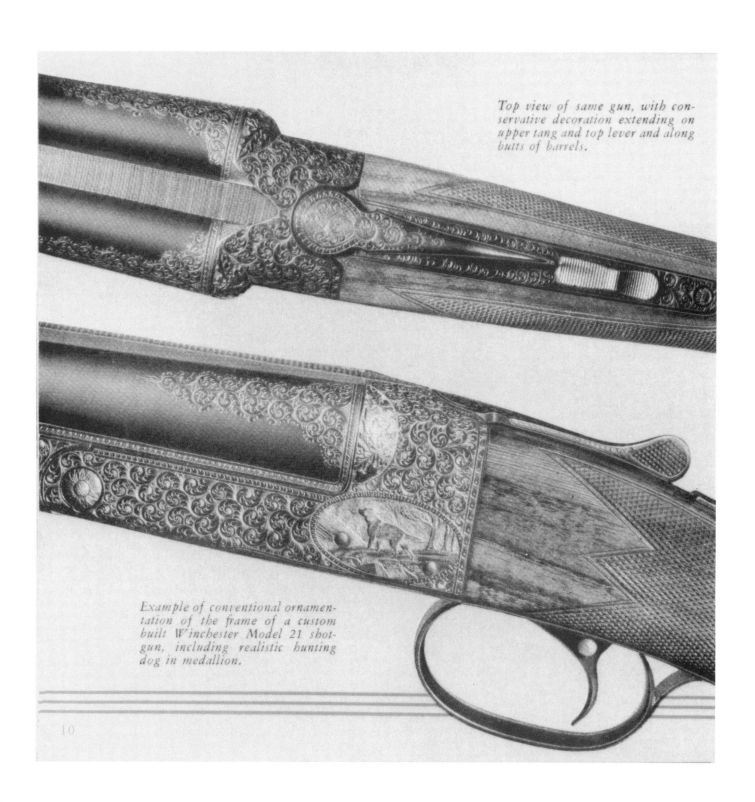

Top view of same gun, with conservative decoration extending on upper tang and top lever and along butts of barrels.

Example of conventional ornamentation of the frame of a custom built Winchester Model 21 shotgun, including realistic hunting dog in medallion.

10

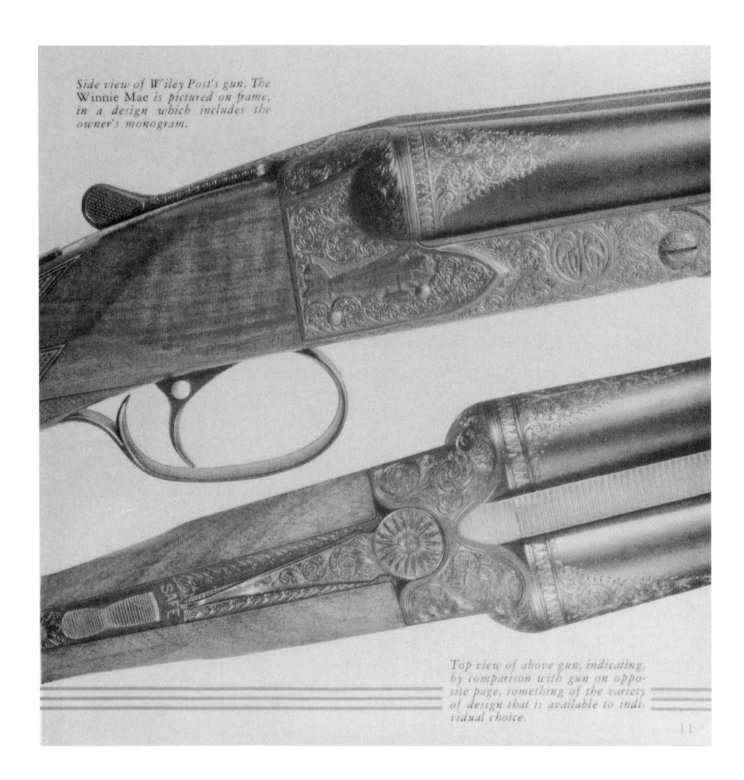

Side view of Wiley Post's gun. The Winnie Mae is pictured on frame, in a design which includes the owner's monogram.

Top view of above gun, indicating, by comparison with gun on opposite page, something of the variety of design that is available to individual choice.

11

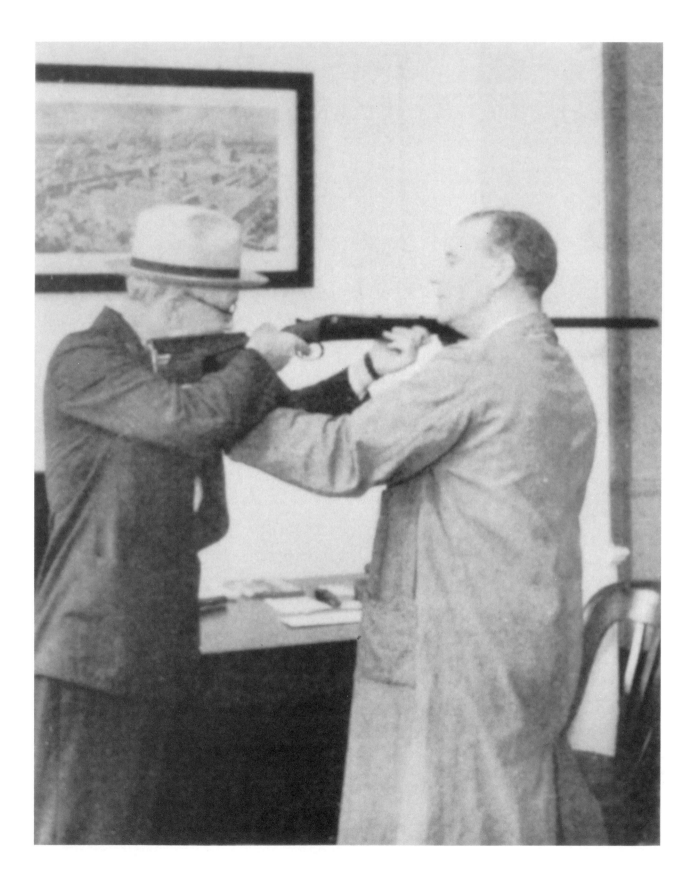

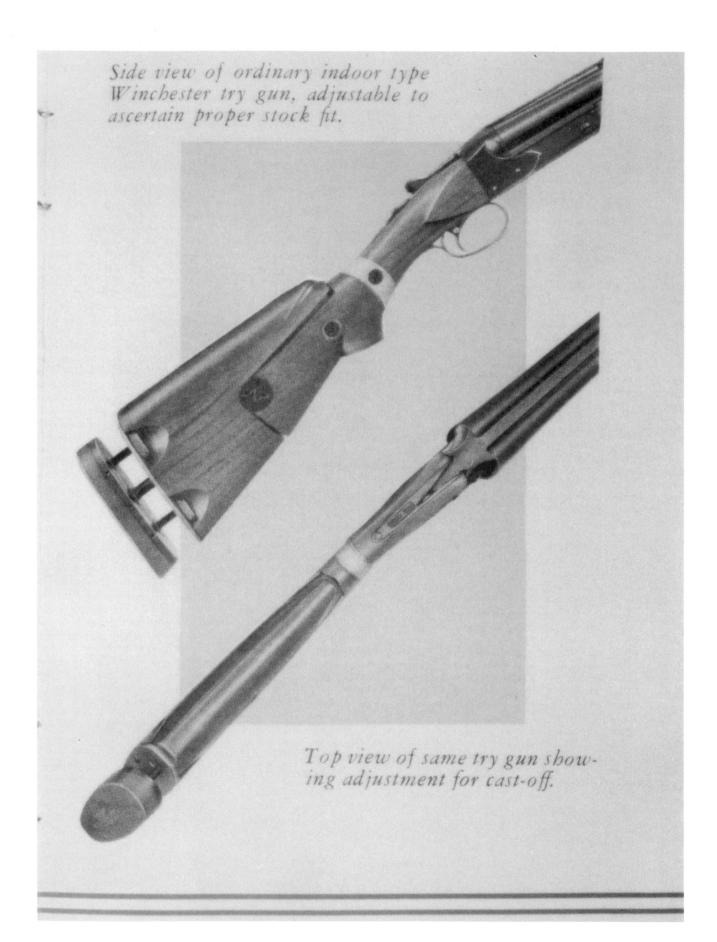

Side view of ordinary indoor type Winchester try gun, adjustable to ascertain proper stock fit.

Top view of same try gun showing adjustment for cast-off.

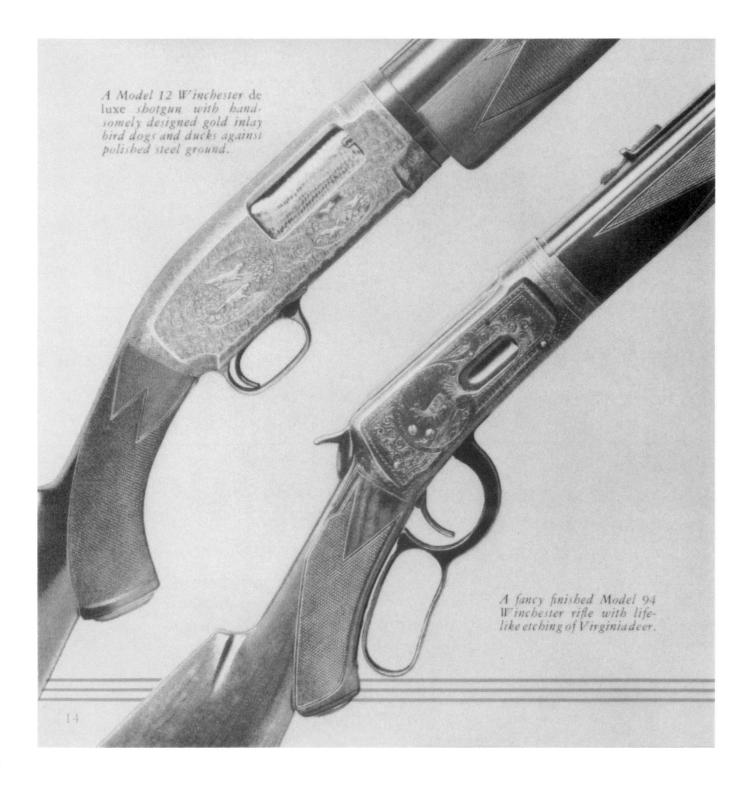

A Model 12 Winchester de luxe *shotgun* with handsomely designed gold inlay *bird dogs* and *ducks* against polished steel ground.

A fancy finished Model 94 Winchester rifle with lifelike etching of Virginia deer.

14

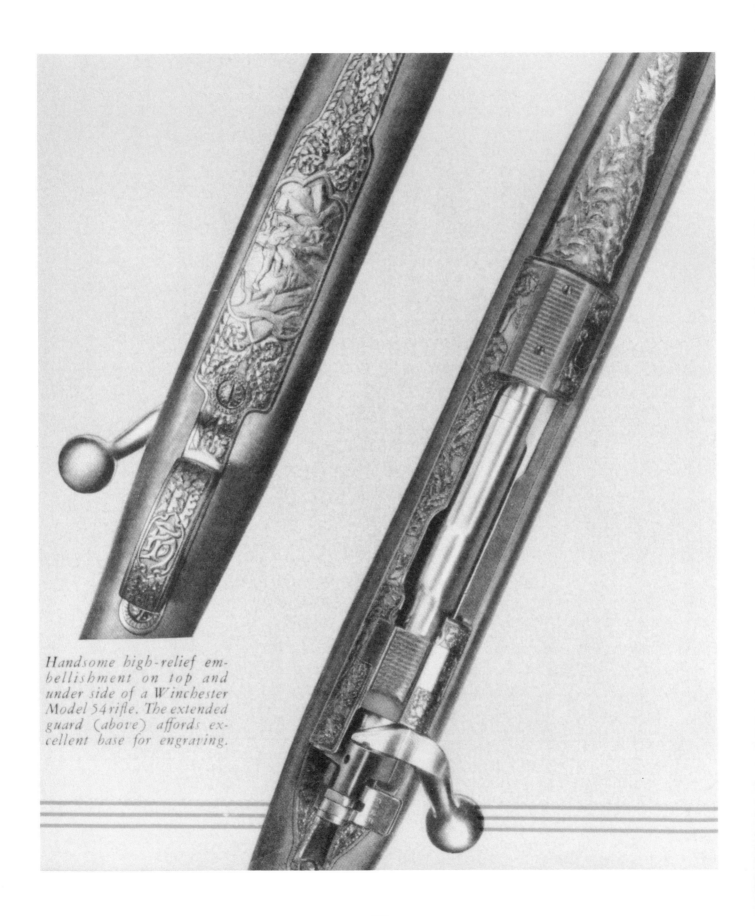

Handsome high-relief embellishment on top and under side of a Winchester Model 54 rifle. The extended guard (above) affords excellent base for engraving.

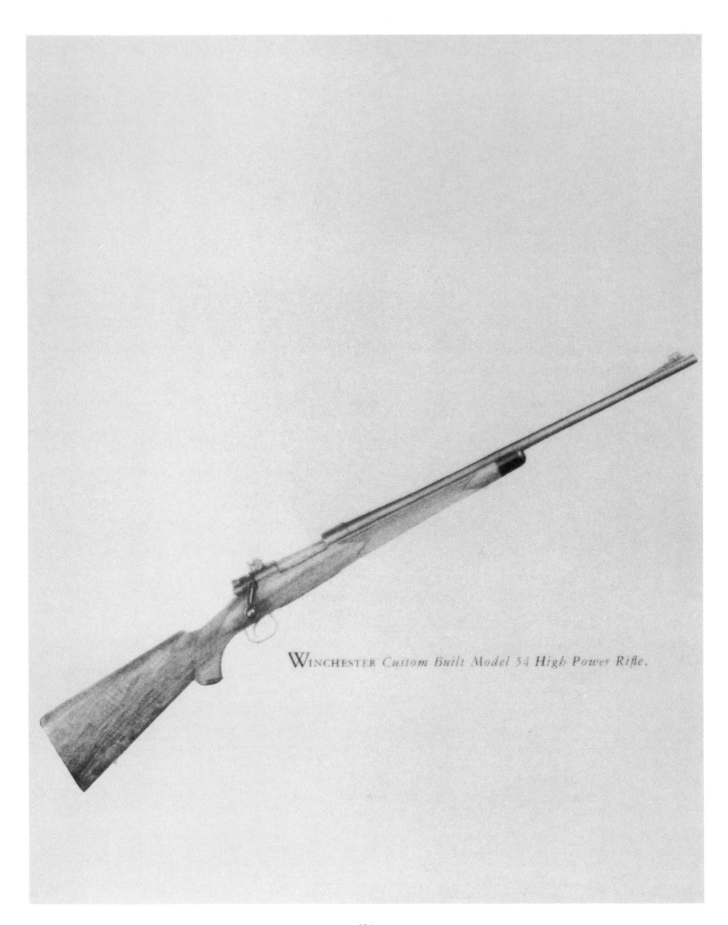

Winchester *Custom Built Model 54 High Power Rifle.*

Front Cover (verso) – a Model 21 shotgun with Number 6 engraving

Page 3 – pistol grip caps

Page 6 – relief panel from a Model 21 shotgun

Page 7 – relief panel from the Model 21 shotgun illustrated on page 10

Page 8 and 9 – a Model 21 shotgun with Number 6 engraving

Page 10 – a Model 21 shotgun with Number 6 engraving

Page 14 – a Model 12 shotgun and a Model 94 rifle

Rudolph J. Kornbrath

Page 2 – the Wiley Post Model 21 shotgun

Page 5 – a monogram

Page 11 – the Wiley Post Model 21 shotgun

Page 15 – a Model 54 rifle made for Ben Hayes

Sadly, the collaborative efforts of Kornbrath and Ulrich on behalf of the Winchester company were to be short-lived. Despite an upsurge in orders for engraved arms after the publication of the Custom Built catalog, they were to decrease in 1936 to the extent that A.G. Ulrich was able to fulfill them. Kornbrath's account ledger reveals that his

last work for the Winchester company occurred in the last third of 1935[21]

Sept. 20   3 Model 21 guns #3-9.50
            #4-24.00
            #5-34.00   72.50 Pd
            3 Model 21 guns#1-4.80
            #2-7.75
            #6-59.00   70.55 Pd

Sept. 25   1 Model 21 gun Gold inlay
            3 Birds - 1 Dog   50.00 Pd

Oct. 26   1 Model 21 gun Scroll &
            Game scenes, 2 sets of
            Barrels
            Order # 75143-F1   30.00 Pd

Nov. 11   Model 21 Scroll & Game
            scenes #6 engraving 56.00 Pd

Tragically, in late November or early December 1936[22], Kornbrath suffered a stroke, leaving him partially paralyzed and unable to work for the remainder of his life. Struck down at the height of his abilities, his work was best memorialized by the following comment made some three years earlier in an article published in the July 2, 1933, edition of *The Hartford Daily Courant*:

"Engraving, because of its inflexibility, is an art which does not readily lend itself to fluency. And yet, despite this fact, Mr. Kornbrath's work has the ease, the grace and the charm of a well-executed drawing or painting. This master engraver has completely surmounted the difficulties of depicting in steel what he has once envisioned, or perhaps sketched on paper."

Endnotes

1. At its peak (circa 1906), the Design and Engraving Laboratory employed as many as six engravers: Herman Ulrich, John Ulrich, Leslie Ulrich, John A. Gough, Angelo Stokes and William Stokes.

2. George R. Watrous, 1927 Sales, page 3. Winchester Repeating Arms Company Archives, Olin Corporation.

3. The letters and other documents regarding this order are in the possession of the original owner's family.

4. For an example of Paul Bonet's work, see Mark Wrey, editor, **Christie's Review of the Season 1985** (Phaidon-Christie's, Oxford, England: 1986), page 217.

5. For a complete account of the Model 21's development, see Ned Schwing, **Winchester's Finest**, op. cit., pages 13-32.

6. Each of the surviving sketches is inscribed "OK GRW."

7. In particular, Olin admired the Model 21's handling characteristics, the dovetailed construction of the barrels and the strength of the blued receiver. With respect to the letter, a test was carried out in 1932 to determine the strength difference between a blued and a case-hardened receiver. The results of this test revealed that a case-hardened Model 21 receiver had a tensile strength of 94,200 pounds per square inch and an elastic limit of 85,400 pounds per square inch. In contrast, a blued Model 21 receiver had a tensile strength of 174,600 pounds per square inch and an elastic limit of 160,950 pounds per square inch. Letter to F.W. Olin from Edwin Pugsley dated April 11, 1932. Model 21 Production File, Winchester Arms Collection Archives, Cody Firearms Museum.

8. George R. Watrous, 1932 Sales, page 3. Winchester Arms Collection Archives, Cody Firearm Museum.

9. A review of Kornbrath's correspondence and accounts, preserved at the Buffalo Bill Historical Center, reveals that he had only passing contact with the Winchester company prior to 1932.

10. The photograph reproduced in Plate 507 is annotated on the reverse "J.M. Olin 1930," in Kornbrath's hand.

11. Two of the extent design sketches contain the monogram "WA Co" for Winchester Arms Company. On the second of these, the monogram was altered to read "WRA Co" (Winchester Repeating Arms Company) by J.M. Olin.

12. The cost for the engraving was written by Kornbrath on the reverse of the design sketch reproduced in Plate 510.

13. Letter to Capt. Paul A. Curtis dated June 13, 1933 (Kornbrath Pagers, Buffalo Bill Historical Center). While it has been suggested that this shotgun was engraved in 1934, the content of the letter cited above demonstrates that the work was done in 1933. The specific portion of this letter is as follows:

"The other set of photos will make you acquainted with a 12 gauge Winchester double which I engraved for Mr. Olin, president of that concern. Please note in particular that there was absolutely no scroll work used in the decoration of this gun. Instead of that each side of gun represents a separate scene extending all over the side and up along barrels. While the left side shows a duck shooting scene, the right side shows Game Bird Shooting. All this work was modeled in high relief including the cloud effect, after a rather detail lacking pencil drawing by Mr. Fred Foster who if I am not mistaken is the art editor of the National Sportsman. Perhaps these will interest you more as it is

rather something new in the line of gun engraving. Please also see short write up in this months Sporting Goods Dealer under the heading "Shooting Streight [sic]" by Mr. Charles S. Landis."

14. The cost for the engraving was written by Kornbrath on the reverse of the photograph reproduced in Plate 512.

15. The reverse of several photographs of this shotgun are inscribed in pencil with the name Ben Hayes. Hayes is also listed in a compilation of clients' names drawn up by Kornbrath in 1934 and 1935.

16. The reverse of several photographs of this shotgun are inscribed in pencil with the name C.A. Tilt. Tilt is also listed in Kornbrath's compilation of clients' names.

17. Patent application draft, Kornbrath Papers, Buffalo Bill Historical Center.

18. Letter to Capt. Paul A. Curtis from R.J. Kornbrath dated June 13, 1933, op. cit.

19. A significant number of pulls, pencil design sketches and factory photographs of A.G. Ulrich's work are preserved in the Kornbrath Papers. Likewise, a large number of similar items originally given by Kornbrath to Ulrich were at one time in the latter's possession and later became the property of his assistant, John Kusmit.

20. Though this booklet is undated, the issuance date is confirmed by advertising circulars sent to dealers in April 1933. Model 21 Production File, Winchester Arms Collection Archives, Cody Firearms Museum.

21. R.J. Kornbrath, Accounts Ledger, page 69. Kornbrath Papers, Buffalo Bill Historical Center.

22. While the date of Kornbrath's stroke is unknown, the last date he billed a client for any work was Nov. 21, 1936. Kornbrath Accounts Ledger, op. cit.

23. **The Hartford Daily Courant**, July 2, 1933, page 6.

ALDEN GEORGE ULRICH'S LEGACY: 1936-1981

Although the timing may have been purely coincidental, one must wonder whether or not Alden George Ulrich's decision to hire an apprentice in late 1936 was not influenced in some way by Rudolph J. Kornbrath's stroke. Certainly, they were of a similar age (Ulrich being forty-eight and Kornbrath fifty-four), and Kornbrath's illness may have given pause to Ulrich. Whatever the case, John Kusmit was hired at that time as Ulrich's assistant[1].

While engraving orders did not return to their 1932 to 1935 levels until after World War II, Alden George Ulrich did complete a number of important commissions during the interim. One of the more unusual of these was an engraved and gold inlaid High Standard Model A semiautomatic pistol, serial number 4 (Plates 560 and 561) done in 1941. Ordered by Carl Swebilius, president of the High Standard Company, this pistol was subsequently presented to Edwin Pugsley. At the same time, Swebilius contracted with John Kusmit to engrave another High Standard pistol (a Model B, serial number 7911), which was to be presented to John M. Olin. Though the acceptance of private commissions by Ulrich and Kusmit was not common during this period, it must be remembered that Swebilius was actively involved with Winchester at this time (see Chapter Seven). Therefore, his hiring of the two Winchester engravers to do special work for him would have not met with any opposition from the company's management, especially given who the recipients of the two pistols were to be.

During the immediate postwar period, Alden G. Ulrich and John Kusmit engraved a large number of Winchester arms that were to be presented by John M. Olin to various senior officers of the Allied Armies. Among the recipients were Generals Eisenhower, Bradley and MacArthur of the United States Army, Admirals Halsey and Nimitz of the United States Navy and General Arnold of the United States Air Force. Foreign officers to receive Winchester firearms included Lord Louis Mountbatten of Burma, Field Marshal Montgomery, Field Marshal Slim, General De Gualle and Chiang Kai-Shek[2].

One of Alden Ulrich's last major works was to be the Model 1894 carbine, serial number 1,500,000, which was presented to President Harry S. Truman on May 8, 1984, by John M. Olin (Plates 562 and 563). Ulrich's lasting contribution to the Winchester firm was, however, to be his development of a standardized set of engraving patterns which could be used on the Model 12 and 21 shotguns and the Model 70 rifle[3]. These patterns were to influence Winchester engraving until the sale of the company in 1981, and even beyond.

496

Plate 560
High Standard Model A semiautomatic .22 caliber pistol, serial number 4, engraved and gold inlaid by Alden George Ulrich in 1941, for Carl Swebilius, president of the High Standard Company. This pistol was later presented by Swebilius to Edwin Pugsley. Cody Firearms Museum. Buffalo Bill Historical Center.

Plate 561
The right side of the presentation High Standard semiautomatic pistol illustrated in Plate 560.

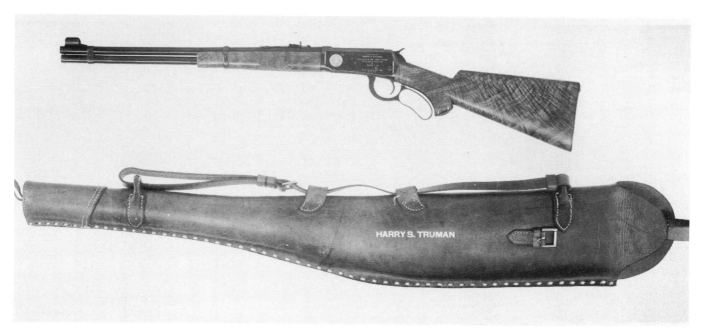

Plate 562

*W*inchester Model 94 carbine, serial number 1,500,000, engraved by Alden George Ulrich for presentation to President Harry S. Truman on May 8, 1948. Olin Corporation Photograph.

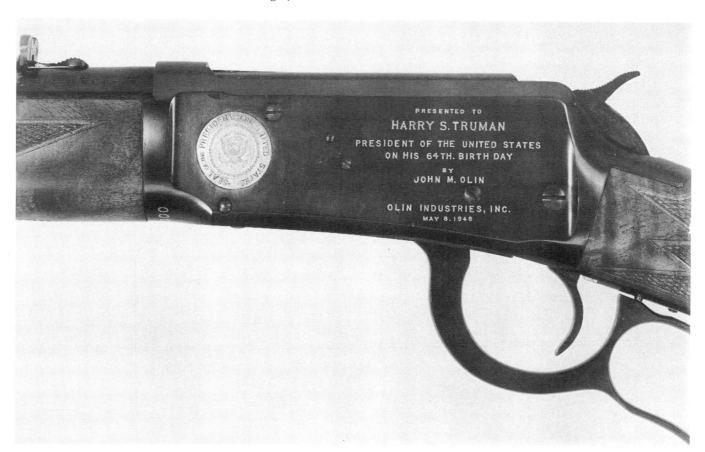

Plate 563

*D*etail of the gold inlaid inscription and presidential seal on the Model 94 carbine illustrated in Plate 562. Olin Corporation Photograph.

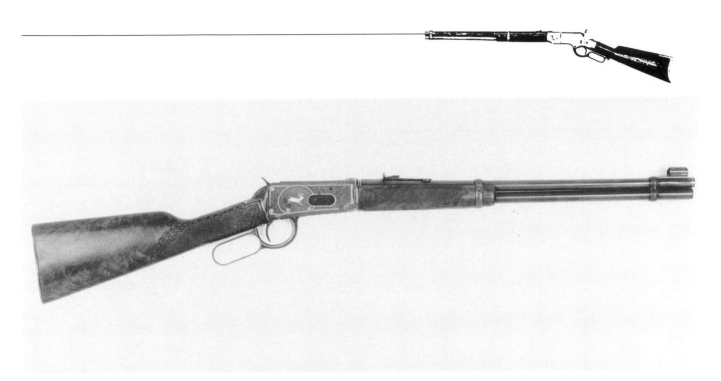

Plate 564

Winchester Model 94 carbine, serial number 2,500,000, engraved and gold inlaid by John Kusmit. Olin Corporation Photograph.

Plate 565

Right receiver detail of the Model 94 carbine illustrated in Plate 564.

Plate 566
*L*eft receiver detail of the Model 94 carbine illustrated in Plate 564.

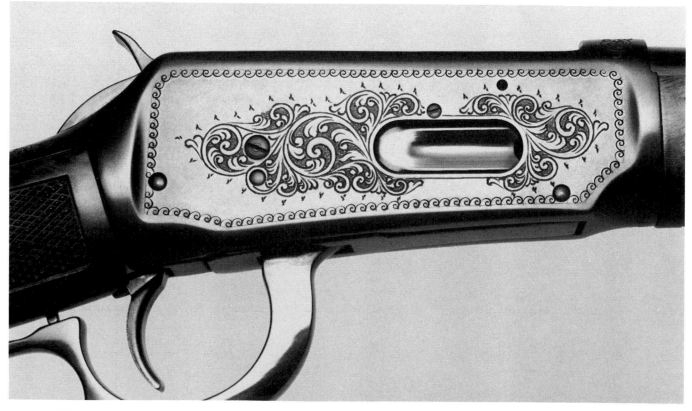

Plate 567
*R*ight receiver detail of a Winchester Model 94 carbine, serial number 4,413,000, engraved by Nick Kusmit. Cody Firearms Museum. Buffalo Bill Historical Center.

500

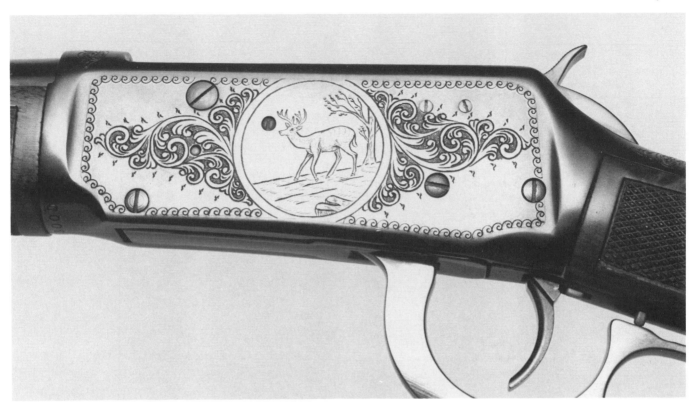

Plate 568
*L*eft receiver detail of the Model 94 carbine illustrated in Plate 568.

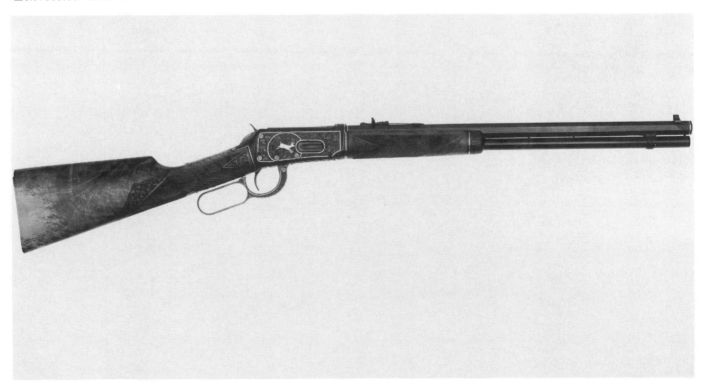

Plate 569
*W*inchester Model 94 carbine, serial number 3,500,000, engraved and gold inlaid by Alvin A. White in 1978 or 1979, for the Winchester-Western Division of Olin Corporation. Olin Corporation Photograph.

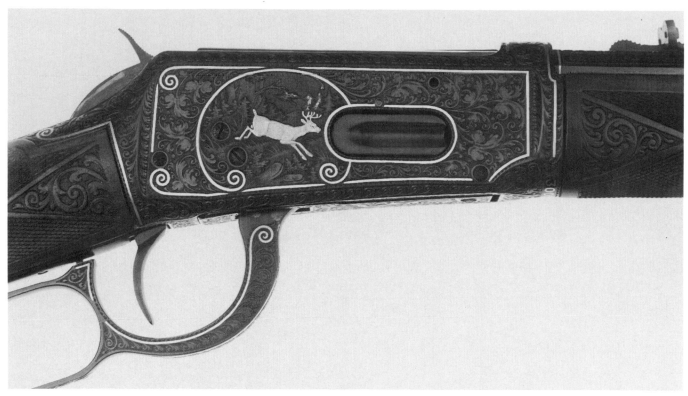

Plate 570
*R*ight receiver detail of the Model 94 carbine illustrated in Plate 570. Olin Corporation Photograph.

Plate 571
*L*eft receiver detail of the Model 94 carbine illustrated in Plate 570. Olin Corporation Photograph.

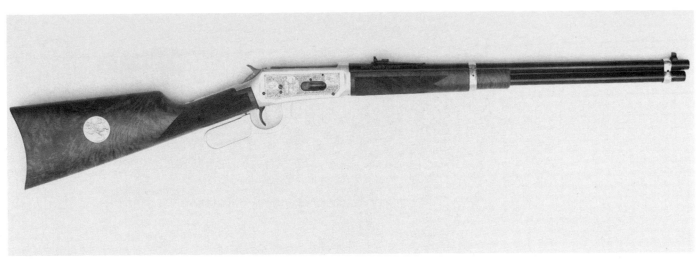

Plate 572

*W*inchester Model 94 carbine prepared as a sample for the Antlered Game Commemorative by the workshop of C. Giovanelli in Brescia, Italy. Olin Corporation Photograph.

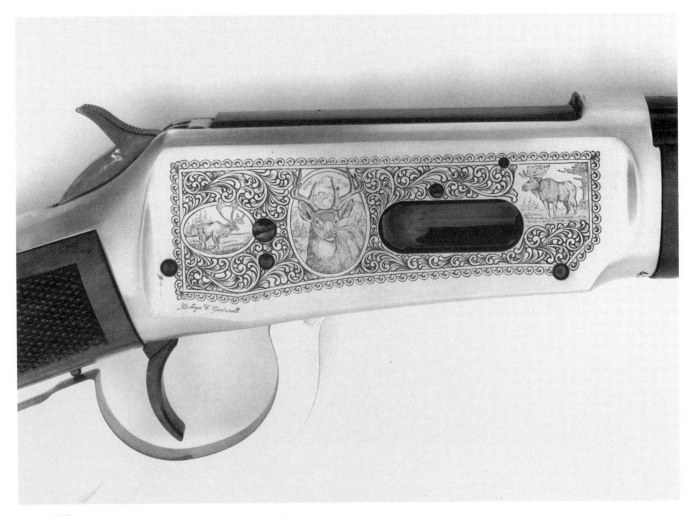

Plate 573

*R*ight receiver detail of the sample Model 94 Antlered Game Commemorative Carbine illustrated in Plate 573. Olin Corporation Photograph.

After Ulrich's sudden death on Oct. 18, 1949, he was succeeded by his former pupil, John Kusmit. The following year, Kusmit hired his younger brother, Nick, to be his apprentice[4].

The Kusmits were to continue the traditions established by A.G. Ulrich until they both retired in 1981. As might be expected, John Kusmit's work resembled that of his teacher and yet in other ways differed markedly. He had learned Ulrich's techniques for cutting relief panel scenes exceedingly well, and his work in that style is almost indistinguishable from his teacher's. Yet, his scrollwork resembled that of Kornbrath rather than Alden Ulrich. John Kusmit's artistry, though, was to flourish in his gold work, and it is the quality of that particular genre that he is best known for today (Plates 564-566). While similar to his older brother's engraving, that produced by Nick Kusmit seemed to draw its inspiration from models dating from the turn of the century (Plates 567-568).

During the 1970s, a number of arms were to be engraved for the Winchester company under contract by non-factory craftsmen. Chief among these was Alvin A. White. One of the best examples of his work is a Model 94 carbine, serial number 3,500,000, completed in 1978 or 1979 (Plates 569-571).

As the Winchester company became more and more involved both in the establishment of foreign operations and the production of commemorative firearms, it was natural that they would explore the possibility of having arms decorated abroad. After considerable searching, the company contracted with the Giovanelli workshop in Brescia, Italy, to design decorations which could be impressed by a roll die on commemorative arms (Plates 572-574)[5].

Though this brief account of Winchester engraving ends with the sale of the company in 1981, the Kusmits were to influence a new generation of engravers through the apprentices they trained during the 1960s and 1970s[6]. Thus, the legacy of the Ulrichs, Stokes, Gough and Kornbrath lives on.

Plate 574

Left receiver detail of the sample Model 94 Antlered Game Commemorative Carbine illustrated in Plate 573. Olin Corporation Photograph.

Endnotes

1. R.L. Wilson, Winchester Engraving, op. cit., pages 385-386.

2. List of Presentation Arms 1943-1946 Commissioned by John M. Olin. Winchester Arms Collection Archives, Olin Corporation Photograph.

3. R.L. Wilson, Winchester Engraving, op. cit., pages 360-364.

4. Ibid, pages 405 and 406.

5. In addition to the manufacture of roll dies, Giovanelli also engraved and gold inlaid Winchester firearms for the European market.

6. Among the apprentices and journeymen trained during this period were Jasper Salerno, Joseph Crowley and Pauline Muerrle. For a discussion of their work, see R.L. Wilson, Winchester Engraving, op. cit., pages 425-433.

SOURCES & BIBLIOGRAPHY

UNPUBLISHED DOCUMENTS

Corporate records of the Winchester Repeating Arms Company (1867- 1931) and the Winchester-Western Division of Olin Corporation (1931 ff). Olin Corporation, Stanford, Connecticut.

Design, development, financial, patent, production and sales records of the Volcanic Repeating Arms Company, New Haven Arms Company, Winchester Repeating Arms Company and the Winchester-Western Division of Olin Corporation (1854-1981). Winchester Arms Collection and Archives (Gift of Olin Corporation), Cody Firearms Museum, Buffalo Bill Historical Center, Cody, Wyoming.

Thomas E. Hall, Select Catalogue of the Winchester Gun Museum, typescript, 8 volumes. Winchester Arms Collection Archives (Gifts of T.E. Hall and Olin Corporation), Cody Firearms Museum, Buffalo Bill Historical Center, Cody, Wyoming.

Credit ledgers of the R.G. Dun company. Baker Library, Harvard University, Massachusetts.

Thomas G. Bennett diaries. Bennett Family Papers. Private Collection.

John M. Davies diaries and papers. John C. Davies, New York, New York.

Major General William B. Franklin aide-memoire (1865-1867). Records of the Colt's Patent Fire Arms Manufacturing Company, Record Group 103, Connecticut State Library, Hartford, Connecticut.

Francois de Suzanne letter books. de Suzanne Family Papers. Charles Dupont, Paris, France.

BIBLIOGRAPHY

Achtermier, William O. **Rhode Island Arms Makers & Gunsmiths 1643-1883** (Man at Arms; Providence, RI: 1980).

Bowman, Hank Wieand. **Famous Guns From The Smithsonian Collection** (Fawcett Publications, Inc.; Greenwich, CT: 1966).

Bourne, Richard A., Co., Inc. **Public Auction Antique Firearms and Related Items, March 17 and 18, 1982** (R.A. Bourne Co., Inc.; Hyannis, MA: 1982).

Brophy, Lt. Col. William S. **Marlin Firearms A History of the Guns and the Company That Made Them** (Stackpole Books; Harrisburg, PA: 1989).

Calvo, Juan L. **Armamento Reglamentario Y Auxiliar del Ejercito Espanol. Libro No. 3 Modelos Portatiles de Retrocarga 1855-1922.** (Juan Luis Calvo Pascual; Barcelona, Spain: 1977).

Chinn, Lt. Col. George M. **The Machine Gun, History, Evolution, and Development of Manual, Automatic and Airborne Repeating Weapons** (U.S. Navy; Washington, DC: 1953).

Christie's East, **Public Auction of Antique and Modern Firearms at the Buffalo Bill Historical Center, July 5, 1984** (Christie, Manson & Woods International Inc.; New York, NY: 1984).

Earle, John E. and Dodge, William C. **Before the Hon. Commissioner of Patents. In the matter of the application of B. TYLER HENRY, for extension of Letters Patent granted to him Oct. 16, 1860, re-issued Dec. 8, 1868, for Magazine Fire Arms. Brief in the part of Applicant.** (Hoggson & Robinson; New Haven, CT: 1874).

Elgger, Karl von. **Die Kriegrfeuerwaffen der Gegenwart** (N.P.; Leipzig, Germany: 1868).

Francotte, Auguste and Gaier, Claude. **FN 100 Years The Story of a Great Liege Company 1889-1989** (Didier Hatier; Brussels, Belgium: 1989).

Fuller, Claude E. **The Whitney Firearms** (Standard Publications, Inc.; Huntington, WV: 1946).

Hatch, Alden. **Remington Arms In American History** (Remington Arms Co.; Ilion, NY: 1992).

Houze, Herbert G. **Cody Firearms Museum** (Buffalo Bill Historical Center; Cody, WY: 1991)

To The Dreams Of Youth: Winchester .22 Caliber Single-Shot Rifles (Krause Publications; Iola, WI: 1993).

Jakobsson, Th. **Svenskt Lantforsvar fran Medeltid till Nutid: Armemuseum** (Armemuseum; Stockholm, Sweden: 1946).

Jinks, Roy G. **History of Smith & Wesson** (Beinfeld Publishing, Inc.; North Hollywood, CA: 1977).

Johnson, Thomas C; Burton, Frank F.; Pugsley, E.; Hall, T.E.; et al. **Inventory of the Winchester Repeating Arms Company Firearms Reference Collection** (Lynham Sayce Co.; Salt Lake, UT: 1991)

Kines, Beverly R. and Clark, Henry A., Jr. **Standard Catalogue of American Cars 1805-1942** (Krause Publications; Iola, WI: 1992).

Lorain, Pierre and Boudriot, Jean. **Les Armes Americaines de la Defense Nationale 1870-1871** (Presses de l'Emancipatrice; Paris, France: 1970).

Marcot, Roy M. **Civil War Chief of Sharpshooters Hiram Berdan Military Commander and Firearms Inventor** (Northwood Heritage Press; Irvine, CA: 1990).

Spencer Repeating Firearms (Northwood Heritage Press; Irvine, CA: 1990).

Marsh, Roger. **The Automatic Weapons Design Series Number 2: The Grant Hammond, Savage and Schouboe .45 Automatic Pistols** (R. Marsh; Hudson, OH; 1945).

McDowell, R. Bruce. **Evolution of the Winchester** (Armory Publications; Tacoma, WA: 1985).

Moore, C. Kenneth. **Colt Single Action Army Revolvers and the London Agency** (Andrew Mowbray Publishers, Inc.; Lincoln, RI: 1990).

O'Brien, Kathryn E. **The Great and the Gracious on Millionaires Row** (North Country Books, Inc.; Utica, NY: 1978).

Parsons, John E. **The First Winchester The Story of the 1866 Repeating Rifle** (Winchester Press; New York, NY: 1969).

Patent Office, H.M. **Patents For Inventions. Abridgements of Specifications-Class 119, Small-Arms. Period-A.D. 1855-1866** (His Majesty's Stationary Office; London, England: 1905).

Ploennies, Wilhelm von. **Neue Hinterladungs-Gewehre** (Edward Zernin; Darmstadt and Leipzig, Germany: 1867).

Rattenbury, Richard. **The Browning Connection** (Buffalo Bill Historical Center; Cody, WY: 1982).

Winchester Promotional Arts (Buffalo Bill Historical Center; Cody, WY: 1978).

Royal Army. **Reports of a Special Committee in Breech-Loading Rifles; together with Minutes of Evidence** (Queen's Printer; London, England: 1869).

Ruth, Larry L. **War Baby! The U.S. Caliber .30 Carbine** (Collector Grade Publications, Inc.; Toronto, Canada: 1992).

War Baby! Comes Home. The U.S. Caliber .30 Carbine-Volume II (Collector Grade Publications, Inc.; Toronto, Canada: 1992).

Schneider, Hugo and Rhyn, Michaelam. **Bewaffnunq und Ausrustung der Schweizer Armee seit 1817. Eidgenossische Handfeuerwaffen** (Verlag Stocker Schmid; Dietikon-Zurch, Switzerland: 1979).

Schneider, Hugo; Rhyn, Michaelam; Krebs, Oskar; Reinhart, Christian, and; Schiess, Robert. **Bewaffnung und Ausrustung der Schweizer Armee seit 1817. Handfeuerwaffen System Vetterli** (Verlag Stocker Schmid; Dietikon-Zurich, Switzerland; 1970).

Schwing, Ned. **The Winchester Model 42** (Krause Publications; Iola, WI: 1990).

Winchester's Finest The Model 21 (Krause Publications; Iola, WI: 1990).

Winchester Slide-Action Rifles Volume I: Model 1890 & Model 1906 (Krause Publications; Iola, WI: 1992).

Winchester Slide-Action Rifles Volume II: Model 61 & Model 62 (Krause Publications; Iola, WI: 1993).

Sellers, Frank M. **American Gunsmiths** (The Gunroom Press; Highland Park, NJ: 1983).

Sharps Firearms (Beinfeld Publishing, Inc., North Hollywood, CA: 1978).

Skennerton, Ian D. **The British Service Lee, The Lee-Metford and Lee-Enfield Rifles & Carbines 1880-1980** (Arms and Armour Press; London, England: 1982).

Stadt, Ronald W. **Winchester Shotguns and Shotshells** (Armory Publications; Tacoma, WA: 1984).

Stevens, R. Blake and Ezell, Edward C. **The Black Rifle-M16 Retrospective** (Collector Grade Publications; Toronto, Canada: 1987).

The SPIW-the Deadliest Weapon that Never Was (Collector Grade Publications; Toronto, Canada: 1985).

Stockbridge, V.D. **Digest of Patents Relating To Breech-Loading And Magazine Small Arms, (Except Revolvers,) Granted In The United States From 1836 to 1873, Inclusive** (U.S. Patent Office; Washington, DC: 1874).

Sutherland, Robert Q. and Wilson, R.L. **The Book of Colt Firearms** (R.Q. Sutherland; Kansas City, MO: 1971).

Tivey, Ted. **The Colt Rifle 1884-1902** (Clouston & Hall Publishers; Queensland, Australia: 1984).

United States Army, Ordnance Department of the. **Ordnance Memoranda No. 15. Report of the Board of Officers Appointed in Pursuance of the Act of Congress Approved June 6, 1872, for the Purpose of Selecting a Breech-System for the Muskets and Carbines of the Military Service** (U.S. Government Printing Office; Washington, DC: 1873).

Report of the Board of Ordnance Officers Convened In Pursuance of the Act of Congress Approved November 21, 1877, To Select a Magazine Gun for the U.S. Military Service (U.S. Government Printing Office; Washington, DC: 1878).

[Weber-Ruesch] **Die Entwicklungsgeschichte der WINCHESTER Gewehre** (Weber-Ruesch; Zurich, Switzerland: N.D. [1883]).

Wegelli, Rudolf. **Katalog der Waffen-Sammlung im Zeughause zu Solothurn** (c. Gassmann; Solothurn, Switzerland: 1905).

West, William. **Browning Arms & History** (W. West; Santa Fe Springs, CA: 1972).

Williamson, Harold F. **Winchester The Gun That Won The West** (Combat Forces Press; Washington, DC: 1952).

Wilson, James H. **Life and Services of William Farrar Smith** (John M. Rogers Press; Wilmington, DE: 1904).

Wilson, Robert Lawrence. **Winchester An American Legend** (Random House; New York, NY: 1991).

Winchester Engraving (Beinfeld Books; Palm Springs, CA: 1989).

Winchester The Golden Age of American Gunmaking and the Winchester 1 of 1000 (Buffalo Bill Historical Center, Cody, WY: 1983).

Winchester, Oliver F. **The First Requisite of a Military Rifle** (Winchester Repeating Arms Company; New Haven, CT: 1870).

Woodend, Herbert. **British Rifles: A catalogue of the Enfield Pattern Room** (Her Majesty's Stationery Office; London, England: 1981).

Yobell, H. von. **Des Zundnadelgewehres Geschichte und Konkurrenten** (E.G. Mittler & Sohn; Berlin, Germany: 1867).

Yoshioka, Dr. Shin-ichi. **Japanese Firearms: An Outline of the Yoshioka Collection** (Osaka Tourist Bureau; Osaka, Japan: 1983).

PERIODICALS

Erlach, Franz von. "Der Henry-Stutzen," **Allgemaine Schweizerishe Militar-Zeitung** (Basel, Switzerland), Volume II, Number 45, Nov. 9, 1866.

Foster, Paul. "Winchester's 'Forgotten' Cartridges, 1866-1900," **Gun Digest Treasury** (Chicago, IL) 1956.

Houze, Herbert G. "Additional Notes on Winchester .22 Caliber Single Shot Rifles," **The Gun Report** (Aledo, IL), Volume 39, Number 10, March, 1994.

"A Reevaluation of the Henry and Model 1866 Serial Numbering," **Man at Arms** (Lincoln, RI), Volume 13, Number 4, July/August 1991.

"Fact & Fancy: A Critical Reassessment of the Origins, Development and Purpose of the Experimental Revolvers Produced by the Winchester Repeating Arms Company During the 1870's," **ARMAX The Journal of the Cody Firearms Museum.** (Cody, WY), Volume IV, Number 1, 1992.

"The Appearance of Evidence: A Brief Examination of the Life and Work of Herman Leslie Ulrich," **ARMAX The Journal of the Cody Firearms Museum,** (Cody, WY), Volume IV, Number 2, 1993.

"The End of a Marque: The Final Production of the Winchester Model 1873," **The Gun Report** (Aledo, IL), Volume 36, Number 12, May, 1991.

"The Design, Development and Initial Production of the Hotchkiss Magazine Rifle 1876-1879," **ARMAX The Journal of the Cody Firearms Museum,** (Cody, WY), Volume III, Number 2, 1991.

"The Sale of English Arms," **The Winchester Repeater** (St. Louis, MO), Volume 15, Winter 1994.

Mayberry, Gerald R. "The Sharps Rifle in Frontier Montana," **ARMAX The Journal of the Cody Firearms Museum** (Cody, WY), Volume IV, Number 2, 1993.

Pugsley, Edwin. "Confidential Report on the Development of the U.S. M1 Carbine," **ARMAX The Journal of the Winchester Arms Museum** (Cody, WY), Volume II, Number 1, 1988.

Schreier, Konrad F., Jr. "Winchester Center Fire Automatic Rifles," **ARMAX The Journal of the Cody Firearms Museum** (Cody, WY), Volume III, Number 1, 1990.

Sword, Wiley. "Winchester Model 1866 Serial Numbers-Another Perspective," **Man at Arms** (Lincoln, RI), Volume 14, Number 1, January/February 1992.

Triggs, James M. "William B. Ruger," **Arms Gazette** (North Hollywood, CA), Volume 4, Number 12, August 1977.

"Sturm, Ruger & Co. The First 29 Years," **Arms Gazette** (North Hollywood, CA), Volume 4, Number 12, August 1977.

INDEX

V

W

Z

Other selected titles by Krause Publications
that may provide further information or
complement this book:

Winchester's Finest: The Model 21 by Ned Schwing
Winchester Model 42 by Ned Schwing
Winchester Model 94 by Robert C. Renneberg
Winchester Slide-Action Rifles,
  Volume II by Ned Schwing
Standard Catalog of Firearms,
  4th Ed. by Ned Schwing & Herbert G. Houze
To the Dreams of Youth—Winchester .22 Caliber
  Single Shot Rifle by Herbert G. Houze

Encyclopedia of Ruger Semi-Automatic Rimfire
  Pistols 1949-1992 by Chad Hiddleson
Ruger 10/22 by William E. Workman
301 Venison Recipes
Advanced Whitetail Details
Deer Hunters Almanac
Game Wardens vs. Poachers, Tickets Still
  Available by James L. Palmer
Hunting Coyotes East and West (Video)
Illusions of Animal Rights by Russ Carman
Musky Mastery by Steve Heiting
Trout at the Walnut Tree by Richard Tate
Turkey Hunting with Gerry Blair
When the Land Calls by Mary Ellen Pourchot

**krause
publications**

700 E. State Street • Iola, WI 54990-0001
Telephone: 715/445-2214

Please call or write for a free catalog.